GENTLE FLAME

1. Sir Dudley North, later fourth Lord North, as portrayed by Cornelius Johnson.

GENTLE FLAME

The Life and Verse of
Dudley, Fourth Lord North
(1602–1677)

DALE B. J. RANDALL

DUKE UNIVERSITY PRESS
Durham, N.C.
1983

Library of Congress Cataloging in Publication Data
Randall, Dale B. J.
  Gentle flame.

  Bibliography: p.
  Includes index.
  1. North, Dudley North, Baron, 1602–1677. 2. Authors,
English—Early modern, 1500–1700—Biography. I. North,
Dudley North, Baron, 1602–1677. II. Title.
PR3605.N84R36 1983   821′.4 [B]   82-21143
ISBN 0-8223-0491-0

To

LETTIE PERRIN RANDALL

and

CECILIA UNZICKER RANDALL

Ex animo.

CONTENTS

LIST OF PLATES

1. Sir Dudley North, later fourth Lord North, a portrait by Cornelius Johnson, reproduced here through the courtesy of the Earl of Guilford, frontispiece.

2. Kirtling (or Catlage) as it appeared in the eighteenth century, an engraving from a drawing by the Rev. Cooper Willyams, *Topographical Miscellanies* (1792), facing p. 76.

3. "On Serena Sleeping," a poem by North from the Perkins manuscript, fol. 7r, facing p. 100.

PREFACE

Among the author's underlying thoughts while working on the present volume, one of the most persistent has been the truism that both history and literary history are selective. Were it not so, the burden of the past would long since have proved intolerable. On the other hand, confining our attention to major figures, events, and works insures that our sense of the past will be not merely fragmentary but skewed. Whatever we do, our sense of the past will never be altogether accurate, of course, but by restricting our attention to major historical figures and major literary works we inevitably deprive ourselves of some of the lesser sounding boards that helped to give resonance to even the greatest men and works in their own time and place.

The present study therefore invites a reader first to contemplate the life of Sir Dudley North, the fourth Lord North, a man who played a minor role in the events of his day, and then it offers a close view of his verse, which is representative of its period and has various kinds of interest, yet is, when all is said, also minor. The book is built of two parts, in other words, both closely related and both showing how North's life and writing illuminate each other. The book as a whole, moreover, is grounded on the assumption that North's life and writing will be seen to cast a few rays of light on other seventeenth-century English lives and writings. Indeed, it is grounded on the belief that such illumination is mutual.

To proceed on the assumption that Sir Dudley North's life and verse are interesting both in themselves and also in relation to other lives and verse is by no means to inflate either the historical prominence of the man or the literary quality of his work. Assuming that the reconstruction of nearly any seventeenth-century life would be worthwhile (the life of a cobbler of Canterbury, say), there ought to be something of interest in an attempt to reconstruct the life of a gentleman born in the reign of Elizabeth, reared in that of James, elected to Parliament under Charles, and retired to his chief country seat in the time of a second Charles. Especially is this true when the bare bones of his story may be fleshed out with a variety of indentures, wills, and account books, all of which help us to a better understanding of both the man and his milieu. Of course North's story is incomplete. As Francis Bacon knew, the remnants left by history are like planks from a shipwreck,[1] and

---

1. *The Twoo Bookes of Francis Bacon. Of the Proficience and Advancement of Learning, Divine and Humane* (1605), Cc2v, Cc3r.

naturally one would like to trade certain bits of flotsam for others—a name, a date, a motive—that have disappeared forever. Nevertheless, when all the demurrals are in, one has good cause in North's case to be grateful for how much has survived.

As for North's writing, clearly his efforts in both prose and poetry are of interest for their place in both history and literary history. Anyone willing to spend a brief while on North's prose (which includes published writings on household economics, political history, religion, and biography) and then another brief while on his verse (published here for the first time) will be able to glimpse a particular seventeenth-century Englishman's views on a good many subjects, and, in the process, gain a reasonably rounded sense of the man as well as something of his time. Hence North's prose is quoted frequently here. Yet the hard fact is that only one of North's publications is noted in the Oxford *Bibliography of British History: Stuart Period, 1603–1714* (1970), and it is listed as anonymous, with a tentative attribution to one of his sons. Even more striking, all three of North's published volumes (or, counted another way, his four volumes) are unrecorded by the compilers of the monumental *New Cambridge Bibliography of English Literature* (I, 1974; II, 1971). It is no wonder, then, that North's writing goes unrecognized by Douglas Bush and James Sutherland in their important histories of seventeenth-century English literature.[2] Most striking of all, however, the latest *British Museum General Catalogue of Printed Books* (1963: photolithographic edition to 1955) not only confuses North's publications with those of his father but entirely overlooks North himself. So far as virtually all scholars of the period are concerned, Sir Dudley North long ago sank from sight.

It is scarcely surprising, then, that some of North's poems are probably irrecoverably lost. On the other hand, the fifty that are introduced here constitute a collection that is not extraordinarily small. Setting aside questions of quality, one might compare North's canon of fifty poems with the fifty that we have from Henry Howard, Earl of Surrey. From Sir Walter Raleigh we have about forty poems; from John Cleveland, perhaps forty-three; and from Andrew Marvell, sixty. Certainly some Renaissance English writers were vastly more prolific than any of these men, but this particular set of figures allows one to realize that Sir Dudley North's pen was relatively more busy than one otherwise might have thought. The poems do, indeed, have what one might term "critical mass."

It should be noted also that, except for a very few errors which are recorded in the annotations, the presentation of North's poems in the present volume conveys virtually all of the accidentals of the copy text—a manuscript

2. Bush, *English Literature in the Earlier Seventeenth Century: 1600–1660* (2nd ed., Oxford, 1962); and Sutherland, *English Literature of the Late Seventeenth Century* (Oxford, 1969). These are vols. V and VI of *The Oxford History of English Literature*.

which is now in the William R. Perkins Library, Duke University.[3] The reasons for attempting this sort of accuracy are several: (1) the manuscript, in Lady North's hand, is apparently close to North's own holographs of the poems; (2) the manuscript is generally accurate and legible, and therefore reproducible with a relatively high degree of accuracy and minimal editorial guesswork and intrusion; (3) the few errors that do occur may be readily indicated in the notes; (4) no such errors and none of the vagaries of punctuation seriously obscure North's meaning; and, (5) such a transcriptional method better conveys to a reader the fact that, whatever kinship one may feel for the seventeenth century, it was a time with habits of language and punctuation that differ interestingly and unpredictably from our own.

Elsewhere in the book as well, quotations from both unpublished and published materials are reproduced as accurately as possible, though economic constraint has prohibited the printing of words with superscript letters; characters in such words have been lowered silently, and (as occasion usually demands) the words have been expanded. For the same reason, the "r's" and "v's" that are normally printed as superscripts to indicate rectos and versos have here been lowered and italicized. In book titles, the use of "i's" and "j's," "u's" and "v's" has been modernized.

Aside from the consolidation of far-flung materials, the most difficult problem in preparing this volume has been deciding whether or not to preserve the order of the poems as they appear in the copy text. Recognition of the claims of *respect des fonds* led at first to an attempt here to deal with the poems as they occur sequentially in the Perkins manuscript. The attempt proved confusing, however, because of such checks as intervening prose passages, the insertion of verse within the prose, and the presence of blank leaves between segments of writing. After various alternative methods of ordering had been considered, the most attractive appeared to be one that was capable of suggesting the genres of North's poems and sometimes their relative earliness and lateness, but without insisting on any chronology. No order imposed from outside the manuscript could ever satisfy all readers, of course, but now, with even a rapid glance, any reader may see something about the range and proportions of North's poetic types.

It may be well to observe here in passing that generic ordering was by no means unheard of in North's own time. When the dramatist Thomas Heywood published his *Pleasant Dialogues and Dramma's* (1637), for instance, his table of contents set apart from one another such genres as dialogues, emblems, elegies, epithalamions, and epigrams. For a more famous example one might turn to John Donne's *Poems*, which even in its earliest form (1633) grouped works roughly according to type, and in subsequent seventeenth-century editions became more rigid in its assignment of poems to such cate-

---

3. The phrase "virtually all" alludes to the fact that superscript letters are printed without the periods and colons that sometimes accompany them in the manuscript.

gories as songs and sonnets, epigrams, satires, funeral elegies, and divine poems. It is true that North's father apparently disdained ordering in his volume called, significantly, *A Forest of Varieties* (1645), but he also conveyed a modicum of uneasiness about his casualness when he wrote on the title page of various copies "or rather A wildernesse." Sir Dudley North himself, furthermore, referred to his own poems as a "rapsody, or masse of things, soe different in nature" that they "can very hardly appear good"[4]—apparently the comment of a man sensitive to the fact that jostling kind against kind did little to enhance the quality of his poetic efforts.

It should be observed, too, that when Lady North copied out Sir Dudley's poems on another occasion, she produced another manuscript as disordered as the one used as copy text here, but one that is disordered in different ways. It would seem that Lady North in both instances simply was taking up her husband's poems as she came to them (perhaps sometimes on individual loose sheets and sometimes in clusters), then copying them out in her volume of blank pages much as one might place unsorted snapshots in an album. Should such an ordering have been preserved here? Any reader who thinks so and misses the kaleidoscopic shifting of generic perspective that one finds in many Renaissance books (Ben Jonson's *Forrest*, for instance) is invited to turn to Appendix C, where he may see precisely how North's poems are deployed in the Perkins manuscript. For good measure, he may turn also to Appendix D and consider the contrasting arrangement in the Rougham manuscript of North's verse.

With the theoretical decisions all made, the research completed, and the writing done, the author finds now that he is indebted to more people than he may reasonably name here. It is nonetheless gratifying to be able to thank Roger and Pamela North of Rougham Hall, who made available not only the Rougham manuscript of Sir Dudley North's poems but also a number of other North family papers. Facilitating the use of these documents and performing further kindnesses as well were J. R. S. Guinness and Barbara Boone. In addition, the Earl of Guilford has graciously consented to the use of his portrait of Sir Dudley North as a frontispiece.

A scholar's accumulation of debts to librarians is an everyday fact of life, but the author's debt to librarians for aid with the present project has come to be enormous. At Perkins Library, Gertrude Merritt (formerly Associate University Librarian) deserves special mention, as do John L. Sharpe, III (Curator of Rare Books), Mattie U. Russell (Curator of Manuscripts), William R. Erwin, Jr. (Assistant Curator of Manuscripts), and Florence Blakely (formerly Head of Reference), Mary W. Canada (currently Head of Reference), and their staffs. At The Folger Shakespeare Library, Nati H. Krivatsy helped to solve several hard problems, and Lilly Stone Lievsay, among a number of

---

4. See his "Dedication" herein, p. 128.

memorable kindnesses, called attention to books in the Folger collection that once belonged to the North family. Ann Hyde (Department of Special Collections, Kenneth Spencer Research Library, University of Kansas) was not only generous with her time and skill but also successful in managing the difficult duplication of North family documents. Further special thanks are due to Margaret Crum and Mary Clapinson (both of the Bodleian Library) and to Jean M. Ayton (Central Library, Manchester), W. W. S. Breem (Inner Temple), N. C. Buck (St. John's College Library, Cambridge), C. R. H. Cooper (Guildhall Library, London), Rosemary Graham (Trinity College Library, Cambridge), H. E. Peek (Cambridge University Library), and J. S. G. Sommers (All Souls College Library, Oxford).

Fellow academics have been more than generous both in responding to questions on the work while it was in progress and in posing questions of their own as the work took final shape. It is a pleasure, therefore, to express warm and particular thanks to John L. Lievsay, as well as to Francis Newton, George Walton Williams, and A. Leigh DeNeef, and to John N. King, William H. Willis, and Giles E. Dawson.

Also far too helpful to be forgotten here were A. Colin Cole (then Windsor Herald at Arms), Oliver Van Oss (Master, The Charterhouse), Elspeth A. Evans (National Portrait Gallery), W. J. Smith (Greater London Record Office), John E. Feneley (Principal, Centre for Medieval and Renaissance Studies), and Douglas M. Lanier (graduate student, Duke University). And coming along with sharp-eyed cheerfulness during the closing days of the project has been J. Samuel Hammond (Head, Music Library, Duke), who has prepared the index.

Furthermore, the author has been aided by various grants from the Duke University Research Council. For these he is most grateful, as he is for the opportunity to have lectured on the subject of Sir Dudley North while serving as a Senior Fellow in the tenth session of the Southeastern Institute of Medieval and Renaissance Studies, and, with funds from the National Endowment for the Humanities, to have served as a Folger Shakespeare Library Senior Fellow.

Immediately following the tendering of these thanks the author hastens to relieve all of his benefactors of responsibility for such follies and errors as remain. He has caught himself in too many slips along the way to think that his work is now free of them. Furthermore, he is sobered from time to time by the recollection of one of Sir Dudley North's own remarks on the making of books: "*I never coveted the honour of the Press*," writes Sir Dudley in a passage never meant to see print; "*much less should I do it in a time of so much prostitution.*" [5]

---

5. From a letter in *Some Notes Concerning the Life of Edward Lord North* (apparently printed posthumously in 1682), p. 38.

Then again, North himself, on balance, was a hopeful man who allowed two of his books to go to the printer. Perhaps it is fitting, therefore, to close with the hopeful words of one of his contemporaries. Backed with good classical authority, Henry Peacham remarks that "as in the same pasture, the Oxe findeth fodder, the Hound a Hare; the Stork a Lizard, the faire maide flowers; so we cannot, except wee list our selves (saith *Seneca*) but depart the better from any booke whatsoever."[6] It is, in any case, a consummation devoutly to be wished.

6. *The Compleat Gentleman* ("Inlarged" ed., 1634), p. 54.

A NOTE ON DOCUMENTATION

ABBREVIATIONS OF PUBLICATIONS

BCP   *The Booke of Common Prayer, and Administration of the Sacraments, and Other Rites and Ceremonies of the Church of England* (1603; i.e., 1604).

Catechisme   Nowell, Alexander, *A Catechisme, or First Instruction and Learnyng of Christian Religion*, tr. T. Norton (1577).

CSP   *Calendar of State Papers*, various volumes.

Forest 45   Dudley North, third Lord North, *A Forest of Varieties* (1645).

HMC   Historical Manuscripts Commission, various volumes.

Light   Dudley North, fourth Lord North, *Light in the Way to Paradise: With Other Occasionals* (1682).

Lives   Roger North, *The Lives of the Right Hon. Francis North, Baron Guilford; the Hon. Sir Dudley North; and the Hon. and Rev. Dr. John North*, ed. Augustus Jessopp, 3 vols. (1890).

Narrative   Dudley North, fourth Lord North, *A Narrative of Some Passages in or Relating to the Long Parliament* (1670).

Observations   ———, *Observations and Advices Oeconomical* (1669).

OED   *The Oxford English Dictionary. . .* , ed. James A. H. Murray, Henry Bradley, W. A. Craigie, C. T. Onions (Oxford, 1933).

Puttenham   George Puttenham, *The Arte of English Poesie* (1589).

Some Notes   Dudley North, fourth Lord North, *Some Notes Concerning the Life of Edward Lord North, Baron of Kirtling, 1658*, published with separate pagination, but (often) bound with North's *Light in the Way to Paradise* (1682).

Stone   Lawrence Stone, *The Crisis of the Aristocracy: 1558–1641* (Oxford, 1965).

ABBREVIATIONS OF REPOSITORIES

BL   British Library, London

Bodl.   Bodleian Library, Oxford University

Perkins   William R. Perkins Library, Duke University

PRO   Public Record Office, London

Spencer   Kenneth Spencer Research Library, University of Kansas

OTHER SHORTENED REFERENCES

Unless otherwise specified, scriptural quotations are from the Authorized Version of 1611. With a few exceptions, well-known literary works are referred to simply by title, section, and line. The place of publication, if not indicated, may be assumed to be London.

PART ONE

THE LIFE

THE FAMILY BACKGROUND

Sir Dudley North, fourth Baron North (1602–1677), was a conservative, Christian gentleman who lived to a ripeness and saw much.[1] Born at the close of Elizabeth's reign, he was knighted by James, participated uneasily in the Long Parliament until shortly before the stormy close of Charles's life, retreated to manage the affairs of his family seat in Cambridgeshire during the days of "Leviathan" Cromwell, and enjoyed a reasonably content old age, surrounded in his library by quantities of books, papers, and parchments, including a pardon from Charles II. Through the years, like many another English gentleman, North occasionally took to his pen. Apparently he had doubts about appearing in print, partly because of a natural reticence, partly because he realized that his skills were limited, and partly because gentlemen were supposed to be uneager to appear in the marketplace. On the other hand, in his sixty-seventh year, he finally did offer the reading public his *Observations and Advices Oeconomical* (1669), a handbook in which he endeavored to tell how a great house might be managed without a great fortune. The following year he published *A Narrative of Some Passages in or Relating to the Long Parliament.* Then finally, five years after his death, his family made a collection of his miscellaneous prose writings (devotional, discursive, and biographical) and for the first time placed his name on a title page: *Light in the Way to Paradise* (1682). Students of the seventeenth century, therefore, have long had some cause to know of Sir Dudley North. Nevertheless, it is only with the discovery of a manuscript that has lain in private hands for about three hundred years that we discover North to have been a writer of verse. Introduction of the life and verse of this minor seventeenth-century writer is the purpose of the present book.

1. There has been no previous biography of North, but helpful sketches appear in the following: [Arthur] *Collins's Peerage of England*, aug. Sir Egerton Brydges, IV (1812), 466–469; Lady Frances Bushby, "Memoirs of Some of the North Family During the Tudor and Stuart Dynasties" (typescript, 1893), Bodl. MS. Eng. hist. c.408; Augustus Jessopp, *DNB*, ed. Leslie Stephen and Sidney Lee, XIV (Oxford, 1959–1960 rept.), 596–597; [George Edward Cokayne], *The Complete Peerage. . .* , ed. H. A. Doubleday and Lord Howard de Walden, IX (1936), 656–657; and Mary Frear Keeler, *The Long Parliament, 1640–1641: A Biographical Study of Its Members* (Philadelphia, 1954), p. 286. Much useful data may be gleaned also from Roger North's *Lives* of three of Sir Dudley's sons (Francis, Dudley, and John), a work available in various forms, including the edition of Augustus Jessopp (1890), used here, and its reprinting with a new introduction by E. Mackerness (1972).

*   *   *

In a biography that he wrote in 1658 Sir Dudley North speaks of Edward, first Lord North, as "the common Parent and raiser of our Family," the man "*to whom we owe our eminency, if any we have.*"[2] Identifying himself as the grandchild of Edward's grandchild,[3] Sir Dudley gives a favorable but largely factual account of the striking career of his ancestor. Born about 1496 into a family which had come to London from Walkeringham, Nottinghamshire, Edward North studied at St. Paul's School under William Lily, continued his education at Peterhouse, Cambridge, and eventually was called to the bar. His rise thereafter suggests something of both the man and his time. After serving as Advocate for the City of London, he rose to be Clerk of the Parliament and then King's Serjeant-at-Law. These posts made his abilities increasingly conspicuous, and in 1540 he was named treasurer of the Court of Augmentations, a court which had come into being recently because of the flood of business following the phenomenal "augmentation" of royal holdings when the monasteries were dissolved. In the years 1540–1543 North served as sheriff of Cambridgeshire and Huntingdonshire, and in 1542 he was knighted. Three times he served in Parliament (1542–1544, 1547–1552, and 1553), and in 1544 he ascended to the chancellorship of the Court of Augmentations—at first a joint appointment with Sir Richard Rich, and later one that he enjoyed alone. Vast wealth passed through Edward North's hands, and a certain amount of it doubtless found its way into his pockets.[4] Still more important to his family's future, however, is the fact that as a trusty servant of the King he received extensive grants of abbey and other crown lands. Lawrence Stone observes that "Wentworth, Windsor, Cromwell, Seymour, Eure, Russell, Paulet, Wharton, Wriothesley, Darcy of Chiche, Paget, Rich, Shef-

2. *Some Notes Concerning the Life of Edward Lord North, Baron of Kirtling, 1658* (hereinafter cited as *Some Notes*) was published with its own separate pagination but is usually bound in the volume called *Light in the Way to Paradise*; passages cited here are from p. 2 and A2v. The fullest published schematic pedigree of the Norths is in George Baker, *The History and Antiquities of the County of Northampton*, pt. II (1826), pp. 526–527. Bushby and *DNB* (various articles) give the best prose accounts, *The Complete Peerage* the most succinct. A few of the many manuscript sources include BL MSS. Harl. 806 (79r–80v), Harl. 1,529 (99r), Add. 5,819 (78r–80r and 114v–120r), and 19,143 (175v–176r); County Record Office, Shire Hall, Cambridge, P101/1/1; and Bodl. MSS. Tanner 180 (75r), Rawl. B.314 (20v–21r), and North c.25 (70–76). Valuable guides to further materials in the Bodleian's massive collection are C. M. Borough, "Calendar of the Papers of the North Family" (1960; Bodl. R.13.111), and Mary Clapinson, "Index to the Calendar of North Family Papers in the Bodleian Library" (1972; Bodl. R.6.104).

3. *Some Notes*, p. 32. At various points in the present volume a reader is likely to be aided by Appendix A, "A Genealogical Chart of the North Family."

4. Helpful perspective is provided by Walter C. Richardson, *History of the Court of Augmentations 1536–1554* (Baton Rouge, La., 1961), pp. 330–331: "It appears to have been taken for granted that a public official would appropriate to his own use a certain portion of the revenue passing through his hands as a justifiable supplement to his salary, which was frequently inadequate."

field, Herbert, Browne, North, and Williams were substantially, and in some cases almost entirely, the product of the great share-out among officials, soldiers, and courtiers of the property seized from the Church between 1536 and 1553."[5] Making his position yet stronger, North in 1546 joined Henry's Privy Council.

As early as 1532, four years before the monastic dissolution began, North had become sufficiently affluent to acquire the seat of Kirtling (or, familiarly, Catlage) in Cambridgeshire.[6] Kirtling at the time was an old moated castle near the border of Suffolk, some six miles southeast of Newmarket in the southeastern corner of the county.[7] North razed the castle and on its site, within the large moat, erected a splendid, sprawling, red-brick mansion which in the next century was to provide the fourth Lord North with most of his knowledge about great-house economy. Approached by an imposing new gatehouse with fifty-five-foot turrets, and situated "on a prettie *Hill,*" the new Kirtling was said to have "a most statelie *Rise* by very many *Steppes* up into the *House* wherein you may behould a great Part both of *this Shire* & *Suffolke. . . .*"[8] As a matter of fact, the same source continues, "saving that yt standeth somwhat upon a *wett Soile,* yt is hardlie paraleild in *both Sheires.*" To the old Norman church that stood close to the grounds of the house, Edward added a large family chapel, and eventually he was buried in a fine black marble tomb between the chancel and the chapel. There his successors might ponder his motto, *Serva Fidem,* and his arms, a lion passant amidst three fleurs-de-lis.

North's capabilities had been considerably enhanced through the years by his acquisition of a wealthy wife. At the age of about thirty-three he married

5. Stone, p. 192.

6. The facts of the matter constitute a legal thicket, but as of 31 January 1532 Robert Browne "gave graunted bargayned and solde" Edward North the manor of Kirtling. Doubts then arose as to the validity of the title, so North in 1536 requested "that yt may be enacted by your Grace [Henry VIII] wyth thassent of the Lords spuall & temporal & the Comons in the present Parliament assembled and by aucthoryte of the same, that your sayd Orator his heyres & assignes shall and may from hensforth peasably have holde and enyoye to them & to ther heyres . . . the forsayde Manor of Kertlyng. . ." (*The Statutes of the Realm,* III [1817; reprinted 1963], 700; also Bodl. MS. North c.44, no. 1). It was 1538, however, before a grant for Kirtling was made by Henry to North in consideration of a thousand marks previously paid out and an annual rent of £33/6/8 (Bodl. MS. North c.84).

7. It was situated in the hundred of Cheveley. The castle had belonged to the barony of Tony, but ownership of the property itself may be traced to Harold, Earl of East Anglia.

8. BL Add. MS. 5,819, 79r. *Topographical Miscellanies* (1792) gives an interesting "Description of the Mansion" and a picture reproduced here as Plate No. 2. Only the gatehouse now survives. Nikolaus Pevsner observes that the latter "represents that moment in Tudor architecture, when the Middle Ages and the Renaissance met"; despite generous crenellation, a two-story oriel window over the entrance is clear evidence that defense was never a serious purpose of the structure (*Buildings of England,* vol. X, *Cambridgeshire* [1954], p. 339). Other sources include E. W. Brayley and John Britton, *A Topographical and Historical Description of the County of Cambridge* (n.d.), pp. 136–138; H. A. Tipping, "Kirtling Tower, Cambridgeshire: A Seat of Lord North," *Country Life,* LXIX (24 January 1931), 102–108; and County Record Office, Shire Hall, Cambridge, MSS. G. N. Maynard, vol. IX, pp. 18–21.

Alice, daughter of Oliver Squire of Southby, Hampshire, and widow of Edward Myrffin (still earlier, she had been the widow of John Brigadine). The union of Edward North and Alice resulted not only in the rearing of the new mansion at Kirtling but also in the birth of four children, two of whom are of special concern here. Thomas (1535?–1601?) was to become the most famous writer that the North family ever produced. Though he had other skills as well, it is as a translator of Guevara, Bidpai, and, above all, Plutarch that he is remembered.[9] Knighted about 1591, Sir Thomas was both a skillful writer himself and the source of skillful writing in others, most notably Shakespeare, who turned to North's Plutarch when writing his Roman plays. The other North offspring of concern here is Roger, who was to become the great-grandfather of Sir Dudley.

In 1543, when both his family and his fortunes were burgeoning, Edward North acquired a second notable property. In Finsbury, about half a mile north of St. Paul's and not far beyond the old walls of London, stood the Charterhouse, fourth of the Carthusian monasteries to have been erected in England (ca. 1341).[10] In 1535 its prior had been hanged, drawn, and quartered at Tyburn, and in 1537 the monastery was surrendered. For a while thereafter the huge establishment was used for nothing more glorious than storing the King's tents and pavilions, but in February 1543 Edward North had a grant of the Charterhouse and proceeded to turn the old stone structure into a magnificent dwelling. Thanks to the monks, it was even supplied with pipes for running water. The Charterhouse may have proved to be a greater house than the Norths required, however, in view of their other holdings, for on 31 May 1565, only five months after Edward North died (31 December 1564), his executors and son Roger sold most of the property to the Duke of Norfolk. As matters evolved, the Charterhouse was to change hands several more times after this, but an important detail to bear in mind here is that many years later the Norths still retained that portion of the property lying east of the chapel, and this remainder was itself sufficiently commodious not only for a mansion but also for courts, stables, gardens, and orchards.[11]

9. *The Lives of the Noble Grecians and Romanes, Compared Together by That Grave Learned Philosopher and Historiographer, Plutarke of Chaeronea* . . . (1579).

10. Publications relating to the Charterhouse—usually with glimpses of the Norths—are extensive; see, for example, Philip Bearcroft, *An Historical Account of Thomas Sutton Esq. and of His Foundation in Charter-House* (1737); James Peller Malcolm, *Londinium Redivivum*, 4 vols. (1802–07); "By a Carthusian," *Historical Account of Charter-house; Compiled from the Works of Hearne* [i.e., Samuel Herne, *Domus Carthusiana*, 1677] and Bearcroft, Harleian, Cottonian, and Private MSS. (1808); *The Carthusian: A Miscellany in Prose and Verse* (1839); Lawrence Hendriks, *The London Charterhouse: Its Monks and Its Martyrs* (1889); William F. Taylor, *The Charterhouse of London* (1912); Gerald S. Davies, *Charterhouse in London: Monastery, Mansion, Hospital, School* (1921); and David Knowles and W. F. Grimes, *Charterhouse: The Medieval Foundation in the Light of Recent Discoveries* (1954).

11. Herne, *Domus Carthusiana*, pp. 170–173. Numerous details may be gleaned also from Spencer MS. uncat. North 17 : 15 (18 January 1631), an agreement between the North family and the Earl and Countess of Rutland. Bearcroft says that the North house spread over into what in

Aside from the Charterhouse and Kirtling, one more of North's properties should be noted. Harrow had long served as the occasional residence of the primate of all England; in fact by the time of Henry VIII it had been associated with Canterbury for some eight hundred years. In 1544, however, Archbishop Cranmer surrendered the Harrow Rectory to Henry, and in 1547, after various intermediate steps, both the Rectory Manor and the Manor of Harrow were merged and turned over to Edward North. In the years to come, Kirtling and the Charterhouse were both to figure intimately in family affairs, but the great manor at Harrow on the Hill was the "flower" of the North estates.[12]

After Henry VIII died (1547) and the new court of young Edward VI was established, North for reasons now unknown resigned his chancellorship of the Court of Augmentations.[13] He retained his seat in the Privy Council, however, and at the close of Edward's reign (1553) resumed his ascent. Despite the fact that he had come out for Lady Jane Grey as Edward's successor, North soon was welcomed into the Privy Council of Queen Mary. In fact, it was Mary who raised North to the dignity of baron of the realm (1554). Obviously believing that such prolonged continuity of favor posed some puzzling questions, the fourth Lord North suggested that his predecessor had a behind-the-scenes arrangement with Mary even at the time that he was publicly espousing the cause of "Queen Jane."[14] Be this as it may, in the same year that Mary herself died (1558), yet another royal Tudor, Elizabeth, did North the honor of visiting the Charterhouse and even held court there for six days before making her entry into the city. In 1559 North was appointed by Elizabeth to be Lord Lieutenant of Cambridgeshire and the Isle of Ely, and in 1561 she visited him again at the Charterhouse. For some reason she de-

his time had become Rutland Court and "the Houses adjoining on to *Goswell-Street*" (p. 202). In 1656 the property entered the history of English drama as the site of the performance of William Davenant's *Siege of Rhodes*, an entertainment frequently regarded as the first English opera. Earlier that same year no less than four hundred spectators had been expected to assemble in a hall of the mansion when Davenant's *First Day's Entertainment at Rutland House* was performed (Leslie Hotson, *The Commonwealth and Restoration Stage* [Cambridge, Mass., 1928], p. 150). Part of the Charterhouse property was retained as a residence for the Norths, nonetheless, at least as late as 1667 (Bodl. MS. North c.4.149). It should be observed also that the larger part of the Charterhouse, to the west, was purchased in 1611 by Thomas Sutton (reputedly the wealthiest commoner in England), who arranged for its conversion to a hospital (almshouse) to maintain men past working age and to educate the children of poor parents (e.g., Richard Crashaw, Roger Williams, Joseph Addison, Sir Richard Steele, John Wesley, and William Thackeray).

12. Diane K. Bolton, "Harrow," *A History of the County of Middlesex*, vol. IV, ed. J. S. Cockburn and T. F. T. Baker, in *The Victoria History of the Counties of England*, ed. R. B. Pugh (1971), pp. 203–204. The term "flower" is from Sir Dudley North's son Roger (BL Add. MS. 32,523, 5r). See also Daniel Lysons, *The Environs of London*, II, *County of Middlesex* (1795), 559–588; and Walter W. Druett, *Harrow Through the Ages* (3rd ed., Uxbridge, 1956).

13. Richardson remarks that "There is little doubt that his resignation was forced upon him by political pressure, although there is no absolute proof of this" (p. 189).

14. *Some Notes*, p. 18.

cided to remove him from her Privy Council, but by that time a monarch's willingness to dispense with North's services as Councillor was much less remarkable than the fact that his political instinct had allowed him to thrive so well and so long as he did.

When Alice, Lady North, died in 1560, North, now in his middle sixties, decided to remarry. For his second wife he took another rich widow, Margaret, daughter of Richard Butler and widow of Sir David Brook. Then in his final four years he seems to have turned mainly to the country duties and peace of Cambridgeshire.

Edward North, first Baron North, was succeeded by his eldest son, Roger (1531–1600), whom Camden calls "Vir viuido ingenio, animo consilioque par." [15] From early times when the young Princess Elizabeth tied a red silk scarf on Roger's arm at a tournament[16] until both were comfortable old opponents at primero (he owned a book on how to win at cards, but his greater skill was losing), Roger was a man who manifested both spirit and wit. As a youth he is supposed to have attended his father's old college, Peterhouse.[17] Then in his mid-twenties he married Winifred, widow of Sir Henry Dudley and daughter of Richard, Lord Rich, sometime associate of Edward North in the Court of Augmentations. Winifred was to bear Roger two sons, John and Henry, the first of whom was the grandfather of Sir Dudley North, and the second, founder of the Mildenhall, Suffolk, branch of the family.

Roger served in Parliament for Cambridgeshire in 1555, in 1558–1559, and in 1563–1564. Then in 1564 he assumed his seat among the Lords. Meanwhile he had been created Knight of the Bath at Elizabeth's coronation (1559) and granted admission to Gray's Inn (1561). Queen Elizabeth employed various means to demonstrate her confidence in Roger. She sent him on diplomatic missions, first to Vienna in 1568 with the Earl of Sussex, and most notably in 1574 as Ambassador Extraordinary to France; and in 1588 she appointed him Lord Lieutenant of Cambridgeshire and the Isle of Ely. In 1577 he was able to reciprocate somewhat by entertaining her lavishly for three days at Kirtling, playing her in to supper with his own band of minstrels, augmented for the occasion by those of his good friend Leicester.[18] Still a vigorous man at the age of fifty-five, he commenced a career as soldier. So successful was he, in fact, that after the battle of Zutphen (1586), where he displayed particular courage, Leicester gave him the title of Knight Banneret. The highest worldly ascent, however, of Roger, second Baron North,

15. *Annales Rerum Anglicarum, et Hibernicarum.* . . (1615), p. 217.
16. Frances Bushby, *Three Men of the Tudor Time* (1911), p. 44.
17. John Venn and J. A. Venn, comp., *Alumni Cantabrigienses*, pt. I, vol. III (Cambridge, 1924), p. 266.
18. Bushby, "Memoirs," p. 71. See William Stevenson, "Extracts from 'The Booke of the Howshold Charges and Other Paiments Laid out by the L. North. . .,'" *Archaeologia*, XIX (1821), 283–301.

came in 1596: already a Privy Councillor, the old soldier and sometime primero player became Treasurer of the Royal Household.

Roger North was by no means the man of letters that his brother Thomas
was. Thomas, after all, was one of the best prose stylists of the age. On the
other hand, Roger North valued writing. In his personal copy of the *Canterbury Tales*—which today remains one of the finest of all surviving copies and
is known as the Ellesmere manuscript—there are several poems scrawled in
his hand and accompanied by his signature and his motto, *Durum Pati*.[19] "My
inward mane," he writes, "to hevenly things would trade me / But aye this
flesh doth still and still dissuade me." When he died at his house in Charterhouse Yard in December 1600, the old courtier and soldier was given a funeral at St. Paul's, then carried down to Cambridgeshire to be buried with
the pomp and circumstance of heralds in the chapel that his father had added
to Kirtling's parish church. There, on a fine six-poster tomb, a stone man in
armor was placed, his head on his helmet, his sword by his side, and the
North crest at his feet. At his feet also were Roger's words, inscribed in large
gold letters: *Durum pati*.

The family title fell not to a son, but to "my loving nephew [i.e., grandson]
Dudley Northe, . . . eldest sonne of my eldest sonne."[20] Dudley's father, Sir
John (1551?–1597), had died previously while still in his forties. Not much is
known of him. In 1562 he was a fellow commoner "of immature age" at Peterhouse, Cambridge, and in 1567 he moved to Trinity when his tutor, John
Whitgift, assumed the mastership there.[21] Then in May 1572, after six years
of study in *humanioribus literis graecis et latinis*, he was admitted M.A. The
continuing importance of Cambridge University in the lives of the Norths becomes increasingly clear—not surprisingly, considering that Kirtling was so
near. Equally clear are the signs of a genuinely bookish strain in the family.

John went traveling on the Continent in 1576, returned home in 1578 (his
father thought a stay of twenty-six months was brief), and soon embarked
again, this time with a band of volunteers for the wars in the Low Countries.
Back in England once more in 1580, he married Dorothy, daughter and coheiress of his father's friend Dr. (later Sir) Valentine Dale, Master of the
Court of Requests. The fact that another of Roger's good friends, Robert
Dudley, Earl of Leicester, was the godfather of the first son of this marriage
would seem to provide the best reason why Dudley became an important
Christian name in the family.[22]

19. *The Ellesmere Chaucer Reproduced in Facsimile*, pref. Alix Egerton, I (Manchester, 1911).
See also Bushby, *Three Men*, pp. 88–89. W. C. Hazlitt included Roger North in his *Contributions
Towards a Dictionary of English Book-Collectors* (1898), p. 22.

20. Bushby, "Memoirs," p. 105.

21. Bushby, "Memoirs," p. 123; Venn and Venn, pt. I, vol. III, p. 265.

22. The entry in the baptismal register of St. Gregory by St. Paul's, London, gives the date of
Dudley's birth as 18 September 1582 (Guildhall Library MS. 10,231). In time, five more children

In 1582, with a commission from the Duke of Anjou, John sailed off again to the Netherlandish wars. He returned to England to serve as M.P. of the shire for Cambridge (1584–1585, 1586–1587, 1588–1589), was knighted in Dublin in 1596, and, back in London the following year, died on 5 June of a summer "calenture." [23] The inveterate letter-writer John Chamberlain reported that Sir John was "thought to have left his lady but a mean widow," [24] yet funds were forthcoming to erect a fine monument to his memory in the church of St. Gregory by St. Paul's. [25] Then in 1604, after an interval of about seven years, his widow, Dame Dorothy, married Sir James Ouchterlony, one of the carvers to England's new king.

---

resulted from this union: John, K.B. (discussed here later); Roger, a notable seaman and one of Sir Walter Raleigh's captains; Gilbert, who became a Gentleman Usher to Charles I; Elizabeth, who married Sir Jerome Horsey, the traveler, and settled in Buckinghamshire; and Mary, who married Sir Francis Coningsby of Hertfordshire.

23. BL MS. Harl. 7,029, 269r; and Bushby, "Memoirs," p. 127.

24. *The Letters of John Chamberlain*, ed. Norman Egbert McClure, I (Philadelphia, 1939), 31.

25. Some fifty years later, much to the dismay of the third Lord North, the church was demolished in the name of urban renewal (*Forest 45*, pp. 233–235).

SIR DUDLEY'S FATHER

At about the time that Sir John North died, his fifteen-year-old son Dudley, later third Lord North (1582–1667), matriculated as a fellow commoner at Trinity College.[1] Dudley was to encounter "dangerous diseases" at the University,[2] but it was his good experiences there at his father's college that proved to be most important. Over half a century later he put into words some of the gratitude that he felt toward his alma mater: "whatsoever fruits of Piety, or shadows of Knowledge or Virtue have found growth within me," he wrote, "next to God, I owe them unto you. . . ."[3]

He said nothing so kind about his mother or grandfather. Old Roger, who had seen his chief heir fall sick and die, and then suffered a breakdown in his own health, had become so fearful for the future of the family that he stirred himself to action and married off his eighteen-year-old grandson late in November of 1600. Dudley never recuperated from the experience. Forty-five years later, in fact, he put some of his frustration into print: "had I been left single, young as I was, I was resolved never to have married, but so as to have set my self at ease for house-keeping, and other charges which attend it, according to my quality."[4] Nevertheless, "My Predecessor after a long and desperate sicknesse lived just enough to marry me. . . ."[5]

At the time of Roger's death the North family's properties were extensive, but Dudley complained bitterly of his situation. "In truth," he wrote, "my estate was so scantie that my endeavours could intertain no further aim then to be able to subsist."[6] In part it was a problem of available cash as opposed to other sorts of property. Considering that he was baring private grievances in print, the particularity of Dudley's complaint is startling: "I had my quality left unto me with an estate of revenew not above six hundred pounds *per Annum de claro*. . . ."[7]

1. John Venn and J. A. Venn, comp., *Alumni Cantabrigienses*, pt. I, vol. III (Cambridge, 1924), p. 265. Dorothy North recorded that when her eldest child was about fifteen, her daughter Elizabeth was about eleven; John, about ten; Roger, about nine; Mary, about seven; and Gilbert, about six months (BL Harl. 7,029, 269r).

2. *Forest 45*, p. 123.

3. *A Forest Promiscuous of Several Seasons Productions* (1659), A3r.

4. *Forest 45*, p. 128. This passage is dated 22 August 1637.

5. *Forest 45*, p. 131.

6. *Forest 45*, p. 127.

7. *Forest 45*, pp. 120–121. Stone places the gross rentals of North in 1602 between £900 and £1,799 (p. 760). Bolton reports that in 1604 the year's profits for the estate at Harrow were £204

There were also other dimensions to what the young man perceived as his plight. Roger died on 3 December 1600, and that same day his daughter-in-law, Dame Dorothy, wrote to Sir Robert Cecil requesting the wardship of her son and the lease of his lands during the remaining two and three-quarters years of his minority.[8] She protested that Dudley's marriage had been arranged "without her consent, or almost privity" and that the money given in marriage had been taken from her son.[9] Dudley himself, on the other hand, wrote to Cecil to move the Queen to grant him his own lands during his minority, arguing that if his mother were to control them, it would "far more hinder his estate than profit hers."[10] Not only had his grandfather impelled him into marriage; it now appeared that his mother wished to profit from the situation.

The sixteen-year-old bride, whose own happiness cannot have been great, was Frances Brockett, daughter of Sir John Brockett of Brockett Hall and his second wife, Elizabeth, herself the daughter of Roger Moore. Until recently Sir John had been the head of the distinguished Hertfordshire family,[11] but in 1598 he died without male issue, and his considerable holdings were divided among six daughters, of whom Frances was the youngest. Many years later North avowed in print that "Love rather alien'd is then bred by force."[12] Nor did he scruple to affirm that "Grossely hee erres, who thinkes that words or law / Can sympathy of heart and love perswade."[13] Still more directly, he complained of his own "mariage in a short fortune," going so far as to say that the "shortness" was the cause of dulling "the edge and alacrity of my spirits."[14] The extent of his frustration may be grasped in part by the fact that at the time he published these observations—with rather transparent anonymity—his wife was still very much alive. It is impossible now to separate fact from feeling in the matter of this marriage, but a tidbit of contemporary gos-

("Harrow," *A History of the County of Middlesex*, vol. IV, ed. J. S. Cockburn and T. F. T. Baker, in *The Victoria History of the Counties of England*, ed. R. B. Pugh [1971], p. 225).

8. HMC, *Calendar of the Manuscripts of the . . . Marquis of Salisbury. . .*, pt. X (1904), p. 405. Cecil had become Master of the Court of Wards in 1598. Lawrence Stone offers interesting insights into the unofficial selling of wardships for Cecil's own profit (*Family and Fortune: Studies in Aristocratic Finance in the Sixteenth and Seventeenth Centuries* [Oxford, 1973], esp. pp. 22–23).

9. HMC, *Calendar of the Manuscripts of the . . . Marquis of Salisbury. . .*, pt. X (1904), p. 410. The proceedings were designed to benefit his grandfather's executors, she said.

10. He wrote to Cecil on 12 December 1600 (ibid., p. 47). See also HMC, *Calendar of the Manuscripts of . . . the Marquis of Salisbury. . .*, pt. XIV, *Addenda* (1923), p. 197; here Roger's executors may be found asking Cecil to name those to whom the lands of the new Lord North should be granted to his use during his minority, since he and his mother could not agree.

11. See, for example, Bodl. MS. North a.16(R); Walter C. Metcalfe, ed., *The Visitations of Hertfordshire*, Publications of the Harleian Society, XXII (1886), 32; William Berry, *County Genealogies, Pedigrees of Hertfordshire Families* (n.d.), pp. 132–134; and Edward J. Brockett, comp., asstd. by John B. Koetteritz and Francis E. Brockett, *The Descendants of John Brockett* (East Orange, N.J., 1905), pedigree following p. 266.

12. *Forest 45*, p. 45.

13. Ibid.

14. *Forest 45*, p. 125.

sip may be glimpsed in a diary entry by John Manningham: "I hear that the yong Lord North was married to Mrs. Brocket, . . . being constrayned in a manner through want of money while he liued in Cambridge; he has some 800*l*. with hir. Shee is not yong nor well fauoured, noe maruaile yf he loue hir not."[15] Manningham certainly was wrong in one matter: Frances Brockett, two years younger than her bridegroom, was quite young enough.

After the wedding took place and after his grandfather had been laid away in the chapel that Edward North had built, the new Lord North proceeded to claim as much freedom as he could. Thinking himself to be fundamentally of a sanguine temperament, though now he was periodically distraught by melancholy, he could not help feeling that "imploiment" might lighten "this weight of my disease."[16] As it turned out, most of his attempts at employment were to prove either temporary or abortive. On 7 February 1602 he was admitted gratis to the Inner Temple,[17] but already on 17 May 1602 Chamberlain was informing Dudley Carleton that "The Lord Norths licence to travayle was signed the last weeke. . . ." Chamberlain adds that "some thincke he will make no great haste for that his Lady is with child" (Lady North was then about three and a half months pregnant with young Dudley).[18] On 17 June, nonetheless, Chamberlain wrote Carleton, "Your cousen Saunders tells me that he and the Lord North begin theyre travayle about a weeke hence, and meane to take theyre way by the Lowe Countries and see this sommers service";[19] and on 27 June he reported that North and Saunders had left some three or four days earlier.[20] The trip ended in disaster. Saunders fell ill and died of the plague, and North sought to protect himself from contagion by undertaking what proved to be an "inordinate, and indiscreet use" of a "new Treakle."[21] This treacle, North later concluded, "wholly altered and disanimated me."[22] He arrived back in England safely, but to this period he traced the worsening of his melancholy. Melancholy, deepened and darkened by "the study of *Mountaynes Essayes*,"[23] became a dominant factor in his life and, perforce, in the lives of those who lived with him.

Meanwhile North's written comments on this period omit any mention of the birth of his son. With the disappearance of better records one must turn again to John Chamberlain for what appears to be the only surviving notice

15. *Diary of John Manningham, of the Middle Temple, . . . 1602–1603*, ed. John Bruce (Westminster, 1868), p. 50.

16. *A Forest Promiscuous*, p. 120. He says in the same passage that he considered going to fight the Turks, "and then came Peace and Truce."

17. F. A. Inderwick, *A Calendar of the Inner Temple Records*, I (1896), 447.

18. Chamberlain, I, 147. Although it was relatively common for a young man to travel on the Continent shortly after his wedding, it also is certain that North felt ensnared by marriage.

19. Chamberlain, I, 150.

20. Chamberlain, I, 152.

21. *Forest 45*, pp. 214, 122.

22. *Forest 45*, p. 214.

23. *Forest 45*, p. 153.

of the event. On 15 October 1602 Chamberlain noted that North's wife was still with child, but on 4 November he was able to report that "The young Lady North is brought to bed of a sonne. . . ."[24] Apparently the news comes from London, and a fair assumption is that the birth took place at the Charterhouse.

Now "pent" by a wife and child, North soon would be "pent" by wife and children.[25] Eventually there were four boys and two girls.[26] Furthermore, there was a continuing responsibility to various sets of servants. More responsibility meant more worry, and more worry exacerbated North's melancholy. Presumably one physician told him that he thought too hard and had too much mind for his body.[27] Making matters worse, his body began to grow pursy, and to counter a tendency to overweight, he undertook a disastrously "misguided sobriety of diet."[28] At least so far as his own temperament was concerned, he exactly hit the mark when he concluded that "Moderation is the hardest of vertues. . . ."[29] Turning to study for solace, he proceeded to study too much, devoting himself to foreign languages with ungentlemanly fervor (perhaps with an eye to making himself fit for a suitable post). Moreover, despite what observers at the time might have thought, he later claimed that he was all the while taking "an inordinate care for the ordering" of his estate.[30] Before long he embarked on "dividing my *London* house where (in al events) there would be least losse, and then lived many years in the lesser part."[31] The Charterhouse thus continued to be important in the lives of the family, but the young lord had not learned how to spend wisely, much less to economize, and later he regretted the "many thousands I laid out in building at *London*."[32]

In the end, although all of North's various activities "proved . . . such miserable helpers as melancholy men use to finde,"[33] he did not stop trying to put his life on a better course. Since his previous travels had been tragically

24. Chamberlain, I, 165–166, 169–170.

25. He uses the term in *Forest 45*, p. 118.

26. Besides Dudley, fourth Lord North, there were Charles and Robert (died young); John (admitted fellow commoner, Peterhouse, Cambridge, 1 July 1629; admitted to Lincoln's Inn 3 February 1631; married 20 July 1634 to Sarah, daughter and coheiress of Henry Seckford, widow of Charles Drury of Rougham, Suffolk; he married twice subsequently, but his first wife "best deserves to be remembered; for she left him an estate in St. John's-Court by Smithfield, upon the ground where the chief house and garden was placed; and now a set of fair houses are built, making three sides of a square, and is called North's-Court" [Roger North, *Lives*, I, 4–5]); Dorothy (married first, Richard Lennard, Lord Dacre of the South [1624]; second, Challoner Chute of the Vyne [1650]); and Elizabeth (died at Tunbridge Wells, August 1624).

27. *Forest 45*, p. 130.

28. *Forest 45*, p. 118.

29. *Forest 45*, p. 150. A prime example of North's lack of moderation is a certain vow he later referred to, a "vow made by me which cost me a great part of my estate, having against my intentions intangled my conscience thereby" (*Forest 45*, p. 121). The nature of the vow is unknown.

30. *Forest 45*, p. 118.   31. Ibid.

32. *Forest 45*, p. 121.   33. *Forest 45*, p. 118.

interrupted, it must have seemed reasonable to him to return abroad. In January 1603, when his son was two or three months old, North was writing to Sir Robert Cecil from Paris.[34] In July 1604, he complained to Cecil about being delayed in another departure—the source of trouble being his own neglect to obtain a pass.[35] And in April and May of 1605 he was among those appointed to attend the Earl of Hertford on his embassy to Brussels.[36] In June of the same year he may be glimpsed in Antwerp, gambling, attending the theater, and playing tennis. From thence he returned to Brussels (where he stayed with the Ambassador) and then set off for Trier, Metz, Reims, and eventually Paris, where, having King James's "leave to consummate this summer on this side the sea,"[37] he passed several months, gaming and playing more tennis.[38] By the time that he returned again to England on 20 November 1605, it was clear that this latest effort to beguile his melancholy had resulted not only in a further shrinking of his means but also in a further weakening of his once-robust health.

When physicians advised North to retire into the country, he decided to go to Eridge House, the hunting seat of Lord Abergavenny down in the wilds of Sussex. After a lengthy visit there, however, finding that seclusion made him worse instead of better, he set out to return to London. It was at this time, about two miles from Eridge, that he came across a certain pool of water with unusual iridescent splotches. The story is told that he borrowed a wooden bowl from a countrywoman, tasted the water, carried a sample up to London to be scrutinized, and hence is to be credited with discovering those waters which within his own lifetime were to become famous as the Tunbridge Wells.[39] Subsequently he came back to drink the waters for about three months, then returned once more to London with his health improved.

North's various attempts at travel and seclusion had finally become so extended that he felt out of touch with the court. Now, "for a strong diversion, and under so brave a patronage as that of Prince *Henry*," he "readventured" —that is, made his second entry into courtly life.[40] Henry was a youth in-

---

34. HMC, *Calendar of the Manuscripts of . . . the Marquis of Salisbury*, pt. XII (Hereford, 1910), p. 603. He assured Cecil that "The hope of my affairs in England is only sustained on your favour"; Cecil died in 1612.

35. HMC, *Calendar of the Manuscripts of . . . the Marquess of Salisbury*, pt. XVI, ed. M. S. Giuseppi (1933), pp. 191–192.

36. HMC, *Report on the Manuscripts of . . . the Marquess of Bath*, IV, ed. Marjorie Blatcher (1968), 200.

37. HMC, *Calendar of the Manuscripts of . . . the Marquess of Salisbury. . .* , pt. XVII, ed. M. S. Giuseppi (1938), p. 293.

38. Bodl. MS. North b.12 (85r–90v, 113r–121r).

39. *Forest 45*, p. 134. The story is told with variations in several places, including Lodwick Rowzee, *The Queenes Welles* (1632); Thomas Benge Burr, *The History of Tunbridge-Wells* (1746); Edward Hasted, *The History and Topographical Survey of . . . Kent*, vol. I (Canterbury, 1778); and Margaret Barton, *Tunbridge Wells* (1937). North also appears to have made known the waters of Epsom (*Forest 45*, p. 134).

40. *Forest 45*, p. 132.

clined towards sports, and North's name now begins to crop up in records of tilting, most notably in June 1610 at the spectacular creation of Henry as Prince of Wales.[41] One observer reported that the pomp and glory of that occasion "cost the noble men no lesse then a thousand poundes apeece, and some of them a great deale more."[42] For North the whole business was a courtly gamble. As Chapman has a character say in one of his masques, "I haue heard of some Courtiers, that haue run themselues out of their states with I[o]usting. . . ."[43] In fact, it was a gamble in more than one sense; on 23 March 1612 North was seriously wounded when a splintering lance wielded by the Earl of Montgomery during a practice session tore into the flesh of his arm. Moreover, the expense of both manly vigor and cash was to be in vain. In December of 1612 one finds Lord North—now thirty years old—participating in the funeral procession of Prince Henry, dead at eighteen.[44]

With the wind knocked from his sails once again, North was becalmed at court. Attaching himself to the Prince had not been the best way to endear himself to the King. Moreover, it was not until a good many years later that North could see and say that "Place forceth no man to expence. . . ."[45] At Caversham House in April 1613 he danced before Queen Anne in a Campion masque (wearing a suit of embroidered green satin), and the following December (in purplish-red and white) he performed in Ben Jonson's *Challenge at Tilt at a Marriage*, a celebration of the most famous match of the day, that of the King's favorite, Robert Carr, Earl of Somerset, and the Lady Frances Howard.[46] In fact, North's name continues for a long while to pop up in connection with courtly events. We find various members of his family being knighted. In May 1619 we find him among the barons at Queen Anne's funeral—and Baroness North among the ladies.[47] Then in 1620, when his seaman brother Roger set off on an unauthorized colonizing venture to "those parts of the Continent of America neare and about the Riuer of Amazones," there was a different sort of news concerning North: King James had clapped him into the Fleet for being clandestinely involved in the business.[48] Although

---

41. John Gough Nichols, *The Progresses, Processions, and Magnificent Festivities, of King James the First*, II (1828), 361.

42. John Noies, in HMC *Report on Manuscripts in Various Collections*, III (1904), 262. North's young son Dudley, now seven, probably sat among "the litell sonnes of the nobilitie" at the creation itself (pp. 259–260).

43. *The Memorable Maske of the Two Honourable Houses or Inns of Court; the Middle Temple, and Lyncolns Inne* (n.d., but performed 15 February 1613/14), C1r–v.

44. Nichols, II, 497.

45. *Forest 45*, p. 183.

46. Nichols, II, 638, 629; and II, 729. In 1616, following the revelation of the murder of Sir Thomas Overbury, North was summoned (along with other peers) to attend the trial of Somerset and his wife; presumably he was "one of approved wisdome and integrity" (*Acts of the Privy Council of England, 1615–1616*, vol. XXXIV [1st pub. 1925; reprinted Nendeln, Liechtenstein, 1974], 504–505). It appears that he did not attend.

47. Nichols, III, 538, 541.

48. In a proclamation dated 15 May 1620 James expressed his ire at the "rash, vndutiful and insolent attempt" of the adventurers (*A Proclamation Declaring His Majesties Pleasure Concerning*

some of the nobility came calling on him there, a man of North's sensitivity cannot have suffered imprisonment for several days with much equanimity. Nevertheless, he continued to play the courtier. In 1621, when the Venetian Ambassador held a grant to raise three thousand soldiers, North, now almost forty, gained a certain prominence by putting himself forward as one of the chief competitors to manage the affair: "I will serve as Colonel with a regiment of 2,000 foot. . . ," he proposed. "I will serve by sea or land. . . ."[49] It was a large gesture, but nothing came of the matter.

While North was failing to find a post suitable to his taste, talent, character, and (he later implied) moral values, his financial base was continuing to erode. In the fall of 1622 he sold Sir William Russell the manors of Stetchworth, Patmore, and Madfreyes, together with some other property, for £9,000.[50] In the winter of 1623 he took steps to cut down the Weald Wood at his great estate at Harrow, although "No man," he wrote, "more abhorred . . . felling, and selling, then my selfe. . . ."[51] Observing, like everyone else, that King James was aging rapidly, North doubtless weighed how he might fare at the court of a new king. Meanwhile he kept his hand in public affairs by attendance at the House of Lords.[52]

In 1625, when James died and Charles came to the throne, it soon became obvious that a change in monarchs was to mean no change in royal favorites. Referring to Buckingham, James's final and dearest favorite, North's brother John wrote that "our great Man of Power, the Duke . . . disposeth of all more absolutely than ever."[53] North himself was moved to compose a series of admonitory prose characters in which he described such figures as a good king and a good courtier. Although too wise to circulate them freely, he had whatever satisfaction might be gained from privately venting his view that a king

---

Captaine Roger North, and Those Who Are Gone Foorth as Adventurers with Him, 1r). The warrant to the warden of the Fleet to receive Lord North is dated 21 May, and the warrant to release him, 26 May (*Acts of the Privy Council of England, 1619–1621*, vol. XXXVII [1st pub. 1930; rept. Nendeln, Liechtenstein, 1974], pp. 201, 207). Chamberlain reports that North was "all the while so exceedingly visited that he had sometimes 6 Earles there at once besids Barons and others" (II, 306).

49. Bodl. MS. North a.2, 243r–v; and Allen B. Hinds, ed., *CSP*, Venetian, 1619–1621, XVI (1910), 620–621.

50. Spencer MS. uncat. North 17:7, indenture dated 21 September 1622.

51. John Cordy Jeaffreson, ed., *Middlesex County Records*, II (1887[?]), 174; and *Forest 45*, p. 119.

52. See Henry Elsing, *Notes of the Debates in the House of Lords . . . 1624 and 1626*, ed. Samuel Rawson Gardiner (Westminster, 1879). In 1614, in a speech in the upper house, North had referred to himself as "the vnworthiest of the house and vnablest to speake," and used notes because *"secundae cogitationes sunt meliores"* (HMC, *Report on the Manuscripts of the Late Reginald Rawdon Hastings. . .* , vol. IV, ed. Francis Bickley [1947], pp. 257–258). If melancholy coupled with a fierce need to excel sometimes tied his tongue, North was doubtless given pause also by the increasingly difficult problems facing Parliament. In about 1625 he attempted to define *"A good Parliament Man"*: "his own interest and allegiance will instruct him to affect to please the King, but his conscience will lead him to assent only to what is wholsome; his sincere judgement, and not implicit faith is to be his guide" (*Forest 45*, p. 87).

53. Printed in Arthur Collins, *Letters and Memorials of State*, II (1746), 360.

should beware of a favorite with "the falshood and voracitie of the Woolfe." [54]
Shortly before the time that Buckingham was removed from the scene by an
assassin's knife (August 1628) matters had grown so bad in the land that
North supported Parliament's famous protest to the King (June 1628), the
Petition of Right. [55] In 1629, it is true, he was chosen—perhaps because he
knew Italian better than most courtiers did—to greet the Venetian Ambassador. [56] In June 1630, furthermore, he was one of only six barons chosen to
bear a rich canopy over the infant Prince Charles at his christening. [57] It
should have been clear to North in the mid-1620s, nonetheless, that he never
would duplicate the courtly success of his forebears.

Evaluating the basic outline of North's story, one historian of our own time
has chosen to cite him as an example of conspicuous consumption. North
illustrates, says Lawrence Stone, "the cost of attendance at Court in the hope
of office, which in the long run was likely to empty the purse of the average
baron, unless the Crown came to the rescue. This was the cause of the ruin of
the Sandys [sic], the Windsors, and the Norths." [58] Little wonder that North's
heir, the second Dudley North, was to spend most of his adult life trying to
increase the family holdings, and that eventually he turned his hand to writing a volume on household economy.

Sir Dudley's son Roger (the third Lord North's grandson) scribbled a paragraph describing North's situation at court and explaining how it finally
changed:

> The Strait Circumstances wch the vanity of K. Ja. 1s Court had
> brought upon the first Dudley Lord North . . . , by following the hu-
> mour of the age, & Neglecting to Embrace opportunityes that offered for
> his advancement [marginal note: "would not accept of Revertions, &
> lived to bury .2. generations" [59]], began to pinch. . . . When, as Wis-
> dome is Never too late, so then upon advice of a phisitian to sell the
> flower of the Estate & pay Debts, & give children their portions, & for-
> sware london & the Court, the advice was ffollowed, tho as his lo[rd-
> shi]ps say'd it was a bitter pill, and the Great Estate at Harrow upon the
> Hill sold, the Mony distributed & the family Retired to the place of their
> honor. . . . [60]

54. *Forest 45*, p. 85.
55. The petition may be viewed in its parliamentary context in *Ephemeris Parliamentaria; or A Faithfull Register of the Transactions in Parliament, in the Third and Fourth Years of the Reign of Our Late Sovereign Lord King Charles* (1654), pp. 175–177.
56. The Ambassador, Giovanni Soranzo, regarded North as one of England's leading noble-men (Allen B. Hinds, ed., *CSP*, Venetian, 1629–1632, XXII [1919], 128; see also p. 445).
57. Edgar Sheppard, *Memorials of St. James's Palace*, II (1894), 33.
58. Stone, p. 186; see also p. 584.
59. The point is that North was too impatient to wait for a post to fall vacant, yet lived to an advanced age.
60. BL Add. MS. 32,523, 5r.

On 6 January 1631, along with other lesser holdings, North had sold off the manor of Woodhall (£3,443/14/6), the manor of Hedgestone (£1,800/2/6), the manor of Roxeth Place (£3,156), and, perhaps the most wrenching thing he ever had to do, the manor of the Harrow Rectory and the manors of Harrow and Sudbury (£13,000).[61] Nor was this all. Before the month was out, on 18 January, for the sum of £4,500, he sold his two chief mansions at the Charterhouse to the Earl of Rutland.[62] Resolved now to live at Kirtling, as Roger says, North "lived upon the small remainder More splendidly & More honourably then ever before in the Greatest profusion. and if the tradition of it be true, in More Grandure then any other family in that part of England. ffor his lo[rdshi]ps being a Courtier, & withall a person of Much Witt, & More fancy, affected a state answerable to his Education, & former cours of life, & had his meals served with officers with white staves. . . ."[63]

Strategic retreat did, indeed, help North to continue living in a style commensurate with his "former cours of life," but the financial maneuvering that proved necessary must have been more than a little sobering to the family. Even before the great shedding of property in 1631, on 23 December 1629 North had

> Conveyed & setled the Mannor of Kirtling with diverse other Mannor lands Avowsons Tythes & other hereditaments in the county of Cambridge To the vse of himselfe & his assignes during his naturall [life] & from & after his decease To the vse & behoofe of Sir John Carleton[,] Sir John Cutts & Sir Thomas Read & their heires for the naturall life of the Lady ffrances then wife to the said Lord North vpon trust to prmitt Sir Dudley North oldest sonne of the said Lord North & his heires to enioy the premisses solong as he or they should pay vnto the said Lady ffrances the sume of 850li per annu[m] halfe yearely. . . .[64]

Lady North's sisters Margaret, Elizabeth, and Mary had married, respectively, into the families of Cutts, Carleton, and Reade. Now by means of the interested aid of these in-laws, North was enabled to save face with the world.

With compelling reasons for retreat to the country, North later wrote that "My years, fortunes, the times and other circumstances have confined my course and discourse, to a resolved retirednesse, as unnaturall to the respects of my places of birth, education, and conversation, as solitarinesse to mankind; no man was ever more affected to an intelligent and well-spirited

61. Spencer MS. uncat. North 7:1; the document also specifies a good many additional details. See Daniel Lysons, *The Environs of London*, II (1795), 563, 564, 565, 567, 583, 590.

62. Spencer MS. uncat. North 17:5 (18 January, 6 Charles). A second document (Spencer MS. uncat. North 17:6), bearing the same date, confirmed the sale and provided that Rutland be allowed to take over without any trouble or interruption.

63. BL Add. MS. 32,523, 5r.

64. Bodl. MS. North b.20, 308r; Bodl. MS. North b.26, 145r, apparently written by Sir Dudley in 1667, is a hasty draft for a revision of the earlier document.

society then my self, I have formerly sought it and enjoyed it with greedinesse, I have now lost it. . . ."[65] Sometimes he tried to put a good face on the matter: "I hope to fall handsomely to an honest country course, and play the Paterfamilias better then others have discharged themselves towards mee. . . ."[66] He did, indeed, invest more time and interest in Kirtling. Repair work there was expensive (workmen were less accurate than in earlier days, and they loitered more),[67] and hop-poles would never prove as interesting as lances, but at least North tried to view his situation positively. "The Country life," he wrote, "is assuredly most naturall, pleasant, setled, and profitable to the *English* breed and course."[68]

A brief comment from Sir Simonds D'Ewes even suggests that by this time, if not before, North and his wife had reached a certain accord. At any rate, D'Ewes enables one to glimpse the Norths together and acting in concert. Always conservative and pious, D'Ewes reports with distaste how he has encountered the Norths at the home of Lord and Lady Coventry. Himself an invited guest to a Sunday dinner of hot venison, D'Ewes notes that he had gone "before their [the Coventrys'] service begann, and heard from Mr. Macchines a verie learned sermon. About the middle whereof came in my Lorde North and his Ladie unexpected, whoe did soe fill upp all the dinner-time with the needles and vaine discourse of a dogg they had which died a little before, as it shewed them to bee ill-catechized in the principles of religion."[69] The trouble with the anecdote, of course, is that it probably reveals more about D'Ewes than about the Norths.

Ironically, it was an attempt that North made to return to London in the winter of 1638–1639 that may have shown him finally that Cambridgeshire was his proper sphere. Writing from the city in January, he confessed that "as I am without power, so am I worne out of fashion and acquaintance, and I find little new worth the seeking and imbracing; friendships are grown rare, dissimulation, cost and ceremony have extirpated them; Generosity is hardly to bee found; All distrust, cunning, pride. . . ."[70] A lover of London all his life, he found that he was no longer comfortable there.

From this time on, one catches glimpses of North as a man concerned about the welfare of his eldest son, devoted to his remaining friends, and interested in religion. On the other hand, he sometimes behaved like a testy,

65. *Forest 45*, pp. 220–221.
66. *Forest 45*, p. 217.
67. *Forest 45*, p. 120.
68. *Forest 45*, p. 159. The fact is that many Englishmen of the time were beginning to manifest an increased interest in the possibilities of rural retirement. Maren-Sofie Røstvig goes so far as to say that "The trend in favour of a retired, introspective existence at this time grew so strong that it almost amounted to a compulsion" (*The Happy Man: Studies in the Metamorphoses of a Classical Idea*, I [rev. ed., New York, 1962; 1st ed., 1954], 80).
69. *The Autobiography and Correspondence of Sir Simonds D'Ewes, Bart.*, ed. James Orchard Halliwell, II (1845), 215–216.
70. *Forest 45*, p. 69.

impulsive, frustrated, displaced courtier. Perhaps these two contrasting sides of North's character merged in his readiness to indulge his emotions and in his refusal to work anything out patiently. Because of the importance of Lord North in the life of his son Sir Dudley, at any rate, the complex and conflicting evidence about his character must be weighed.

In February 1639, when the King summoned all peers to York, North was inclined to demur because of "infirmity of body and fortune," but he attended nonetheless and promised to supply horses to the King—fewer than others, on the grounds that he was "the least estated lord of the kingdom." [71] During this period when political sides began to form, North evidently was inclined toward the royalists. On 24 April 1640 he voted against the King on an important issue that came before the Lords,[72] but on 22 October that same year Charles appointed him joint Lord Lieutenant of Cambridgeshire with William, Baron Maynard. Apparently North could see good reasons for not joining either side. In 1645 he wrote that *"the direfull extremities and convulsions which my unhappy Country, and my self in it have suffered these last yeeres make good with me the saying of* Ingentes curae stupent: *Partiality found much, ingenuity little freedom: the first surprize was such as caryed me to an affectation of dissolution rather then to endure the spectatorship of the growing miseries & approaching tragedies; nay, spectatorship was not allowed. . . ."*[73] When detachment proved impossible, North again took lodgings in London.

Roger North later scrawled an account of how his grandfather's attempt at "dissolution" led back, by a circuitous route, to the very eye of the storm. In order to absent himself from civil strife, and in particular to avoid taking the oath required by the Solemn League and Covenant of 17 August 1643, North sought seclusion at the country house of his daughter Dorothy, Lady Dacre, in Kent. As Roger explains it,

> at length Some lords, called him old fox, and being Resolved to bring him out amongst them, obteined an order for a comittee of lords to goe downe, & tender him the Covenant; which was done, & he tooke it; ffor, however he had No Stomack to Conforme, yet having bin a Courtier & a man of pleasure, he was Not disposed to be Either Martir or Confesser In a case of State, and as soon as these lords had done with him, without More adoe he Shaved off his spade-beard (which he had let grow long) and went to london, and In Every thing he could opposed their proceedings. and from a Sullen absentee, became an active patroniser of the suffering Cavaliers, & seldome went to or from the hous without his hands full of papers, and a bustle of Suitors & petitioners, & most especially ladys of the Cavalier party at his heels, as If he were a Comon sollicitor

71. John Bruce and William Douglas Hamilton, ed., *CSP*, Domestic, 1638–1639 (1871), p. 472; and HMC, *Report on the Manuscripts of the Duke of Buccleuch. . .* , I (1899), 279.
72. William Douglas Hamilton, ed., *CSP*, Domestic, 1640 (1880), p. 66.
73. *Forest 45*, A2r.

for them; which made the then raging powers wish they had let him alone with his beard, not Stired his humors.[74]

Thenceforth his name appears repeatedly in the official records of the day, perhaps most importantly in 1645 when he was placed on a six-man commission for managing Admiralty affairs. On 10 February 1647 one finds him voting for the readmission of certain royalist lords who had been deprived of their seats in the Upper House back in 1644,[75] but the hard truth was that there would be no royalist stemming of the tide.

When two regiments of soldiers suddenly appeared at Whitehall, presumably to protect Parliament from a city mob, three peers, including North, requested leave of absence. On 6 December 1648 the last remnants of the King's party were purged from the Commons, as were some moderates like North's own son, Sir Dudley. Then two weeks later, on 19 December, when the King's danger was clear, Lord North went with three others to visit General Thomas Fairfax at his headquarters, in part, it has been thought, to discuss a plan to save Charles's life.[76]

The beheading of the King in January 1649 exhausted the passions of few men, and North still had sufficient public visibility to attract the pen of satire. If certain ladies, wrote Henry Neville, "want a *pouder'd and patch't old fool* to wait upon Them, let them send to my L. *North*, whose Coach and himself will be ready at a Call. . . ."[77] This was sharp enough, to be sure, but North's own words on both old age and himself could be nearly as harsh: "Age is a disease and breeds a morositie, yeeres and experience of good and bad, right and wrong, have made me nice and hard to please, whether in diet, conversation, or good order, wee have much adoe to become pleased in our selves, as much in others."[78]

Alongside the continuing strain and contention that somehow seem always to have marred his life, North's last years were made at least somewhat pleasanter by his success at involving various members of the Kirtling household in music. For a while the composer John Jenkins came to live and work at Kirtling.[79] Furthermore, North had long since disburdened himself of the management of his complex business affairs by placing them with a certain

74. BL Add. MS. 32,510, 17v–19r. An example of the materials not published in Roger's *Lives*, this passage throws light on a letter of 25 August from the Speaker of the House of Lords to the Earl of Lincoln and the Lords Bruce, Dacre, and North, bidding them forthwith to attend (HMC, *Fifth Report of the Royal Commission on Historical Manuscripts*, pt. I, *Report and Appendix* [1876], 103).

75. Charles Harding Firth, *The House of Lords During the Civil War* (1910), p. 155.

76. Firth, p. 206; but cf. David Underdown, *Pride's Purge: Politics in the Puritan Revolution* (Oxford, 1971), p. 168.

77. *Newes from the New-Exchange, or The Commonwealth of Ladies* (1650), p. 20.

78. *Forest 45*, p. 189.

79. See pp. 82–84. In the very last months of North's life one finds money being laid out on his behalf for music paper (Bodl. MS. North b.12, 351r).

prideful renunciation on the shoulders of his eldest son. Moreover, he claimed that he had managed to turn his mind mainly to godly things.

None of this is to suggest that there would be any thoroughgoing mellowing of North's character. Some of his family found him not merely overnice, but "very tyrannical and vindictive." [80] Roger North is quite outspoken about his grandfather: "he cared not whom he persecuted nor how unjustly or unreasonably, if it tended, as he thought[,] to justify any thing he had done. . . ." [81] But the composer Jenkins saw his patron in a different light. Although funerary verse is by definition suspect regarding the virtues of the deceased, it is noteworthy that after North's death Jenkins wrote of him not merely as "A True Mecenas & the muses Friend" but also as a man who had been "Just, pious, prudent, Charitable, good." [82] Complex as North was to the end, the truth probably lies not in a simple mean between such extreme statements, but in a dynamic, kaleidoscopic mix of them.

North himself, in addition to recording his pious devotional habits, acknowledged his "violence of spirit." [83] He made no bones about hating "fetters and circumscriptions, more then Religion, government, and reason cast them upon mee. . . ." [84] Furthermore, even when not resorting to a glaring eye or a sudden turning of his back, he sometimes must have been seething. He clearly had no trouble imagining how, without the grace of God, he might "transforme my selfe into an Angell of light, and play the Devill in my heart." [85] Very likely he knew himself better than his family ever fathomed. "I am naturally over solicitous in what I undertake," he wrote, "impatient and exact. . . ." [86] He understood that he had a weakness for excess. He says, "I have ever been over-hard to please in conversation, my present affections and habit make me now more dainty"; and to this observation he adds a query that is almost touching: "what shall I doe?" [87] Early and late, he was sensitive, impatient, and proud, capable of both spirited wit and profound moroseness. And at least sometimes his self-searching led him to peer through the facets of his own cantankerousness, wit, and sensitivity and to see at bottom the underlying, cold truth of his life. After all of his intellectual and emotional thrashing about, his most courageous confession of all comes as something of a shock: "I have been both agent and authour of my misery, and sufferings, I

80. *Lives*, I, 34.
81. Ibid.
82. Bodl. MS. Rawl. D.260, 34v–35r; also BL Add. MS. 18,220, 37r–v. Lord Holland in earlier years claimed to "know no man less swayed with passion, and sooner carried with reason and justice; and that at all times, a man could promise himself no less from Lord North" (cited by Lady Frances Bushby in her entry on North in *DNB*, XIV, 595). There is also an epigram to North by John Davies of Hereford, headed "To the Truly Noble Lord, Deservedly Al-be-loved, the Lord North" (*The Scourge of Folly* [1611], p. 219).
83. *Forest 45*, p. 214.   84. *Forest 45*, p. 66.
85. *Forest 45*, p. 182.   86. *Forest 45*, p. 217.
87. *Forest 45*, p. 174.

have been both Criminall and tormenter; God made me strong, I have made my self weak. . . ."[88]

On Epiphany in 1667, the year that he would have turned eighty-five, Dudley, third Lord North, "Remoued from Catlidge to Heauen."[89] Three days later the earthly remains of the long-exiled courtier, the sometime poet, tilter, soldier, masquer, and musician, were placed in the family chapel at Kirtling's church. This time there was no magnificent monument but simply a handsome black marble slab with the arms of North impaling a cross fleury for Brockett. In his wake the old Lord left Frances, his wife of some sixty-six years, and, as his successor, Sir Dudley, now fourth Lord North.

*   *   *

About two decades before his death, the third Lord North published privately (presumably for his closest friends) a miscellaneous collection of works called *A Forest of Varieties*, dedicated to Elizabeth of Bohemia, sister of his long-dead patron Prince Henry. Some of the pieces in this volume had been written when all three were together at James's court. Then in 1659, his seventy-seventh year, he dedicated a revised and augmented version of the book, now called *A Forest Promiscuous of Various Seasons Productions*, to another and nearer lady, his alma mater, Cantabrigia. Though almost universally overlooked by students of the period, North's work in these volumes has considerable interest.[90] It includes not only a wide variety of poems but also miscellaneous commentaries on poetry, as well as letters, characters, and other short prose forms, all of which, despite their avowedly unrevised rambling, provide insights aplenty into North and his time.

As for literary standards, North observes rather disdainfully that "The Poetry of these times abounds in wit, high conceit, figure, and proportions; thinne, light, and emptie in matter and substance; like fine colored ayery

---

88. *Forest 45*, p. 154.

89. So said the Earl of Thomond, North's old friend (Bodl. MS. North c.4, 7 January, "fatall 1666," i.e., 1667).

90. Apparently the only study is by Robert J. Parsons, "Autobiographical and Archetypal Elements in the Verse of the Third Lord North," unpub. Ph.D. diss., Duke University, 1980. Margaret Crum, however, includes a few incidental critical observations in "Poetical Manuscripts of Dudley, Third Baron North," *Bodleian Library Record*, X (1979), 98–108; and North is mentioned in passing by L. A. Beaurline, "'Why So Pale and Wan': An Essay in Critical Method," *Texas Studies in Literature and Language*, IV (1963), 553–563; *The Works of Sir John Suckling: The Non-Dramatic Works*, ed. Thomas Clayton (Oxford, 1971); and Rosalie L. Colie, *Resources of Kind: Genre-Theory in the Renaissance* (Berkeley, Calif., 1973), p. 6. Beaurline also has written on "Dudley North's Criticism of Metaphysical Poetry," *Huntington Library Quarterly*, XXV (1962), 299–313; Beaurline suggests that North "is a rather ambiguous figure, who looks back to Elizabethan and forward to Augustan times" (p. 313). The most readily available sample of North's criticism is the snippet included in Edward W. Tayler's *Literary Criticism of Seventeenth-Century England* (New York, 1967), pp. 158–166.

bubbles or Quelque-choses, much ostentation and little food; conceits, similes, and allegories are good, so the matter bee carried along in them, and not interrupted by them."[91] He contrasts himself to writers of the new verse: "These tormentors of their owne and their Readers braines I leave to bee admired in their high obscure flight, (while my selfe will bee happy, if I can procure but a familiar delight to a superficiall reading) they affect to shew more wit then love. . . ." Regarding his own work, he recommends that a reader "expect not the strong Master-pieces and quintessentiall lines, which these curious times, and the refined ambitious Spirits of our age produce. . . ." He adds, "in defiance of Critiques, my births are naturall, easie, and hasty, sometimes foure peeces to my breakfast in the beginning of a morning; I am as impatient as any woman of a long and painfull labour. . . . I love not Verses of the ragged staffe, but wish them fluent and gentle, which was wont to be a commendation."[92]

The phrase "which was wont" is a valuable clue. Elsewhere in some critical comments that he seems to have addressed to Lady Mary Wroth, niece of Sir Philip Sidney, North might be expected to commend Sidney's writings; he does so, however, in such terms as to suggest a reason why he feels rather out of step with his own time: Sidney's "works flourish in applause of all," writes North, "by a happy and familiar display of their beauties to the meanest. . . ."[93] One of the rare modern commentators on North speaks of him as sometimes sounding "neo-Sidneyan."[94] Although born a decade later than John Donne and Ben Jonson, he believes neither in wreathing iron pokers into love-knots (Coleridge's criticism of Donne's metaphysical lines) nor in working toward the precision of the Jonsonians. He does profess to believe in poetic clarity (rather as Jonson recommends perspicuity) and usually he manages to turn out verse that is both clear and reasonably witty, but what is conveyed most consistently in his practice is his belief in facility, brightness, and dexterity— what the sixteenth century called *sprezzatura*. His own phrase is *a delivre*.[95] As this might suggest, his verse is uneven. "My Writings are somwhat like a Mart," he acknowledges, "Much choice, not all allowable; better and worse. . . ."[96]

Since North's poems, "better and worse" alike, are so little known, it may be helpful to include one of them here. The following example (untitled, like a good many of his works) is of particular interest because, beyond giving a

91. *Forest 45*, p. 2. This and the next quotation, both from the same page, appear to have been composed when James was king.
92. *Forest 45*, p. 213.
93. *Forest 45*, p. 3.
94. Crum, p. 107. Sidney was a distant relation of the Norths.
95. *Forest 45*, p. 5. According to Randle Cotgrave it means *"Loosely, freely, at full scope, with good libertie"* (*A Dictionarie of the French and English Tongues* [1611], Aaiiir).
96. *Forest Promiscuous* (1659), p. 325.

glimpse of his technique, it gives in figurative form an epitome of some of the
major problems of his life:

> Iockey and his Horse, were by their Master sent
> To honour him in hunting, run, and race;
> To put in for the Bell,[97] and take content
> In honest sort, fitting faire time and place.
>
> In pride of nature, fit for any sport,
> Jolly and lusty both, at first they were,
> But shortly after both of them fell short,
> What by mischance, by ill-advise and care.
>
> Soon he became engaged to a match,
> Which cost him dear, both on the By and Main;
> He thought himself no easie peece to catch,
> But knew not to resist so strong a train.
>
> He now conceits he could not hope to win,
> Except his horse were straightly dieted.
> Such course he takes, but thrives so ill therein,
> His beast grows joylesse, faint, and famished.
>
> He who depended much upon his beast,
> Grew much dejected; study, care, and thought,
> To set all right, and doe all for the best,
> Brought him as low, as first his Steed was brought.
>
> After much time, Art, Cost, the Beast became
> As vigorous and lusty as before:
> Ill now they sorted, th'one wilde, th'other tame,
> Zeale to his Master helpt to make him poore.
>
> Jockey must ride, the Beast would run away,
> He strove and pul'd, and us'd his best of Art,
> To check his pride, and force him to obey,
> So long till both were sinking out of heart.
>
> The Master now came in, to this disorder,
> And finding Jockeyes want of strength and skill,
> By his all-taming art, brought all in order,
> And fashioned horse and man unto his will.
>   Thus right, and each to other fitted well,
>   They are to run, and cannot misse the bell.[98]

97. I.e., try for first place.
98. *Forest 45*, pp. 175–176.

Immediately after the poem North writes, "You may call this . . . a fit of Melancholy, but my hope and resolution is by Gods grace, never to be other, then my conclusions make me to appeare. . . ." Call it what one will, the poem sheds considerable light on the third Lord North.

EARLY YEARS

When Sir Dudley North became the fourth Lord North in 1667, he was sixty-four. Though he had managed most of his father's business affairs for some thirty-five years and had lived much of that time in the same house with him, and though he had married late and well and sired a large clan of talented and successful offspring, Sir Dudley's life had been much shaded by that of the older man. Doubtless observing early that his father was equable when not crossed, Sir Dudley had managed to suppress a part of himself over a period of many years and in ways that probably should be interpreted as showing strength, not weakness, of character. However the matter is to be interpreted, one needs to know that Sir Dudley is said to have remained standing with hat in hand when in the presence of his father, and at the age of sixty-three to have stood at the chair of state in the House of Lords as an eldest son of a peer.[1] Of course there were social, catechetical, and even scriptural grounds for doing so: "Obey them that haue the rule ouer you" (Hebrews 13.17).

Born in the latter part of 1602, probably at the Charterhouse, young Dudley was doubtless brought up by women in his early infancy. He himself would later write that the "government" of small infants "doth belong to the Mother, . . . as the Father is as then uncapable of it. The Mothers care of them is as duly theirs, as is naturally the Milk of her Breasts." On the other hand, he adds, "Male Children when they become disciplinable fall under government of the Father, whose duty in the first place, is to infuse into them the general Principles of Religion. . . ."[2] Aside from conjecture based on

1. Roger North understandably finds both of these details noteworthy (*Lives*, I, 35). Beyond the fact that Sir Dudley had to stand while many younger men sat as members of the House of Lords, he would have appeared strikingly old when grouped at the dais with other eldest sons of living peers. Lawrence Stone is able to find other seventeenth-century examples of great deference to parents (*The Family, Sex and Marriage in England 1500–1800* [New York, 1977], esp. p. 171), but Sir Dudley's case is more extreme than most because of his age. According to Stone's figures, the median age of heirs (born 1600–1649) of squires and above was about twenty-six at the time of their fathers' deaths (p. 53).

2. *Observations*, pp. 15–16. Since Sir Dudley usually expresses conventional views, one of his implications here regarding parental duty should be noted as untypical. Lawrence Stone points out that normally "the infants of the landed, upper bourgeois and professional classes in the sixteenth and seventeenth centuries [were] sent out to hired wet-nurses for the first twelve to eighteen months" (*The Family, Sex and Marriage*, p. 107). Cf. North's poem No. 25, l. 81: "Our Gentry they suck rudenes from theyr hyred Nurse." On the other hand, some among the upper

such passages as these and on how children of high birth usually were reared, one can say little about the fourth Lord North's earliest years. The two best indicators, however, appear to come from his father and from his son Roger. His father later set down the belief that a proper gentleman "will educate his sonne to be like himselfe, and not infuse Grammar and Philosophie into him in such sort as if nothing else concerned him and his well-being. And therefore hee will bring him up to the true understanding of honour and true reputation. . . ."[3] Perfectly consonant with this is Roger's much later observation that the third Lord North "bred his eldest son Dudley . . . after the best manner; for, besides the court, and choicest company at home, he was entered among the knights of the Bath. . . ."[4]

Certainly the Norths' Charterhouse home was suitable for "breeding" and "choicest company." James Howell mentions it among "handsome Palaces."[5] An inventory made of the place when Dudley was five indicates that it was richly appointed with paintings and maps, with velvets and silks, and with tapestries and carpets of Turkey work.[6] The inventory allows us to know that North *père* stored some of his own writings in a chamber "at the Staires head," and that other writings, his books, and a little French pistol in a bag might be found in his closet—a retiring room that was luxuriously "hanged aboute with guilt leather." Apparently someone with an eye as well as a purse had assembled the furnishings of North's closet, since a large chair and two high stools "of the same guilt leather" might also be found there, as well as a carpet of matching material for the table. Perhaps the finest piece in the room was a chair from Spain, its frame inlaid with ebony, its seat upholstered with red velvet. The furnishings of Lord North's chamber were also chosen by someone who cared how things looked. There were green silk curtains at the window (and beneath the window a statue), a green and white silk tester and valance for the bed (with silk and silver fringe), a green rug and a white one for the floor, and a green carpet for the table and another for the cupboard, and a large chair and two high stools "of sea green velvett." In the "greate Chamber" there were playing tables, chessmen, and his lordship's viol (music was important to him), and, upon the walls, five "Tapesterie hangings with bells." Along with much else the wardrobe held seven more French pistols and "twoe Armoures of my Lords made fitt for his body in it." It is true that the furnishings of young Dudley's own quarters, the nursery, were not all new—the tester and valance of the bedstead were both of "ould damask,"

---

classes had noticed that infants who were breast-fed by their mothers had a survival rate about twice that of infants turned over to wet-nurses.

3. *Forest 45*, p. 91.
4. *Lives*, I, 6.
5. *Londinopolis* (1657), p. 343.
6. The facts in this paragraph come from "The Inventorie of Charterhowse July . . . 1608." A transcription of this document made by Mr. Francis Bickley has kindly been furnished by Mr. Oliver Van Oss, The Master of Charterhouse.

and the red rug on the floor was "ould"—but there is evidence enough that the boy spent his early years amidst creature comforts and cultural refinements proper to his rank.

On 3 November 1616, about the time he turned fourteen, he was created a Knight of the Bath in honor of the creation of Charles as Prince of Wales. During James's reign the value of most titles was shrinking at an alarming rate because of the King's rather heedless selling of favor, but the K.B. which young Dudley now received was maintaining its integrity, and Lord North probably reasoned that the expenditure of the £340 or so that it called for was a sound investment.[7] On Saturday, 2 November, the boy was escorted to the Parliament House at Westminster, where he and twenty-five fellow candidates were served a supper, all at one table and every one seated beneath an escutcheon of his arms. Each then retired and after suitable ceremonies was bathed in a linen-lined tub. The next morning each was invested in what passed for a hermit's gray habit, and eventually each was clad in a crimson robe (signifying he should be a "martial" man) lined with white (in token of sincerity) so that he might properly attend his Prince.[8] Then, with trumpets sounding and the heralds going on before, young Dudley and the other candidates—including his Uncle John—rode from Westminster to the court, where the Marshal met them and conducted them to the King, seated beneath his cloth of state. There James gave them their knighthood. In view of the later course of their lives, it is of interest that the ritual required Sir Dudley to swear to live and die for his king. Dudley's Uncle John, brother to Lord North, did, indeed, serve for many years at Charles's court as a Gentleman Usher of the Privy Chamber.

Although James Cleland, a social adviser of the time, went so far as to say that a young nobleman was likely to find the court a better place to be than one of the universities,[9] the Norths usually spent a while at Cambridge. Late in life Sir Dudley wrote of spending "*some few years*" there.[10] If he was recalling and recording the facts accurately (and he was generally good about this), and if his phrase suggests at least three years ("*some few years*" surely sounds like more than two), and if, as seems to be the case, he left Cambridge in 1619, he arrived not later than 1616, the year he was knighted and turned fourteen. Like his grandfather, he almost certainly was "of immature age" when he arrived. Unfortunately, the matriculation records of his college, St. John's, do not survive for the period of his residence, and he never took a

7. Stone, p. 83. There was also the fact that, left unknighted, the eldest son of a baron was only an esquire.

8. John Gough Nichols, *The Progresses, Processions, and Magnificent Festivities of King James the First*, III (1828), 221, 215–222; and *The Manner of Creating the Knights of the Antient and Honourable Order of the Bath* (1661).

9. "Of the Best University for a Young Noble Man," Ἡρωπαιδεία, *or The Institution of a Young Noble Man* (1607), pp. 34–37.

10. *Observations*, A3*v*.

degree. Furthermore, even if the records did survive, they might not help in tracing Sir Dudley; many young men, especially of his class, did not trouble to matriculate, and few took degrees.

Certainly Sir Dudley was a fellow commoner at St. John's in 1619. Simonds D'Ewes writes in his diary of being acquainted at that time with "manie of our fellowes and some other fellowcommoners especiallie of the nobilitie as with Sir Dudlie North eldest sonne to the Lorde North. . . ."[11] As the second richest and second largest of the Cambridge colleges (only Trinity was richer and larger), St. John's naturally attracted the scions of noble families. Being a fellow commoner, moreover, assured one of unusual freedoms and privileges. At suitably high cost, a fellow commoner could dine with the dons. His lodgings were separate, as suited his rank, and he was allowed to bring servants. A life adorned with privilege, however, had its own kind of limitations, and Sir Dudley's son Roger later regretted that being a gentleman commoner had kept him from playing football with the common scholars, indeed from mixing with them at all.[12]

Just how Sir Dudley spent his time at Cambridge is impossible to say. The walks, bowling-ground, and tennis court of St. John's bred in his acquaintance D'Ewes "a serious delight and marvellous content."[13] D'Ewes, on the other hand, was far too earnest to be badly distracted by them; it is his own academic efforts that he writes about most fully. He is quite explicit, in fact, regarding his studies for his tutor, Richard Holdsworth.[14]

The figure of Holdsworth may be worth special attention here. A Fellow at St. John's from 1613 to 1620, and later Master of Emmanuel and, for a time, Vice Chancellor of the University, Holdsworth was one of the better and more forward-looking scholars of the day, eventually one of the best-known preachers in London. In D'Ewes's words, "Mr. Richard Holdsworth, my tutor, read unto me . . . one year and a half . . . in which he went over all Seton's Logic, exactly, and part of Kerkerman's and Molineus. Of ethics, or moral philosophy, he read to me Gelius, and part of Pickolomineus; of physics, part of Magirus; and of history, part of Florus. . . . I . . . read over Gellius' Attic Nights, and part of Macrobius' Saturnals. Nor was my increase in knowledge small. . . ."[15] Beyond the possible relevance of these readings to

11. "D'Ewes Diary," *The Eagle*, IX (1875), 375.

12. *Lives*, III, 14.

13. *The Autobiography and Correspondence of Sir Simonds D'Ewes, Bart.*, ed. James Orchard Halliwell, I (1845), 109.

14. *Autobiography*, I, 121. D'Ewes describes Holdsworth as "one of the most eminent scholars of the University of his time, and since inferior to few in the kingdom for depth of learning and assiduity of study" (*Autobiography*, I, 107). His "Directions to Students" is now Emmanuel College MS. 48; it is published in Harris Francis Fletcher, *The Intellectual Development of John Milton*, vol. II, *The Cambridge University Period 1625-32* (Urbana, 1961), pp. 623-664.

15. *Autobiography*, I, 121. See Andrew G. Watson, *The Library of Sir Simonds D'Ewes* (1966). The *Dialectica* (1st ed., 1545?) by John Seton (1498?-1567) of St. John's College was one of the most used and admired logic texts at the University (Fletcher, p. 140).

Sir Dudley as a student, one might add that in later years, when he took upon himself the task of preparing one or two of his own sons for college, it was to Molineus that he turned for a text.[16] If such a fact is scarcely admissible as a clue, the fact that Holdsworth was, indeed, known to the Norths is worth a moment's thought. In later years he was a welcome guest at Kirtling.[17] Conceivably in earlier years he had been Sir Dudley's tutor.

When the Queen died in March of 1619, Cambridge brought forth a little anthology called *Lacrymae Cantabrigienses: In Obitum Serenissimae Reginae Annae.* The volume contained offerings from many Cantabrigians, including Mildmay Fane, George Herbert, and Sir Dudley North (*"Eques balnei. Col. Ioh."*).[18] This first recorded flight into verse by North (he was sixteen at the time) is one of the briefest in the book, a modest six lines. It is only fair to add that the lines are not merely conventional but also neat and effective.

A possible second glimpse of the young man at St. John's is a good deal more hazy, and again the surviving physical evidence is literary. This time it is a small folio manuscript of a five-act comedy named "Alphonsus," written in Latin and now preserved in the Houghton Library at Harvard.[19] The play concerns Alphonsus, Duke of Urbino, and his long-lost daughter, Parthenia, and its connection with the North family is quite specific: written on the first leaf is the inscription "Ex libris Caroli North 1653." To understand this, one must skip over the years to April 1651, when Sir Dudley North's second son, Charles, at the age of sixteen, was admitted as a fellow commoner at Sidney Sussex College, Cambridge.[20] But the binding and the several neat, italic hands in the manuscript appear to be earlier than the inscription, and written above it are the letters "E. D. P. D. N." Possibly these may be rendered "Ex Dono Patris Dudleii North."[21] Certainly Sir Dudley had literary leanings, and certainly St. John's College had long been noted as a center of theatrical activity. Had the young man some involvement in the writing or production of a play? Or did he know someone so involved? Or, indeed, had the play come into his hands after he left Cambridge? In Sir Dudley's known writings there is no sign of interest in the drama.

16. *Lives,* III, 13 (re Roger) and II, 275 (re John). Molineus (Pierre du Moulin, *Elementa Logica* [Leyden, 1596, and other editions]) was considered appropriate for the first year of logic.

17. *A Forest Promiscuous* (1659), p. 217; from a letter dated 6 December 1639, at which time Holdsworth was Master of Emmanuel. In any case, one may deduce something of what the youth found at the University in William T. Costello's *The Scholastic Curriculum at Early Seventeenth-Century Cambridge* (Cambridge, Mass., 1958) and vol. II of Fletcher's *Intellectual Development of John Milton.*

18. *Lacrymae Cantabrigienses,* p. 26. The poem is No. 27 herein. Although there is no discernible relationship between Sir Dudley and George Herbert, one's sense of the milieu of both may be enhanced by Donald A. Lawniczak, "George Herbert and His Classmates at Cambridge: 1609–1628," unpub. Ph.D. diss., Kent State University (1967).

19. MS. Lat. 329.

20. John Venn and J. A. Venn, comp., *Alumni Cantabrigienses,* pt. I, vol. III (Cambridge, 1924), p. 265.

21. This plausible suggestion has been made by the cataloguers at the Houghton Library.

Sir Dudley's reasons for leaving Cambridge must also be surmised. The simplest answer might be that he had been there long enough, but the case is perhaps more complex than that. In later years he wrote with pride of "our Universities, which have no parallel," [22] but he also wrote of himself as "*one of those who have taken from the* Cantabrigian Helicon *least water*." [23] Indeed, in great contrast to his father, he wrote (in the passage cited here earlier) that "*In the prime of my youth I past (or rather lost) some few years at the University of* Cambridge." [24] It may be that his very youth had proved to be problematic. His age at departing, sixteen, was about the average age for entry. [25] Another crucial fact may be that St. John's was by no means enjoying its finest hour under its current master, Owen Gwynn, and such abuses as had grown up through the years were rather out of hand. The laxness of the University had reached the attention of the King himself, who attempted to restore some of the standards of better days, but without notable results. [26] The rather strait-laced Simonds D'Ewes did manage to continue his studies there, but only with particular effort: "the main thing which made me even weary of the College was, that swearing, drinking, rioting, and hatred of all piety and virtue under false and adulterate nicknames, did abound there and generally in all the University. Nay, the very sin of lust began to be known and practised by very boys; so as I was fain to live almost a recluse's life, conversing chiefly in our own College with some of the honester fellows thereof." [27] D'Ewes reports that he was "everie day growing moore warie of mine acquaintance and avoiding the visitations too frequent and unnecessarie either to give or take them." [28] One may suspect that Sir Dudley, however he may have comported himself during this period, was in certain fundamental respects not unlike the conservative, bookish D'Ewes. On the other hand, some of the nobility at the time apparently tended to feel that Oxford and Cambridge were little more than a species of preparatory school and that a young man's real college was in London, at court or one of the Inns of Court. [29] Many a youth went to college, stayed briefly, and then moved on to his Inn while still a very young man. In any case, whatever the reasons, Sir Dudley left Cambridge in 1619. [30]

22. *Observations*, p. 115.

23. *Some Notes*, p. 41. Apropos of this comment one might note his observation in later years that some youths were less devoted to Apollo than to Bacchus ("A Satyre. 1636," herein No. 25, l. 86).

24. *Observations*, A3v.

25. James Bass Mullinger, *The University of Cambridge from the Royal Injunctions of 1535 to the Accession of Charles the First* (Cambridge, 1884), p. 398.

26. See Thomas Baker, *History of the College of St. John the Evangelist, Cambridge*, 2 vols., ed. J. E. B. Mayor (Cambridge, 1869).

27. *Autobiography*, I, 141–142.

28. "D'Ewes's Diary," *The Eagle*, X (1878), 2–3.

29. See Edward Miller, citing H. C. Porter in *Portrait of a College: A History of the College of Saint John the Evangelist Cambridge* (Cambridge, 1961), p. 36.

30. A voice from later years is that of the physician Henry Paman. Although not born until after Sir Dudley's departure, Dr. Paman attended Emmanuel and St. John's, and became a fel-

One of his father's friends, John Selden, working from Sir John Fortescue's Latin, said that young men traditionally went to the Inns of Court to "learn singing and all kinds of music, dancing and such other accomplishments and diversions (which are called revels) as are suitable to their quality, and such as are usually practised at Court. At other times . . . the greater part apply themselves to the study of the law." [31] The standard rationalization for pursuing the latter goal was set down by William Laud: "almost all young gentlemen spend part of their time in one or other of the Inns of Court, and afterwards, when they return to live in their several countries [*sic*], steer themselves according to such principles as in those places are preached unto them." [32] Like others in his family, Sir Dudley would, indeed, eventually become much involved in the affairs of his county. Uncontentious and retiring by nature, except when his temper was aroused, he certainly was not cut out for a lawyer, but knowing something of the law was bound to be useful, and on 10 August 1619, not yet seventeen, he was admitted to Gray's Inn. [33]

As the Inn which the aristocracy most favored, Gray's would seem to have been a natural place for Sir Dudley. His few sentences of autobiography, however, include no mention of Gray's. Following a comment on Cambridge, he says simply that *"Then I came to have a tast of the Court. . . ."* [34] The important thing for some young men at the Inns was that residence there made attendance at court easier. But many who went for wool came back shorn. North next says, with a touch of wry wit, *"my Father soon called me from thence* [i.e., from the court], *knowing by dear experience the Air of that place to be such, as few elder Brothers can long breath there without falling into a Consumption."* If one accepts the timing implied here, Lord North learned his lesson long before he managed to put it into effect in his own life. In any case the son would now profit from the father's mistakes.

The elliptical quality of Sir Dudley's comments makes them difficult to interpret, but apparently he first entered military service at about this time. Military service was held to be yet another kind of school, a proving ground for honor that prepared a young man for right governing. Sir Dudley's father wrote that a good soldier is "a Corrector of Vice and disorder in others, and therefore must in no sort admit them in himselfe. . . ," [35] and Sir Dudley

---

low of St. John's and Public Orator of the University. On 3 July 1671 he wrote as follows to Sir Dudley: "There is not any Person that has gone out of our gates whom wee haue reason to belieue a more firme and stedfast friend to us then your Lp, of wch you haue giuen us soe great an assurance both from your words and actions" (Bodl. MS. North c.4, no. 262).

31. Quoted by Foster Watson, *The Beginnings of the Teaching of Modern Subjects in England* (1909), pp. xxxi–xxxii. Selden's translation of Fortescue's *De Laudibus Legum Anglie* appeared in 1616.

32. John Bruce, ed., *CSP*, Domestic, 1633–1634 (1863), pp. 340–341.

33. Joseph Foster, *The Register of Admissions to Gray's Inn, 1521–1889* (1889), p. 156. That same month saw the admission of Kenelm Digby and Robert, Lord Rich.

34. *Observations*, A3v.

35. *Forest 45*, p. 100.

himself later observed that the military "Profession is fit to be understood, not only by Princes, but by the Gentry universally, it being their proper vocation, as appears in some measure by the ensigns of Nobility, their Coats of Arms impressed upon a Shield." [36]

In January 1620 the Privy Council met at Whitehall to discuss an expedition to recover the Palatinate on behalf of King James's daughter Elizabeth and her husband, Frederick, the Elector Palatine. Sir Horace Vere, England's ablest military leader, was named commander of the English forces in June. [37] "Never was service more popular," writes Clements Markham. "The flower of the young nobility pressed forward for the honor of serving under Sir Horace Vere, and volunteers crowded to the standard in the city of London by beat of drum." [38] Vere's favorite nephew, Henry de Vere, Earl of Oxford, and Robert Devereux, Earl of Essex, were given the task of raising troops, and on 22 July a well-equipped little army sailed from Gravesend. The English faced impossible odds abroad, however, and Oxford and Essex returned to London on 11 November 1620 to urge the need for reinforcements. That same month, having to go into winter quarters, Vere parceled out his forces to the three major Palatinate strongholds. He put Sergeant-Major General John Burrough at Frankenthal and Sir Gerard Herbert at Heidelberg, and occupied Mannheim himself. Matters seem never to have gone well for the English, however, and in a letter dated 19 March 1622 James Howell reported that "Sir *Arthur Chicester* is come back from the Palatinate, much complaining of the small Army that was sent thither under Sir *Horace Vere*, which should have been greater, or none at all." [39] Chicester did manage to round up more funds while in England, but despite these and despite Vere's commitment and skill it turned out that the entire expedition was doomed. Vere was forced to surrender Mannheim in October 1622.

Because of the friendly associations between Lord North and Elizabeth and Frederick, Sir Dudley's presence in Vere's expedition is not difficult to suppose. Hard facts in the matter are difficult to come by, but in 1625 Prince Frederick remembered and recommended various officers who previously had "served in the Palatinat," and among the "Lieftenants" now to be "recomended . . . to Captaines places by his Highnes" was Sir Dudley North. [40]

36. *Observations*, p. 119.
37. Roger North, writing much later, is surely mistaken in saying that his father served as a captain under Francis Vere, who died in 1609, when Dudley was a child of seven (*Lives*, I, 6). On the other hand, it had long been fashionable for young gentlemen to serve for a while under either Francis or Horace Vere, even if they did not intend a lifelong military career. See Clements R. Markham, *The Fighting Veres: Lives of Sir Francis Vere . . . and of Sir Horace Vere* (1888).
38. Clements Markham, pp. 397–398.
39. *Epistolae Ho-elianae*, ed. Joseph Jacobs (1890), p. 112.
40. PRO, SP 63/267, 20r–v. In 1625 an invasion of Ireland by the Spanish appeared likely, and it seemed necessary to "secure" Ireland by repairing old forts and building new ones, and by sending armed forces from England. Orders went out for levying 2,250 foot soldiers for the Irish

Since he was not yet eighteen at the time of the formation of the 1620 expedition, Sir Dudley's appointment as lieutenant probably was less an acknowledgment of his ability in the field than of his social rank and military heritage. Knowing as little as we do of the matter, however, it is conceivable either that he returned to England amongst those accompanying Oxford and Essex (November 1620) or that he stayed abroad long enough to become more deeply involved. In the spring of 1622, at any rate, well before the surrender of Mannheim, Sir Dudley—or someone on his behalf—was arranging to have him enter a second Inn of Court, this time the Inner Temple.[41]

Another piece of evidence linking Sir Dudley with the Palatinate provides a more unequivocal *terminus ad quem* for his service there. On 22 September 1622 his Johnian friend D'Ewes recorded that the "miserable newes was the taking of Heidleberg in the Palatinate with the castle. . . ,"[42] and the following day in London he sought out Sir Dudley as an authoritative source for some details. Had Sir Dudley, as a relatively recent soldier there, been making a special effort to keep abreast of the news? Referring to the fall of Heidelberg, D'Ewes writes, "I had the former newes confirmed by Sir Dudlye North whome I went to see and that Sir Garrett [i.e., Gerard] Herbert, the captaine, was slaine after three pikes first valiantlye brooken, being then shott in the head. This hapned through the cowardice of the Dutchmen in the outworkes, as hee fullye dilated it to mee."[43] For North to be an eyewitness he would have had to be in Heidelberg as recently as 19 September. Perhaps, then, talking with D'Ewes in London, he was quoting what he had been told by someone else—either an eyewitness who had traveled posthaste or some intermediary.[44]

service. The record of Prince Frederick's recollection of Sir Dudley comes from about February, when some thirty men were to be named for assignment as officers to the three provost-marshals of Munster, Connaught, and Ulster. The next document in the PRO volume is a similar one headed "A list of the Captaines to haue the cõmaund of the Companies to be now leauied for Ireland" (24v), and lists Sir Dudley's name ninth in a list of thirty-two (25r). See Robert Pentland Mahaffy, ed., *Calendar of the State Papers Relating to Ireland . . . 1647–1660* (1903), pp. 46–48.

41. The records of the Inner Temple (where his father was a member) note on 12 May 1622 the formal confirmation of his special admission, the admission itself having taken place at least somewhat earlier: "Where this last vacation Mr. Treasurer [Sir Thomas Coventry] at the request of Mr. Stapleton did specially admit into this Society gratis Dudley North, son and heir of the right honourable Lord North and of Mr. Philip Parker, the same admittances now at the p'liament are confirmed" (citation from unpublished typescript, "Admissions to the Inner Temple," ed. R. Lloyd, 3 vols. [1950–1960], kindly furnished by W. W. S. Breem, Librarian, Inner Temple).

42. *The Diary of Sir Simonds D'Ewes (1622–1624)*, ed. Elisabeth Bourcier (Paris, 1974), p. 97.

43. *Diary*, ed. Bourcier, p. 98. Arthur Wilson writes that "*Heidelberg . . .* was taken by Assault, Sir *Gerard Herbert* the Commander of the Castle slain, after he had repulsed the Enemy from the Assault, breaking six *Pikes* upon them with his own hand" (*The History of Great Britain* [1653], p. 211).

44. The city of Heidelberg was taken September 6 (new style)/16 (old style) and Herbert was

Sir Dudley's reminiscences are brief and unspecific, and they contain no reference to soldiering in the Palatinate. Indeed, they have his removal from court followed by his moving in with Lord and Lady North: "*Afterwards I lived with my Parents at their* London *habitation, and having no employment I surfeited of Idlenesse, taking my pastime with some of the most corrupt young men of those dayes.*"[45] This is strong language: there is no vice that does not keep company with the idle. Sir Dudley was uncomfortable in bad company, however, and his very discomfort suggests that any "fowle Terrene affections" he may have experienced were not deep-dyed.[46]

Registration at the Inner Temple in May of 1622 clearly proved no solution. Still only nineteen in 1622, Sir Dudley soon was asking his father to let him escape from the dangers of London (a request which hardly suggests that he had sojourned long with an army), and the family's attempt at a new resolution of the young man's situation is recorded in the Acts of the Privy Council under 26 December: "A passe for Sir Dudley North, knight, to travaile for three yeares. . . ."[47] Two is the best number of servants for a young traveler, says the social adviser James Cleland; a young gentleman needs a pursebearer and a page.[48] Sir Dudley's license granted him permission "to take with him two servantes, trunkes of apparell and other necessaries, not prohibited, with a proviso not to goe to Rome." The coda here should come as no surprise. Many a good Englishman, like the learned Joseph Hall, deplored the possibility that an English youth might go abroad and "*freely quaffe of the puddle of popish superstition.*"[49]

In his verse Sir Dudley suggests that travel sometimes changes young men for the better.[50] Theoretically, travel was supposed to provide a political knowledge of other lands, hence, like the Inns of Court and soldiering, improve one's capability for public life. George Parks notes that in about 1620 it began to be assumed that the traveler also would be alert to foreign arts and manners.[51] In the present case one might point not only to Sir Dudley's felt need for a change of sky but also to a few other scraps of evidence. Most notably, Sir Dudley himself wrote later of "*being present at* Madrid *and* Paris,

---

killed September 7/17. Soon thereafter the castle fell, the articles of capitulation being dated September 9/19 (PRO, SP 81/27, 32r). D'Ewes's dating is old style.

45. *Observations*, A3v–A4r.

46. The phrase is from his poem beginning "When after chyldhood . . ." (No. 48, ll. 38–39).

47. *Acts of the Privy Council of England, 1621–1623*, vol. XXXVIII (1st pub. 1932, rept. Nendeln, Liechtenstein, 1974), pp. 376–377.

48. Ἡρωπαιδεία, p. 252. A younger man needs a tutor, too, he says. In 1604 Sir Dudley's father had gone accompanied by a younger brother, a gentleman associated with "my Lord of Devonshire," and three servants (HMC, *Calendar of the Manuscripts of . . . Salisbury*, XVI, 192).

49. *Quo Vadis?* (1617), A4v.

50. "A Satyre" (No. 25, l. 87).

51. George B. Parks, "Travel as Education," in *The Seventeenth Century: Studies in the History of English Thought and Literature from Bacon to Pope by Richard Foster Jones and Others* . . . (Stanford, Calif., 1951), pp. 264–265.

*when the several Marriages for our then Prince of Wales were treated on in those
Courts. . . .*"[52]

At least some Englishmen believed that God chose to express His thoughts
on the projected Spanish marriage when, in the summer of 1623, lightning
struck away the crown and vane from the top of the gatehouse at St. James's,
Prince Charles's home at the time.[53] Charles and the royal favorite, George
Villiers, then Marquess of Buckingham, had become infatuated with the idea
of going to Spain to woo the *infanta* and thus unite England with her cordial
foe. King James fretted about "so farre and hazairdouse a jorney" for the two
people he loved best, holding sensibly "that it is without exemple in manie
aages past that a kings onlie soone showlde goe to woe a nother kings daughter, before the mache were concludit. . . ."[54] The young men, nonetheless,
were determined. On 17 February 1623 they donned false beards and set out
in secret, and on 7 March turned up in Madrid, thus launching a series of
negotiations which ultimately led to some embarrassing farewells and the decision of both that it was better to war with Spain than to marry her *infanta*.

On 24 February Simonds D'Ewes wrote of learning from his tutor "that
now the King had opened the list or role of names, which the Prince had left
sealed, of all those whome his pleasure was should follow him."[55] On 3 April,
Sir John North, Gentleman Usher of the Privy Chamber, embarked from
Portsmouth on the *Adventure*, and in less than five days he arrived in Spain.[56]
(Less than a month earlier, knowing that he was to travel to "partes beyond
the Seas," Sir John had composed a will in which he made bequests to various
relations and provided adequately for his "dearly beloued brother" Lord
North but designated that the healthy remainder of his estate should go to
"my Loueinge nephewe," Sir Dudley.[57]) With his own license to travel in
hand since Christmas, Sir Dudley now joined Sir John. So did a good many
other Englishmen with the time and inclination for a jaunt. According to
Arthur Wilson, "the *Prince* was so circled with a *Splendid Retinue* of his own
people, that it might be said, *There was an English Court in the King of Spain's
Pallace*."[58] Abraham Darcie records the names of both Sir Dudley and
his uncle among "the Noble Peeres and worthy Gentlemen of Great Britaine,

52. *Observations*, A4r.
53. *A True Relation of Some Passages Which Passed at Madrid in the Year 1623* (1655), p. 8.
54. PRO, SP 94/27, pt. 1, 22r.
55. *Diary*, ed. Bourcier, p. 122.
56. Richard Wynne, "An Account of the Journey of the Prince's Servants into Spain, A.D.
1623," in vol. II of *The Autobiography and Correspondence of Sir Simonds D'Ewes, Bart.*, ed.
James Orchard Halliwell (1845), p. 415.
57. Bodl. MS. North c.29, 50–51. Sir John had personal property at the time at Lord North's
place at Charterhouse, at his own quarters in St. James's, and at the home of Sir James Ouchterlony, who had married his mother (now deceased) in 1604.
58. *History*, p. 229.

that were in Spaine, to Attend on the Most Mighty and Gracious Prince CHARLES, our incomparable Prince." [59]

Since fear of infection from the popish puddle nearly always ran high when Englishmen thought of going to Spain, it is no surprise to find Darcie assuring Sir Dudley, Sir John, and others that "you are such Patrons, as haue euer manifested a rare and confident protection of GODS vnspotted Religion and Worship: but in your late Honovrable employments in forraine parts, vnder our Illustrious PRINCE, they haue receiued a more apparent testimony of your true HEARTS RELIGION and ZEALE, when soiourning for a time, (as one may say) in the very Tents of KEDAR, and beholding with your bodily eyes, many superstitious Idolatries, you yet retained firme and vnshaken, the treasure of a sincere faith, and inuiolable conscience. . . ." [60]

Although they had proved themselves thus, Sir John and many others were ordered to return home well before the royal charades came to an end. When the Prince was given to understand that the Spanish were disinclined to accommodate his many followers, he proceeded to reduce his train. Most of the English resolved to return by sea, but Sir John decided to go as far as possible by land, via Burgos, San Sebastián, and thence France. [61] Perhaps Sir Dudley went with him.

When Prince Charles and Villiers, now Duke of Buckingham, returned to London on 6 October that year, the English were overjoyed that Charles was unmarried and unharmed. Shops closed, bells rang, and bonfires blazed, and subsequently the North family library proved to contain two copies of a work called *Gratulatio Academiae Cantabrigiensis de Serenissimi Principis Reditu ex Hispaniis Exoptatissimo* (Cambridge, 1623). [62]

Negotiations for a French match had their awkwardness, following, as they did, so hard on the heels of the negotiations with Spain. Nevertheless, a bride would be acquired for the Prince this time. Thinking of the complex processes required on both occasions, Sir Dudley later spoke of himself as being *"a partial witnesse of the artifices, and uncertainty of such Negotiations."* [63] Obviously, then, his visit to France antedated the nuptials of Charles and Princess Henrietta Maria in 1625. Moreover, he writes elsewhere that he was in France when "the learned Lord *Herbert* of *Cherbury*," author of *De Veritate* (Paris, 1624), was English Ambassador there. [64] Herbert, who had left England on the day of Queen Anne's funeral in 1619, later that same year suggested a match between Charles and Henrietta Maria. In July 1621 the vola-

59. Darcie's book, formerly attributed to Isaac Casaubon, is called *The Originall of Idolatries: Or, The Birth of Heresies* . . . (1624); citation is from leaf following title page.
60. Verso of leaf following title page and a1r.
61. Wynne, p. 457.
62. Both copies are now at the Folger Shakespeare Library, Washington, D.C.
63. *Observations*, A4r.
64. *Light*, pp. 30–31.

tile Ambassador was recalled to England, only to be sent abroad again to serve from February 1622 to April 1624. In his second satire, "Of Travellers: (from Paris)," written before he held the post, Herbert tells of young Englishmen who come

> To *Fauxborgs St. Germans*, there take a Room
> Lightly about th' Ambassadors, and where,
> Having no Church, they come, *Sundays*, to hear,
> An invitation, which they have most part,
> If their outside but promise a desert. . . .[65]

A bit cryptically, Herbert records how the young travelers found their way to the Embassy on Sundays, ostensibly to hear a good English sermon but actually to hear some sort of invitation, an invitation which they were likely to receive if their "outside" promised well and especially, one may assume, if they were well connected. Very likely Sir Dudley was one of these young men in later years.

Sir Dudley also visited Italy. Since his grandfather had lived for a while in Venice,[66] and since his father was regarded by the Venetians as one who "always displayed the most favourable disposition towards our republic,"[67] Venice is almost certain to have been on the young man's Italian itinerary. In later years Sir Dudley wrote of the sensible dress of the Venetians and described them as a "wise and frugal People," hardly a stereotypic view among Englishmen at the time.[68] He also referred to Italian books in his collection, and his own copy of at least one of these, Guarini's *Il Pastor Fido* (Venice, 1605), still may be seen at the Bodleian.[69] Furthermore, at one point in his posthumous *Light*, North offers a glimpse of that sort of religious temptation to which all Englishmen of the day were supposedly subject whenever their toes touched papist soil: "being very young . . . in *Italy* I was in continual disturbance by a Gentleman of our own Nation, who laboured very much to win me to the *Romish* profession, and would not desist, till I assured him that I would never forsake the Religion wherein I was trained up, without a full hearing what would be said by our Divines, which was impossible to be effected there."[70]

"*From thence*," says North, referring to his travels, "*I was employed as a*

65. *The Poems English and Latin of Edward, Lord Herbert of Cherbury*, ed. G. C. Moore Smith (Oxford, 1923; rept. 1968), pp. 14–15.

66. John Walter Stoye observes that when Sir Dudley's paternal grandfather, Sir John, returned to England from abroad, he "kept his accounts and even described his ordinary journeys in East Anglia and the Midland counties for at least two years in the Italian which he had learnt in Venetia" (*English Travellers Abroad 1604–1667* [1952], pp. 201–202).

67. Allen B. Hinds, ed., *CSP*, Venetian, 1619–1621, XVI (1910), 552; n.b. also p. 82. Clearly the relationship did not suffer from the fact that the Venetian ambassadors were neighbors of the Norths in Charterhouse Square.

68. *Observations*, p. 68. Another knowledgeable reference occurs on p. 78.

69. It is now Bodl. MS. North g.1.

70. *Light*, p. 17.

Soldier in Holland, *about three years, Commanding a Foot Company in our Sovereigns Pay.*"[71] On 23 June 1624 the Privy Council issued a notice beginning thus:

> Whereas the States Generall of the United Provinces have by their ambassadors humbly sollicited his Majestie aswell to renue the ancient defensive league betweene his kingdome and their Provinces as also to permitt them for the better confirmation thereof to raise some good number of voluntarie souldiers within his dominions to be imployed in their service in these hazardous times when the Emperor and the Romish Catholique League are preparing and drawing downe towardes their countries divers great and threatning troopes. . . .[72]

The short of it is that James gave permission for raising five thousand soldiers, partly because his daughter Elizabeth, her hapless husband, and their children were now refugees in the Low Countries. The Earls of Oxford, Essex, and Southampton, and Robert Willoughby were appointed colonels to enlist the required men, and in mid-summer, 1624, the Earl of Oxford signed the following document:

> Be it knowne vnto all men by theis p[rese]nts that I Henry Vere Earle of Oxenford Lord high Chamberlaine of England haveing receaued Comission from the Ambassadors of the States generall of the Vnited Provinces to Commaund as Collonell ouer .1500. men which nomber I am to leavy heare in England by vertue of his Majesties Permission soe signified by letters from the Lords of his Majesties most honorable Privy Councell to the Lieuetennants of euery County within his Majesties said Realme of England I Doe authorisz you Sir Dudley North knight one of the Captaines vnder my Regiment and your Officers to raise .115. men beinge the full nomber of your company and them to embarke and Conduct for the Service of the said States of the Vnited Provinces accordinge to such Directions, as I haue, or shall heareafter giue you. In Wittness wheareof I have hearevnto sett my hand, and Seale at Armes this xxxth Day of June Anno Dni 1624[.][73]

That same year Gervase Markham rhapsodized on "What Glories attend a *Souldier*."[74] He also printed the names of the chief officers and under officers of the four regiments—thus recording not only Captain Dudley North's name but also those of his chief comrades in arms.[75] Elsewhere Fran-

---

71. *Observations*, A4r–v.
72. *Acts of the Privy Council of England, 1623–1625*, vol. XXXIX (1st pub. 1933; rept. Nendeln, Liechtenstein, 1974), p. 249; PRO, SP 84/118, 98r–v.
73. Bodl. MS. North a.2, 272r.
74. *Honour in His Perfection* (1624), p. 2.
75. Markham, *Honour*, A4r.

cis Markham explained that "A Captaine of Foote or of the Infantrie, is the highest of all priuate Commanders and yet the lowest of all that command in cheife. . . ."[76] Captains of Foot were supposed to be "Gentlemen both of Blood and Qualitie" and were expected to have ensigns carry their colors. (Sir Dudley's arms at the time were those of North—a gold lion and three silver fleurs-de-lis on an azure ground—with a cadency label of three points; his ensign was a youth named Costrydge.)[77] It was presumed that any captain's command would be divided more or less equally between pikes and muskets and that he would be able to "suppresse . . . all euill liuers, & where Instruction workes no cure, there let sharpe examples make others fearefull."[78] On the other hand, "the Father should be no more tender ouer his Children then the noble Captaine ouer his well deseruing Souldier, for that will linke and ioyne them together as men made of one peece. . . ."[79] Markham describes a flawless model, but one may suspect that Sir Dudley, not yet twenty-two, tried hard to match it. He acquired such military books as Samuel Marolois's *Fortification ou Architecture Militaire* (The Hague, 1615) and Henry Hondius's *Description & Breve Declaration des Regles Generales de la Fortification* (The Hague, 1625). Other relevant books that come down to us with his inscription are Thomas Scott's *Belgick Pismire* (1622), which explores the relations between Great Britain and the United Provinces; and Harry Hexham's *A Tongue-Combat, Lately Happening Betweene Two English Souldiers in the Tilt-boat of Gravesend, the One Going to Serve the King of Spaine, the Other to Serve the States Generall of the United Provinces* (1623—i.e., probably early 1624); and an English translation from Paolo Sarpi called *The Free Schoole of Warre* (1625).[80]

On 12 July, less than two weeks after Sir Dudley received his commission, Oxford's men embarked from Gravesend. On 16 August they arrived at Rotterdam, whence they departed next day for Utrecht and then Arnheim. When at last the company was scattered over the countryside to cover nine different posts, Sir Dudley was sent with his men to Woerden, and there, some nine miles northeast of Gouda, he was in command.[81]

It is little wonder if Sir Dudley was warmed by Oxford's attention. The Earl was about ten years older than he and still possessed plenty of dash and color. He bore the title of one of England's most distinguished families and, like earlier Veres since Norman times, was hereditary Lord Great Chamber-

---

76. Markham, *Five Decades of Epistles of Warre* (1622), p. 133. One section is dedicated to Dudley, Lord North (pp. 105–108).

77. Markham, *Five Decades*, p. 134; PRO, SP 84/121, pt. 2, 278r; Folger MS. V.a.258. The lieutenant assigned to Sir Dudley was named Purfrey.

78. Markham, *Five Decades*, p. 135.

79. Markham, *Five Decades*, p. 136.

80. Sir Dudley's copies of these five works are now in the Folger Shakespeare Library. The French translation of Hondius was by Albert Girard, the English one of Sarpi by W. B.

81. PRO, SP 84/119, 179r; SP 84/118, 172r; and SP 84/121, pt. 2, 274r.

lain of England. Moreover, although it is true that his youth had been given over to loose living, Oxford subsequently had become greatly refined while living abroad (so says the historian Arthur Wilson).[82] Then, as we have seen, he served between June and November 1620 in the expedition to relieve the Palatinate. In the summer of 1624 he returned abroad once again to military service and thereafter conducted himself with much gallantry, especially in attempting the relief of Breda in 1625. Unfortunately he was wounded during the latter attempt, suffered sunstroke, and died at The Hague.

Henry de Vere, eighteenth Earl of Oxford, requires attention here not only because he commanded North's regiment but because the name "Verus" figures in one of North's early poems.[83] Since the Vere family was large, one cannot be sure, but it is not unlikely that North's poem honoring "Verus" is addressed to Henry de Vere. In his own writing about the Earl, Gervase Markham certainly uses the Vere/Verus pun that catches Sir Dudley's fancy.[84] Moreover, Sir Dudley's poem conveys a young man's praise of "Verus" as one especially favored by Venus and Mars. One could invent no celestial sponsors more appropriate for Henry de Vere.

Not all was well with Sir Dudley, however. Having escaped from loose companions in London, he encountered yet more in Holland. "*I ran hazard again,*" he writes, "*of being lost in debauchery, and especially in the Vice-rampant of that People. But by Gods grace I came home scot-free, though I served under a* Scotch *Colonel.*"[85] The man whose nationality provides North with a pun here was quite probably John Seton,"[86] and the chief vice of the Hollanders was drink. John Donne writes of the "spungy'hydroptique Dutch,"[87] and John Marston has a character observe, "amongst a hundred Dutchmen, four-score drunkards."[88] Considering what might have happened, it is pleasant to be able to add that Sir Dudley himself later became the very model of happy moderation in imbibing.

Unfortunately, the English expedition to the Low Countries failed. The Spanish general, Spinola, besieged Breda, and Maurice, Prince of Orange, General of the States's army, seemed unable to take significant action. When Breda surrendered (1625), the German mercenary Count Mansfeld went to get reinforcements for the States in England. Mansfeld assembled so many raw recruits, however, that, once abroad, they became more a burden than an asset. That same year brought the death of the prematurely aged Prince Maurice, and although his brother Frederick Henry, who succeeded him as General of the States's Army, was a bolder soldier, he unfortunately lost

82. *History*, p. 161.
84. Markham, *Honour*, p. 9.
86. Markham, *Honour*, A4v.

83. "The Favorite of Loue and Honour" (No. 1).
85. *Observations*, A4v.

87. "Elegie: On His Mistris," l. 42 (*The Complete Poetry of John Donne*, ed. John T. Shawcross [New York, 1968], p. 63).
88. *The Malcontent*, III.i.94.

"many gallant Men (especially *English*)."[89] In short, for all its brave promise, the expedition brought the English much grief.

Meanwhile, in November 1624, the Earl of Southampton and his son, the young Lord Wriothesley, both in Holland, had died of the "pestilence"—a fact which is bound to have struck Captain North because he and Captain Wriothesley had been fellow commoners together at St. John's College in better days, in fact had been created Knights of the Bath at the same time. Simonds D'Ewes was surely touched by the loss. Perhaps flattered a bit by his attention, D'Ewes had greatly enjoyed conversing with young Wriothesley and sharing verses with him, and held him to be "no lesse happy in inwarde accoutrements then great by outwarde birth. . . ."[90]

With the death of King James, with a prolonged and virulent outbreak of plague, and with fear of a Spanish invasion of Ireland, some Englishmen recalled grimly that 1625 was the year of the Romish jubilee.[91] But worse was to come. A good deal of trouble in the latter half of the 1620s may be traced to the cheerful callousness of James's favorite, who now was the favorite of Charles. The Duke of Buckingham's abuses of power eventually became so bad that in 1626 Parliament took the extraordinary measure of trying to impeach him. Although the date of Sir Dudley's return from the Low Countries to England is unknown, he later estimated his time abroad as about three years, and the unwontedly strong expression of feeling in his poem called "1627" supports the probability that at that time he was viewing the deplorable state of current events from home ground.[92] Whereas three years earlier there had been hope of an Anglo-French alliance against Spain (after all, the new Queen was French), England now was at war with both Spain *and* France. Buckingham, brimming with self-esteem and decked with the title of Lord High Admiral, decided to lead an expedition to relieve the Huguenots of La Rochelle. He sailed in June, arrived in July at the Isle of Rhé, outside La Rochelle's harbor, and returned to England in November with less than half of his men. It was one of the most shameful defeats England had ever known, and it accomplished nothing. There is little doubt, therefore, about Dudley North's target in "1627," which decries an unnamed "Great Lord" and compares him with Erostratus, who burned the great temple of Ephesus in order to be remembered.

The following year, at twenty-five, North himself entered the political

89. Wilson, *History*, p. 286.

90. *The Eagle*, X, 4–5. Cf. below, headnote to North's "To my deerest freind deceased" (No. 28). Wriothesley's father, Southampton, is best known in literary history as Shakespeare's patron, but in his own time he would have been more conspicuous for the lavish favors that he himself (unlike Sir Dudley's father) had received from the King.

91. It should be indicated at this point that I have found no evidence on whether or not Sir Dudley served in Ireland following his nomination to a captaincy by Prince Frederick early in 1625 (as cited in note 40).

92. The poem is printed here as No. 24.

arena, where his rank, if not his inclinations, led him to continue participating off and on for nearly fifty years. On 29 February 1628, in a list of members returned to service in Parliament, his name is recorded for the borough of Horsham in Sussex, which he represented in 1628–1629.[93] One may think of him as watching and listening intently to Sir John Eliot and Sir Edward Coke (the latter now in his mid-seventies but still a dominating figure), to John Pym and John Selden. The Commons worried over such information as that concerning a certain printer who had put out the prayer book with the word "minister" changed to "priest" and the word "elect" excised.[94] Eliot warned how Arminianism "creepes and Undermines, and howe Poperie comes upon us" and, more precisely, how in the figure of Richard Neile, Bishop of Winchester, was "contracted all the dainger wee feare."[95] On 7 February 1629 Sir Dudley North rose to his feet, doffed his hat, and

> informed the house that one Docter Moore attendinge the Bishopp of Winchester vpon an occasion, the Bishopp tould him, that hee had often times heard him preach before kinge James and that hee [Moore] Vsed to preach against Poperie (which hee said was well liked of then) but nowe you must not doe soe, wherevpon the Docter said, if occasion serued, hee would not spare to doe the like nowe.
>
> To whome the Bishopp farther said that the tymes were not the same, and therefore [Moore] nowe must not.[96]

Members of the Commons were riled constantly by religious undercurrents such as this, as well as by a good many other matters, and they emitted an increasingly loud and angry rumble of protest.[97] Speaking of vipers in their midst, the King on 10 March dissolved Parliament.

It would appear that Sir Dudley was spending a considerable amount of time in London during this period. In 1630 he was named to a committee on buildings there, along with his Uncle John and his Gray's Inn contemporary Kenelm Digby.[98] At twenty-eight, he should have been able to go about such duties with a certain *savoir-faire*. He had now had a taste of the university, the court, and, it appears, two Inns of Court. He had traveled on the Continent, put in a respectable military stint, and participated in public affairs. Furthermore, he had begun to assist his father with managing a baron's business, "for as soon as my years gave me Capability, he not onely acquainted me with matters of his Estate, but would sometimes take my advice, and frequently

---

93. *Members of Parliament*, I (1878), 478.

94. "A True Relacōn of euerie Daies proceedings in parliament since the begininge thereof this present Session 1628" (i.e., Jan.–March 1629), Spencer MS E205, item 61.

95. "A True Relacōn. . . ," 101v–102r, 71r.

96. "A True Relacōn. . . ," 70v.

97. See Wallace Notestein and Frances Helen Relf, ed., *Commons Debates for 1629* (Minneapolis, 1921).

98. PRO, SP 16/171, item 3.

make use of my endeavours. . . ."[99] Because his father regarded them as important, "Dancing, Horsemanship, Languages, and the like" were inevitably among Sir Dudley's accomplishments,[100] although in the long run his own favorite occupations were to be music and books. As for writing, he had been composing verse off and on for at least a decade.

In the picture painted about this time by the fashionable portraitist Cornelius Johnson, Sir Dudley is a well-turned-out young man.[101] Though his face is rather dominated by his nose, it is softened by a light moustache and a frame of wavy hair, and his eyes are sober, clear, and steady. One understands how a father might say to such a man, "God hath blest you . . . with [a] good and constant temper and affections. . . ."[102] From beneath a crisp, broad ruff there gleams a soldier's gorget, and draped over both of these with artful casualness there is a silken band with a jeweled pendant bearing the motto of the Knights of the Bath. Dignity and reserve are predictable qualities in most portraits of the time, but somehow they are particularly appropriate to this young subject. In 1630 Sir Dudley was every inch a gentleman and lacked only a wife to be complete.

99. *Observations*, p. 62.

100. *Forest 45*, p. 88.

101. The painting is now at Waldershare Park, and the Earl of Guilford has kindly allowed its use as the frontispiece of the present volume. Johnson (or Jonson or Janssen van Ceulen) was of Flemish origin but liked to pass as English (C. H. Collins Baker, *Lely and the Stuart Portrait Painters*, I [1912], 74). Cf. Ralph Edwards, "Oil Miniatures by Cornelius Johnson," *The Burlington Magazine*, LXI (1932), 131–132.

102. *Forest 45*, p. 158.

MARRIAGE AND RESPONSIBILITY

In his handbook on how to manage a great house Sir Dudley includes advice on choosing a wife. A man "cannot use too much circumspection," he writes, "being to give her an irrevocable Estate for life in his Person."[1] He agrees with Martial that the prospective lady should not be "too rich in Revenue . . . lest she become too imperious and upbraiding," and with noble tongue in cheek he recommends that she be selected so as to prove "no lesse useful in the day than agreeable at night."[2]

His father, who might be expected to have learned something about the matter, expressed the forward-looking view that parents ought "to leave their Children full freedome with their consent in so important a case."[3] "I thank God," wrote North *père* in 1637, "with all my necessitie, I have left my Sonne both his freedom of choice, and Wives portion."[4] On the other hand, it would be a mistake to overlook North's muddying admission elsewhere that "I would when my fortune was whole, have matched my Sonne then very young, and have assured my Lands upon him for a reasonable portion; it could not bee."[5]

Lord North's views would have been of particular interest to Dame Mary Montagu, widow of Sir Charles Montagu, who on 15 December 1630 expressed some doubts on the subject in a letter addressed to her husband's eldest brother, Edward, Lord Montagu, at Barnwell Castle:

> being desirous to take your advice to bestow my daughters . . . makes me to intreat your advice for my daughter Ann, whom I should willingly bestow on a wise and religious husband, which were able to live of himself, for when I have matched my daughters, I think that which I shall leave [i.e., have for personal use] will but maintain me. The Countess of Manchester [one of her sisters-in-law] came to me in London, whom wish well [*sic*] to my daughters, and told me that Sir Dodly Noth would fain match himself with my daughter Ann, but I do not know what to

---

1. *Observations*, p. 6.
2. *Observations*, p. 4.
3. *Forest 45*, p. 141. According to Lawrence Stone, "North was the first in English history to take the extreme radical position" (*The Family, Sex and Marriage in England 1500–1800* [New York, 1977], p. 274).
4. *Forest 45*, p. 121.
5. *Forest 45*, p. 131.

think by him, for his father hath sold his land at Harrowe the Hill and his land at the Cherter House, so that they say that my Lord will give him 10,000*l.*, but how I may be sure of it I do not know.[6]

She wanted to know whether Anne, if she married Sir Dudley, would acquire much more than a husband.

Part of the answer is indicated in later jottings by Anne herself: "When I marryed in 1632, my lord's father gave him as his portion £4000 in money, which with what I brought was the use of it to maintain us till it could be disposed of in land to be settled for my jointure and upon the children."[7] The marriage bond itself, dated 31 March 1632, provides more details: a deposit by Lord North of £4,000 was to be matched by a £4,000 deposit by Dame Mary, and the two sums were to be put forth to interest for the present but in due course used for buying land, and thence go to the heirs of Sir Dudley and Anne (if none such, to the heirs of Sir Dudley; and, again, if none such, to the heirs of Lord North himself).[8] Both settlement and suitor, presumably, were satisfactory. Meanwhile no harm was done to the Norths' reputation when the report got about that Mistress Anne would bring to the marriage an impressive £10,000.[9]

About seventeen at the time of her mother's inquiry, Anne Montagu was an intelligent, brown-haired girl with a mind of her own and family connections of some consequence. She was the second daughter and coheiress of Sir Charles Montagu of Cranbrook Hall (which was a fine place about a half-mile north of Ilford village, Essex) and of his second wife, Mary, daughter of Sir William Whitmore of London. The most notable of the Whitmores was doubtless Mary's brother George, a wealthy and prominent merchant of the day, owner of the then-famed Balmes House in Hackney, a moated mansion remarkable for its six pairs of Doric pilasters. This uncle to Anne was Sheriff of London in 1621–1622 and Lord Mayor of London in 1631–1632, and on 27 May 1632 he was knighted.[10] The Montagus, nonetheless, Anne's paternal relations, were generally a more prominent family than the Whitmores, and

6. HMC, *Report on the Manuscripts of Lord Montagu of Beaulieu* (1900), pp. 113–114.

7. Anne's notes are included in Roger's *Lives*, III, 311–313; present passage, p. 311.

8. Spencer MS. uncat. North 1J:47:43.

9. *Seventh Report of the Royal Commission on Historical Manuscripts*, pt. I, *Report and Appendix* (1879), p. 548. Maurice Ashley helps us put into perspective the figures involved: "Dowries might vary between £1,000 and £3,000 for an ordinary squire, might range up to £5,000 or so for a baronet or minor peer, and up to £10,000 or £12,000 for an earl or Minister of State. To get one's daughter married into the peerage [as in the present case] £8,000 would be a modest price. . ." (*The Stuarts in Love, with Some Reflections on Love and Marriage in the Sixteenth and Seventeenth Centuries* [1963], p. 27). See also J. P. Cooper, "Patterns of Inheritance and Settlement by Great Landowners from the Fifteenth to the Eighteenth Centuries," in *Family and Inheritance*, ed. Jack Goody, Joan Thirsk, and E. P. Thompson (Cambridge, 1976), pp. 192–327.

10. William Robinson, *The History and Antiquities of the Parish of Hackney in the County of Middlesex*, I (1842), 157, 161, 162. A good deal of information on the Whitmores is given by William H. Whitmore, *Whitmore Tracts* (Boston, 1875).

they seem to have attained special favor under King James. As the fourth son of Edward Montagu of Boughton, Anne's father, Sir Charles, who in earlier years appears to have served under Elizabeth as a captain of a cornet of horse and quartermaster general of the army in Ireland, was among the first men to be knighted by James (18 April 1603). Obviously a bright fellow, he at some point began to serve as a financial agent and adviser to his family, and eventually to think of himself as a "mony man."[11] Clearly he was in a good position to enjoy as well as benefit from having powerful brothers. Sir Henry was made Lord Chief Justice (1616), Lord High Treasurer (1620), Baron Montagu of Kimbolton (1620), first Earl of Manchester (1626), and Lord Privy Seal (1628); Sir Sidney was made Master of Requests (1618); James, after serving as Dean of the Chapel to King James, became a bishop (and thus a peer of the realm), first, Bishop of Bath and Wells (1608) and later Bishop of Winchester (1616)—the latter in the same year that he worked with the King on the editing of his majesty's *Workes*; and Sir Edward, a friend of Buckingham, was created first Baron Montagu of Boughton (1621). The day was to come when Anne's cousin Edward, second Earl of Manchester, would lead an army against the crown, but in 1620 King James said that he advanced Sir Henry not only for himself but for love of all the Montagu family.[12]

Anne's father died in 1625, when she was about twelve, and her mother, appointed Sir Charles's executress, proceeded to obtain from the King a grant of the wardship and the lease of Anne's lands during her minority. Not only did this prove very costly for Dame Mary; she also found that the yearly expense of maintaining Anne was great.[13] Presumably it would all be worthwhile, however, since proper rearing would help to set off the girl's natural qualities to advantage and prepare her for a good match. Despite the passing of Charles, there certainly were plenty of matchmaking advisers around in 1630 when Henry's wife, Margaret, first informed Mary of Sir Dudley North's interest. After Mary turned to Edward for advice, he, in turn, set about gathering facts in order that a proper evaluation of the situation might be made.[14] By the time all the necessary decisions in the matter had been

---

11. The latter phrase is cited by Esther S. Cope in *The Life of a Public Man: Edward, First Baron Montagu of Boughton, 1562–1644* (Philadelphia, 1981), p. 13; several other facts in this paragraph are derived from the same source. See also Walter C. Metcalfe, ed., *The Visitations of Northamptonshire Made in 1564 and 1618–19* (1887), pp. 37, 114–115; and BL MSS. Harl. 807, 104r, Harl. 4,204, 233r, and Add. MS. 39,177, 113r. Falk records that "Sir Francis Galton, founder of the science of eugenics, . . . investigated the almost unbroken rhythm of Montagu prosperity" and concluded that it was based on "sheer ability: the possession of natural gifts of an exceedingly high order" (*The Way of the Montagues: A Gallery of Family Portraits* [n.d.], p. 11). Falk himself recognized that "family influence" was also an important factor.

12. Reported by Sir Charles Montagu, 13 December 1620 (HMC, *Report on the Manuscripts of the Duke of Buccleuch*, I [1899], 255).

13. Spencer MS. uncat. North 1J:48:190, a document dated 28 April 1632.

14. Edward wrote to his brother Henry, Earl of Manchester, who replied 4 January 1630: "The other day Mr. Tansfeld [Robert Tanfield], speaking with me, told me the same you writ,

reached and the marriage had taken place, Mistress Anne was in her nineteenth year, Sir Dudley in his thirtieth.

Although there is reason to think that Sir Dudley had a certain manly glint in his eye, most courtships of the day among the nobility and upper gentry were rather formal and stilted, and probably the present one was not different. The sole surviving evidence on the subject would seem to be Sir Dudley's series of poems addressed to a mistress named Serena. Whether he found this idealizing name in Spenser, Raleigh, or Drayton, or in Roman literature or somewhere else, one cannot say. Perhaps he recalled that he and his Cambridge friends had put forth a volume that was subtitled *In Obitum Serenissimae Reginae Annae.* In any case, he is likely to have had Mistress Anne Montagu in mind when writing at least some of his poems. Some, he says, are "levelled at obiects of Love, not reall, but imaginary"; but others, he assures Anne, "are not without a reall obiect, nor were it iniurious to any, if you should assume it to your selfe, to bee the person intended." [15] Anne appears to have been an attractive young woman characterized more by spirit and brains than by conventional beauty, but the poems give only conventional glimpses of the beloved playing a lute, sleeping in beauty, or feigning coldness. One never can say that *here* North has in mind Anne, not the ideal beloved. Perhaps the ideal is never wholly absent from the verse. In any case, this cluster of amatory poems constitutes North's wittiest writing and includes one poem that leads us to anticipate that Hymen will bring the wooing game to a close. [16]

Sir Dudley North and Mistress Anne Montagu were joined in matrimony on 24 April 1632. [17] The ceremony took place at St. John-at-Hackney, Middlesex, where previously, in May of 1630, Anne's elder sister Elizabeth had been married—not very happily, it turned out—to Sir Christopher Hatton. [18] The North-Montagu match proved to be a good one on several counts and was destined to thrive for some forty-five years. After the death of both husband and wife, in fact, it seemed to their son Roger, working with such recol-

---

which North would have dissembled; but let that pass; you will find land enough for your money. My sister Charles [i.e., the wife of Charles] is very busy about a match with Sir Chr. Hatton [for her daughter Elizabeth]. I bade her stand upon large demands and good assurance, for he doth not seek a wife, but his friends for him seek a good bargain. . ." (HMC, *Report on the Manuscripts of . . . Buccleuch,* I, 269).

15. From his dedication to the poems, p. 128 herein.

16. No. 21 ("Come lett vs end our sorrowes with a Kisse").

17. County Hall, Greater London Record Office, P 79/JN1/21.

18. Daniel Lysons, *The Environs of London,* II (1795), 489. Elizabeth's later years may be glimpsed in vol. I of *Correspondence of the Family of Hatton,* Camden Society Series 2, vol. XXII, ed. Edward Maunde Thompson (1878), esp. p. 50; and in *Lives,* II, 294–295. According to herself, Elizabeth proved to be a much-put-upon and long-suffering wife, one who could seriously sign herself "the afflicted EHatton" (BL Add. MS. 29,571, 68*r*), but to her son Charles she was an outrageous and habitual fomenter of trouble, one who "travell'd from House to House in Town and Country bemoaning conterfeit Calamity's and overlooking real ones" (BL Add. MS. 29,571, 156*r*).

lections as he could summon up and looking back through eyes somewhat misted by sentiment, that

> If Ever perfect Congugall amity were Intirely preserved with out the least interruption, it was there. altho the lady was a fortune that would intitule her Expectations to an opulent[,] Much More an Easy Course of life . . . , yet . . . during all her life [she] was perfectly happy in the opinion of her Match, & went thro all the troubles of her life with an alacrity, & agreeable patience Never Enough to be admired. . . .[19]

The life before the newlyweds was not without problems, to be sure. We later find Sir Dudley remarking a common practice among the gentry of the day:

> A new Married couple, if they be young, shall do well not to engage themselves in House-keeping too suddenly, but to Sojourn with their Parent, or some other Friend, for some years, that they may have time to observe what order is to be held, and to provide themselves of Houshold stuff, and of other utensils, in some measure, for otherwise they will be like fresh-water Soldiers going to a Military Command, before they are fitted with Arms, and understand the use of them, or what belongs to the exercising of their Soldiers.[20]

On the other hand, the old ex-soldier Sir Dudley had good cause to qualify this advice. He goes on:

> When the Heir becomes a Married man and Master of a Family of his own, yet sometimes the Parent thinks his Sons presence so necessary to him, as he will summon him again to Sojourn, which must be inconvenient, unless the Son hath brought himself by improvidence to an impossibility to live by himself. This I know by experience; for having many Children I was called home by my Father several times, who finding the inconvenience of two considerable Families in a house, returned me as often to my own home, which was not onely a doubling of charge, but a very great hinderance to me in my whole course.[21]

Certainly Dame Anne did not approve of the way theory was put into practice at Kirtling. "My lord's father obliged us to live in the country with him, & to pay £200 a year for our board, which wee did, tho' sometimes wee were not there above 7 months of the yeare."[22] It is well to bear in mind that Lord North apparently turned over many of his business affairs to Sir Dudley. In a letter dated 19 December 1637, North assured his son that "you may in my little Fortune (which I have wholly committed unto your disposing) have a

19. BL Add. MS. 32,523, 6r. 20. Observations, p. 97.
21. Observations, pp. 98–99. 22. Lives, III, 311.

full and free faculty of managing and ordering all according to your good
pleasure and discretion." [23] A few sentences later he adds: "Since your self
hath been a witnesse and an Overseer of my ordinary expenses, . . . you are
not now without experience, you have not been without advice, God blesse
them unto you. . . ." On the other hand, there was no doubt in Anne's mind
that she and her husband were not well treated. After 1636 or so, she explains, "my lord's father thought it convenient that wee should keep a coach
of our owne, & so wee bought a coach & 2 horses and had a coach man to
encrease the number of the [our] little family, & then our boord was increased
to £300 a yeare." [24] One might observe that, as the parents of an ever-increas-
ing number of children, she and her husband scarcely could have avoided
increased expenses, Lord North or no. The problem would seem to have
been, however, not that Lord North was charging his son, nor that as time
passed he increased the charge, but rather—as Roger stated the case—that he
"Exacted rigorously More than the value of their board, Servants & children. . . ." [25] In the seventh year of their marriage, when Lord North raised
the cost of lodging at Kirtling yet another hundred pounds, to £400 a year,
Sir Dudley decided to buy an estate for himself at nearby Tostock in Suffolk,
some six miles east of Bury-St.-Edmunds. Unfortunately, the intricate domestic entanglements between the "two considerable Families in a house"
were not ended so simply. In fact, there were still more complications from
1640 to 1648, when Sir Dudley was in Parliament and his immediate family
was sometimes with him in London. Then in 1649 they were all back at Kirtling. Intermittent sheltering under the parental roof had now stretched on for
some seventeen years, and one can understand the edge in Anne's words
when, late in life, she tried to record the facts of the case. She recalled that in
1650 "wee removed again to Tostock, & after that time were never more in a
settled way, but a year or two in one place & then in the other, which was
both trouble & charge to us." [26]

The estate at Tostock, purchased from one Henry Lambe, Gent., was a
good one. It was situated in fertile, rolling countryside and cost something
over £6,000. Sir Dudley's Uncle John wrote to say, "I think you haue don
very well to fixe vpon that house & land by Bury, which wilbe a fine retreate
for you in winter, when you shall like to go thither, as I hope you meane to

23. *Forest 45*, p. 157.
24. *Lives*, III, 311.
25. BL Add. MS. 32,523, 5v. Nor did the board that the younger family paid at Kirtling
cover all their expenses there. In Anne's words, "At the time that wee lived borders we found
[i.e., had to furnish] all necessarys for our selves & children. . . ." For instance, Sir Dudley
provided "beds & furniture to them, & linen & washing & horse corne, till the latter years, all
fruit & spice & sugar that was used in the chambers & [my Lo:] never had so much as [the least
bitt of] household stuff, linnen, plate, &c., as long as he lived from his father. . ." (*Lives*, III,
313; the last two sets of bracketed words are added from the manuscript, now at Rougham Hall).
26. *Lives*, III, 312.

keepe so fine a seate for your owne dwelling." [27] With only nineteen hearths, the mansion was modest according to Kirtling's standards, [28] but Sir Dudley and Anne tried to make it a real home. Inevitably, therefore, Tostock required a considerable outlay for repairs and upkeep.

There were also various other kinds of strain on the family finances. There was the gradual acquisition of more land (new property at Norton Wood, Saxham, Drinkston, Ashley, and elsewhere); there were sons to be sent to the University—"tho' with as much providense as could be, yett in the quality of noblemen"; [29] and there were daughters to be married off as well as possible. Under the circumstances, perhaps what Sir Dudley and Dame Anne achieved in the way of "economy" is remarkable enough. Anne claimed that her husband never was master of so much as £1,000 a year, and for the last five years of his life not even of £700 a year. [30] Anyone knowing the family's expenses, she contends, would not be surprised to find that at his death he left debts of some £1,500.

Through the years Sir Dudley—who was himself a man of some "naturall heat and courage" [31]—managed to maintain a middle position between his steady, strong-minded wife and his erratic, strong-minded father. The egocentric old lord, who would have had to expend noteworthy effort to "put my self out of my own wayes to accommodate yours," [32] may well have wondered sometimes if he had failed to pass on a certain spark to Sir Dudley. "If any thing prejudice you," North warned his son, "it may prove your tender and infirme constitution, with a minde bent to the more noble speculative and generous thoughts, but you must something force and stiffen your self, to carry an eye, and take a pleasure, in super-intending what concernes you. . . ." [33] The elder North sometimes sensed but never fully understood that there was, indeed, an abiding potential for passion in his son. Though Sir Dudley nearly always managed to subdue his own will to his father's, it was only at some cost to himself. In fact, a recurring concern in the younger man's writing, including one poem composed when he was about sixty, [34] is the liberty that circumstances have denied him. The most outspoken of his statements occurs in one of his essays:

27. Bodl. MS. North c.4, 50r (a letter dated 6 September 1638). Some further connections between Suffolk and various members of the North family are suggested in Alfred Suckling, *The History and Antiquities of the County of Suffolk*, 3 vols. (1846, 1848; Ipswich, 1952).
28. *Suffolk in 1674, Being the Hearth Tax Returns*, Suffolk Green Books, no. 11, vol. XIII (Woodbridge, 1905), p. 287. Great mansions had from twenty to fifty hearths. See also W. A. Copinger, *The Manors of Suffolk*, VI (Manchester, 1910), 243–244, 347.
29. *Lives*, III, 313.
30. This information was excised from the transcription of Anne's words in *Lives*, III, but is preserved in the original version of her cryptic jottings at Rougham Hall.
31. *Forest 45*, p. 194.
32. *Forest 45*, p. 158.
33. Ibid.
34. "A Riddle. 1663" (No. 37).

> Of all my inward conflicts, none hath appeared more like an Earth-
> quake in shaking the whole frame of my nature, than that which raised it
> self upon the consideration of (and sitting down under) some pressures
> carrying with them a constant deprivation of outward freedom; which
> freedom . . . hath been always too far considered by me as the ground of
> external happiness.[35]

Any life, of course, is complex; Sir Dudley had also encountered restraints
during his years as a soldier. Furthermore, in his elegy on the death of his
father, he speaks of the elder man's "abounding vertues."[36] Nonetheless, a
"tyrannical" father (Roger's adjective)[37] would appear to be the best explanation for the son's most distressing "inward conflicts" (Sir Dudley's phrase).
All things considered, there were reasons to be glad that Sir Dudley's mind
was, indeed, "bent to the more noble speculative and generous thoughts."

On one occasion, as we shall see, Sir Dudley did challenge his father publicly, but by and large he appears to have accepted the need for a hierarchy of
authority and to have put his mind and effort to the challenges of managing a
large estate. Given the times, this meant that he learned a great deal about
constraint of a financial sort. Years later, when he decided to share some of
what he had learned by committing it to writing, he suggested significantly
that "It hath been observed as a great unhappinesse to our Nobility and Gentry that generally they are over-housed."[38] Too often, the "Builders of . . .
great Houses were persons either of wast, or rising fortunes, and they contrived their Mansions to be fit for their present or approaching condition, and
no man will doubt, but Estates are much diminished. . . ."[39] A great house,
he says, "is like to great Personal titles, causing the owner to hoise up more
Sail, then the bottom can beare. . . ." Quite clearly he is writing from first-
hand knowledge:

> All men know (and some of us by experience) the great charge of fitting a
> large House, and keeping it in sufficient repair, together with the un-
> comfortablenesse (and seeming shame) of living there attended by a
> small Family [the term includes servants], so as it is hard to give advice
> to persons in such condition, especially if they be fettered so as they can-
> not transplant themselves. . . .[40]

It was one of the major problems of his life.

Another problem was numerous progeny.[41] Sir Dudley and Anne's first-

---

35. *Light*, p. 96.
36. "An Elegie vpon the Right Honble Dudley Lord North. . ." (No. 31), l. 5.
37. *Lives*, I, 34.   38. *Observations*, p. 88.
39. *Observations*, p. 89.   40. *Observations*, p. 90.
41. It may be of interest to juxtapose the fact of the Norths' fruitfulness with the figures of
Lawrence Stone, who suggests that the mean number of children born to peers' sons who themselves, like Sir Dudley, were born in 1600–1624 was less than five (*Family, Sex and Marriage*,

born was delivered at Anne's mother's home, Cranbrook Hall, in November 1633 and named Frances, probably as a compliment to Lady North; but the infant died in December of the following year. The eventual inheritor of the North title and estates, Charles, was the second child, born in September 1635 at Kirtling. If one pauses to note that his name echoed that of both the current King and the heir apparent, one should not forget that it likewise was the name of Anne's father. Charles was to marry well and acquire a title of his own even before his father's death. Edward, perhaps named for the family's founder, was born at Kirtling in September 1636, but apparently died young. The naming of Francis in October 1637 would appear to have been a further attempt to pass on a family name. The event certainly moved Sir Dudley to write a poem expressing the wish that this "third Sonn" enter the church.[42] Instead, he became Lord Keeper of the Great Seal. A female infant born on Christmas Day, 1638, was named Mary; she would die when only twenty-four, shortly after giving birth to a son. In the spring of 1640 Sir Dudley had to go up to London, and Anne, back home and eight months pregnant, wrote on 4 April to give him news about the rising cost of oats and the leasing of the great pasture, as well as to send some licorice juice for his cough and ask that he send her a hundred needles.[43] The next month Dorothy was born. Dudley, the third in the family to bear the name, arrived in May 1641. As a child he was kidnapped by a beggar for his clothes.[44] Rescued by a servant, he grew to be the sort of lad who loved to bet on cockfights, swim in the Thames, and shoot London Bridge at low tide. Blessed with intelligence and luck, he survived even school (he was the least bookish of the sons) and became a wealthy merchant. Anne, perhaps named for her mother, was born at Kirtling in November 1642, shortly after the start of the Civil War. Katherine was born 3 February 1644 but survived only a little over a year. The tenth child, John, was born at midnight on 4 September 1645, when the family was staying in Drury Lane. He proved to be the most studious of all, from the time he was sent off to grammar school at Bury-St.-Edmunds until he became Master of Trinity College (which his grandfather and great-grandfather had attended).[45] Elizabeth, born 4 January 1647, when the family was living in King Street,

---

p. 65). Details in this paragraph are drawn from a variety of sources, including Bodl. MS. North c.25; Kirtling Parish Registers 1585–1649 (P101/1/1, County Record Office, Shire Hall, Cambridge); and notations by Roger in the Rougham Hall manuscript of Sir Dudley's poems.

42. "Made vpon the birth of my third Sonn" (No. 26). N.b. the headnote to this poem.

43. Anne to Sir Dudley, 4 April 1640 (Huntington MS. North 14).

44. *Lives*, II, 2.

45. Although John was the most academic of the sons, it might be observed that Sir Dudley and Dame Anne also sent Francis, Dudley, and Roger, and perhaps Charles and Montagu to the same school at Bury-St.-Edmunds; see S. H. A. Hervey, *Biographical List of Boys Educated at King Edward VI. Free Grammar School, Bury St. Edmunds. From 1550 to 1900* (Bury-St.-Edmunds, 1908), pp. 277–279.

Westminster, was to marry well but die in childbirth.[46] The next daughter, born in January 1648, also in King Street, was called Christian, which was both an old family name and a reflection of her parents' abiding piety. If the name was ambiguously capable of evoking Puritan overtones in the ears of some hearers, Sir Dudley was, after all, a member of the Commons. In 1649, however, after Parliament had been purged of moderates such as Sir Dudley, the Norths retired to Kirtling, and a thirteenth child, Montagu, named for his mother's family, was born in July. Then, some eighteen years after the birth of the first child, the fourteenth and final one, Roger, was born at Tostock on 3 September 1651. His tuition began under Kirtling's chaplain, Ezekiel Catchpole (who was also the parish clergyman), and later included study at Jesus College under his brother John, who was a fellow there. Still a bit later he ascended to high worldly places, but the fact remains that Roger is best known for his painstaking biographies of his brothers Francis, Dudley, and John.

Included in Roger's voluminous writing is a nostalgic description of the little town of Kirtling in his boyhood:

> The town was then my grandfather's, consisting of tillage farms, and small dairies, so that business was usually done by noon, and it was always the custom for the youth of the town, who were men or maid servants, and children, to assemble, after horses baited [fed], either upon the green or (after haysel [hay season]) in a close accustomed to be so used, and there all to play till milking time, and supper at night. The men to football, and the maids, with whom we children commonly mixed, being not proof for the turbulence of the other party, to stoolball, and such running games as they knew. . . .[47] I mention this because it seems to me to have been a better condition of country living than I ever observed anywhere else, and being at those years free from all cares, made a happier state than all honour and wealth can boast of.[48]

Although Roger's writing tends to warm into a nostalgically rosy glow sometimes, it invariably lights up some facts of interest. He later described his mother and father as "parents of just and honourable principles if any such ever were,"[49] and, again looking back to his childhood, reported that

> Wee were taught to Reverence our father, whose care of us then consisted cheifly in the Gravity and decorum of his comportment, order and sobriety of life, whereby no Indecent or Mischevous Impressions took

46. Roger writes that the King Street house, "though a sorry one," was "remarkable for being the first and only brick house in that street for many years" (*Lives*, II, 2).

47. Stoolball was an old country game resembling cricket, the "stool" being a wicket.

48. *Lives*, III, 9–10.

49. Peter T. Millard, "An Edition of Roger North's *Life of Dr. John North* with a Critical Introduction" (D.Phil. thesis, Linacre College, Oxford, 1969), p. 6.

place with us from his example, and when he deposed his temper [i.e., his habitual gravity], and condescended to entertein the little credulous Impertinents, it was with an agreable as well as moral Effect, tending either to Instruct or Encourage what was good, and to defie the Contrary. . . .[50]

His mother, he says,

was learned (for a Lady) and Eloquent. Had much knowledg of history, and readyness of witt to express herself, especially in the part of Reproof, wherein she was fluent and pungent. And not onely her children but servants dreaded her Reproof, knowing how sensibly she would attag[51] them. . . . But without occasion given to the Contrary, she was debonair, familiar, and very liberall of her discours to entertein all, and ever tending to goodness, and morality.[52]

Father and mother alike were bent on instilling in their children such beliefs and behavior as Richard Hooker himself might have approved.

Furthermore, with the exception of Charles, the boys were all groomed for occupations of some sort. In Roger's words,

wee were without Remission held close to the Methods proper to Fitt us for them. And wee were given to understand early, that there was no other means of living to be expected, then what came out of our Industry. . . . Wee were not deluded by a vaine, pompous way of living . . . , But with all the parsimony Imaginable . . . ; and what learning in philosophy and arts we had it came cheap, being pick't up by our owne care. . . .[53]

Here the rosy hue goes down to gray, and one is left with the age-old difficulty of a son to see his father.[54]

In these middle years, one of Sir Dudley's duties was serving as a justice. The sense of responsibility that pervaded his entire life and often reached out

50. *Lives*, III, 1–2.

51. Not in *OED*. Apparently a form of either "attach" (i.e., accuse, charge) or "attack" (set upon with hostile action or words).

52. *Lives*, III, 4. The contrasting images of the father and mother that are conveyed in these two passages by Roger are corroborated indirectly but strikingly in a passage by Sir Dudley himself: "The second person in a Family is the Wife, who if she be industrious, and prudent, flies at all within dores, and pitty it is that any obstacle should be met withal, which is well illustrated by the Queen at the game of Chesse, where the King, or Master, keeps his gravity by going but one draught at once, but the Queen as his Lievtenant, is not limited for way, since she hath power to march every way, nor for distance, so as she keep within compasse of the Chesse-board, which you may understand to be the House or Family" (*Observations*, pp. 57–58).

53. *Lives*, III, 6.

54. In a more characteristically cheerful mood Roger writes: "It Must be sayd ffor the honor of the provident pair, that whatever hardship they endured, Nothing of due Education was wanting to any of the children Nor Convenient portions & disbursṁts, upon Every occasion of advantage to them. . ." (BL Add. MS. 32,523, 5*v*.).

to touch the lives of others may be glimpsed in some of the scrappy passages that he jotted in a notebook on his justiceship.[55] During Easter Week, 1639, for instance, he met with a handful of other men to review the accounts of certain church wardens and overseers from various towns. On 20 January he had sent one Joseph Clarke to jail for stealing a coat and pair of breeches from Will Wybrows at Kirtling. On 19 September, concerned about two men who had refused to take apprentices, he thought it best to bind them to answer their refusal at the next assizes. And on 8 July 1640, he noted that certain men had been whipped in accordance with a statute from Elizabeth's reign. There is even one rueful confession of a mistake: "I tooke Gawins word for his appearance at sessions to give in Evidence. I should have bound him."

It turns out that another Cambridgeshire justice, one Michael Dalton, was gaining contemporary renown as the author of an invaluable book entitled *The Countrey Justice, Conteyning the Practise of the Justices of the Peace out of Their Sessions*. Originally composed as some private notes for Dalton's own use, the book was published first in 1618, then revised and amplified in many subsequent editions. The matter is of interest here because Dalton knew Sir Dudley. Surviving yet today in private hands is a small manuscript abridgment (with eighty-one pages of text and two of index) entitled "The Authority & Office of a Justice of Peace," inscribed by Dalton and presented "To the Right Honorable Sir Dudly North, Knight of the Bathe."[56]

Beginning in the 1630s Sir Dudley also endeavored to improve the family's finances by involving himself in drainage of the fens. Godfrey Davies writes that with fen drainage "well over half a million acres were added to the cultivated land in England. The outstanding example is the draining of the Great Level of the Fens, which had stretched through six counties, from Lincoln to Cambridge—a vast morass, with a few islands here and there."[57] Sir Dudley had long lived near the fens, and he also had observed at first hand the skill of the Dutch in treating problems relating to land and water management. Repeatedly now his name crops up in connection with fenland matters. On 2 June 1637 the "undertakers" of the Great Level ("lying along the river Witham from Lincoln to Bourn") agreed to sell two hundred acres of Gosberton Fen for £600.[58] In January 1638, when some £12,000 were being raised for the drainage of the Eight Hundred Fen, Sir Dudley was among the "adventurers" assessed.[59] His knowledgeability in the business is suggested by his being named on 20 May 1646 to a commission to investigate matters relating to the fens.[60] In May of 1649 Parliament produced "An Act for drayning

---

55. All of the quotations in this paragraph are from a notebook now at Rougham Hall.
56. For this information I am indebted to Mr. John R. S. Guinness of London.
57. *The Early Stuarts: 1603–1660* (Oxford, 2nd ed., 1959; 1st pub. 1937), p. 281.
58. John Bruce, ed., *CSP*, Domestic, 1637 (1868), p. 184.
59. John Bruce, ed., *CSP*, Domestic, 1637–1638 (1869), p. 151.
60. W. M. Palmer, "The Fen Office Documents," *Proceedings of the Cambridge Antiquarian Society*, XXXVIII (1939), 120.

the Great Level of the Fens" and proposed a completion date of 1656.[61] In fact, this same act appointed Sir Dudley (along with Lt. Gen. Oliver Cromwell) as one of the Commissioners to assist with adjudging questions arising from its execution.[62]

Some of Anne's jottings record the fen business without enthusiasm. She writes: "the Lincolnshire fen being declared drained, they took proportions out of every bodies' land, & my lord choose rather to buy the part of his which the undertakers had taken than to part with his land, so layed down £600, for it was [he had been?] at cost to enclose & lett it at a good considerable rent; but the times changing all was throwne out & that money & cost lost."[63] Land drainage was an enormously good idea, nonetheless, and Sir Dudley remained involved in it for a number of years.

When Sir John North, uncle to Sir Dudley, died toward the close of 1638 at the age of about fifty-one, it was reported that the King was "very sorry" to lose "a good chesse player to keepe him company at that sport."[64] Unfortunately things were in a muddle because no will could be found. It was only after a week had passed and Lord North and his other brothers already had taken steps to administer the estate that someone turned up the will which Sir John had made back in 1623 just before sailing to Spain on the *Adventure*. Now Sir Dudley, as chief heir, had the difficult task of challenging his father's action. Although Sir John had specifically designed his will to avoid contention,[65] an unseemly scramble took place. John's sometime chess-playing partner, the monarch himself, was the recipient of petitions from both Lord North and Sir Dudley. In his, Lord North wrote of the "great trouble, charge & wast of time" likely to ensue if the King did not intervene in the matter. He did not mince words: because his son was "chalengeing after legacies paid the whole estate to belong and be intended to him, great and vnnaturall dissention and inconvenience may growe. . . ."[66] Sir Dudley, learning that the King was, indeed, going to make a ruling on the following Sunday, asked that he either assume that it had been Sir John's intention to make Sir Dudley his primary beneficiary or else have the registrar of the prerogative court of Canterbury attend his majesty with depositions.[67] The upshot was that Sir John's will was upheld. Lord North, however, was not to be totally outmaneuvered.

---

61. C. H. Firth and R. S. Rait, ed., *Acts and Ordinances of the Interregnum, 1642–1660*, II (1911), 130–139.

62. Among the books that later turned up in the North family's library was Cornelius Vermuiden, *A Discourse Touching the Drayning of the Great Fennes* (1642). Helpful perspective is provided by H. C. Darby, *The Draining of the Fens* (Cambridge, 1940).

63. *Lives*, III, 311.

64. HMC, *Sixth Report of the Royal Commission on Historical Manuscripts*, pt. I: *Report and Appendix* (1877), 285.

65. Bodl. MS. North c.29, 50 and 51.

66. PRO, SP 16/531, item 96; and William D. Hamilton and Sophia Crawford Lomas, ed., *CSP*, Domestic, Addenda: March, 1625–January, 1649 (1897), p. 388.

67. PRO SP 16/531, item 971; Hamilton and Lomas, ibid.

Anne makes no overt reference to the business but she does observe that the old man, in view of Sir Dudley's "encrease of fortune & children wee had in the house,"[68] raised their board (as we have seen) to £400 per year.

Uncle John deserved a better memorial. An affectionate and patient man, he had long tried to maintain close contacts with the family at Kirtling, writing them weekly letters from Theobalds or Hampton Court or Whitehall, or from his lodgings in the gatehouse at Charterhouse. He wrote even when his brother and nephew were both too busy to reply, telling of events at court (a masque, a funeral), advising them to leave Kirtling when a visit by the Elector Palatine was threatening (though Lord North would call on the Elector in London), and looking forward to good times when the family could be together.[69] At least now the kindly courtier's good will bore fruit for Sir Dudley.

The same year that Sir John died, 1638, brought Sir Dudley himself near death. Writing from his Charterhouse quarters on 31 August 1638, Uncle John had observed—ironically, in retrospect—"I never heard of the death of more of my acquaintance in so short a time. . . ."[70] Up at Kirtling Lord North wrote that "a most pestilent and mortall small Pox [has] seised and carryed many of eminent rank and vertue."[71] Extremely important to Lord North was the fact that Anne, Lady Rich, wife of Robert, Lord Rich, and only daughter of William Cavendish, second Earl of Devonshire, had fallen ill and died while visiting at Kirtling. Poems on the death of Lady Rich were produced by Henry King, Sidney Godolphin, Thomas Barrington, Arthur Wilson, and Edmund Waller. Lord North himself wrote four, and Sir Dudley, one.[72] In fact, the Reverend Dr. John Gauden was still writing on the subject twenty years later in *Funerals Made Cordials*, a version of the funeral sermon that he preached on Lady Rich's son. The death of a virtuous and attractive young woman at Kirtling seems to have obsessed Lord North for a while. At the very time she lay ill, moreover, his own eldest son was badly stricken. Writing on 22 September 1638, North recalls "the sight of my Sons extreamity, lying as I thought (and little lesse it was then) strugling with death. . . ."[73]

More than half of Sir Dudley's life, it turned out, lay ahead.

68. *Lives*, III, 312.
69. See Bodl. MS. North c.4, passim.
70. Bodl. MS. North c.4, no. 48.
71. *Forest 45*, p. 79.
72. Most of these are included in "The Shadow of the (Sometimes) Right Faire, Vertuous, and Honourable Lady Anne Rich Now an Happy, Glorious, and Perfected Saint in Heaven," a manuscript volume (Bodl. MS. Eng. misc. e.262); see also *Forest 45* (pp. 77–80) and Sir Dudley's "An Elegy composed vpon the buriall of Ann Lady Rich" (No. 29).
73. *Forest 45*, p. 63. Sir Dudley was still unwell in November (*Forest 45*, pp. 191, 194), but on 3 November one finds both him and Sir Christopher Nevill (a sometime resident of the Charterhouse) involved in an indenture tripartite to help manage the mangled financial affairs of Katherine Lennard, daughter of Sir Dudley's widowed sister, Dorothy, Lady Dacre (Spencer MS. uncat. North 17:4).

CIVIL STRIFE AND RETIREMENT

Though a private, bookish sort of man, averse to violence and inclined to preserve the values and ways of an earlier time, Sir Dudley found himself *"called to Publick affairs"* [1] in one of the most turbulent periods in English history. Pulled in different directions by conflicting instincts, duties, goals, and necessities, he became a reluctant supporter of Parliament, one who could argue—and in later years argue publicly—for monarchy. Beneath the shifting tides of men and events, the ground he chose to stand on was his conviction that he could serve both his country and his private interests best by working within the Parliament for moderation. This is the ground he continued to hold until men of moderation had outworn their usefulness and he was expelled from the Commons. [2]

When he wrote later about his four elections to the Commons (in 1628–1629, 1640, again in 1640, and 1660), North found it difficult to separate personal cost—a perennial problem—from the larger subject of public duty. He observed that his *"Service and approaches were excessive chargeable, and of no profit as to my particular. One of these was that fatal Parliament* [November 1640] *which set the whole Kingdom on fire, seeking to enervate or unsinue all Government, and that it might the better be effected, divers of us their Members were by Club-law forced from our station. Yet it pleased God (even by that Parliament . . . when we were re-admitted), to put all again in such a way as the old Government was perfectly restored in a succeeding Assembly."* [3]

In later years North repeatedly found occasion to assert his belief in the English monarchy, especially in his *Narrative of Some Passages in or Relating to the Long Parliament* (1670), which bears the title-page motto *"Rebellion is as the Sin of Witchcraft"* (I Samuel 15.23). Well aware that some men would

---

1. *Observations*, A4v.

2. John R. MacCormack, *Revolutionary Politics in the Long Parliament* (Cambridge, Mass., 1973), p. 322, attempts to graph Sir Dudley's political course from "probable core moderate" to "probable latent moderate" to "probable fringe moderate" to "fringe moderate." See also D. Brunton and D. H. Pennington, *Members of the Long Parliament*, introd. R. H. Tawney (1954), and Mary Frear Keeler, *The Long Parliament, 1640–1641: A Biographical Study of Its Members* (Philadelphia, 1954).

3. *Observations*, A4v–A5r. North's words here acknowledge that the Long Parliament reconvened briefly in early 1660. It allowed London to elect a mayor, cashiered Lambert, sent for General Monk, called for another Parliament, and, on 16 March, dissolved itself (see Browne Willis, *Notitia Parliamentaria* [1750], pp. 240–241).

recall only too well how he had retained his seat in the Long Parliament until he was forcibly ejected, he felt the need to introduce his recollections with what his son Roger called an "apologetic, or rather, recantation preface."[4] Whether it is because Sir Dudley aimed to be discreet or because he was working from scraps of memories and scattered notes, his "narrative" conveys a general aura of truthful vagueness. Here and there, however, it quickens with a cluster of details that help us to see the writer a bit more clearly. Throughout his book, moreover, we see evidence of the kinds of pressures, changes, and difficulties that were faced also by other loyalist gentlemen and aristocrats of the time.

On 28 August 1640, along with a number of other lords, Sir Dudley's father put his name to a petition beseeching the King to ponder such "evils" of the day as the current expedition against the Scots, innovations in religious practice, the rise of popery, the urging of ship-money, and the long intermission of Parliaments.[5] At last, cornered by events and burdened by the blunder of having previously dissolved Parliament (5 May 1640), the King could no longer afford to be deaf. On 3 November the Parliament known later as the Long Parliament was convened. "Never Parliament was assembled," wrote Sir Dudley, "when the people were in a higher discontent. . . . The encrease of Ceremonies had made them fear the approach of a Religion hateful to them. The late business of Ship-money, together with some other impositions without consent of Parliament, caused them to apprehend the loss of property in their estates. . . ."[6] Nevertheless, before the very first month was over, Sir Dudley was pledging £1,000 to Parliament's campaign to raise money for the King's army.[7]

A short time later, in January 1641, the King's devoted friend and servant Thomas Wentworth, Earl of Strafford, Lord Lieutenant of Ireland, was denounced as a traitor and taken to the Tower. Sir Dudley later recalled:

At or about the time of *Straffords* Trial, there was a general licentiousness used. The Parliament-houses were daily haunted with a rabble of tumultuating people, crying out for that which they called justice. There was also a Liberty assumed, and connived at, to Print and publish what every man thought fit, which for the most part was in defamation of the Governors Ecclesiastical and Temporal. Within the City of *London* the Pulpits were almost wholly possest by Presbyterian-Ministers, whose eloquence was altogether employed the same way.[8]

4. *Lives*, I, 6.
5. William Douglas Hamilton, ed., *CSP*, Domestic, 1640 (1880), pp. 639–641.
6. *Narrative*, p. 8.
7. *The Journal of Sir Simonds D'Ewes*, ed. Wallace Notestein, I (New Haven, 1923), 52; see also p. 452.
8. *Narrative*, pp. 14–15.

As the wind of words gathered dangerous force in the streets and pulpits and in political pamphlets, it became clear that sooner or later the storm would break. The early plans to impeach Strafford had to be abandoned because he could not be shown to have violated any laws, but in May, with the signature of Charles on the death warrant, Strafford was beheaded before a huge crowd on Tower Hill. Parliament then settled in for several months of corrective legislation, and in August, at a time when the lives of few Englishmen can have remained untouched by Parliament's actions, Sir Dudley North was one of five commissioners named "for disarming Popish recusants and other dangerous persons in the County of Cambridge."[9]

Long a devout Church of England man, Sir Dudley had fretted in 1636 about members of the clergy who were willing to "nourish strife at home for trifles, and vntye / The peace of Nations to mayntayne theyr Hyerarchye. . . ."[10] Clerics, he complained then, were making themselves into statesmen. Of course Sir Dudley had no idea how far some of his countrymen would eventually carry criticism of this sort, and when all was said and done he himself remained a Church of England man. In his *Light in the Way to Paradise* he later avowed that he had no desire to engage in religious polemics. He was more concerned with devotion than details of dogma, more committed to morality than details of worship. Nevertheless, he proceeded to explain why he never could accept such Roman Catholic tenets as the Pope's supremacy (only Christ can head the Church) or transubstantiation (were not Christ's body *and* the bread present at the first communion?).[11] He also pointed out that "our *Non-conformists* . . . seem to be but ill Directors."[12] Presbyterians and Independents alike, whatever their virtues, were too strict, and sometimes destructively so.[13] He himself was thoroughly at home only in "our Church of *England*"[14] and believed it "a great commendation of the *Common prayer-book*, to say that it complieth with Antiquity as far as lawfully may be done."[15] Somewhat ironically, however, he was one of those Anglicans whose rather stable position in the *via media* could be viewed as somehow becoming increasingly liberal because the Laudians were moving the Church of England farther and farther to the right, imposing a strictness

9. Noted by H. C. Darby and E. Miller in *The Victoria History of the County of Cambridge and the Isle of Ely*, ed. L. F. Salzman, II (1948), 405.

10. "A Satyre. 1636" (No. 25), ll. 35–36.

11. *Light*, pp. 23–24. Considering the facts of the case, I think there is minimal danger in citing a later writing to explain Sir Dudley's earlier religious position.

12. *Light*, p. 27.

13. *Light*, pp. 24–27. One may safely discard Alfred Kingston's statement that "Sir Dudley was a rigid Presbyterian, and his wife was a not less rigid, but more zealous, Independent" (*East Anglia and the Great Civil War* [1902 ed.], p. 314); Kingston misread a passage in Roger North's *Lives*.

14. *Light*, p. 8.

15. *Light*, p. 29.

comparable to that which Sir Dudley found distasteful in the Presbyterians and Independents.

For North, the basic points of faith were few. Man's proper end in life is glorifying God, but because of his radical sinfulness, man forms the wrong kind of attachments to the present world. If he is to be saved, it is through the sacrifice of Christ and the grace of God. As North puts it in one of his prayers, "*We confess, that of our selves without thy especiall grace we cannot step one step towards thee, by our actings in any Religious duty; yet by means of that grace we are enabled so far to act, as to obtain acceptance at thy hands in Jesus Christ. . . .*"[16] The ins and outs of sin and redemption were very nearly his whole concern in religion.

The similar religious positions held by Sir Dudley and his father are caught in the following passage, written in 1640 by the elder North and darkened with political implications: "Gods Service and Worship is the substantiall and Morall part. Episcopacy, and this or that Form, but the Ceremoniall, and I would be sorry to see cutting of throats for Discipline and Ceremonie: Charity ought to yeeld farre in things indifferent: But must all the yeelding be on the Governours part? God forbid, that we should yeeld to every fanatical opinion, and to fal into a way of *Enthusiasts*. . . ."[17] It was enthusiasm, nonetheless, that would carry the day.

The year 1642 was a turning point, for on 4 January King Charles made the mistake of attempting in person to arrest five members of the Commons, and such a furor resulted that he found it best to retire from Whitehall to Hampton Court. "After this," Sir Dudley observed, "there were many addresses to the King by the Parliament, but not any, that could be in the least measure pleasing to him."[18] Sir Dudley had cause to recall in particular the occasion when, in response to a silent but eloquent gesture of protest on his own part, the Commons named him to a delegation as a means of reproof. Although he is usually frugal in dispensing details, it is possible to reconstruct the facts that, following his angry gesture on 9 February 1642, he, together with John Colepeper, Alexander Carew, and Giles Strangways, was appointed to attend the King the next morning. In Sir Dudley's words,

> It happened that Mr. [John] *Pim* had newly and publickly . . . used some words of disrespect to the King, wherewith his Majesty exprest himself to be offended, and thereupon the House of Commons . . . took a resolution to send his Majesty a paper, in full justification of that which Mr. *Pim* had said, . . . and appearing dissatisfied with it, [I] immediately went out of doors, which being observed by a back friend[19] of mine, he named me one of the four to carry it. This unwelcome news

16. *Observations*, K3v.
17. *Forest 45*, p. 236.   18. *Narrative*, p. 19.
19. "A pretended or false friend; an enemy who pretends friendship" (*OED*).

was brought to me to my own house by one of our Serjeants, with a copy of the order, which must not be disobeyed, and so we went and delivered the paper to his Majesty at *Hampton-Court*, which being read, he began to discourse upon it, as if he expected reason from us, and seem'd to address his Speech more particularly to me (perhaps having heard of my dislike) but Sir *John Culpepper* then Chancellor of the Exchequer and chief of the four, told his Majesty, we had not power to speak one word, whereupon we were dismissed, and returned to *London*.[20]

One is left to surmise Sir Dudley's frustration at failing to satisfy either side in the matter.

On 5 March 1642 Sir Dudley's father was nominated once again to serve as Lord Lieutenant of Cambridgeshire. This time, however, the nominator was not the King but the Parliament, and now the Lord Lieutenants and justices were supposed to begin actual impressments and call the militia out for drill. This was not at all like wishing to go fight the Turks or offering to lead soldiers on behalf of the Venetians. Increasingly now, Englishmen of all ranks were presented with the problem of whether to cast their lot with King or Commons. On 8 June, after several months of what he called "this time of imminent Danger," Lord North nominated Sir Dudley to serve in his stead.[21]

Probably Sir Dudley's hands were already full. Having pledged money in 1640 for the King's army, he was listed in early June of 1642 among those members of the Commons advancing horses, money, and plate for defense of the Parliament.[22] An additional irony is that it was agreed a short time later (1 August 1642) by the masters and seniors of his old college, St. John's, to present the King with certain pieces of the college plate, including, among other "Standing Pieces and . . . Boules," the very gift which young Sir Dudley himself had made at the time he went to the University.[23] Justifiably worried about the shape of coming events, he now sought official permission to carry

20. *Narrative*, pp. 19–21. The King and Commons had exchanged messages on the licensing of persons traveling to Ireland. The Commons had affirmed that "many of the chief Commanders, now in the Head of the Rebels," as well as "*Irish* and other Papists," had been licensed by the King despite "the Order of Restraint of both Houses" (*Journals of the House of Commons*, II [n.d.], 423); for Charles's reply, sent from Dover, 22 February, see pp. 453–454. The whole wrangle is summarized in *His Majesties Message Concerning Licenses Granted to Persons Going into Ireland* (1641; i.e., 1642).

21. Bodl. MS. North c.44, no. 25.1. Oliver Cromwell regarded North *père* as Lord Lieutenant as late as 19 July (William Douglas Hamilton, ed., *CSP*, Domestic, 1641–43 [1887], p. 354). It is the opinion of Louis Tebbutt, however, that Lord Lieutenants probably did not function after war broke out ("The Lord Lieutenants of Cambridgeshire," *Proceedings of the Cambridge Antiquarian Society*, XLI [1948], 53).

22. F. Kyffin Lenthall, "List of the Names of the Members of the House of Commons That Advanced Horse, Money, and Plate. . . ," *Notes and Queries*, XII (1855), 358; "Sir Dud. North will freely give sixty pownds."

23. Thomas Baker, *History of the College of St. John the Evangelist, Cambridge*, ed. John E. B. Mayor, II (1869), 633. Although the King's request for college plate (dated 24 July 1642) had hinted at its threatened "sequestration" by the enemy, "Even a college like St. John's, the focus

twenty muskets down to Kirtling.[24] In July, Oliver Cromwell was sending down arms for Cambridge, and Sir Dudley was in charge of reimbursing this fellow member of the Commons whom later he would call "Leviathan *Cromwell*."[25] In mid-August the Commons instructed the local Deputy Lieutenants to serve in Lord North's absence,[26] and on 22 August Charles raised his standard at Nottingham. It was no longer a war of "Manifestoes and Declarations."[27]

About two weeks later, under the date 6 September 1642, we find "Instructions agreed upon by the Lords and Commons in Parliament assembled, for Sir *Dudley North*, Knight, *Oliver Cromewell*, Esquire, Members of the House of Commons, and Committees to be sent into the County of *Cambridge*, and Isle of *Ely* . . . for the Preservation of the Peace. . . ."[28] In his *Narrative* Sir Dudley recorded what he saw:

> . . . the house of Commons ordered me to go into the Countrey for which I served, where I found all full of terror, the common people generally apprehending, that the Cavaliers (as the Royallists were then called) were coming to plunder them. This fear was artificially put into them, as I could easily perceive: for the Countrey was full of strange fictions of their inhumane carriage in other countreys, and being at my usual Mansion [Kirtling], we had scarcely any rest (no not in the night) for Messengers giving the allarm, and the manner was to bring a paper of intelligence without any subscription, and this must be taken for truth, without any farther proof. These allarms generated strange, wild, and indigested propositions, such as were not to be hearkned unto by any person of Judgment and experience, yet they were some way tending to the great design of raising the terror to a height, and putting arms into the hands of Schismatical people under the name of Voluntiers, and by those means to form a new power to be disposed of upon occasion in any part of the Kingdome. . . . But since the Kings forces did not really make any approach towards us, and since I had not accepted of any Command to oblige my stay in the Countrey, I made my return to *London*, and applyed my self to my constant course of attending in Parliament. . . ."[29]

North reports that "then there were also Ordinances of Parliament (which kind of law grew now in fashion) framed, and past for constituting asso-

in the University of the Royalist element, put up only certain articles of plate" (Frederick John Varley, *Cambridge During the Civil War: 1642–1646* [Cambridge, 1935], p. 79).

24. *Journals of the . . . Commons*, II, 654.
25. *Narrative*, p. 3.
26. Clive Holmes, *The Eastern Association in the English Civil War* (Cambridge, 1974), p. 52.
27. *Narrative*, p. 29.
28. *Journals of the House of Lords*, V (n.d.), 342.
29. *Narrative*, pp. 36–38.

ciations, whereof the *Eastern* was chief, and much promoted by *Cromwel*, who founded his greatness there. . . ." [30] The Eastern Counties Association, which was to play a major role in the war, was founded in December 1642. Aside from its general importance in the history of the time, it is significant here because on 16 August 1643 the Earl of Manchester, cousin to Anne North, arrived in Cambridge to serve as its Commander-in-Chief. Though Manchester had commenced a courtier, even married one of Buckingham's kinswomen, he later had become a puritan. Now, whatever private misgivings any individual members of the family might have had, the Norths were allied conspicuously with the Parliamentary leadership. [31] Among other matters, Manchester authorized the commission of William Dowsing to carry out Parliament's ordinance of 28 August 1643 for the destruction of stone altars, of rails about altars, and of crucifixes, images, and pictures. [32] Dowsing carried out his orders even at Kirtling, where his victims included *"Three superstitious Pictures & 14 Angels* in the *Chancell* on the *Roof*, which the *Lord North's* man promised to take of[f], & the *windowes* broken down. . . ." [33] Manchester wintered at Cambridge and, in accord with an ordinance of 22 January 1644, undertook the reformation of the University. Since passions on all sides ran high, it is difficult now to winnow fact from feeling in the matter, but surely one may say that it was a dark day for most Johnians when soldiers were quartered in the college. [34]

Even while he was being drawn deeper into an involvement with the Parliamentarians, it is likely that Sir Dudley regarded himself as standing at the side of rather than with those whom he called fire-loving "Salamanders." [35] One indication of this fact—and a subtle one, for it is capable of being interpreted in opposite ways—was his refusal to accept remuneration for his work in the Commons. Roger North explains that, "wheras other's in like case had 4. [pounds] a Month allowed by the vsurping powers, he never had a cross, nor would he take any, beleeving it would taint that service which he thought his duty with the Imputation of selfishness." [36] Mindful always of his

30. *Narrative*, p. 39. Philip Warwick wrote: "What this word *Ordinance* signified was grown so unintelligible, that I could never meet with any, who cleerly could expound it either by good books or authority. . ." (*Memoires of the Reigne of King Charles I* [1701], p. 168).

31. Then again, oversimplification is dangerous. Sir George Whitmore, Anne's uncle and sometime Lord Mayor of London, was imprisoned for being an ardent royalist.

32. Varley, pp. 33–34.

33. BL Add. MS. 5,819, 120r.

34. *Querela Cantabrigiensis: Or a Remonstrance . . . for the Banished Members of the Late Flourishing University of Cambridge* (Oxford, 1646), supposedly by John Barwick, probably conveys outraged feelings accurately, if not facts.

35. *Narrative*, A6v.

36. BL Add. MS. 32,523, 5v. The word "cross" here means simply "coin." Practices varied widely, but it was increasingly common for a constituency to agree to elect a candidate if he would sign a pledge not to charge whatever the current wages were. Although Roger presents his father's action in a moral light, most such arrangements were a simple outgrowth of practical politics (see, for example, Edward Porritt, asstd. by Annie G. Porritt, *The Unreformed House of Commons*, I [Cambridge, 1909], 153–154).

own financial problems, Sir Dudley probably participated with quiet alarm as Parliament went about raising the money it needed: by sequestration of delinquents' estates; by "requiring a twentieth part of goods and a fifth part of every man's revenue"; and, "last and surest, . . . a monthly tax for the army. . . ."[37] Sir Dudley was the first man named from Cambridge to oversee the "Ordinance for the speedy raising and levying of Money for the maintenance of the Army Raised by the Parliament . . . by a Weekly Assessement. . ." (24 February 1643).[38] He was the first named from Cambridge to oversee the "Ordinance for Sequestring notorious Delinquents Estates" (27 March 1643).[39] Again, he was named first for Cambridge to oversee the ordinance for "taxing such as have not at all contributed or lent, or not according to their Estates and Abilities" (7 May 1643).[40] Despite all this, however, the paradoxical possibility remains that Sir Dudley may have been loyal to the institution of the monarchy, perhaps even to the person of the King. Much later his son Roger would claim that Sir Dudley was "misled" in his actions during this period,[41] but the only sure fact would seem to be that Sir Dudley believed he could best safeguard the things that were most important to him by working within the Commons.

The better to attend to his Parliamentary duties, he moved his family to the city. In Anne's words, "wee . . . lived by ourselves [i.e., not with Lord North] most at London till about '49,"[42] and, indeed, it was here in Drury Lane and King Street that some of their children were born.

Although war had broken out in 1642, it was Anne's view that "In '44 the troublesome times began. . . ."[43] By all odds the greatest event of 1644 came on 2 July, when an army of twenty-six or twenty-seven thousand Parliamentarians fought and badly defeated an army of ten or eleven thousand Royalists at Marston Moor. The city of York surrendered soon thereafter, and a good many Royalist officers fled to the Continent. Now the control of the north was settled. The Earl of Manchester, however, one of the chief victors, returned to the eastern counties and, put off by the rise of Independency among his men, contrived to do as little as possible, thereby incensing Cromwell, who was now Lieutenant General. The poem which Sir Dudley entitled "August .15. 1644" records his own efforts to hold on to some enduring values at a time when the world seemed to be crumbling. The very next day brought to light Parliament's "Ordinance for the speedy establishing of a Court Martiall, within the Cities of London, Westminster. . . ," and his father was named one of the commissioners to constitute the court.[44] Then on 14 October 1644 Sir Dudley himself was put in charge of collecting money from the county of Cambridge for the purchase of pistols and armor for Cromwell's regiment.[45]

37. *Narrative*, pp. 40–41.
38. Firth and Rait, I, 85.
39. Firth and Rait, I, 145.
40. Firth and Rait, I, 146.
41. *Lives*, I, 6.
42. *Lives*, III, 312.
43. Ibid.
44. Firth and Rait, I, 486–487.
45. Firth and Rait, I, 530.

While Sir Dudley was forced by circumstances to take to the roads between London and Cambridge, Manchester was forced to do battle at Newbury (27 October 1644).

When the ordinance for the New Model Army was passed on 17 February 1645 (Parliament's forces had to be reshaped), Sir Thomas Fairfax was named Commander-in-Chief. Of course still more money was needed. The monthly charge for the county of Cambridge was set by Parliament at £2,171/6/8, and once more, inevitably involved, Sir Dudley North was first on the list of the administrative committee for the county.[46] The following June brought what was to be the major event of the war for many in the eastern counties—the relatively near Battle of Naseby. Here, Sir Dudley wrote in later years, "there was so absolute a defeat of his Majesties forces, as the after strivings were but as labouring for breath, by a person not long before his decease."[47] The ambivalence of his feelings must have been intense. Nevertheless, after the siege and surrender of the Royalists at Oxford in June 1646, Sir Dudley continued to carry out Parliament's instructions and continued to work with Cromwell.[48]

On 30 October 1648 he wrote a letter to Sir John Potts expressing tentative hope that the Treaty of Newport, recently negotiated with the King, might meet with success and thus "put to the blush all those that shall endeavour to continue the miseries of this kingdom. . . ."[49] Actually the treaty was something of a marvel, for in it Charles had agreed to abolish the whole ecclesiastical hierarchy except for the bishops and to suspend episcopal government for three years. His concessions came too late, however. As Sir Dudley told Potts, "I find, by those that pretend to have observed the temper of the house, that unless there be a yielding *in terminis*, there is no great hope of a happy winding up within doors. . . ."[50]

Perez Zagorin's wise generalization may be applied to Sir Dudley North at this time: "The advance of a revolution steadily destroys the ground on which moderates try to keep a stand between contending extremes."[51] In late November and even in the first week of December Sir Dudley was placed on more Parliamentary committees (he was supposed to expedite the sale of lands lately belonging to bishops and archbishops, and help to settle the militia in Cambridge), but despite all the cooperation he had manifested, his Parliamentary days were numbered. On the morning of 6 December 1648 he heard shouts of soldiers in the street, and that day, along with many others, he was "purged." He tells the story himself:

46. Kingston, p. 376; Varley, p. 98.
47. *Narrative*, p. 69.
48. *Journals of the . . . Commons*, V, 31; and *The Writings and Speeches of Oliver Cromwell*, ed. W. C. Abbott, asstd. by Catherine D. Crane, I (Cambridge, Mass., 1937), 432.
49. Henry Cary, *Memorials of the Great Civil War in England*, II (1842), 49; also Bodl. MS. Tanner 57.2, 395r.
50. Cary, p. 48.
51. *The Court and the Country: The Beginning of the English Revolution* (New York, 1970), p. 222.

they resolved . . . upon the seclusion of all those Members [of the Commons], whom they had found to be principled opposite to their interest; and so having had good trial upon our great debate concerning the personal Treaty, and time to make a Catalogue of such persons names, as they intended to seclude, during one days adjournment made by the House after having spent a whole night in that debate, they sent their Red-coats early in the morning before the next sitting, who passed the Streets with great cries, and so possess themselves of the House of Commons-door, admitting only those Members, whose names they found not in their Catalogue, and seizing upon many of the rest who would have entred. I question not, but upon this occasion (as upon all others of great importance) they held a solemn fast among the chief Commanders, to ask counsel of God, for the doing of that which they their selves had already resolved upon, which . . . is one of the greatest hypocrisies that the world hath known. The House of Commons being thus moulded according to their desire, they presently fell upon the formalities of that most hideous (and not to be paralell'd) murther of our Royal Sovereign. . . .[52]

Before the next month was out, King Charles had been tried and beheaded. "*I never had the least disloyal thought in relation to my Prince,*" Sir Dudley wrote later, "*and my endeavours always tended to a reconciliation of the business, with a production of peace. . . .*"[53] No cause, he felt, could justify armed opposition to one's king, "*and if I were at any time enforced (for I never did it willingly) to act in the way of opposition contributory to the war, it was with hope, that at last there would be a happy agreement.*"[54] In the Bodleian Library one now may see the pardon which was issued to Sir Dudley North in 1660 under the aegis of King Charles II.[55]

In 1649, with little need for a town residence, Sir Dudley and his family returned to Kirtling, where Lord North put their board back at £300 per year. Notwithstanding the change in financial arrangements, the members of the younger family moved to Tostock in 1650, and thereafter, as we have seen, "were never more in a settled way, but a year or two in one place & then in the other. . . ."[56] Consequently it is in the records of both Cambridgeshire and Suffolk that we now catch glimpses of Sir Dudley serving as a justice of the peace.[57] It seems that the less vehement of the secluded members were

---

52. *Narrative*, pp. 84–85.
53. *Narrative*, A6v–A7r.   54. *Narrative*, A7r.
55. Bodl. MS. North c.85, no. 15; dated 3 September 1660.
56. *Lives*, III, 312.
57. Beginning in *The Names of the Justices of Peace, in England and Wales . . . 1650* (1650), p. 7. See also Keeler, *The Long Parliament*, p. 286; Bodl. MS. Tanner 226, 187r; PRO C 193/13.5 and C 193/13.6. We also find him (along with his Uncle Roger and his sister, Dorothy, Lady Dacre) petitioning the Committee for Compounding. From 2 July 1650 until 19 March of the following year, Sir Dudley was involved in a case that concerned the sequestered estate in York-

regarded as appropriate persons to serve as justices. North himself writes that "a Gentleman of quality . . . living in the Countrey can hardly keep himself out of employment, under the Lievtenancy or Commission of the Peace; and this may contribute something against the inconveniencies of Solitude."[58] He had first served as a justice of the peace before the outbreak of the war—concerning himself with problems of tippling, gaming, and swearing, of papists and rogues.[59] Now returned to such chores, he issued an order on 19 July 1654 for a mother and daughter to sit three hours in the stocks or pay fines for swearing. Most interesting, perhaps, we find him conducting marriages—for example, that of "Tho Hood & Elizabeth Larke of Ashly, single persons, marryed at Catlidge . . . sept 18. 1654."[60] According to the Interregnum statute of 24 August 1653, "the said Justice of Peace may and shall declare the said Man and Woman to be from thenceforth Husband and Wife; . . . And no other Marriage whatsoever within the Commonwealth of England, after the 29th of September . . . shall be held or accompted a Marriage according to the Laws of England. . . ."[61]

It did the Norths no harm in this period that Sir Dudley's sister Dorothy was now married to Challoner Chute of the Vyne, Hampshire. Dorothy's first husband had been Richard Lennard, thirteenth Lord Dacre, whom she had married in 1625. When Dacre died in 1630, his young widow returned to live at Kirtling, thus complicating domestic arrangements there for several years; in fact, she remained at Kirtling, Anne later recalled, until 1635 or 1636 before moving on to a house of her own.[62] Then in 1650, at the age of about forty-five, Dorothy took Chute as her second husband. Chute must have been a remarkable man. Although he had formerly undertaken the defense of Archbishop Laud, he also had earned the respect of non-royalists (he was an "eminent chancery practiser," says Roger),[63] and in the Parliament of Richard Cromwell he rose to be Speaker of the Commons. Having held the post only briefly, however, Chute died in 1659, and two years later the Lords decreed that his widow had forfeited her privilege of peerage by marrying him.[64]

The period following Sir Dudley's removal from Parliament must have been at least comparatively placid for him. Although Anne's mother, Dame Mary Montagu, died in July 1652, entrusting Sir Dudley with the problems

---

shire of Cuthbert Morley and the extreme necessity of his wife, Katherine (*Calendar of the Proceedings of the Committee for Compounding, &c., 1643–1660*, pt. IV [1892], pp. 2,394, 2,398).

58. *Observations*, pp. 124–125.

59. Flyleaf of his notebook, Rougham Hall. After the Restoration he was to continue (Crown Office Docquet Book, PRO C 231/7, p. 181).

60. North's notebook, Rougham Hall.

61. Firth and Rait, II (1911), 716.

62. *Lives*, III, 311.

63. *Lives*, I, 18.

64. George Edward Cokayne, *The Complete Peerage* . . . , ed. Vicary Gibbs, asstd. by H. Arthur Doubleday, IV (1916), 13.

of executorship,[65] his immediate family was thriving. His last son, Roger, was born in September 1651, and in 1653 his old college, St. John's, admitted Francis. Meanwhile the family was becoming increasingly involved in making music. A resident music master was added to the household, and Francis, at seventeen, was presented with a new viol.[66] There were also books to be read and at least some time for contemplation. "I professe not to know any pleasure," wrote Sir Dudley, "exceeding . . . Contemplation in matters Divine."[67] And there was his own writing. One sad occasion for an elegy was the death of Anne's sister Mary in December 1657,[68] but in 1658, having garnered as many relevant old documents as possible, he assigned himself the pleasant task of writing the biography of Edward, first Lord North. In short, together with his obligations as justice and his continuing interest in drainage of the fens, there were occupations enough in the country, and he did not yearn for the strain and cost of the city.

There is little wonder that when the Restoration of the monarchy came at last in 1660, Sir Dudley chose "with most humble & hearty thankfullnesse [to] lay hold upon his Majesties . . . free & generall pardon. . . ."[69] (His petition was witnessed and signed by Harbottle Grimston, speaker of the Convention Parliament, on 5 June 1660.) Neither is it surprising that Sir Dudley "declaired as much as he could not to stand for Knight of the Shire. . . ."[70] According to Anne, however, "when the time came[,] many pressing my lord's father about it, he layd his comands upon him to stand. . . ." Characteristically, Sir Dudley obeyed. Characteristically, too, Anne recorded that it cost Sir Dudley £240. On 20 April 1660, however, Samuel Pepys recorded the startling news that Sir Dudley North, "against all expectation," had lost the Cambridge county election.[71] Sir Dudley himself must have had mixed reactions. In any case, there is never one gate shut but another one opens, and when Parliament convened on 25 April, Sir Dudley North was there, sitting not for the county but for the borough of Cambridge.[72] After that he did

65. See John Le Neve, *Monumenta Anglicana: . . . 1650, to the End of . . . 1679* (1718), p. 14. Obviously Dame Mary, who lived to the age of seventy-seven, had come to trust the man whom she called in her will (25 February 1649) "my good sonne" (Spencer MS. uncat. North 1J:48: 184). The Bodleian has receipts to Sir Dudley from various beneficiaries.

66. From notations in Sir Dudley's account book, now at Rougham.

67. *Observations*, p. 121.

68. See "An Elegy made vpon the Death of Mary Lady Baesh" (No. 30).

69. Bodl. MS. North c.44, no. 27.

70. *Lives*, III, 312.

71. *The Diary of Samuel Pepys*, ed. Robert Latham and William Matthews, I (Berkeley, Calif., 1970), 112. In the entry for 3 March Pepys had reported going after dinner to the Earl of Manchester's home, Warwick House in Holborn, where the company had included Sir Dudley (I, 75). Under Charles II, Manchester would become Chamberlain of the Household, Privy Councillor, and Chancellor of Cambridge University.

72. Edmund Carter, *The History of the County of Cambridgeshire* (1819), p. 55; and Brunton and Pennington, p. 92.

not stand for election again. When next he sat in Parliament, it was as the successor to his father. At last become fourth Baron North, Sir Dudley was summoned to the House of Lords on 24 January 1667, and seven days later, at the age of sixty-four, he took his place on the barons' bench.[73]

---

73. *Journals of the House of Lords*, XII (n.d.), 96.

LATER YEARS

Though the streets were strewn with flowers and the fountains ran with wine when Charles II returned to London in 1660, the joy and relief felt by many Englishmen were succeeded by more disasters: the sale of Dunkirk (1662), the return of the plague (1665), the Great Fire (1666), the fall of Clarendon (1667), and the secret Dover treaty (1670). It was just as well for his peace of mind that Sir Dudley North finally managed what he called a *"full retreat into the Countrey."*[1] At his country seat in Cambridgeshire the walls were hung with many portraits of noble and powerful people whom he and his father had known at court, men and women caught and fixed in the glowing colors of Cornelius Johnson, Paul van Somer, and perhaps Van Dyck—and all silent now in the country air. Weariness and relief sound in Sir Dudley's words, published in 1669: *"now at last I am come to reside at the chief Mansion-house of our Family, where I have no other ambition then to end my dayes with a peaceable and pious dissolution; So much of myself tyred and retired, which I may well be, since the World can scarcely shew me any thing new."*[2]

When finally he became his own man, North devoted himself more than ever to the pleasures and chores of housekeeping. *"I have been a Housekeeper a great part of my dayes,"* he writes, *"and more especially in these my latter years, at which time Men are accustomed to take matters into consideration more maturely. . . ."*[3] North's reflections on housekeeping, which probably derive partly from experiences at Tostock but mainly from those at Kirtling, may be said to have borne fruit in his *Observations and Advices Oeconomical.* One of the major concepts that North offers in this book—and a striking one it is, in view of England's recent turmoil—is that a large household and a monarchy have much in common. Neither household nor monarchy, he writes, "can well subsist without due subordinations, and good order."[4] Hence Sir Dudley's need to bow to his father's wishes through the long preceding years. He believed in order, pattern, and discipline. Though he did not find it fitting either in his life or his book to concern himself with matters of housewifery (luckily Anne was expert at such things), he ranges broadly in his *Observa-*

---

1. *Observations*, A5r.
2. *Observations*, A5r–v.   3. *Observations*, A7v.
4. *Observations*, p. 35. Lawrence Stone, in his study of *The Family, Sex and Marriage* (New York, 1977), quotes King James as saying that "Kings are compared to fathers in families: for a King is truly *parens patriae*, the politic father of his people" (p. 152).

tions over various subjects relating to the operation of a great house, and somehow he manages always to seem traditional, a champion of the tried and true old ways. On the subject of architecture, for instance, he regrets that nowadays "the Hall (or basis of Hospitality) is either wholly left out, or so contrived as to be without Chimny or Fire-hearth, which in Winter time should draw Company together, and give chearfulnesse to a Family." [5] (Kirtling had a great hall with a fireplace and a music gallery.) North discerns that the new styles in building are conducive to social fragmentation, on the one hand, and lack of privacy, on the other. "Great Staire cases are also affected, which fill a house with noyse," he writes, "and uniformity [i.e., 'after the *Italian* manner'] doth often deprive us of inward Rooms, and of Closets, with other little retiring places. These considerations and some others make me lesse forward, then the generality, in crying down the pretended rusticity of our Ancestors. . . ." [6]

North's observations cast light on various aspects of life at Kirtling. "A considerable Family ought to be furnished with Houshold-stuff accordingly," he writes, "but it is far from necessary to have it wholly modern (or *a la mode*, as they call it). . . ." [7] Outdoors, he says, it is good economy to maintain a fishpond; Kirtling had a pond, a stew, and a moat some fifty yards wide. [8] It also had a cony warren, a dove house, and a deer park, North *père* having made the last of these in the 1630s. [9] With little interest himself in husbandry—he advises no more tillage than necessary—Sir Dudley nonetheless holds that a gardener is the most useful of servants. A gardener, "besides his care in Gardens of pleasure, by his improvement of the Orchard and Kitchin Garden may bring great plenty with little charge to the Kitchin, and so by consequence to the Table, from which ariseth the chief honour of Housekeeping." [10]

5. *Observations*, pp. 92–93.

6. *Observations*, p. 93. One of the "inward Rooms" at Kirtling was an octagonal closet in a tower, whence there was access to the leads; tradition had it that Elizabeth lived in hiding here for a while during Mary's reign (see "Cambridgeshire," in *Topographical Miscellanies, Containing Ancient Histories, and Modern Descriptions, of Mansions, Churches, Monuments, and Families* [1792], n.p.). Although North is not mentioned in Mark Girouard's *Life in the English Country House* (Harmondsworth, 1980; 1st pub. New Haven, 1978), Girouard's study does much to clarify North's comments on architecture and other matters.

7. *Observations*, p. 99.

8. In a book entitled *A Discourse of Fish and Fish-Ponds* (1713) his son Roger writes as follows: "I must remember, that once, at the Command of my [grandfather] Lord *North*, I did . . . proceed to the making one great Pond, and one Stew, at *Catledg*, which are still to be seen, but neglected; and besides, the Regard to Profit by the Fish they would maintain and supply, the very Ornament of them was worth the Charge. I was limited to 10*l.* besides the Work of his Lordship's Horses, which I compute to be 4*l.* more; so the whole did not cost 15*l.* and yet a full Acre of Ground lay under Water, and all was compleated in 12 days" (p. 18). Even the subject of the North family's fish-ponds draws in the theme of financial constraint.

9. *Observations*, p. 103; *Forest 45*, p. 222. On the other hand, Kirtling is said to have had a "park of wild animals" at least five hundred years before Edward, Lord North, acquired the estate (observed in "Note B" in *Lives*, III, 314).

10. *Observations*, p. 54.

With little charge: the phrase is telling. Despite years of careful management, Sir Dudley never shook off financial problems. His son Roger went so far as to write of the Norths as "a half-decayed family with a numerous brood and worn-out estate. . . ."[11] At the time he himself wrote, Sir Dudley viewed the family as weathering "*a time when Revenues of the Gentry are fallen beyond what could have been imagined of late years. . . .*" Still worse, revenues were likely to continue meager, "*if not to incur a farther diminution.*"[12]

In a large and complex establishment, of course, a steward was an absolute necessity. As Sir Dudley put it, "A Steward of the houshold (stiled *Oeconomus*, to shew his usefulnesse in a Family) is his Masters right hand in presence, and his Deputy in time of absence."[13] When Sir Dudley's father was still alive, there sometimes had been strain about who held the post. Roger tells how Dudley North *père* once turned a fine and faithful old steward out of Kirtling, thereby leaving the position open for a couple of ill-equipped French servants whom he favored, one his sycophantic *valet de chambre* and the other a former page whose chief talents appear to have been dancing, singing, and playing the violin.[14] Sir Dudley had more practical views. Since a steward "hath a general Command over his fellow Servants," says Sir Dudley, he "ought to be a man of understanding, and somewhat of an Austere nature, that they may not too farr press upon him in way of familiarity, but rather stand in awe of him."[15] Furthermore, "He must be of a higher condition then the rest, which will draw respect."

Because stewardship involved keeping records, the passing years brought on the gradual accumulation of various accounts of the family's expenses and goods on hand. In 1661, for example, five pints of "Sallet Oyle" were set down as costing the Norths 5/3, and three pecks of oatmeal 4/3.[16] Lemons, oranges, barrels of oysters, and loaves of sugar had to be purchased, but butter (thirty-eight pounds in a week) and cheeses (fourteen in a week) were made at home, bringing the total number of cheeses on hand to one hundred and twenty. (It was dairy country.) Separate categories were set up for dairy, larder, granary, and pantry. According to one pantry entry for the week ending 16 May 1662, there were fourteen and a half hogsheads of ordinary beer stored in the cellar. Stocked in the larder were joints of mutton, pieces of beef, sides of pork, and flitches of bacon.

Food aside, there were expenses for brown thread, starch, holland for sheets, sealing wax, paper, chamber pots, and nails. There was a need for

11. *Lives*, I, 405.
12. *Observations*, A7r.
13. *Observations*, pp. 47–48.
14. *Lives*, I, 34–35; St. John's College, Cambridge, MS. Bb, James 613, pp. 52–54.
15. *Observations*, p. 48.
16. Facts in this paragraph and the next two are drawn from various manuscripts, including Bodl. MSS. North c.49 and d.49; County Record Office, Shire Hall, Cambridge, L95/12; and the Account Book ending 1677, Rougham Hall.

2. Kirtling (or Catlage), Cambridgeshire, seat of the Norths.

mops, pails, and scouring sand, for brooms and besoms (the latter being a sort of broom made of brush or twigs). "Extraordinary" expenses included payment to the rat-catcher (10s. a quarter), a lock with two keys for the billiard room door (10/6), and "An Almanack to hang up in the hall" (2d.). Two dozen candles were required for a single week in March, but only one dozen for an August week. After the purchase of a renovated, secondhand coach, there was need for "A livery coachmans cloke."

Workers of various sorts were a constant necessity, of course, at both Kirtling and Tostock, and sometimes an extra hand was also required. A millwright was brought in to work three days at the mill (3s.), and John Taylor was called to kill blackbirds (4d.). Goody Thomas was paid for one day of washing (4d.), Goody Grigg for two days of weeding (10d.), and Goody Gatewood for six days of gathering stones (2s.). Sir Dudley himself, meanwhile, one may think of as quietly accepting the need to pore over minutely detailed records of how money had been paid out for gelding pigs, drenching cows, mending plows, cutting wood, mending kettles, sweeping chimneys, binding faggots, and, always, weeding, weeding, weeding. Of course he needed assistance with all the records, and Anne, providentially, was good at the job.

Among the countless details recorded for the Norths' complex household, some touch on family matters more intimately than others. In the spring of 1653, for instance, Dr. Thomas Buckenham, who served as the family's physician for many years, received £1 for his consultation when Anne required attention.[17] (Conveniently situated in Bury-St.-Edmunds, Dr. Buckenham could take the roads either eastward to Tostock or westward to Kirtling.) Gloves for Sir Dudley (a continuing expense) were 15/2, and a candlestick for his closet (one of those "little retiring places" he liked) came to 4s. In 1655 a new scabbard and the mending of his sword cost 5s., and his copy of Fonseca's *Consultationes* (a medical book) cost the same.[18] Admission to the Middle Temple for his eighteen-year-old son Francis, the future Lord Keeper, was a remarkably good investment of £3/8/6.[19] Pleasure, on the other hand, must have been the motive for mending a "Gittar" and acquiring a parrot and parrot paraphernalia. One even learns that in later years North took up tobacco, and one may hope that as a result he found at least a little solace from his physical ills.[20]

17. The name "Buckenham" takes various forms in the family records, but Dr. Thomas Buckenham (1613–1682) seems likely to have been the proper man; John Venn and J. A. Venn, comp., *Alumni Cantabrigienses*, pt. I, vol. I (Cambridge, 1922), p. 247.

18. Roderigo de Fonseca, *Consultationes Medicae Singularibus Remediis Refertae* (Venice, 1620; also other editions). Cf. *Lives*, I, 18. Because Challoner Chute, treasurer at the time, was the young man's uncle, he swept the money into Francis's hat and gave it to him.

19. Cf. *Lives*, I, 18. Because Challoner Chute, treasurer at the time, was the young man's uncle, he swept the money into Francis's hat and gave it to him.

20. Since sobriety and dignity pervaded North's life, one is heartened by nearly any glimpse of him at ease, such as his tobacco expenditures provide. Consider, for instance, the rare little

When North reached his mid-sixties it was time for a pair of spectacles (together with their case, they cost 1/6). Then came the need for mourning cloth and a black marble marker for his father (£64/6), as well as scarlet cloth for making new parliamentary robes for himself (£20/19) and, for good measure, a bag to hold them (10s.). To Robert North, a faithful but taciturn amanuensis and "clerk for his justice business"[21] who somehow managed for a while to conceal that he was a relative, the new Lord North even entered payment (6s.) for "coppying my booke of Oeconomy"—doubtless the *Observations and Advices Oeconomical*.[22]

Despite all of North's care in matters economic, there were continuing financial strains in his family. Young Montagu was disappointed in the amount his father provided for his trip abroad.[23] When Francis was called to the bar, his allowance was cut from £60 to £50.[24] Sir Robert Wyseman, intending to marry Elizabeth North, protested (but then accepted) a marriage settlement he regarded as too small.[25] When even Charles, who was to inherit the North title and most of the property, dared protest in January 1669, his father was moved to justifiable remonstrance:

> . . . for my carryage towards you, & especially in matters relating to your marryage, I can appeale to all the world, whether or noe I have not yeilded as farr, as could have been desyred, frō. a Father having such other dependances vpon him as I have. Sure I am, I have not one penny of a wyfes portion, as is vsual with other fathers, soe as that little which I

anecdote that his son Francis enjoyed telling about the time when he himself was a beginning lawyer. Sir Dudley had asked the young man—and the question itself is characteristic—"What good did you do, Frank?" And the young man replied that he had enough to manage in doing no hurt, "which made the old man merry enough that he should breed his son to a trade of being paid for doing no hurt" (*Lives*, III, 168).

21. *Lives*, I, 395.

22. Robert North was the grandson of Sir Charles North of Walkeringham, who in turn was second cousin to Edward, first Lord North. Roger North gives a few facts about Robert (most notably, that he was a melancholy fellow), but one would like to know more about him because he was "esteemed by Sir Dudley North to the degree of a favourite" (*Lives*, I, 394, 395).

23. Bodl. MS. North c.4, 293r (8 August 1672).

24. *Lives*, I, 40.

25. Bodl. MS. North c.4, 297r and 301r: "I do not thinke it good manners in mee, to presse you further," he told Sir Dudley. Roger explains that Sir Dudley attempted to raise £1,500 apiece for the portions of Elizabeth and Anne by selling off "some skirts of his estate." When the land remained unsold, Francis managed to bring forward a match between Elizabeth and Wyseman—a good man and rich, but old (*Lives*, I, 401). Although their contributions may have been small in comparison with that of Francis, apparently John and Roger also chipped in, the three brothers' contribution totaling £1,228/10 (Spencer MS. uncat. North 1J:48:145). Elizabeth later married William, second Earl of Yarmouth. When it came to marrying Anne, an older daughter, Sir Dudley decided he could manage a portion of only £1,200. Francis himself bought the proffered lands, Anne went to live with Francis in London, and there she met her comfortable fate in Robert Foley, despite the fact that he was fifteen years her junior (*Lives*, I, 402). Mary married Sir William Spring of Pakenham, by Bury, in Suffolk; and Christian married Sir George Wenieve of Brettenham, also in Suffolk. According to Sir Dudley's own notes, Mary fared surprisingly well with a portion of £2,500, plus clothing and extras of about £100, and Christian least well with £1,000, plus about £50 (Bodl. MS. North b.12, 347v).

could part with all in present came freely to you. . . . I would not have you forgett the old saying That free horses must not bee too much spurred. . . .[26]

On 9 November 1675 the old gentleman put his name to an indenture designed to prevent his debts—at that time totaling over a thousand pounds—from encumbering the estate of his successor.[27] Whether or not Charles was an agreeable fellow, his father was determined that the estate he inherited be as sizeable and as nearly intact as possible. It is little wonder, then, that there is an edge to Lady North's words when she recalled later how much her husband was in debt at the time of his death.[28]

Such was the character of Dudley and Anne that, financial constraints notwithstanding, they earned and held the esteem of their children. Even Charles, who became the most detached of the lot, managed at one crucial point to address them as "the most indulgent parents that ever sonne was happy in."[29] Roger, the youngest, wrote most. His longest-lived happiness, he claimed, was the fact that he was "descended from Religious, vertuous, wise, and sound parents. That they were so is granted by all that knew them, and that I am happy from their vertues I know and can affirme."[30]

Time was to mend the fortunes of some of the North offspring to such a degree that the famous Judge Jeffreys reputedly complained "that nothing could happen or fall but a North was presently to be considerable, as if they had a monopoly of preferment."[31] On the other hand, Charles, the heir, was something of a case apart. In the spring of 1660 he briefly joined the fleet that went to bring Charles II home, making music on shipboard with Pepys, who observed that young North seemed "to be a fine gentleman and at night did play his part exceeding well at first sight" (2 May 1660).[32] The part which Charles chose to play in politics, however, eventually served to widen the affective gap between himself and his brothers. In March 1680 he was spoken of as one of the "malcontent lords" meeting with the dangerously dissident Earl of Shaftesbury,[33] and in 1681 he seems actually to have been in some danger of losing his life for being of Shaftesbury's party.[34] Years later Roger

26. The draft of this letter is in Anne's hand (Bodl. MS. North c.10, 45r).
27. Spencer MS. uncat. North 2A:32:38.
28. She writes, "he hath left a debt upon security of about 11 or £1200 besides some £300 other debts" (Lives, III, 313).
29. Bodl. MS. North c.4, no. 165 (letter of 24 May 1667).
30. Lives, III, 1.
31. Lives, III, 178.
32. The Diary of Samuel Pepys, ed. Robert Latham and William Matthews, I (1970), 123. Another entry records Pepys's impression that Charles was "an ugly fellow; but a good scholar and sober gentleman" (VIII [Berkeley, Calif., 1974], 600).
33. Letter of 18 March 1680 from Sir Charles Lyttelton in Edward Maunde Thompson, ed., vol. I, Correspondence of the Family of Hatton, Camden Society, ser. 2, vol. XXII (Westminster, 1878), 223.
34. F. H. Blackburne Daniell, ed., CSP, Domestic, 1 Sept. 1680–31 Dec. 1681 (1921),

wrote of him discreetly but sourly as having been one of the "faction."[35] The following anecdote, whether or not it is true, suggests something about the width of the political and personal rift that had opened up between Charles and the rest of the Norths:

> when his second brother Francis was about to be made Lord Guil-ford, . . . [Charles] went to the king . . . and informed him he thought his majesty ought to know, that in his opinion his brother the Lord Keeper was not by any means worthy of the honour which he had heard his majesty was about to bestow upon him. The king listened in surprise and silence for a few moments, and then replied, laughingly, "He had always heard there was one fool in the North family, and now he knew who it was!"[36]

All in all, Charles's wisest move may have been marrying Katherine Moseley, widow of Sir Edward Moseley and daughter of William, first Baron Grey of Warke (1667), in consequence of which (probably) he was summoned to the House of Lords as Lord Grey of Rolleston (1673).

The other sons, for all their differences in temperament, were much more in harmony with one another. Francis became Solicitor General and was knighted (1671), rose to be Attorney General (1673) and Lord Chief Justice of the Common Pleas (1675), and, some five years after his father's death, Keeper of the Great Seal (1682) and Baron Guilford (1683). John Evelyn, the diarist, a gentleman of discernment, remarked on the human qualities that underlay Baron Guilford's phenomenal rise: "He is a most knowing, learned, ingenious gent, & besides an excellent person, of an ingenuous sweete dispo-sition, very skillful in Musick, Painting, the new Philosophie & politer stud-ies. . . ."[37] Moreover, it is not too much to say that "In his rapid climb . . . , he pulled his brothers up with him and became, in effect, the saviour of the family."[38]

Dudley, a handsome, robust fellow, began as his mother's favorite and went on to become "perhaps the richest and most respected member of the Turkey Company"[39]—at one point bringing home a Turkish slave called

---

p. 450. He was also the target of some striking verbal accusations, as in Adam Elliot's *A Modest Vindication of Titus Oates the Salamanca-Doctor from Perjury*. . . (1682).

35. *Lives*, II, 230.

36. Told by Charles Augustus North in an untitled seven-page pamphlet which provides some notes on the fourth Lord North's *Some Notes Concerning the Life of Edward Lord North* (1889), p. 1.

37. *The Diary of John Evelyn*, ed. E. S. deBeer, IV (Oxford, 1955), 299.

38. Peter T. Millard, "An Edition of Roger North's *Life of Dr. John North* with a Critical Introduction," D. Phil. thesis, Linacre College, Oxford, 1969, p. 15.

39. William Letwin, "The Authorship of Sir Dudley North's *Discourses on Trade*," *Econo-mica*, XVIII (1951), 36. On the basis of the *Discourses upon Trade* (1691), Letwin observes, "Economists have extolled Sir Dudley for his profound understanding and precise logic, and have acclaimed him a great, if not the greatest, predecessor of Adam Smith" (p. 35); but Letwin argues for Roger North's significant involvement in the volume.

Shatein, whom he presented to his mother.[40] Dudley was to win the friendship of his King, to be knighted (1682), and to become one of the Lords Commissioners of the Treasury (1684).[41] One modern historian calls him an "unofficial chancellor of the Exchequer."[42]

John North, to whom Greek is said to have become almost vernacular, was ordained deacon in 1669 and priest in 1670,[43] preached before Charles II on the subject of debauchery and profaneness (Charles ordered the sermon printed[44]), and for a while served as Clerk of the Closet to the King, "lodging in Whitehall upon the parade of the court, near the presence chamber."[45] Clearly his inclination toward Arminianism did him no harm at court. Somewhat more in keeping with his character and taste, however, John was appointed Regius Professor of Greek at Trinity College, Cambridge (1672).[46] At the instigation of John Maitland, the powerful Duke of Lauderdale, who much admired his abilities, the University made John a doctor of divinity in 1676. Later that same year John Evelyn recorded hearing "Dr. *North*, sonn to my Lord *North*, a very young, but learned, & excellent person on 53 *Isa*: 57. . . ."[47] Furthermore, just a few weeks before Sir Dudley's death, the young cleric must have pleased his old father greatly by succeeding Isaac Barrow as master of the college (12 May 1677).[48]

Even Roger, the youngest, managed to make himself "a piece of a courtier, and commonly on Sundays went to Whitehall."[49] As a young man he had kept his father's manor court (Francis kept his grandfather's),[50] and finally he rose to be steward to the see of Canterbury (1678), Solicitor General to the Duke of York (1684), and, after the King's death, the new Queen's Attorney General (1686). The second Earl of Clarendon thought of him as one of only

---

40. *Lives*, II, 151.

41. In his *Examen* (1740), Roger claims that "no single Person in *England* had more Esteem with the King, as long as his Majesty lived, than Mr. *Dudley North* had" (p. 602).

42. David Ogg, *England in the Reigns of James II and William III* (Oxford, 1955), p. 143; it is only fair to add that Ogg also deems him "unscrupulous." Lord Macaulay previously had used the same adjective to describe this third Dudley. At the same time he spoke of him as "one of the ablest men of his time," a man of "profound knowledge, both speculative and practical" (*The History of England from the Accession of James the Second*, I [1858], 518, 519). Dudley married Anne, daughter of Sir Robert Cann of Bristol and widow of Sir Robert Gunning of Cold Ashton, Gloucestershire.

43. John's certificate of ordination, signed by Benjamin Laney, Bishop of Ely, and dated 30 October, is at present Spencer MS. uncat. North 17:14.

44. *A Sermon Preached before the King at Newmarket October 8. 1671* (Cambridge, 1671). John also published *Platonis de Rebus Divinis Dialogi Selecti Graece & Latine* (Cambridge, 1673).

45. *Lives*, II, 300.

46. He resigned from the professorship on 6 April 1674 (Millard, p. 52).

47. *Diary*, IV, 87.

48. Folger MS. W.b.96, 40r.

49. *Lives*, III, 170.

50. Theoretically such a court was presided over by the lord of the manor, but in practice it was presided over by his deputy. The jurisdiction of such a court was restricted to the boundaries of the manor, and its business concerned such matters as small debts, property succession, leases, and rights and services of tenants (*Lives*, III, 106).

two honest lawyers he had ever met.[51] After the Revolution of 1688, however, like his father and grandfather before him, Roger withdrew into the relative peace and quiet of the country, and frequently thereafter had recourse to his pen.[52]

Of the daughters of the house, Mary might be singled out for mention because, as Roger explained, she was the "foundress" of a group of "wittified" young ladies. Their "symbol was a sun with a circle touching the rays and, upon that in a blue ground were wrote αὐτάρκης in the proper Greek characters, which her father suggested."[53] As they themselves were well aware, Sir Dudley and Dame Anne had produced a remarkable array of children. According to Roger, "the Most transcendent happyness that Made their old age Comfortable & pleasant was the growth & disposition of their Children."[54]

Besides the dominating and unifying force of religion in the family there was also, through the years, the harmonizing influence of music. Sir Dudley wrote that "Of pastimes within dores Musick may challenge the next place to Study, and is more sociable, for it entertains many at the same time."[55] The family's delight in music was apparently shared by all—by the elder Lord North, by Sir Dudley and Dame Anne, by Francis (who wrote a treatise on music), and by Roger (who turned out some two thousand manuscript pages on the subject).[56] Roger records that even some of the servants were drawn into the musical activities at Kirtling in the time of the old Lord North:

> the servants of parade, as gentlemen ushers, and the steward, and clerk of the kitchen, also played, which, with the young ladies', my sisters, singing, made a society of music, such as was well esteemed in those times. And the course of the family was to have solemn music three days

51. Noted by R. W. Ketton-Cremer, "Roger North," *Essays and Studies*, ed. Dorothy Margaret Stuart, n.s. XII (1959), 75. Roger married Mary, daughter of Sir Robert Gayer of Stoke Poges.

52. A good attempt to define Roger's political stance may be found in T. A. Birrell, "Roger North and Political Morality in the Later Stuart Period," *Scrutiny*, XVII (1950–51), 282–298. An account of his voluminous writing is given by Peter T. Millard, "The Chronology of Roger North's Main Works," *Review of English Studies*, n.s. XXIV (1973), 283–294. See also Lois Green Schwoerer, "Roger North and His Notes on Legal Education," *Huntington Library Quarterly*, XXII (1959), 323–343; and, especially, F. J. M. Korsten, *Roger North (1651–1734): Virtuoso and Essayist* (Amsterdam, 1981).

53. *Lives*, I, 46.

54. BL Add. MS. 32,523, 6v.

55. *Observations*, pp. 119–120. Kirtling, the Norths, and Sir Dudley's *Observations* provide the basic subject matter of my "Country Delights for the Gentry: A View from 1669," *South Atlantic Quarterly*, LXXX (1981), 222–232.

56. Roger later recalled how his father "translated the Italian old song which his daughter had learned: 'Una volta finira,' &c., 'Time at last will set me free,' &c., and gave it to me to set. . ." (*Lives*, III, 82); the song may be traced in the Vatican Library manuscript catalogue of music manuscripts in the Biblioteca Chigiana (Q.IV.8, 86). On Roger and music the best source is *Roger North on Music*, ed. John Wilson (1959). On Francis see Michael Foss, *The Age of Patronage: The Arts in England 1660–1750* (Ithaca, N.Y., 1972), pp. 102–103; and Francis's treatise entitled *A Philosophical Essay of Musick* (1677).

in the week, and often every day, as masters supplied novelties for the entertainment of the old lord. And on Sunday night voices to the organ were a constant practice, and at other times symphonies intermixed with the instruments.

This good old lord took a fancy to a wood he had about a mile from his house, called Bansteads, situate in a diluvial soil, and of ill access. But he cut glades and made arbours in it, and no name would fit the place but Tempe. Here he would convoke his musical family, and songs were made and set for celebrating the joys there, which were performed, and provisions carried up.[57]

As Roger's words suggest, the North household included a music master for a good many years. From about 1652 to 1660 Henry Loosemore (1600?–1670), the organist and composer, appears to have served as resident organist and music teacher at Kirtling. Then from 1660 to 1666 his brother George seems to have succeeded him as organist, probably assisting John Jenkins. Jenkins (1592–1678) was not simply a fine performer on the lute and viol but also one of England's most notable composers. In earlier years his skill on the viol had impressed the King himself, and in 1634 he had taken a prominent part in the presentation at court of James Shirley's extravagant Inns of Court masque called *The Triumph of Peace*. In later, more difficult times, when England's peace had been shattered, he "passed his time at gentlemens houses in the country," continued to compose voluminously and well, and is said to have become "the best-loved English master of the mid-seventeenth century."[58]

Looking back in his *Observations*, Sir Dudley recorded that music had pro-

57. *Lives*, III, 68.

58. *Memoires of Musick*, ed. Edward F. Rimbault (1846), p. 86; Wilson, *Roger North*, p. xxii. Anthony à Wood considered Jenkins "the mirrour and wonder of his age of musick" (*The Life and Times of Anthony Wood, Antiquary, . . . Described by Himself*, ed. Andrew Clark, I [Oxford, 1891], 209). In our own time *The New Grove Dictionary of Music and Musicians* calls him "supreme in consort music, especially for viols," the composer of "works whose pre-eminence in their kind is beyond question" (art. by Andrew Ashbee, ed. Stanley Sadie, IX [1980], 596, 597). Some of Jenkins's original scores may be seen at the Bodleian Library, and a generous sampling of Jenkins's music may be heard on Meridian Records, No. E77020, directed by Peter Holman (1978). For commentary of various sorts see Christopher Simpson, *The Division-Violist* (1659); J. A. Westrup, "Domestic Music under the Stuarts," *Proceedings of the Musical Association . . . , 1941–1942* (Leeds, 1942), pp. 19–53; Helen Joy Sleeper, ed., *John Jenkins (1592–1678): Fancies and Ayres* (Wellesley, 1950); Hans Ferdinand Redlich, "John Jenkins," *Die Musik in Geschichte und Gegenwart*, vol. VI (Kassel, 1957), cols. 1876–80; Percy M. Young, *A History of British Music* (1967), esp. pp. 215–217; Pamela J. Willetts, "Autograph Music by John Jenkins," *Music & Letters*, XLVIII (1967), 124–126; Carolyn Coxon, "A Handlist of the Sources of John Jenkins' Vocal and Instrumental Music," *Royal Musical Association Research Chronicle*, IX (1971), 73–89; Margaret Crum, "The Consort Music from Kirtling, Bought for the Oxford Music School from Anthony Wood, 1667," *Chelys*, IV (1972), 3–10; and Andrew Ashbee, "John Jenkins, 1592–1678," *Consort*, XXXIV (1978), 265–273. After the Restoration, Jenkins's name regularly appeared in lists of court musicians, but it is not likely that he spent much time at court (Ashbee, p. 272). Roger remarks that John Lilly also frequently assisted with the music at Kirtling (Wilson, p. 37).

vided him with "great subsistence" in his retirement. "When I found my self subject to be pensive," he confessed,

> then by Musical Ayres, Corantoes, and Sarabands, I was rendred more chearful;[59] and when I desired to become Serious, the work was done for me by hearing Almayns, Fancies, and Pavans; variety is most pleasing, and much of this is afforded even in the diversity of Musical Instruments, as the Lute, Harp, &c. but certainly no Musick can bear up with the Vocal, to which some suppose a continuance in Heaven it self; but however that be, Musick is found useful in the Service of God here below (even with the most rigid who must have singing Psalms). . . . I professe not to know any pleasure exceeding Musick, saving that of Contemplation in matters Divine.[60]

Books and writing were certainly other outlets essential to the "subsistence" of North. For less studious men he could recommend hunting, hawking, fishing, and bowling. (In the old days, his Uncle John had used to look forward to the bowling green at Kirtling, and Sir Dudley doubtless knew that bowling was recommended for his own chief ailment—the stone.)[61] He himself, however, was an indoors man, and perhaps especially so as the years slipped by and he became, as one of his upper servants discreetly pointed out, somewhat more portly ("I . . . humbly intreat your lo[rdshi]pe to beleeve that the dublet now is wider then any that I ever yett made for your lordshipe. . .").[62] As for indoor amusement, Sir Dudley went so far as to condone moderate gaming after dinner to while away the long winter evenings. Nevertheless, he writes, "Of Countrey delights, Study may deserve the first place, whereby our Gentry may in some sort converse with persons of the greatest rank and wisdom. . . . In all wayes whereby delight is sought there must be variety, and therefore those Families enjoy a great advantage in the way of satisfaction, which are furnished, and inriched with plenty of good Books."[63]

The old library at Kirtling was a retreat within a retreat, a place where North could "*entertain*" himself "*frequently by turning over old Books (whereof I have good store in several Languages).* . . ."[64] Some of his books had belonged to his father and his grandfather. And there were more books at Tostock. Though avowedly no systematic student, Sir Dudley found occasion

59. One of the many surviving manuscripts of Jenkins's compositions (written for "Bassus" and bearing the name of Charles North) contains airs, corantoes, and sarabands, and includes a composition by Francis North (Bodl. MS. North e.37).

60. *Observations*, pp. 120–121.

61. Bacon's "Of Studies"—on p. 294 of Sir Dudley's own copy of *The Essayes or Counsels* (1629), now at the Folger Shakespeare Library.

62. John Hallam to Sir Dudley, 1669; Huntington MS. North 45.

63. *Observations*, pp. 116–117.

64. *Observations*, A5v.

in his own writing to cite Sidney and Selden, Martial and Horace, Machia-
velli and Guicciardini. It is of particular interest that he writes in 1669 of having *"lately perused"* a book *"consisting of certain politick and prudential Considerations, written by three distinct* Italian *Authors in an articular way."* [65] The
volume in question was some edition or other of the *Propositioni, overo Considerationi in Materia di Cose di Stato*, by Guicciardini, Lottini, and Sansovino,
and the matter is worth mentioning because the *Propositioni* proves to have
been the model for his own *Observations and Advices*.[66] Further evidence of
Sir Dudley's books takes various forms. We have earlier noted his copies of
Battista Guarini's pastoral drama and of Roderigo de Fonseca's medical book,
and his little collection of military books which seem to relate to his period of
soldiering abroad. His father may be found bidding him recall the advice to
be found in the *Théâtre d'Agriculture* (Paris, 1600) of Oliver de Serres,[67] and
he himself may be found praising the style of *"the Great* [Hugo] Grotius,"
commending Grotius's learning and buying one of his books on the Nether-
lands.[68] It helps us to understand a bit better the range of Sir Dudley's interests when we come upon his signature in Gerard de Malynes's *Center of the
Circle of Commerce* (1623) and Giovanni Battista Manzini's *Political Observations upon the Fall of Sejanus* (1634).[69] Michael Dalton could be reasonably
sure that Sir Dudley would find a practical use for his writing on justices, and
Brian Walton could count him among the subscribers to his monumental, six-
volume *Biblia Sacra Polyglotta* (1655–1657), which was one of the first publications to be printed in England by subscription.[70] Furthermore, in order
to write the life of Edward, first Lord North, his great-great-grandfather, Sir
Dudley had to delve into the family's collection of manuscripts. In short,
though Sir Dudley published virtually nothing until after the death of his
dominating father, both men, for a long stretch of years, may be glimpsed devoting some of their most pleasant leisure hours to reading and composition.

Sir Dudley's *Observations and Advices Oeconomical* (1669) on how to run a

65. *Observations*, A5v–A6r.

66. For this suggestion I am grateful to my friend Dr. John L. Lievsay. The title page of the
Venetian edition of 1588 continues: *sotto titolo di Avertimenti, Avedimenti Civili, & Concetti Politici. Di M. Francesco Guicciardini. M. Gio. Francesco Lottini. M. Francesco Sansovini. Di Nuovo
posti insieme, ampliati, & corretti, a commodo, & beneficio de gli Studiosi. Nelle quali si contengono,
leggi, regole, precetti, & sentenze molto utili a coloro che maneggiano, cosi i Principati & le Re-
publiche, come ogni altra sorte di governo* (from the copy in Perkins Library; the compilation appeared also in 1583, 1598, and 1608). All three of the constituent works were first published
separately by their authors in the 1570s. Later in his own book, when writing about servants,
North refers to (but disagrees with) "Francis Guichiardin, that excellent Authour in his *Avertimenti Civili. . .*" (pp. 46–47).

67. *Forest 45*, p. 157.

68. *Light*, A3r and p. 2, and account book at Rougham.

69. North's copies of these two books are now in the Folger Shakespeare Library, Washington, D.C.

70. *Lives*, III, 284. See Henry John Todd, *Memoirs of the Life and Writings of the Right Rev.
Brian Walton*, 2 vols. (1821).

great household was his first book to be printed. Two years previously, on 22 January 1667, John had written to his mother: "I hope my Father will bee pleased to follow the steps of my Grandfather in the Vertue of imparting, if not to the world, yett to his owne posterity, those note's[,] observations, or discourses hee has made in his life time, when I haue heard & haue reason to think that many of such a nature doe lye dormant in his hands." [71]

When the time came to impart Sir Dudley's notes and observations to a larger public, the arrangements, fittingly, were entrusted to John. He was, after all, the scholar of the family and possessed not only "a very researching spirit," in Roger's words, but a veritable passion for books. "He courted as a fond lover," says Roger, "all best editions, fairest characters, best bound and preserved." [72] To produce the *Observations* John turned to John Martin, "Printer to the *Royal Society*," on the grounds that Martin turned out books with excellent paper and "a very faire Character." [73] When John went to see him about the project one morning in the last week of May, Martin leafed through the manuscript a bit, then resolved on the spot to accept it. Later that same day John wrote to urge his father to send any additions or alterations with dispatch, because Martin "intends immediately to gett it Licensed" and "it will enter the press immediately." A short time later the little octavo was issued with modest but not excessive anonymity, everyone's assumption being that the author's identity would be known to many. [74] Francis, who had approved of his younger brother's plans and predicted that the project would go well, [75] was able to report to his father on 15 July that "the book is liked" in town." [76]

The *Observations* volume was followed the next year by North's *Narrative* of his experiences in the Long Parliament. This, too, was a little octavo issued anonymously, but it had a title-page acknowledgment that it was by "*a Person of Honor*." To produce this book the family turned to Robert Pawlet in Chancery Lane, perhaps because he was known as a publisher of political pamphlets. Pawlet took the manuscript at once to the licenser, Roger L'Estrange, who proved to have some objections that John deemed "frivolous" (for example, that Pym's name should be expunged and "Scotch" changed to

71. Bodl. MS. North c.10, p. 17.

72. *Lives*, II, 283, 281.

73. John to Sir Dudley, 24(?) May (Trinity College MS. o.11a.3 [38]).

74. When John wrote on 3 June, the manuscript already was being printed (Trinity College MS. o.11a.3 [35]). The book is listed in the *Term Catalogues* under "1669 Trin. 28 June," with the information that it sold for one shilling (Edward Arber, ed., I [1903], 14). On 3 July Francis wrote of having ten copies (Huntington MS. North 15).

75. John to Sir Dudley (Trinity College MS. o.11a.3 [38]).

76. Francis to Sir Dudley (Trinity College MS. o.11a.3 [46]). Francis also writes that "I gave my Brother Charles two of the Bookes, & delivered him the rest to be sent down, & Suppose your Lordship hath them by this time. . . ." In one of the rare published comments on North's writing, William Carew Hazlitt points to the *Observations* as North's "most important work" and "deserving of perusal" (*Inedited Poetical Miscellanies*, priv. circ., 50 copies [1870], n.p.).

"Scottish").[77] Apparently John wrote somewhat huffily to L'Estrange, re-
jecting all but one of the requested revisions, and, when L'Estrange relented
insufficiently, sent the manuscript on to Samuel Parker, chaplain to the Archbishop of Canterbury. Hence the work was published with Parker's *im-
primatur*, bearing the date 12 November 1670.[78]

North's explanation for launching the *Narrative* certainly is conventional,
but it may be true nonetheless: "*some friends looking upon it with too favourable
an eye, will not consent that it should be stifled by a confinement to one family or
place. . . .*"[79] It is, of course, perfectly understandable that he and his politi-
cally mobile sons might want as many people as possible to know why he had
remained in the Long Parliament so long.

North's third volume, a miscellany called *Light in the Way to Paradise, with
Other Occasionals*, was published some five years after his death, during the
Easter term of 1682.[80] Once again the choice of publisher was reasonable
enough: William Rogers, operating in Fleet Street near St. Dunstan's in a
shop at the "Sign of the *Sun*," was a man destined to become known mainly
for his theological publications.

The sixty-eight-page devotional work that lends its title to the volume
makes use of the important and ubiquitous idea of life as a pilgrimage. Trace-
able back to Hebrews 11.13 ("they were strangers and pilgrims on the earth")
and John 14.6 (Christ's "I am the way"), it is merged here with the idea of
necessary illumination, as in Psalms 119.105 ("Thy word is a lampe vnto my
feete: and a light vnto my path"). The title page affirms that "*Light is sowne
for the Righteous*, Psal. 97.11," and the final page brings both author and
reader to an anticipation of the "presence extraordinary" of "God and the
Lamb." All in all this opening piece is the thoughtful work of a faithful and
relatively broad-minded son of the Church of England.

Coming next in the volume is a little collection of short essays to which Sir
Dudley himself assigned the name of "occasionals."[81] Here he mulls over and

77. John to his mother, 17(?) November 1670 (Trinity College MS. o.11a.3[37]). L'Estrange,
who had been appointed as a licenser of the press and surveyor of printing presses in 1663, was a
journalist, pamphleteer, and translator.

78. It appeared during Michaelmas Term and, like its predecessor, sold for one shilling
(Arber, I, 58). John asked his parents to send instructions concerning how the books were to be
distributed in London, assuming that the remainder would be sent to Kirtling. Sir Dudley apparently was "content to haue but 20 Copyes" (Trinity College MS. o.11a.3[37]). In the following
century the text was chosen for the opening selection in the first volume of *A Collection of Scarce
and Valuable Tracts on the Most Interesting and Entertaining Subjects. . .* , i.e., Lord Somers's
tracts (1748), pp. 1–32; but it was erroneously attributed to Sir Dudley's son Francis (A3r).
When reprinted by Sir Walter Scott in the second edition of the *Collection* (1811: vol. VI, pp.
565–590), the work was correctly attributed.

79. *Narrative*, A4v.

80. Arber, I, 483.

81. Two of these (X, XI) are included by John L. Lievsay in *The Seventeenth-Century Resolve:
A Historical Anthology of a Literary Form* (Lexington, Kentucky, 1980), pp. 187–192. It might be
noted that, contrary to the implication of the title page, the titular work in North's volume is not

moralizes on such topics as the nature of power and the force of God's providence (both of which figure in his verse). He speaks out for the value of human pleasures (though, of course, one should be moderate in enjoying them) and perhaps touches close to home when he acknowledges that those men who are quicker and more carefree in the game of life not only gain higher esteem but also are in actual fact more serviceable.

Following these essays are a "meditation" dated 17 February 1666, and then a discourse on original sin, another discourse "*sometime intended as an addition to my observations and advices Oeconomical,*" and (with a separate title page) *Some Notes Concerning the Life of Edward Lord North.* Since *Some Notes* follows a page of advertisements and starts with fresh foliation, joint publication of the biography with North's devotional and reflective work apparently was an afterthought.[82] The thirty-six-page piece on the family's founder is accompanied by three letters of presentation (to Sir Dudley's eldest son; to the master, fellows, and scholars of Peterhouse, Edward's college; and to the Vice Chancellor and other "Governours" of the University),[83] and in the final one of these documents North casts a glance back to the period when he put the biography together: it was "*a time of unparallell'd trouble and confusion,*" he recalls, "*when the best conversation of Good men was with their own thoughts, and when Historical Truth was dangerous. . . .*"[84] Though the general tone of

---

at all like his occasionals. Perhaps one has here additional cause (see also pp. 104–105) for suspecting that an agent of the Norths was involved in the publication of these works.

82. One does come across some copies that appear to have been bound and issued separately, for example, BL C.53.c.11.(2.) and G.14414. It may be worth adding that the paper in both *Light* and *Some Notes* bears the same watermark.

83. Copies of the life were also presented to Cambridge University and to St. Peter's College in manuscript form. John North, writing to his mother, tells of sending a blank "Paper booke" to his father:

> And though it proues somewhat larger then I intended, yett it may suit perhaps the better for the place it is designed, viz the University Library, where a little booke would scarce bee taken notice of. & if there shal happen to bee left any spare sheets, if they will not induce my Lord to putt in somewhat more then hee has yett purposed, yett they will serue to sett out the rest, as is comonly done in Manuscript's. But if I may presume to add my opinion I think it would bee very convenient, if my Lord will please a little to inlarge that place in my L. Edwards life, which onely giue's a hint of his appropriating Burwel parsonage to the University. That they may see from an account of the Writing's his Lordship has at Catlidge [Kirtling], as wel that they are mistaken in attributing all to K. Hen. 8, as that wee doe not claim the glory of having a Predecesseur of Our's, their most considerable Benefactour, upon our bare word, & without just title. Which vindication will fitt that place & Person, & confirm that which I my self haue not forborn to giue out concerning it; Not to mention that it may procure some little more respect to mee here, who am at present, and am like to bee a member of the same Body.

Then in a postscript John adds that "The booke cost in all but 6s. which is very reasonable" (Bodl. MS. North c.10, 21r). A folio with polished calf binding and gilt-edged leaves, the book may now be seen in the Cambridge University Library (MS. Ee.5.3), and in it Sir Dudley's prose neatly written by a scribe. Sir Dudley's words on the problematic question of the Burwell beneficence may be read in two passages in *Some Notes* (pp. 34–35, 41–42).

84. *Some Notes,* p. 42.

the biography is that of an admiring descendant, the note struck here suggests a genuinely scholarly impulse.[85]

Clearly the dominating component in this hybrid volume is its titular work. Robert Watt would seem to assume this when he says that *Light in the Way to Paradise* shows that North "was stedfast in the religion of the established Church, and led an exemplary life."[86] Equally notable is one of the criticisms of his book that North himself, in his introduction, tries to forestall: "*Another objection may be, that for so serious a Subject, this discourse is somewhat too Poetical, by fiction of Mounts, Plains, Waters, Rocks, &c. But I shall presume that whosoever hath considered the whole Book of* Canticles, *and* S. Paul's *expressions*, of the Buckler of Faith, Sword of the Spirit, *and such like, will easily pardon this fault. . . .*"[87] The propriety of presenting his pilgrim against an allegorical backdrop was a matter that North thought worthy of reflection and justification.

During the latter decades of his life he had composed prose works on economy, politics, and biography, and from time to time over a period of many years he had composed poems of various sorts, but at last, he says, "*both Reading and Writing are now grown so troublesome to me, as I have reason to dispose my self to a retreat. . . .*"[88] It was time, indeed, while time remained, to consider more intensely—and now, most likely, with his pen lying idle on his desk—a subject which had frequently attracted his thoughts through the years, the nature of the light that is available to a pilgrim on the way to paradise.

Apparently no late portrait of North survives,[89] but his account books yield scattered hints as to his appearance and way of life. In March 1659 he had a black cloth suit trimmed with galloon and loop-lace, which must have been both sober and dignified. Later on, in June 1660, there were a silk mohair suit and cloak; in May 1668, a Flanders serge doublet and hose; and in May 1670, various garments of black bombazine.[90] Money was laid out on his behalf for tobacco and pipes, hair powder, a mended periwig (and then a new

85. Horace Walpole provides one of the rare comments available on this work: "Written sensibly and in a very good style, yet in vain attempting to give a favorable impression of his Ancestor, who appears to have been a very time-serving person. . ." (*A Catalogue of the Royal and Noble Authors of England: with Lists of Their Works*, II [Strawberry Hill, 1758], 31).

86. *Bibliotheca Britannica*, II (Edinburgh, 1824), 710*p*.

87. *Light*, A3*v*–A4*r*.

88. *Light*, A3*v*.

89. Engravings of a portrait of a bearded old gentleman identified as the fourth Lord North may be seen in John Adolphus, *The British Cabinet; Containing Portraits of Illustrious Personages*, I (1799), n.p.; and in Horace Walpole, *A Catalogue of the Royal and Noble Authors of England, Scotland, and Ireland; with Lists of Their Works. . .* , enlarged by Thomas Park, III (1806), plate preceding p. 203. It is almost certain, however, that these pictures depict Sir William Pope, first Earl of Downe, who died 2 June 1631. (For this identification I am indebted to Mr. John R. S. Guinness, London.)

90. Details in this paragraph are drawn from various passages in Bodl. MS. North c.20 and from North's book of accounts at Rougham Hall.

one), and eyeglasses to aid failing sight. Unfortunately, it was necessary to record visits from the doctor and, significantly, the "Charge of proxies in Parliament." As the handwriting of North's personal accounts grows shaky, there are still cattle to be bought (a frequent entry). Even for an old man, there is a need for new stockings.

There are also continuing payments to his durable old mother, who, so far as the records go, remains to the end the most shadowy major figure in his life. Kirtling was the Dowager Lady North's home, after all, and her financial interests were very much tied up in its complex affairs. As for domestic arrangements, she still required a variety of attendants—a gentlewoman, chambermaid, usher, footman, and perhaps others.[91] She still prized her grand old bed hung with embroidered blue plush, her heirloom diamond chain, and her great looking-glass set about with agates; but as time took its toll she also thought sometimes about which of her things should fall to Sir Dudley and which to Anne, and which to her other children, Dorothy and John, and to Charles the heir of the Norths.

Predictably enough, age brought the Dowager Lady North faltering health and little respite from financial concerns. In a letter to Sir Dudley dated 25 March 1667 Anne wrote: "my Lady I prayse God is very well now but this is the first day she hath been out of her chamber since you went away[.] the day after you went she was in so much extremity with Shoutings in Her head that she made me send to Dr. Bucknam who directed many outward things to be apply'd. Which I hope hath done her good. She hath a cold still vpon her, but is hearty & cheerfull & talkes hotly of going to london in Easter terme."[92] The old woman's cheerfulness must have eased matters for everyone concerned, and fortunately it continued. On 17 June 1667 Anne was able to inform Sir Dudley that his mother, "having been very tender with her cold so that she could scarse till friday endure to eat in the dining roome," subsequently "hath been well & at church yesterday but this day complaines a little of a paine of her side but she is cheerfull enough. . . ."[93]

Unfortunately, the elder Lady North had a sufficiently clear knowledge of the ways of the world and a sufficiently dim grasp of financial matters to make her wary and changeable even in dealing with her family. On 27 March 1667 Anne told Sir Dudley "how willing my Lady was to doe any thing that might be for your advantage & no preiudice to her selfe. . . ."[94] But on 16 May Sir Dudley's son Francis lamented her capriciousness: "I am very sorry my Lady [Grandmother] has altered her resolutions of complying in the matter of the settlement, & more that my Lady beleeves so little in me that nothing that I can say can give her any assurance, I hope when my Lady has all her arrears from your Lordship shee will better understand the necessity of it. . . ."[95]

91. PRO, Prob. 11/354.65, 174v–175v.
93. Bodl. MS. North c.4, 173r.
95. Bodl. MS. North c.4, 159r.
92. Bodl. MS. North c.4, 131r.
94. Bodl. MS. North c.4, 135r.

Adding to Sir Dudley's worries in his later years, then, as his own health faltered, was the presence in his home of his aged and ailing mother. When the Dowager Lady North died in late February of 1677, her ninety-third year, her son Dudley was seventy-four years old and would not live to see another birthday.

Anne provides a few additional glimpses of her husband about this time. On 25 March 1677 she writes to her daughter Anne, now the wife of Robert Foley of Stourbridge, Worcester: "I prayse God my Lo: is pretty well & I hope will gather strength apace[;] he hath not yett been at Church but hath walk't in the feild as farr as the maple." [96] As for herself, she adds, "I have been faine to wright & cast account to helpe my lord. . . ." No wonder she adds, "I am tyred with the sight of a penn & inke horne. . . ."

Lord North in later years suffered terribly, and, as Roger reports, "in all the Extremity of the Stone with which he was most Extreamly afflicted," Lady North "had comfort in the good service and help she gave him, and that which would have sunk comon spirits into dispair stired up her Strength & vigor, being Invincible in patience, Indefaticable in care & watching. . . ." [97] On 9 April 1677 she wrote to Francis: "My Lo: hath bin so very ill all the last week that he could not mind or think vpon any thing but this night he is some thing better and bids me rem[ember] him to you & to my Deare daughter[-in-law]. . . ." [98] On 20 May Anne wrote again to her daughter Anne: "wee have been in great trouble all last week our old servant Richard Holmes lying in great extremity of the stone & at this tyme lyes a dying—this hath troubled my Lo: very much & now he hath a fitt of the Strangury & lyes by fitts in very great payne." [99] It was necessary to make numerous payments "To Doct: Bucknam."

At least the comfortable relationship of Lord and Lady North provided both with something of a cushion against life's trials. When Roger later looked back upon his parents, it seemed that Sir Dudley was "never absent from her, Nor she from him." [100] He continues:

Who Ever hath bin acquainted there, will know that the Same room all-waies Conteined both. when all their children were removed, & they left alone, they were as Much Comfort & company to Each Other, as Ever without any Satiety or uneasyness, & this in their ages of infirmity & weakness. and altho he was a Man of Much passion, under the Influ-ence of which, No Man can answer for indiscretions, tho afterwards he

96. BL Add. MS. 32,500, 18r.
97. BL Add. MS. 32,523, 6r; working with characteristic haste, Roger writes "wast" here for "was."
98. Huntington MS. North 1. Francis had married the second daughter, Frances, of Thomas Pope, Earl of Downe.
99. BL Add. MS. 32,500, 21r. "Strangury" is a condition of the urinary organs in which the urine is painfully emitted drop by drop.
100. BL Add. MS. 32,523, 6v.

May Repent of them, yet No occasion Ever made a difference betwixt
them. . . .

When Sir Dudley composed the dedication to his verse, he signed himself
"Entirely and constantly" Anne's,[101] and in writing his will, he went out of
his formal way to acknowledge the "piety vertue and constant affection" of
his "most Deare Wife." [102] He not only named her executrix but also acknowledged that "all I can doe" is "farr Short of her merit. . . ."

At the time he wrote his will (8 May 1675) North described himself as
"very infirme in Body." Although he had long sought comfort from life's various ills by raising his eyes sometimes above and beyond Kirtling and Tostock, and although he wrote now of "haveing learned to fix . . . [his] desires
upon the eternall Mansion" made ready by his "pretious Saviour," North
nonetheless continued to involve himself in affairs relating to the management of his extensive properties. His will draws in the names of some of the
tenants with whom his sons would have to deal when he was gone—Thomas
Farthing, William Bawly, Thomas Ottoway, John Frost, George Cole—such
men as, through the years, he always had tried to treat fairly and generously,
even when his own finances were badly strained.[103] Perhaps most notable of
all in the will, however, is North's concern for Anne. In the document itself
and in its codicil, added in the autumn of the following year (22 September
1676) when he had only a few more months to live, North took care that his
widow might enjoy more ease and comfort than she had ever known in their
years together.

From early the next summer (18 June 1677) there survives a letter in which
Anne says that one could scarcely "imagine what divertizement my Lo: hath
found since our coming hether [to Kirtling] both in looking abroad & within[,] he haveing been so long from hence that every thing hath a new face[,]
but the park & other grounds wee had wont to ayre in are so full of bushes &
molehills that makes it more vneasy then pleasent yett he is every day in the
coach & endures our pace very well. . . ." [104] The old estate itself showed
signs of decline, but it had been his home longer than anywhere else, and it
was where the old man most liked to be.

Not so much as a week later, on Sunday, 24 June, at the age of seventy-
four, Sir Dudley North died. In Roger's words, he "died a miserable martyr
to the stone." [105] Sir Dudley himself, however, at an advanced age, had written, "The truth is, that daily experience sheweth a general abhorrence of
death, whereof the cause is not very easie to be found. It can hardly be the
fear of pain accompanying it, for Death, which is a Cessation of the faculties

101. Dedicatory introduction to his poems (herein, p. 128).
102. Bodl. MS. North c.32, no. 8; also PRO Prob. 11/354.69, 205v–206v.
103. North touches on his attitude as a landlord in *Observations*, pp. 105–106.
104. BL Add. MS. 32,500, 22r.
105. *Lives*, III, 317.

belonging to sense and motion, cometh in a moment that admits no extremity." [106] Of course, his own spirit had been aguish sometimes, but the cause of its general good health through the years is made clear in his *Light in the Way to Paradise*: "I verily think that even here, where Christianity is professed, the number of those who believe a Subsistence after death, is very small, and especially among the vulgar. But the comfort of us Christians is, that all these doubts and difficulties are clearly overcome by Faith. . . ." [107] Given his views, it is fitting that Sir Dudley died on the nativity of John the Baptist, Midsummer Day, one of the happiest of holidays. As age had overtaken him, Sir Dudley had turned to medicine frequently, but all the while he knew perfectly well that his life never really lay in any man's hands. [108] God was at once the true Aesculapius and the only true source of light in the way to paradise.

North left the request that his "Body be buryed without invitation of ffriends and without other Solemnity as privately as may be in the Chancell of Kirtling Church." [109] There at the west end of the chancel, on 27 June, he was laid amongst his predecessors. To mark the place there was a black marble slab with the three fleurs-de-lis and rampant lion of the Norths impaling a fess of three lozenges and a border for Montagu. Underneath was an inscription beginning, "Heic humatus est *Dudlejus North*. . . ." [110]

A widow after forty-five years of marriage, Anne had long since lost her mother, her sister Mary, and more recently her sister Elizabeth, who had died in an explosion at Cornet Castle, her son's home in Guernsey, when the powder magazine there was struck by lightning one December night in 1672. [111] Anne was quite aware how much she now needed her children. "I must with all willingnesse submitt to the good pleasure of the Almighty in all things," she wrote to Francis; "& I know he hath given me so many good Children that they will all helpe to supply my great losse of there ffather in there kindnesse to me." [112] Unfortunately, Charles, now fifth Lord North, was already causing trouble about his inheritance. In subsequent years, he even refused to pay his brothers any of the annuities that their father had settled upon them. [113] Nevertheless, the ties between Anne and the rest of the children were close, and by frequent letters she managed to keep in touch with them, endearing herself still more in her own final years by taking in the three "pretty

106. *Light*, p. 65.

107. *Light*, p. 66.

108. "An Essay in the way of Gratitude" (No. 50).

109. Bodl. MS. North c.32, no. 8. Privacy and minimal fuss were in keeping not merely with the temper of the man, of course, but also with his sense of moderate expenditure.

110. North family inscriptions are given in BL Add. MS. 5,819, 114*v*–120*r* and included in *Monumental Inscriptions and Coats of Arms from Cambridgeshire Chiefly as Recorded by John Layer about 1632 and William Cole between 1742 and 1782*, ed. W. M. Palmer (Cambridge, 1932), pp. 91–93.

111. Thompson, *Correspondence of the Family of Hatton*, I, 103.

112. Written 2 July 1677 (Huntington MS. North 2).

113. Korsten, p. 2.

babes" of Francis when his wife died in 1678.[114] In order to take the children airing, Anne had the old coach brought out of the barn, and Roger records that she was "Never More pleased then when her hous was filled with her Children, & her children's children, with whom she would be merry & free, & Encourage them to be so too. . . ."[115] A realistic adjustment in Roger's picture is made possible by Anne herself, however, for at one point she confesses that the children are "grow'n so wild that I know not how to order them."[116] Doubtless she loved her grandchildren, but sometimes it seemed that her house was too small for them, and often they worried her by being ill. Her nursing skills were called forth not only by her grandchildren, moreover, but also by her son John, whose physical and mental health was deteriorating rapidly during this period.[117]

Although Anne managed for a while to maintain something of the aura of enduring strength that she had projected in earlier years, the signs of her own decline were at last unmistakable.[118] Among other things, she took to fretting over "the troubles coming upon her dear Son the Lord Ch[ief]. Just[ice]. from the Antimonarchicall faction whose fury & Impetuosity She knew by old experience. . . ."[119] On the other hand, it was Roger's opinion that his mother was never really altogether well after Sir Dudley died. Somehow it seemed to Roger that she "was gnawed with cares within when there was nothing without to employ them."[120]

In January 1681, when the weather turned very cold, Anne reported that she was having difficulty keeping warm.[121] On Thursday, 6 February, she wrote of being taken extremely ill the preceding Thursday. She had remained in bed ever since, she said, sometimes in great torment, but finally allowed herself to fancy that she was somewhat better.[122] In this same late letter, sent to Roger in Chancery Lane where he was staying with his brother the Lord Chief Justice, Anne retains both her matter-of-fact practicality and her concern for the well-being of her family. Roger and Francis, she says, may expect a box she has sent containing some "foules & a peec[e] of bacon I beleeve not

114. Anne to Francis, 19 November 1678 (Huntington MS. North 3).
115. *Lives*, III, 213, and BL Add. MS. 32,523, 7r.
116. BL Add. MS. 32,500, 37r.
117. Millard considers John to have become "an advanced hypochondriac" (p. 56). Although it is true that John feared blindness and read Milton for comfort on the subject (*Paradise Lost*, III, 1–55), it is also true that, whatever their causes, John suffered from real physical symptoms, including convulsive fits and paralysis (see, for example, Bodl. MS. North c.5, 77r and 89r; and *Lives*, III, esp. 328–342). John died in 1683.
118. In a letter to one of his sisters Roger writes: "I thinck there never was such an Example in the world as our Mother, who was no Hector, but Never appeared disturbed, during all her painefull Nursings which She had with many of us, & More with My father, so that altho she was as tender as was possible, one would have thought she had an heart of brass. I have heard that upon terible wounds made up, after the work done she would Swoon, but rub'd thro the work like a lyon" (BL Add. MS. 32,500, 93r).
119. BL Add. MS. 32,523, 7v.
120. *Lives*, III, 256.
121. BL Add. MS. 32,500, 53r.
122. BL Add. MS. 32,500, 56r.

to[o] salt to rost & eat cold." About a week later, at the age of sixty-seven, she died, and on 15 February, in accordance with her wishes, she was laid in Kirtling church "as neere to my Deare Lords Body as Conveniently they can." [123] Yet again there was a black marble slab, this time with an inscription beginning, "Hic in Pace requiescit *Hon^{ma} Dña Anna.* . . ." [124]

Roger, to whom Anne entrusted the management of her estate, never set down the facts of her life, but it is clear that he saw her as a loving, selfless mother, kind, strong, and devout. Viewed through the eyes of her youngest son, Anne is idealized nearly as much as she appears to have been half a century earlier when Sir Dudley himself had written of the fair Serena.

The image of Sir Dudley that Roger passes down is rather more restrained, and yet it, too, is grounded on truth. In fact, it is quite faithful to the man whom Sir Dudley, after traveling many post-stages, had become. "He was a christian speculatively orthodox and good," writes Roger, "regularly charitable and pious in his family, rigidly just in his dealing, and exquisitely virtuous and sober in his person." [125] Then Roger adds that all these things are made manifest in what his father wrote. When all is said and done, Sir Dudley North's writing remains the clearest mirror of the man.

123. PRO, Prob. 11/366.61, 106r–v.
124. Palmer, p. 93.
125. *Lives*, I, 6. A bit of extra-familial reinforcement of this character assessment comes from Dr. Henry Paman in a letter to Sir Dudley dated 3 July 1671: "If your Lp were capable of it nothing could soe likely raise a pride in you as the great perfections in your Children, of whom yet nothing lesse could bee expected hauing soe admirable and [sic] example at home" (Bodl. MS. North c.4, no. 262).

PART TWO

THE VERSE

THE PERKINS MANUSCRIPT

The leather-bound volume of manuscript verse and prose which has served as copy text for the verse in the present volume was purchased by Perkins Library of Duke University from Dawsons of Pall Mall (August 1969). Dawsons had acquired the volume through Sotheby & Co. (March 1967) from the collection of the Hon. Dudleya North of Hillside House, Newmarket.[1] Dudleya North, as her name suggests, was a descendant of the writer, Dudley, fourth Lord North, and more specifically of his son Francis. There is prima facie evidence, then, that prior to 1967 and for about three hundred years the manuscript passed from generation to generation within the North family.[2]

The approximate date of the compilation may be surmised on several grounds. The watermark on the paper bears the combined arms of France and Navarre with the subscript "ADVRAND" (i.e., A. Durand). Although Dawsons has identified this mark as Heawood No. 655,[3] the design is closer (though still not identical) to Heawood No. 678 and to another design that Heawood reproduced elsewhere.[4] Variants that are reasonably close to the France-Navarre watermark in the Perkins manuscript occur in such places as a Hollar print (1666), Ashmole's *Garter* (1672), Varen's *Descriptio Regni Japoniae et Siam* (1673), Herbert's *Travels* (1677), and Raleigh's *History of the World* (1677)[5]—works whose dates (1666–1677) provide a plausible time-range for the Perkins manuscript. Furthermore, it is clear that the paper in the Perkins volume comes from the Durand mill in Normandy, southeast of

1. I understand from Peter T. Millard that he came across the volume at Hillside House while engaged in research on "An Edition of Roger North's *Life of Dr. John North* with a Critical Introduction," a D.Phil. thesis, Linacre College, Oxford (1969). John Pitcher has published a chart that records numerous related facts about the dispersal of "The North Papers" (*Samuel Daniel: The Brotherton Manuscript*, Leeds Texts and Monographs, n.s. 7 [Leeds, 1981], p. 9).

2. A spokesman for Dawsons wrote to Perkins Library on 12 March 1970 that "I think it can be assumed that it was owned by successive generations of North family until 1967."

3. Catalogue No. 200 (July 1969), p. 36, citing Edward Heawood, *Watermarks Mainly of the 17th and 18th Centuries*, vol. I of *Monumenta Chartae Papyraceae* (Hilversum [Holland], 1950), pl. 102.

4. *Watermarks*, I, pl. 106; and "Further Notes on Paper Used in England after 1600," *The Library*, 5th ser., II (1948), 144, No. 26.

5. Heawood, "Papers Used in England after 1600," *The Library*, 4th ser., XI (1931), 267; also Heawood, *Watermarks*, I, 79. Heawood observes that sometimes one of the fleurs-de-lis is dropped and the design of the remaining two barely recognizable. "Paper with this mark," he writes, "was perhaps made specially for the English market, as I have not found it in a French book. . ." (*Library*, 4th ser., XI, 268).

Vire, near the village of Maisoncelles-le-Jourdain. Stevenson helps us to put a still finer point on the matter by observing that in seventeenth-century England the name Durand was "a symbol of excellent 'Paper out of France.'"[6] It is perhaps worth adding that Parliament put an embargo on French paper in 1678. English supplies of it would not have vanished overnight, of course, but they must have shrunk quickly.[7]

There are other kinds of evidence—fortunately supportive—regarding the time of compilation of the Perkins manuscript. The latest dated poem in the collection is entitled "A Riddle. 1663."[8] A piece that appears earlier in the volume, however, is a short prose composition labeled "A Sundays meditation vpon Eternity June 17. 1666."[9] Moreover, Lord North's father, Dudley, third Lord North, died in January 1667, providing a *terminus ad quo*, since the volume includes "An Elegie vpon the Right Honble Dudley Lord North by his Eldest Sonne Executor."[10]

Probably we may accept 1677, the year of the younger North's death (which was also the year before Parliament's embargo), as the manuscript's *terminus ad quem*. Certainly the compilation shows Sir Dudley's cognizance that it was being made. The opening sentence of his dedication contains North's assurance to the copyist—his wife, Anne, Lady North—that "Since freely of your selfe you have taken a resolution, to coppy out these imperfect essayes of myne in the way of poetry, . . . it now becomes fitt that I should give you some accompt of theyr condition. . . ."[11] Such a sentence could have been recopied by Lady North, however, at any later date before her own death in February 1681, so we need to seek elsewhere for a suggestion that it actually was recorded while the author himself still lived.

Fortunately some indirect evidence has survived. In a letter that Lady North endorsed "My sonn John. Jan 22 66" (i.e., 1667), John wrote to thank his mother for presenting him with his father's "Verses in a copy taken with your owne hand."[12] At the time of this letter John's father was very much alive, though his grandfather, the third Lord North, had been dead less than a week. John praises his father's verse, then turns to his prose, apparently, when he expresses the hope that "my Father will bee pleased to follow

6. Allan Stevenson, ed., Jubilee Edition of C. M. Briquet, *Les Filigranes*, gen. ed., J. S. G. Simmons, I (Amsterdam, 1968), *35. The book thus provides a bit of evidence of the fact that northern and western France was the chief source of paper used in England down through the first eight decades of the seventeenth century (Heawood, *Library*, 4th ser., XI, 292).

7. "After the Revocation of the Edict of Nantes (1685)," Stevenson points out, "The English again learned how to make white paper for themselves" (*35).

8. Fol. 151r (herein, No. 37). All of North's verses, of course, and his prose dedication are reproduced in the present volume. For clarity the folio numbering used for citations here is based on that now found in the Perkins manuscript, although some of the original leaves of the manuscript were excised before the numbering was made.

9. Fols. 126r–127r.

10. Fols. 128r–129r (herein, No. 31).

11. Fol. 1r (herein, p. 128).

12. Bodl. MS. North c.10, 17r.

On Serena sleeping

Such a sweet stillnes doth the soule possesse,
When dead to sorrow, fill'd with blessednes.
From clogging earth emancipate, and free,
It only tends the great Divinitye.
Tymes vnrelenting messenger, to this
Fayre lovely semblance, ill compared is,
Were women sure, that death were thus attyr'd,
They'd sell theyr liues, and soules to bee admyr'd.
I Heav'n and Lyfe in this fayre obiect see,
Not Earth, and death, theyr image rests on mee
Mee a poore plant bereft of verdure quite
By that too cleere a heav'ns abundant light:
Yett could those veyled Sunns theyr beams contract,
And on theyr mistris hart full warmth reflect,
Her frequent favors then, like tymely rayn,
Might make this plant to flourish once agayne.

3. "On Serena sleeping," a poem from the Perkins manuscript in Lady North's hand.

the steps of my Grandfather in the Vertue of imparting, if not to the world, yett to his owne posterity, those note's[,] observations, or discourses hee has made in his life time. . . ."

The discovery that Lady North copied out her husband's poems for John leads one to wonder whether she made copies for others of her children and, if so, for whom. No full answers to such questions are possible, but it appears reasonably certain that she made a copy for her youngest son. Still preserved at Roger's home, Rougham Hall, at any rate, and containing some of Roger's handwriting, is a copy that provides the chief basis of collation for the verses in this present edition.[13] For whom, then, might the Perkins copy have been intended? As we shall see presently, it may have been for Charles. It seems safe to hypothesize that the eldest son, who was expected to carry on the family's traditions and titles, would have received a copy. Indeed, one section of both the Rougham Hall and Perkins manuscripts is addressed specifically "To my eldest sonn."[14] Moreover, North's opening words here to Charles are worth noticing: "Since it hath pleased God to sett you in a condition, whereby you are likely to bee entrusted, with the honor of your house, and of all which is most pretious belonging to it, I have iudged you the person to whom I might most fittly recomend the ensuing discourse. . . ." Furthermore, with the foregoing three copies of the compilation all coming from Lady North's desk, it is not altogether likely that she would have forgotten her second-oldest son, Francis, or her favorite, Dudley.[15] This, however, leads us dangerously deep into speculation.

To return to the problem of dating: Lady North's labors in making multiple copies—one does not know how many—of her husband's verse and some of his prose must have occupied her free time over a rather extended period. The Perkins manuscript has 148 pages of writing (all of it, incidentally, on the rectos of the leaves), and the Rougham copy, 118 (on both rectos and versos). The time required for her work would help to explain why the Rougham manuscript ends with Lord North's elegy on the death of his father, and the Perkins manuscript with North's "Essay in the way of Gratitude." The elegy on the elder North closes with the fourth Lord North's decision, likely recorded early in 1667, to compose no more poetry: "I . . . dedicate to thee my latest verse, / And Sacrifice my penne, and lawrell at thy hearse."[16] That John's copy concluded with the same poem—then a very new one—is suggested by one of the observations he makes to his mother in his January 1667 letter about the collection: "It only troubled mee that they should bee the

13. Thanks to the kindness and courtesy of Roger and Pamela North of Rougham Hall, and of John R. S. Guinness of London, I made this discovery in August 1977.

14. Perkins, 93r.

15. Francis was the second oldest, and Dudley (his father's namesake) was her special favorite (*Lives*, II, 1). There were a number of other children, too, but even Lady North's patience as a copyist must have had a limit.

16. Fol. 129r (herein, No. 31, ll. 25–26).

last fruits of soe pregnant & Juvenile a fancy." In the final poem of the Perkins manuscript, however, North observes that God has now extended his own life "to great length." [17] Uncharacteristically ragged in style, "An Essay in the way of Gratitude" expresses thanks to God for allowing the writer to survive a terrible bout with kidney stones. One cannot say when that struggle occurred, only that it was in 1677, in his seventy-fifth year, that Lord North succumbed to a subsequent attack of the stone.

In short, when all the evidence is weighed, it appears that the Perkins manuscript is somewhat later than its Rougham counterpart and later than the copy John received, and that probably it dates from the 1670s. Dawsons suggests approximately 1676. [18]

Examination of the volume yields other information. The contemporary calf covers (the front one now detached) are both a faded, uneven brown, blind-tooled with simple borders of double fillet. [19] Within the central panel formed by the border on each cover there is a similar but smaller triple fillet border with simple fleurons extending outward from the four corners. The spine is also tooled, four double fillet lines running down the length and two running parallel at both the top and the bottom. Within the resultant rectangle are four small floral ornaments, two with heads aimed downward from the inner line at the top, and two with heads aimed upward from the bottom inner line. When the volume was new, two narrow black ribbons emerged from small holes in the triple fillet border near the fore-edges of each of the boards so that the book might be tied closed. Now only the knotted stubs of the ribbons survive, protected beneath the cover paste-downs inside the boards.

The volume is the size of an average small quarto, its boards measuring 225 mm × 175 mm, but inside it is gathered as an octavo. In other words, it is a quarto in eights: one sheet of quarto leaves is inserted in another. The leaves measure 220 mm × 172 mm and have horizontal chain-lines. Though with effort one can discern that some have been removed, one hundred and seventy-five such leaves survive, and in its present state the volume may be collated as follows: 1, six leaves only ($1^{1,2}$ = paste-downs; $-1^{4,5}$); 2, six leaves ($-2^{1,7}$); 3–5, eight leaves each; 6, seven leaves (-6^6); 7, eight leaves; 8, six leaves ($-8^{1,2}$); 9, five leaves ($-9^{5,6,7}$); 10–16, eight leaves each; 17, seven

17. Fol. 157r (herein, No. 50, l. 10). I do not mean to suggest that the manuscript is chronologically ordered, but that this particular poem, which does come last, has a late feeling to it. On the other hand, North clearly had his own death in mind even before the death of his father. In his "Appendix to the Occasionalls" North writes that, "Having past my Climactericall [sixty-third year] in the yeare of our Lord 1666 . . . I may well thinke that my own dissolution will speedily overtake mee. . ." (82r).

18. Dawsons Catalogue No. 200, p. 36. Sotheby & Co. is clearly off in suggesting "*mid-seventeenth century*" (*Catalogue of Valuable Printed Books Autograph Letters and Historical Documents* [day of sale: 14 March 1967], p. 58).

19. For aid with the description in this paragraph and the next, I am indebted to Dr. John L. Sharpe, III, Curator of Rare Books, Perkins Library.

leaves (-17^5); 18–21, eight leaves each; 22, seven leaves (-22^3); 23, eight leaves; 24, seven leaves (-24^8; $24^{6,7}=$ paste-downs). Aside from the fact that the first gathering has only six leaves (two others having been torn off, perhaps, before the book was bound), such anomalies as occur here would seem to be the result of the copyist's neat excision of various leaves, probably during the actual copying process and probably in an uncomplicated effort to keep her pages as attractive as possible.

The most puzzling physical attribute of the book is the occurrence of nine small, fragmentary lumps of reddish-orange sealing wax that bear the imprint, also fragmentary, of a seal. The lumps occur on three leaves, an inch or so from each fore-edge, four on $1r$, two on $55v$, and three on $150r$, with torn places on $170v$ where two others obviously were to be found at some earlier time. These lumps pose two questions: why are they there, and who put them there? Because of the singular placement of the wax, because all the lumps are broken, and because certain bits of paper are stuck to some of them, it would seem that two sheets (or perhaps strips) of paper, their edges held with wax, were once placed so as to cover the fore-edge of two sections of the volume, the purpose being to seal off these pages from any would-be reader. The sections which would have been closed run from $1v$ (which is the verso of the present title page) to $55r$, and from $150v$ to $170r$. Both of the sealed-off portions are comprised entirely of North's verse, and the portion that always would have been exposed ($55v$–$150r$) consists, with only three exceptions, of North's prose.[20]

From whom would the poetry have been sealed off, and for whom would the prose have been exposed? Except for one poem ("A Riddle. 1663"), the personal element in the poems is not such that anyone is likely to have worried much about keeping them from family eyes. Under what circumstances might persons outside the family be reading the prose? One cannot reconstruct the situation well enough to justify more than an informed guess, but all of the prose that would have been visible when the inhibitory pieces of paper were in place was published by North's family in *Light in the Way to Paradise* (1682), after North's death, and, indeed, after Lady North's death. Perhaps the poems were sealed off when the volume was submitted for publication.[21] Making this theory more likely is the nature of the wear discernible in the prose sections: the only badly torn leaves in the volume occur here, and

---

20. The three poems which would have been exposed are "As all by Natures fatall course must dye" ($121r$, at the close of North's biography of Edward North; herein, No. 36), the elegy on the death of his father, the third Lord North ($128r$–$129r$; herein, No. 31), and, immediately following, in Latin, "Hymnus sacer" ($129r$; herein, No. 45). In both the sealed-off and the exposed sections there are a few blank leaves.

21. The manuscript lacks "A Discourse sometime intended as an addition to my observations and advices Oeconomical, afterwards printed," which was published in *Light* (pp. 129–135), but that could have been set from another source. Bodl. MS. Eng. th.d.55, $65r$–$69v$, is a manuscript version of this "Discourse."

the leaves are generally soiled. Most striking of all, on one leaf (120r), along with a number of other suspicious smudges, there is a sizeable fingerprint that appears to have been made with black printer's ink.[22]

The wax fragments are especially enigmatic because of the seal which was impressed in them. Photographic enlargement in an attempt to reconstruct and identify the seal yields a design that belongs neither to any known member of the family nor to any known contemporary bookseller.[23] It is reasonably clear that each of the original impressions consisted of a shield parted *per fesse* indented and in chief three crosses *patée* (or *formée*). In other words, a regularly indented line like a large-toothed saw-blade divided the upper and lower parts of the shield, and in the upper portion there were three squarish crosses, the limbs of which were almost triangular, narrow where they met and widening towards their outer extremities. The problem is that one has here the arms of Perceval. The Perceval shield was argent with a chief indented, gules, and three crosses *patée* of the first.[24]

One may set aside fairly readily the fact that such a seal technically should have been used only by the head of the Perceval family.[25] In practice such seals were used by various members of a family. In fact, it may be of consequence that in the North family's home county of Cambridgeshire one may find the Perceval arms on a number of monuments: at Chippenham, for instance, on that of William Percivall, Gent. (buried 28 June 1671) and that of John Percivall (d. 18 November 1669); and at Newmarket (halved with other arms) on that of Mary Percivall, wife of Thomas (d. 1707).[26]

The problem is that some *one* Perceval must be connected with the manuscript. Reasonably diligent search has not resulted thus far in establishing any Perceval link, though it has made a tentative suggestion possible. On 9 August 1679 one Thomas Percivall may be found writing to Francis North and referring to himself as "under great obligations to your family, & desireous upon any occasion to speake my sense thereof. . . ."[27] One cannot help pon-

22. The catalogue of Sotheby & Co., in describing the wax fragments (p. 58), offers the alternate theory that after the verse passages were sealed off and prior to the publication of the prose the volume was turned over to a professional scribe for transcription. One might add that in earlier years, when John was seeing his father's *Observations and Advices Oeconomical* (1669) through the press, he came to lament that an additional manuscript copy had not been made so as to facilitate the process: "it would have been better if I . . . had here another Copy to compare every Sheet by, for this one [?] will bee in continuall Use in the Setting of the Letters. . ." (Trinity College, Camb., MS. o.11a.3[35]).

23. I have examined personal seals used by Charles, Francis, Dudley (the merchant son), and Roger, as well as others; see esp. BL Add. MS. 29,580.

24. Both reconstruction and identification have been confirmed for me by A. Colin Cole, then Windsor Herald of Arms (letter of 11 January 1978). See Bernard Burke, *The General Armory of England, Scotland, Ireland and Wales* (1884), p. 792.

25. Sir John Perceval (b. 1660, d. 1686) does not appear to have had any reason to know about the manuscript, nor does his predecessor, Sir Philip Perceval (b. 1656, d. 1680).

26. William Mortlock Palmer, ed., *Monumental Inscriptions and Coats of Arms from Cambridgeshire* (Cambridge, 1932), pp. 29, 125–126.

27. Spencer MS. uncat. North 1J:47, packet 7:4.

dering what sort of relationship the Norths had with such a man. A Cambridgeshire attorney who lived for a while in Newmarket (about five miles from Kirtling), then moved to London, Percivall was to become deeply involved in the political maneuverings of the day. One finds reports of him speaking seditious and dangerous words, "gathering money for carrying on factious designs in parliament time," [28] making "it his business to go from county to county and . . .[spare] no pains to promote Fanatic elections," and, it was said, generally behaving like "a vile desperate person," "the most active and daring against the government of any man in this county [Cambridgeshire], Norfolk, Suffolk or Huntingdonshire." [29] In particular, Percivall was reported to be "in great vogue with some leading men of the faction." [30] Charles North, significantly, the oldest of the North brothers and fifth Lord North as of June 1677, was by 1679 one of the most prominent men in the dissident "faction." [31] In striking contrast, all of his brothers were faithful to the King. Francis, in fact, Lord Keeper of the Great Seal (1682), was the head of the party in power. John North wrote to his brother Roger with great distaste concerning Percivall and their brother Charles: "I heare None so great with him as percival. Sir Tho Wilby found them together and Percival was going to keep a Court at Catlidge [i.e., Kirtling]. Divinity is quite gone with him but it seems he holds still a Ragg of the Law: And he would not that if he could." [32]

A connection between this Thomas Percivall and the Perkins manuscript is temptingly easy to hypothesize. Conceivably when Charles found it convenient to publish some of his father's prose, he turned over the actual carrying out of the project to one of his hangers-on. It is frustrating to have to add, however, that Percivall's seal on his 1679 letter to Francis does not match the seal as reconstructed from the fragments in the Perkins manuscript. It might be argued, therefore, that the hypothesis should be discarded. On the other hand, an Englishman of the day did not necessarily limit himself to the use of a single seal, a case in point being Roger North.

All things considered, there is at present only one safe stand regarding the presence of the Perceval seal in the Perkins manuscript: until more evidence comes to light, it is best to regard the seal as one of the enigmas of the book. [33]

28. Letters of Thomas Smyth (25 February 1681) and Sir Leoline Jenkins (25 October 1681) in F. H. Blackburne Daniell, ed., *CSP, Domestic*, 1 Jan.–30 June 1683 (1933), pp. 183 and 533.
29. Letter of Robert Brady, Regius Professor of Physic, Caius College, to Jenkins, in Daniell, p. 350.
30. Ibid.
31. See above, pp. 79–80.
32. Bodl. MS. North c.10, 55v.
33. If one argues that the Perkins manuscript belonged originally to Francis, not Charles, one might suggest that the seal-owner was Beaumont Percivall, who matriculated at Oxford 22 March 1661, took his B.A. in 1664, and proceeded to his M.A. in 1668, his B.D. in 1679, and his D.D. in 1684 (Joseph Foster, *Alumni Oxonienses*, III [1891], 1145). Beaumont Percivall in 1683 became rector of Broughton, Oxfordshire (southwest of Banbury), which was only about two miles from Wroxton Abbey. Wroxton was the home of Francis North's wife, Frances, daughter

It remains to be added, however, that there is, indeed, further cause to believe that the Perkins manuscript once belonged to Charles North. As we have seen, it shows signs of passing through a printer's hands: not only were the poems closed off with paper and sealing wax in such a way as to leave the prose accessible, but the pages of prose appear to be smudged with printer's ink. Furthermore, Roger North specifically informs us that it was his eldest brother, Charles, who gave to the press the prose that appears here. In a passage that was excised from the published version of his *Lives*, Roger claims that his father wrote "divers slight Essays, and some verses, w'ch he tituled Light in the way to Paradise. These 2 last, his eldest son caused to be published with his name to it, viz. Dudley the 2d (misprinted for the 2d Dudley) Lord North. These were at first designed to remain with his family in Mss, and not to be published, but there is no harm done. . . ."[34] Despite an error here (the verse in the book is limited to a single short poem[35]), most of the passage rings true. The title-page misinformation appears in *Light in the Way to Paradise* just as Roger describes it, and it is not difficult to believe that all of Sir Dudley's writings that were left unpublished at the time of his death were, indeed, "designed to remain with his family in Mss." Hence we may the more readily accept Roger's statement that Charles, the "eldest son," caused the prose to be published. Roger is not likely to be wrong in such a matter. One might observe, too, that although John had managed the publication of Sir Dudley's writing up to this time, his extreme ill health in 1682 makes it understandable that he played no part in the project. Furthermore, it was precisely during this period that Charles was under attack for his political dissidence. At a time when his name was being dragged through the mud, perhaps it seemed reasonable to him to publish not merely the pious prose of his father but, simultaneously, the biography of Edward North, the first Lord North, which made clear the foundations of his family, including what the family believed about Edward's benefactions. In short, the Perkins manuscript seems not only to have belonged at one time to Charles North; it may have been used by him as a public defense.

Three final facts about the Perkins manuscript should be noted: its bookplate, its first-leaf inscription, and its hand. On the inside of the front cover of the volume is the bookplate of the Earl of Guilford, Wroxton Abbey, bearing the North coat of arms (a lion passant amidst three fleurs-de-lis) with two

---

of Thomas Pope, third Earl of Downe (d. 1668) and his wife Beata (d. 1678), and after their deaths Wroxton became the country seat of Francis North himself. Furthermore, Roger reports that the Norths, long a Cambridge family, did indeed establish connections with Oxford University (*Lives*, II, 296–297). John in particular made efforts to meet the eminent men there. Perhaps one can conceive that in 1682 Francis or someone on his behalf turned to a nearby learned clergyman, soon to be rector at Broughton, to help see his father's prose through the press. For this suggestion and others I am indebted to William R. Erwin, Jr., Assistant Curator of Manuscripts, Perkins Library.

34. "A general preface," St. John's College, MS. Bb, James 613, vol. I, p. [41].
35. An epigram, herein No. 36.

dragon supporters and the family motto, *La virtu est la seule noblesse*. It was not until 1752, during the reign of George II, that the title Earl of Guilford entered the family. If one is willing to press beyond the firm fact that the bookplate therefore dates from 1752 or later, one might hazard the guess that a book owned by Charles is likely to have passed to subsequent Lords North. If it did, then there may be some point in recording that for exactly half a century after 1752 (i.e., until 1802) the Earls of Guilford held the concurrent title of Baron North.

Who were the Earls of Guilford? First to bear the title (from 1752 to 1790) was Francis North, seventh Baron North of Kirtling and third Baron Guilford, the son of Francis, second Baron Guilford. (The latter, in turn, was the son of Francis North of Wroxton, who has concerned us here and whose patent to become first Baron Guilford was dated 27 September 1683. In other words, the first Earl of Guilford was the great-grandson of Dudley, fourth Lord North.) The second Earl of Guilford and eighth Baron North of Kirtling was the first earl's son, Frederick North, who held the two titles only briefly (1790–1792) but who now probably is the best known of all the family. Commonly styled simply Lord North, it was he who served as England's Prime Minister during the American Revolution. Finally, third and last to bear both titles (1792–1802) was Lord North's son George Augustus North, the third Earl of Guilford and ninth Baron North of Kirtling. Upon the death of the latter, the barony of North fell in abeyance among his three daughters.

One might be tempted to conclude that because the Perkins manuscript was recently discovered in the hands of a descendant of Francis North, it originally must have been copied out for him by Lady North. In truth, the branching of the family tree makes it possible to suppose that either Francis *or* Charles was the original owner. After the death without issue of Charles's son William, sixth Baron North and second Baron Grey (1678–1734), the barony of Grey became extinct, and Francis, third Baron Guilford, became seventh Baron North. In other words, the titles of North and Guilford, at first held by brothers, came to be held by a single descendant of both in 1734. Then sometime in 1752 or later, after the descendant—Francis, Baron Guilford and Baron North of Kirtling—became Earl of Guilford, the North family manuscript now known as the Perkins manuscript acquired its present bookplate. Familial lines of descent might account for either Charles or Francis as the original owner. It is other evidence that we have seen that tips the balance of probability towards Charles.

Little need be said about the rubric at the beginning of the manuscript. On the leaf now facing the Guilford bookplate there appear the only words in the volume that were placed there by someone other than Lady North: "Works of Dudley Lord North Son of Dudley Lord North." Judged by its appearance, the label is likely to have been inscribed rather casually at a time when the volume had lost whatever initial sentimental importance it may have had for members of the family, yet long before it had begun to gain its present significance as an historical and literary document.

Finally, the means by which the text of North's compositions is conveyed: Lady North's handwriting, both in her correspondence and within the Perkins and Rougham manuscripts, varies from time to time, most noticeably in the size of her characters, but overall it is as her son Roger describes it, "large, plain, and most legible." [36] It resembles the flowing round hand of the period in that individual letters within words are usually connected, and descenders and ascenders are often looped. On the other hand, Lady North's characters tend to be more oval than circular. Speaking generally, one may say that her hand is a version of that which Martin Billingsley described in 1618 as Roman. In *The Pens Excellencie* Billingsley writes of the Roman as "A hand of great account, and of much use in this Realme, especially in the Vniversities: and it is conceived to be the easiest hand that is written with *Pen*, and to be taught in the shortest time: Therefore it is usually taught to women, for as much as they (having not the patience to take any great paines, besides phantasticall and humorsome) must be taught that which they may instantly learne. . . ." [37]

Unfortunately the precise labeling of Lady North's hand is problematic: there is justification for calling it Roman, italic, Italian, or Italianate. [38] Billingsley's most notable pupil, Charles I, whose handwriting is very much like Lady North's, was said by Oldys to have written "a fair open Italian hand, and more correctly perhaps than any Prince we ever had." [39] By any name, however, and certainly as a result of Lady North's "patience" and "paines," the script in the Perkins manuscript of Dudley North's verse and prose is, except in a few passages, beautifully clear. One can believe that it was a labor of love.

36. *Lives*, III, 286. See Plate No. 3.

37. Billingsley, C4r. See also Giles E. Dawson and Laetitia Kennedy-Skipton, *Elizabethan Handwriting 1500–1650* (1966), p. 10.

38. Dr. Dawson (former Curator of Books and Manuscripts, Folger Shakespeare Library) has suggested to me the phrase "calligraphic italic hand" for the Perkins manuscript (15 February 1978).

39. Quoted by Wilfrid Blunt, *Sweet Roman Hand: Five Hundred Years of Italic Cursive Script* (1952), p. 29. Blunt provides a sample of Charles's writing. Stanley Morison refers to Charles's hand as a "delicate version" of "soft Italianate script" (introd. to Ambrose Heal, *The English Writing-Masters and Their Copy-Books 1570–1800* [Hildesheim, 1962], p. xxxvi).

A DISCUSSION OF THE VERSE

It is true, as Roger North says, that the clearest mirror of Sir Dudley North is his writing. *Stylus virum arguit.* It is true also that North's writing, both verse and prose, provides a splendid example of how letters figured in the life of a cultivated seventeenth-century man of affairs, and hence, perhaps, how letters fit generally into the life of the time. North helps to remind us of the fact that all writing is bound to life in multiple ways.

At the same time, and as this implies, we should remember that all writing is related to other writing and that the best writers provide examples of certain things that we may see also—and sometimes more clearly—elsewhere in the literary chain of being. In the sixteenth and seventeenth centuries all cultivated Englishmen were presumed to have some practice in writing, and in order for us to understand better the highest links in the resultant literary chain, it is well that we know something of those links below the point where it is gold. One does no disservice to Sir Dudley North, furthermore, to state frankly that his place is below the gold. He himself was a realistic and modest man, one who described himself as "noe wayes by nature designed to Appollo his lawrell."[1] Part of the pleasure here comes, in fact, from discovering some three hundred years after his death that he belongs in the chain at all.

The discovery that a certain seventeenth-century gentleman wrote verse is less striking, of course, than the discovery of that verse itself—verse which North himself termed his "collection."[2] The writing of poems for such a man was likely to be a leisure-time avocation for his own personal "ease and satisfaction" (the doublet is North's)[3] or a social grace intended for the eyes of a few friends or relations. Sometimes, of course, it could be both. Set down at various times and on separate sheets of paper, the poems might be either tucked away or handed about, but whatever path the poems took, their preservation was chancy, and preservation with a proper attribution quite remarkable.

A professional writer like Michael Drayton nevertheless felt frustrated when confronting the typical habits of literary amateurs such as North. In publishing *Poly-Olbion* (1612), he says, "there is this great disaduantage against me; that it commeth out at this time, when Verses are wholly deduc't

1. "Dedication," herein p. 128.
2. Ibid.
3. Ibid.

to Chambers, and nothing esteem'd . . . but what is kept in Cabinets, and must only passe by Transcription. . . ."[4] The fact is that Puttenham and others had commented many years before on the practice of circulating verses privately.[5] A seventeenth-century English gentleman could even find classical precedent in Horace's "nam satis est equitem mihi plaudere."[6] On the other hand, the situation was to change considerably in North's own lifetime. His father's friend Selden harumphed that "'Tis ridiculous for a lord to print verses; 'tis well enough to make them to please himself, but to make them public is foolish."[7] Yet North's father himself, protesting that he had been "prest . . . to the presse," published his miscellaneous writings at the age of sixty-three.[8] The conflict in attitudes that is reflected here in Drayton's complaint was to some extent succeeded by that reflected in Selden and the elder North, but both were gradually resolved by the same means: publication grew more acceptable. Donne, Greville, Herbert, Crashaw, Carew, Suckling, and Marvell all sidestepped, minimized, or postponed printing their verse (as had Wyatt, Surrey, Sidney, Raleigh, and Oxford in earlier years). But the times were changing. As Miner observes, "it is a curious thing that the publication of books of Cavalier non-dramatic poetry is for the most part an Interregnum and Restoration phenomenon."[9]

In choosing not to print his own verse, then, Sir Dudley North may have been acting either on his thoroughgoing, old-fashioned conservatism or on his awareness that he was not "by nature designed to Appollo his lawrell." Perhaps both came into play. He allowed some of his prose to go to the press, but that may have been because it at least appeared to be less intimate and to spring forth from fact and reason undistorted by fancy. His poems were another matter. He allowed his wife to gather them together and transcribe them, but his son Roger made it clear that they were "designed to remain . . . in Mss, and not to be published. . . ."[10]

*   *   *

When Lady North collected her husband's unpublished writings and converted them from his crabbed, scratchy script to her own fair one, she was more concerned about preserving them legibly than with putting them in any particular order. The poems as they come from her hand are not grouped ac-

4. "To the Generall Reader," A1r; such "Cabinets" as Drayton refers to were usually small, well-furnished private rooms containing some of their owners' most prized possessions.

5. Puttenham, p. 16.

6. *Satires*, I, x, 76 (H. Rushton Fairclough, ed. [Cambridge, Mass., 1929 ed.; 1961 printing], pp. 122–123).

7. *The Table-Talk of John Selden*, ed. S. W. Singer, rev. W. S. W. Anson (n.d.), p. 188.

8. *Forest 45*, p. 62.

9. *The Cavalier Mode from Jonson to Cotton* (Princeton, 1971), p. 86.

10. "A General Preface," St. John's College MS. Bb, James 613, vol. I, p. [41].

cording to subject or kind. Probably they move generally from earlier to later works, but they are not arranged chronologically, either. In fact, they are interspersed with unrelated prose and sometimes even separated by blank leaves. (Any reader of the present volume who wishes to do so may ruminate on their original ordering—or lack of it—by turning to Appendix C.) The result is so confusing that, in order to suggest likenesses and contrasts among the poems, indeed to enable one to think about them clearly, the present edition arranges them according to genre.

Seventeenth-century writers and readers, after all, were used to thinking of a poem not simply as an entity in itself but as an example of a genre. In his *Forest* North's father—as improvisational a writer as the age has to show— suggests that just as "Musick hath its Anthems, Pavens, Fantesies, Galliards, Courantoes, Ayres, Sarabands, Toyes, Cromatiques, &c.," so "Verses have their Hymmes, Tragedies, Satyres, Heroiques, Sonets, Odes, Songs, Epigrams, Distiques, and Strong lines, which are their Cromatiques. . . ."[11] Furthermore, writers and readers of the time were quite aware of the fact that genre to a certain extent implies content. This is a point made by Scaliger himself, perhaps the major Renaissance student of genre.[12] Recognition of the genre of a work provides a clue into the world projected by that work. It calls to mind a set of gentlemen's agreements concerning the rules likely to pertain within it, including what feelings one may be expected to find and to share. Whatever insight one may lose in the present edition, then, because of a reordering on generic lines, one may gain a sense of some literary relationships in North's verse that might otherwise be obscured.

All this is not to deny that the generic path has potholes. One should be aware, for instance, that it is probably impossible to define any genre without leaving its boundaries vague. One man's song will always be another man's sonnet. Furthermore, it is potentially misleading to mix historical and theoretical genres. Among North's works one finds a kind that he calls an "elegy," and in the present edition one also finds a kind that, for lack of a more precise term, is called "meditative." The former label was known to every poet and poetaster of the seventeenth century, whereas the latter, although suggestive enough to many modern readers, might not have occurred to North himself. In fact, the adjectival "meditative" is a gesture away from genre in the direction of mode: part of the usefulness of the word "meditative" is that it may be brought to bear on poems of various genres.

Critical problems relating to genre are endless and subtle, but one additional warning must suffice at this point, namely that the value of any attempt at generic placement is limited to the extent that whatever is placed before us tends to obscure what *might* have been placed there. The generic ordering

11. *Forest 45*, p. 3.
12. Rosalie L. Colie cites Scaliger and discusses the point in *The Resources of Kind: Genre-Theory in the Renaissance*, ed. Barbara K. Lewalski (Berkeley, Calif., 1973), p. 28.

offered in the present volume may provide the reader with certain perspectives, therefore, and to those who are familiar with the literature of the period it may suggest certain characteristics relating to voice and projected audience. One should realize, though, that the generic decisions made here are not the only ones possible.

*   *   *

Coming first among North's poems, according to the present ordering, are two secular debates. One of these apparently relates to North's early military career, the other to his abiding interest in music and verse. Subject matter aside, both obviously are in some sense a result of the emphasis on logical debate in Renaissance education. In fact both belong to a tradition of verse that sprang from some of the same ancestors as the medieval *débat* and resulted in the seventeenth century in such qualitatively disparate poems as Andrew Marvell's debate between body and soul and Edward Thimelby's between a lady's forehead and cheeks.[13] Although only two North poems are grouped here as debates, it should be noted that they serve to introduce a strategy that is also operative elsewhere in his work, most noticeably in the pastoral poems and certain of the devotional verses. North considered himself to be better endowed with reason than fancy, and although this may not augur well for his poetic flights, it does help us to understand the nature of his verse. By presenting a subject dialectically, as he does especially clearly in the second of these two opening poems, he could not only convey the tension between opposing sides (two is the number of discord), but he could also conclude with some sort of resolution, with a voice of justice or a chorus of concord. Beyond the fact that such structuring has both aesthetic appeal and centuries of schoolroom antecedents, it is thoroughly characteristic of North. A thoughtful traditionalist, he might be said to have devoted a lifetime to working for stability, order, and concord.

Being a man of his time, North naturally wrote some poems that he called "sonnets" (Nos. 3–21). The word then generally referred to short poems of various lengths and forms on the subject of love, as Ben Jonson's Kitely implies in part when he dubs the lovesick versifier Matthew "Songs and Sonnets."[14] Through the years such poems had come to be thickly encrusted with conventions. Even before North's father had been born, George Turberville was protesting that in his work, "although my minde were free, / Yet must I

13. Thimelby's poem may be read in Edmund Blunden and Bernard Mellor, eds., *Wayside Poems of the Seventeenth Century* (Hong Kong, 1963), pp. 73–81.

14. *Every Man in His Humour*, IV.iii.17. Sometimes the meaning of "sonnet" was even more broad. Gascoigne complained about those who held "that all Poemes (being short) may be called Sonets, as in deede it is a diminutiue worde deriued of *Sonare*. . ." (*The Posies of George Gascoigne Esquire* [1575], Uiv).

seeme love wounded eke to be." [15] And North's father himself, who held "love to be the most worthy object of the best and most generous dispositions," nonetheless warned a reader of his poems to "*think them not so Passionate as they appear; for I never was, or could be a whyning or Dolorous Lover; such Pieces were rather variations of Tuning then Humour.*" [16] One result is that it is extremely difficult now to distinguish between the conventional and the personal in Renaissance love poetry. It is only common sense to recognize that a writer, without adhering to facts, might sometimes tap his own experience, but rhetorical convention could be relied on as a safeguard against indecorous intimacy. Simultaneously, rhetoric could provide some genuine interest of its own. It is therefore perfectly understandable that Sir Dudley North in the dedication of his poems to his wife says frankly that many of his lighter efforts "were levelled at obiects of Love, not reall, but imaginary." [17] Immediately thereafter and much more strikingly, however, he observes that "some of them are not without a reall obiect," thus allowing Lady North to think that sometimes she was "the person intended."

Since North's amatory poems are the most witty, ingenious, and carefully polished in his canon, one may suppose that he chose to avail himself of his most careful workmanship in them in order to demonstrate his particular concern and interest. It is true, of course, that if one sets professional poets aside, writing love poetry was something of a game of skill for sophisticates. On the other hand, if it seems now that that game could have appealed only to the brain, not the pulse, part of the reason may be that we are not the players. Even in some of these poems where style itself seems to be the real subject, the rhetorical game may not be the only one in progress. In any case, one finds North sprinkling his sonnets generously with fires and suns, which had been counters used by love poets ever since Petrarch and, before Petrarch, by the Provençal and Latin poets. One finds here such conventions as the cool mistress, the lady sleeping, and the lady playing on an instrument. Quite understandably it is usual nowadays to observe that love poetry comprised of such elements had badly staled by the latter years of the sixteenth century, but that did not stop men such as North from writing it well into the seventeenth. Presumably they realized perfectly well what they were doing. The innovative poems of Donne gained their initial impact partly from the fact that they were playing off conventions which, far from being dead, were by some men still practiced.

Et in Arcadia erat. Changing his fictive vehicle from Petrarchan to pastoral enabled North to say some different things about love. Never mind that North's was not the pastoral of damasked meadows and lowing herds, of

15. Quoted and discussed by Douglas L. Peterson, *The English Lyric from Wyatt to Donne: A History of the Plain and Eloquent Styles* (Princeton, 1967), pp. 122–125.

16. *Forest 45*, p. 7 and sig. A1*v*.

17. "Dedication," p. 128.

purling streams and shaded glens, that it was, in fact, almost bare of bucolic trappings. His two eclogues (Nos. 22, 23) come sufficiently late in the pastoral tradition that such things could be dropped, either assumed or set aside in favor of what seemed more important. Earl Miner has toyed with the term "semi-pastoral" for such works.[18] What North did not find expendable were the dialogue form, the speakers with classical names, and the focus on the dialectic of love. There is even a reminder here that pastoral traditions involved singing, a matter which North himself, with his interest in music, is likely to have considered important. More important to us, perhaps, is the problem of whether we are meant to perceive something beneath the conventional surface of the verse. What more may there be here than the melancholy realization that even Arcady is darkened by inconstancy and death? The evidence is gone that would enable one to say, but both of North's eclogues appear to move upwards from human love towards love of a higher sort. Of course, the presentation of a range in kinds of love is itself another pastoral tradition, a basic matter in, for instance, Spenser's *Shepheardes Calender* (1579) and Fletcher's *Faithful Shepherdess* (ca. 1609). From Petrarch's time onward, there are models from both literature and life.

A consideration of North's satirical writing (Nos. 24, 25) takes us back again to early models. Classical satires had long been taught to schoolboys in England, and by North's time there were many native English satires as well. The poem called "1636," the later of North's two works categorized here as satires, is a clear-cut version of formal verse satire, differing from others of its kind mainly in that it is duodecasyllabic rather than decasyllabic. The earlier of the two poems, "1627," a bitter little piece intended to "dispraise" an individual, might be considered either a satire or a satirical epigram.[19] Because it is unlike North's other epigrams, however, "1627" is perhaps best placed with "1636." Each poem conveys indignation, contempt, and anger. Each implies moral concern. Each is a monologue which to some degree suggests spoken discourse. Moreover, each is written in reaction to a larger, more public world than one generally finds in North's verse. Although the target of "1627" (indeed, its ostensible listener) is a particular man, and that of "1636" is various segments of society, each poem is designed to decry a dreadful falling off in English affairs. Each is the exasperated cry of a conservative as he sees important things in his world going wrong. To be sure, one probably should suggest that such poems give an aesthetic imitation of anger and moral concern rather than an expression of either, but one cuts North off from his various personae only with some loss of comprehension. There was every reason for him to be exasperated by what he saw happening to time-honored

18. Miner, p. 233.
19. William Camden describes epigrams as "short and sweete Poems, framed to praise or dispraise. . ." (*Remaines, Concerning Britaine* [1614; 1st pub. 1605], p. 325).

traditions and values, both during the sway of the Duke of Buckingham ("1627") and during the dangerous calm before the Civil War ("1636").

The term "elegy" had considerable flexibility both in classical and Renaissance times, but from very early and perhaps even in the beginning it referred to a lament for the dead. In North's day the rhetorical treatises were full of precepts on the tone, scope, outline, and *topoi* proper to such verse. Students everywhere were taught to write them—and one result is that North's earliest datable work is a poem from his Cambridge days on the death of Queen Anne.[20] Many a similar poem served its purpose simply by fluttering for a while on a swathe of black funeral cloth,[21] where it illustrated more clearly than verse in any other genre the point that Rosemond Tuve was making when she suggested that the ultimate critical question of the time was not "What does the poem say?" or "How is it said?" but "What is the poem for?"[22] Beyond making a point by its very existence, however (as a lover's sonnet might sometimes do), a funeral elegy was supposed to attend to such things as praising the departed, lamenting the death, and consoling the survivors.

North uses the term "elegy" for three of his five surviving poems on specific deaths (Nos. 27–31). The range of subject in these five is provocative: a queen, a friend or two (one of the two friends may be a young relation), a sister-in-law, and his father. Viewing such a list, which stretches over nearly a half century (1619–1667), one might wonder if North composed other elegies which have not survived, elegies for a sister we know that he lost, for an infant son or daughter, or for his favorite uncle. Furthermore, one might wonder whether there were not only others but also other kinds of poems that never came Lady North's way. Probably North wrote some poems that have not survived.

Even a cursory reading of the five elegies that we have shows North taking up various conventions—for example, the need for complaint, the disparagement of all that is temporal in light of all that is permanent, and the praise of virtue, beauty, and family. Paradoxically, although an elegy was in part intended to vent personal grief, such conventions could end by masking both the characteristics of the deceased and the feelings of the poet. As with the emotion in North's sonnets or satires, then, it is impossible to be sure what he may have felt in writing any of his elegies. Still, there are notable differences among them. The poem on the Queen is a cool but proficient exercise in eulogy, whereas the poem "To my deerest freind deceased" is a rougher work with an apparently genuine note of urgency, a sense of real bereavement. Be-

20. Herein, No. 27.
21. As Thomas Shipman wrote, verse was "The common *Hatchment* . . . of every Herse" (from "The Mourner. 1659," *Carolina: or, Loyal Poems* [1683], p. 32).
22. Tuve, *Elizabethan and Metaphysical Imagery: Renaissance Poetic and Twentieth-century Critics* (Chicago, 1965; 1st ed., 1947), p. 110.

cause so much may now be realized about the relationship between North and his father, however, the most provocative of the group is the poem on the third Lord North. With characteristically dutiful effort, Sir Dudley, himself approaching sixty-five and no longer in good health, took up his pen to do the best that he could in a time of stress. After a few lines the words would not come. Even when his thoughts could not be aligned, though, there was one last literary convention available to him. As Robert Fletcher said in breaking off a poem on the death of a friend, "Angels alone can speak the rest." [23] Sir Dudley broke off and vowed never to write again.

The final groups of North's poems as arranged for this edition might be thought to adumbrate his later progress into moral and religious realms. As he himself says in his dedication, his lighter works were written when his "Muse was in her nonage," and he turned to "more serious" subjects later. [24] Furthermore, the movement from a world of artifice where Love is god to a world of belief where God is love is surely convincing both in biographical and broader human terms. Nonetheless, one should not forget that most of North's poems are undatable and that North apparently was a rather serious fellow all of his life. Probably a wary reader should be ready to glimpse certain gleams of youth here and there even in North's epigrammatic, divine, and meditative verse.

The trouble with the term "epigram" is that it is so broad. To get a hold on what an epigram is, one may do worse than recall that in Greek it refers to words inscribed on something, for that at least keeps to the fore the idea of conciseness. Because of the influence of Martial's work, used as a text in the schools, epigrams also frequently tended to be thought of as poems "ending in a witty or ingenious turn of thought" [25]—a definition which has its use, if only insofar as one is able to ignore many poems, including Roman and Greek epigrams, even some by Martial, which it does not fit. A more subtle observation is that epigrams work with pairs and contrasts, and sometimes with a statement of some sort followed by a comment or question, or a question followed by an answer. On the other hand, even though Renaissance theorists appear to have regarded comparison and contrast as basic to the form, "epigram" remains a baggy generic term.

Turning from definitions to the writings themselves, one finds that in Tudor times a good many English epigram-writers merely stated a sententious truth concisely. Their seventeenth-century successors more frequently tended to write poems that were imitative of Martial, but they also continued to turn out verses of the short, sententious variety. North's own tendency was towards the sententious, although, as we have seen, his bitter "1627" may be

23. Reprinted in Norman Ault, ed., *Seventeenth Century Lyrics* (2nd ed., New York, 1950), p. 311.
24. "Dedication," p. 128.
25. *OED*, III, 241.

regarded as an epigram of dispraise. One might recall also that certain pithy
memorial poems (like Jonson's on his son and daughter) may be considered
epigrams of praise; thus North's poem on the death of Queen Anne may be
viewed as epigrammatic. Scaliger speaks of the riddle as yet another form of
epigram;[26] hence one might place North's "Riddle" (No. 37) under the same
generic heading. Moreover, as Bradner points out, "In the religious field the
sacred epigram, based upon the Bible or the feasts and fasts of the Christian
year[,] acquired a great popularity"[27]—a point one might illustrate by turning to the religious poems of Sir Dudley North.

It may be that North's neatest epigrammatic wit occurs in his elegy on the
Queen, and his sharpest epigrammatic stings in "1627," but beyond these
North also gives us a little clutch of short, sententious poems—called epigrams here (Nos. 32–36)—in which it is possible to discern, as we are sometimes advised to do, a rhetorical contrast between "setup" and conclusion.
One such poem ends with "The Man *thus* born. . . ," another with "*Soe* Lyfe
preserves. . . ," and another with "*Then* court not Toyes. . . ."[28] Obviously
such patterning might appeal to a man who sometimes allowed himself to
think at least comparatively well of his reasoning ability. Within this group of
poems, furthermore, aside from the rather boyish first one, North gives us
contrast of another sort. As is thoroughly characteristic of the man, his faith,
and his time, he sets about diminishing this world in relation to the next.

Most of North's specifically religious poems (Nos. 38–45) relate to the
world of the Bible. In fact, most prove to be contributions to that pool of
scriptural translation and paraphrase which by the middle of the seventeenth
century may fairly be said to have become enormous. Composing a paraphrase or a brief poem on the subject of a particular biblical passage enabled
writers to study that passage closely, to pay it respect, and at the same time to
engage in a pleasurable form of devotion. All of this sounds very much like
Sir Dudley North. Sometimes the poems that resulted must have fulfilled
their purposes by the time they had been set down. One can imagine North,
for instance, retiring to his closet at Kirtling on some particular Whitsunday
in order to write his poem called "Pentecost," and then tucking it away somewhere. On the other hand, some such poems undoubtedly were intended by
their writers to be read by others for *their* edification and, God willing, their
delight. Herein lies a problem inherent in devotional writing: the writer may
be tempted to lose sight of what is most important in his work. By indulging
in what George Herbert speaks of as "Curling with metaphors a plain intention,"[29] he may become guilty of misdevotion. Joseph Caryl suggests that in

26. Julius Caesar Scaliger, *Poetices Libri Septem* (Geneva, 1561), p. 54.
27. Leicester Bradner, *Musae Anglicanae: A History of Anglo-Latin Poetry 1500–1925* (New York, 1940), p. 78.
28. Herein, Nos. 32, 33, 35; emphasis added.
29. "Jordan (II)," l. 5 (*The Works of George Herbert*, ed. F. E. Hutchinson [Oxford, 1964; 1st pub. 1941], p. 102).

dealing with sacred texts the aim should be to "polish and garnish, embroider and bedeck the words of God, not with vain ostentation or pedantic pomp of words, but with sobriety and holy gravity."[30] In North's religious poems it is decorous and appropriate (though perhaps it is a mixed blessing overall) that his characteristic instincts kept him in the straight and narrow paths of sobriety and gravity.

For the matter of his religious verse North turned twice (that is, twice that we know of) to poetic passages in the Old Testament. Once he chose to recast the famed story of Deborah, which contains what is probably the oldest lyric in the Bible, and once he tried his hand at a passage from Solomon's Song of Songs. Both of these poems appear to be examples not merely of religious exercises but also of the dual technique whereby one wrote of scriptural events in such a way as to comment parabolically on contemporary life.[31] On at least four other occasions North turned to the New Testament for subjects, choosing four of its most significant events, the Annunciation, the Passion, the Ascension, and Pentecost. In a Latin poem called "Hymnus sacer" he cast his thoughts more broadly, blending various scriptural elements from both the Old Testament and the New. Opening with words borrowed from the Psalms, he went on to produce a work that is itself a little psalm of praise. And in "Antiphona" he took up the idea of relating religion to music. In fact it turns out that over half of North's divine poems rely upon music in one way or another. Religion and music were both important to him. Perhaps with resident musicians at Kirtling he had the pleasure—certainly his father had enjoyed it—of hearing some of his own divine verses sung.

Writing meditative verse was another widespread form of mental exercise with a spiritual goal. Although it, too, was frequently inspired by scriptural passages, it reached beyond scrutiny of the Bible to scrutiny of God's Book of Creatures, including that most intricate of all creatures, oneself. The practice of meditating—as distinguished from writing meditative verse—was a form of devotion that had been authorized by scriptural example and then endlessly shaped and reshaped by years of Roman Catholic and, subsequently, Protestant practices. Drawing on one's memory and understanding, a meditation (and hence meditative verse) was intended to point above and beyond mere reason. As Bishop Joseph Hall put it, "A man is a man by his vnderstanding part"—for only man among the creatures is so gifted—"but he is a Christian by his will and affections."[32] Meditation, Hall writes, although "It begins in the braine, descends to the heart; Begins on earth, ascends to heauen; Not suddenly, but by certain staires & degrees, til we come to the highest."[33] At least so far as seventeenth-century English views on the subject

---

30. Quoted by Lawrence A. Sasek, *The Literary Temper of the English Puritans* (Baton Rouge, La., 1961), p. 56.
31. See annotations, below.
32. *The Arte of Divine Meditation* (1606), p. 150.
33. *Arte*, p. 85.

were concerned, virtually any subject might be suitable for meditating so long as it served to intensify man's awareness of God and to rekindle his motives for amending his life. After a man's heart was stirred (or stirred again, if need be, or thawed or ignited or properly broken), he had a chance to become a Christian worthy of the name.

The five North poems that are here called meditative (Nos. 46–50) provide an interesting range of types.[34] The first two are similar in that each explores a common and, as it happens, contrasting *topos* of the period, the city and the garden. Both depict a microcosm where fallen man resides, and both point to that state whence man fell. North's decision here to write about generalized man gives both of these poems a reserved, objective quality. These are sober meditative efforts on what oft was thought. In the final three poems, however, North takes a more intimate approach, writing not merely about mankind but about a man. If it is unsafe to say that in these final three poems, all cast in the first person, one has three variations on the authentic voice of North himself, one must nevertheless recognize that North has been tumbling up and down in his mind some of the facts and forces in his life. Commonplaces are still present, naturally, but here they are accoutrements rather than the basic frame for the verse. In the first of these final three poems, the speaker meditates on certain efforts he has made to rid himself of sin. In the second, the speaker wrestles with the fact that he has never felt a sense of freedom. In the third and last, the speaker takes up the topic of illness. Physical illness as a route to spiritual health is one of the subjects treated in manuals of devotion of the day, and the speaker turns to it because he himself has just suffered from an ailment that came close to killing him. Finally, in each of these three poems, as in the first two, there is an appropriate upward surging at the close (at both the beginning *and* close in the last poem) which serves to direct our attention to an eternal realm above the temporal one.

Within North's meditative poems one hears a range of voices that suggests in small something about the range of voices in the overall collection. Though one may grant with Father Ong that "Masks are inevitable in all human communication,"[35] one still can see, through an attempt to align North's life and verse, that there is an intriguingly inconstant distance between the poet and his masks. The purposes for assuming the mask of a Petrarchan lover are not the same as those for assuming the mask of an outraged satirist, and yet these two may both be closer to each other than either is to the mask that North creates to express gratitude to God for an escape from a real illness. The distance between North's life and his verse proves to be a constantly varying, unpredictable, and inevitably mysterious factor.

34. I have analyzed this group of works in "Mode and Voice in 17th-Century Meditative Verse: A Discussion of Five Newly Discovered Poems by Dudley North" in *Medieval and Renaissance Studies*, No. 9, Proceedings of the Southeastern Institute of Medieval and Renaissance Studies, ed. Frank Tirro (Durham, N.C., 1982), pp. 55–86.

35. Walter J. Ong, "The Writer's Audience Is Always a Fiction," *PMLA*, XC (1975), 20.

*   *   *

After considering North's individual poems and the kinds of clusters they comprise, one is better able to generalize about them, as well as to suggest where North fits among writers of his time. To begin with, "of his time" is a problematic phrase because he began to write in the days of James I and lived to see James's grandson Charles reign for some seventeen years. His verse must be viewed against a changing backdrop. Furthermore, he himself observes that his verse moved generally from "light and slight" to "more serious." What he wishes to acknowledge in these phrases, apparently, is that with the passage of the years his poetic center of gravity shifted from secular towards sacred love. As time passed, moreover, he tended to become less concerned with how he was to say something. For example, the heroi-mythical Renaissance paean to young Verus comes early, and the plain-talking poem that tells of his own kidney stones comes late. Looking only at these two works, one might be tempted to hypothesize that North somehow wrote his way out of one age into another (as Marvell did in the same century, and Yeats in ours). North's case, however, as we shall see, is simpler than that.

Although art of any period conveys a stylized version of reality, North's constant recourse to commonplaces such as the ship at sea and the bird in the cage reminds us quite strikingly of the great extent to which Renaissance writers generally depended on imitation. In North's verse one may search in vain for such sparks as genius can impart, but at least North usually demonstrates a sober competence in deploying his time-tested images. The fact that he continued to rely so heavily on them, moreover, in so much of his verse, while others about him were drawn into the magnetic field of the metaphysicals or toward the singing school of the cavaliers, makes him seem an essentially old-fashioned writer, standing in literature, as in life, more for the old than the new.

Had he ever had to choose between them, North almost certainly would have sacrificed image to meaning. It is not simply that he himself considered reason his best literary tool. As Rosemond Tuve has explained, "the Elizabethan thought of the poet's function as close to that of any other thinker —philosophers, preachers, and orators included."[36] Samuel Daniel in his *Defence of Ryme* (1603) had no doubt that "it is matter that satisfies the iudiciall,"[37] and North's own father hoped to "write clearly and strongly, rather then finely and artificially."[38] In fact, along with Sir Philip Sidney, William Camden, Ben Jonson, and others, he held that "Verses are then good, when turned to prose they hold a faire and currant sense. . . ."[39] The more interesting point, however, is not that few voices during the century would

36. Tuve, p. 190.
37. Daniel, *Defence*, ed. G. B. Harrison (1925), p. 13.
38. *Forest 45*, p. 6.   39. Ibid.

have cried up the self-sufficiency of fancy's warbled woodnotes but that thought, reason, and logic manifested themselves in such varied ways. As far as North *père* was concerned, mental gymnastics of the sort that Donne typically executed were too fantastic, whatever their intellectual models. Meanwhile some men were seeking to distill and compress their thoughts into couplets worthy of the best Roman models. For various reasons, North's own work inclines rather more toward neo-classical than metaphysical, and yet it differs from both. Tending towards the sententious and the commonsensical, it typically moves along under no great pressure, hovering only slightly above prose.

Great or small, a poet must convey his images and thoughts through a grid of diction and meter. One should not overlook the fact that Sir Dudley North, whose work embraces both secular and sacred and seems to move generally from the first toward the second, used the Janus-faced word "love" more frequently than any other noun.[40] (Not surprisingly, "love" is also among the words used most frequently by some of the other poets of the century.[41]) North's other favorite nouns include "God" (and "gods"), "soul," "mind," "life," "power," "glory," "time," "death," "fire," "light," and "heart."[42] These are noteworthy as the counters with which his mind was most comfortable. It turns out that North is more a poet of nouns, especially abstract nouns, than of adjectives or verbs (hence it is, perhaps, that his verse conveys less a sense of movement or color than of thoughtful abstraction) and that when his work is compared with that of a wide range of his contemporaries, his favorite nouns include some seventy percent of the nouns most frequently used by others. North's favorite adjectives are fewer than his favorite nouns, and his favorite verbs fewer still. Among adjectives, he turns most often to "fair" (as did a good many other poets, including writers so diverse as Sandys, Waller, Carew, Crashaw, and Cowley).[43] Frequently also he turns to "blest," "great," "true," and "happy." Again the quality of his choices is suggestive: not only do these words seem to point more towards certain realms than others but also, aside from "fair," they have little or nothing to do with the concrete and the sensuous. North relies least of all on his verbs.

40. Dale B. J. Randall and Robert J. Parsons, "A Concordance to the Poetry of Dudley North, Third Baron North, and Dudley North, Fourth Baron North," computer print-out (Cambridge, 1979).

41. Josephine Miles, *The Primary Language of Poetry in the 1640's* (Berkeley, Calif., 1948), p. 4. Miles's samples are drawn from the first one thousand lines of each poet she analyzes; North's English verse totals a reasonably comparable 1,156 lines.

42. Given here in order of frequency. Of North's ten most favored nouns, four ("love," "god," "soul," and "time") occur on Miles's list of the ten nouns used most frequently in verse of the 1640s (pp. 4, 31). The next most frequent nouns in North are "light," "heart," "power," "freedom," "earth," "man," and "grace"; "heart," "earth," and "man" are also on Miles's list of ten most frequent nouns.

43. Josephine Miles and Hanan C. Selvin, "A Factor Analysis of the Vocabulary of Poetry in the Seventeenth Century," in Jacob Leed, ed., *The Computer & Literary Style* (Kent, Ohio, 1966), pp. 117–118.

Aside from some forms that commonly are omitted from concordance tabulation, his most frequent verbs are "make," "find," "see," "die," and a most unusual but idiosyncratically suggestive "prove."[44] Even without diving deeply into the topic, one can perceive that although North's range of diction is, naturally, unique, his word choices also assure in some interesting ways that he will always be heard to have a period voice that subsumes all of his personal ones.[45]

A study of North's metrical practices soon brings to the fore his willingness to experiment—paralleling, one might think, his willingness to experiment with genre. Despite the fact that his canon is not large, North's attempts include iambic dimeter, trimeter, tetrameter, pentameter, and hexameter, and trochaic tetrameter. On the other hand, since it had long been obvious that English falls readily into iambic feet, it comes as no surprise that North's verse is predominantly iambic. His longest poem of all ("A Satyre. 1636") is composed in iambic hexameter, but most frequently he turns to pentameter, and usually he casts it in couplets. All of his English poems take advantage of what Samuel Daniel called this "most excellent instrument" of rhyme.[46] Heroic couplets, of course, were to be the staple for most poets of the Restoration, so one could suppose that North's rather plain, level-headed lines might sometimes have a forward-looking quality. If it is there at all, however, it is minimal, and probably for the simple reason that he found it most natural to continue in the poetic course he had long since begun. Many years before Dryden came along, before Waller and Denham, Ben Jonson had turned to couplets, John Donne had leaned on them more heavily than on any other measure, and young Sir Dudley North had experimented with them. No matter what first moved North to take them up (some held them to be the nearest approach in English to Latin's elegiac distich), the closed or end-stopped couplets that he most frequently wrote were well suited to his temperament. A dependably regular form, they repeatedly gave him the opportunity to create a momentary bit of stability and order, the unified nature of which was enhanced by the iterated chime of rhyme. Furthermore, having created a small unit of order, he could move on, repeat the trick with variations, and thereby suggest such movement as pleased him. Sometimes he thought a bit about the possibilities of supracouplet patterns—most simply, for instance, when couplet answered couplet. And, of course, there was no need for absolutely every couplet to be end-stopped; variations always were possible, especially in a stichic context. All in all, the iambic pentameter couplet was an ideal form for North, one that allowed him to present thoughtful parallels and antitheses, and to work towards solution and concord.

44. The first three of these are reported by Miles as among the eleven most used verbs in verse of the 1640s (*Primary Language*, pp. 4, 31).

45. Cf. Fritz Martini, "Personal Style and Period Style: Perspectives on a Theme of Literary Research," trans. Leila Vennewitz, in *Patterns of Literary Style*, Yearbook of Comparative Criticism, III, ed. Joseph Strelka (University Park, Pa., 1971), 90–115.

46. Daniel, *Defence*, p. 16.

Although it soon will be four centuries since North's birth, the echoing years have sent down to us but two comments on his verse. The first is the effusion of a dutiful son. In January 1667, John North, whose excited approach suggests that he had never before read through his father's poems, declared them

> to bee such as may pass under the most critical eye & censorious Judgement[,] falling soe smooth from off the Toung, entertaining the mind with soe strong sence & fancy, included in most proper words, not stuff'd with farr-fetch'd Allegories & those long continued for want of matter, nor with pityfull Allusion's which can be ascribed to nothing but chance;—to say noe more my nigh relation suffers mee not to giue so high a comendation of them . . . as I am confident I shall receiue from others to whom I comunicate them.[47]

As interesting here as John's sense of discovery is the fact that he praises his father's writing in terms of his own quite contemporary views. Born in 1645, John was now twenty-one. The time for "smoothness" in verse had come round again. Once again allusions and diction were to be deployed with decorous care, no longer imported from too great a distance at too great a cost. Without doubt John's praise is excessive, but it also provides some food for thought.

Less may be said for the second surviving comment on North's verse. In the third quarter of the nineteenth century, among some manuscripts in private hands, William Carew Hazlitt turned up a copy of North's elegy on the death of his father. Hazlitt for some reason decided to print the poem but then, unfortunately, proceeded to cast more shadow than light when he called it "satirical."[48] Whatever normally acceptable definition one chooses to give the word "satirical," it does not suit the facts of the poem, and one is left to wonder if perhaps a weak, conventional elegy struck Hazlitt as so very weak and conventional as to be a deliberate mockery of its kind. In any case, Hazlitt's criticism proves to be weaker and more enigmatic than the poem itself.

Sir Dudley North's own comments on other English poets are few and brief. In widely scattered places he speaks of three, all of an earlier time: Sidney, Spenser, and his father. As he composed the preface to his prose *Narrative of Some Passages in or Relating to the Long Parliament* (1670), North wanted to make a gracious observation about an author's hopes, and his mind reached back across the years to Sidney's *Astrophil and Stella*. A friend is spo-

---

47. Bodl. MS. North c.10, p. 17.

48. *Inedited Poetical Miscellanies*, priv. circ., 50 copies (1870), n.p. One cannot be sure how Hazlitt came across the poem, but from a reference in his edition of *The Complete Poems of George Gascoigne*, I (1869), vi, it is clear that he knew of some North papers in the Corser collection. Jean M. Ayton (Archivist, Central Library, Manchester) kindly informs me that this collection was the property of the Rev. Thomas Corser (d. 1876), sometime rector of Stand, near Manchester.

ken of in the latter as having justly criticized the writing of Astrophil, who thereupon acknowledges that his gentle birth calls for nobler desires, lest "that friendly foe, / Great expectation, weare a traine of shame."[49] Had the passage been fixed in North's mind years before, or had he recently turned back to Sidney? One can be sure only that in his old age, his own "harvest time" not far off, the creator of Serena remembered the creator of Stella. North refers to his other Elizabethan poet as "the most ingenious Poet *Spencer*."[50] Here we have a little more to go on. What North has in mind particularly is Spenser's description of Fair Alma's house (where Concoction is the cook, Digestion the kitchen clerk, etc.), which now appears to be one of the most mechanically allegorical passages in all of Spenser's work.[51] When he made this allusion toward the end of his life, however, writing a six-and-a-half-page postscript to his *Observations and Advices Oeconomical*, North was launched into a little allegory of his own, and the reason Spenser came to mind is obvious as soon as one knows North's own basic schema: "According to this Hypothesis, the Body is to be understood as the House, and *Psyche* (or the Soul) as absolute Mistris of it, which I suppose will not be improper, since the Body is called her Mansion, and the faculties of the Soul, and the organical parts of the Body, may be conceived and treated of as Servants."[52] North could have turned to allegorists more recent than Spenser, but it may be that the models he held most firmly in mind were those he first knew in youth.

North's father, with whom he was associated so closely, so long, and in so many ways, is the third and most recent poet to whom North refers, and probably the single writer to whom he was most indebted. Indeed, the third and fourth Lords North provide a striking pattern of father-and-son poetics. Of the two men, the elder North had the livelier wit, the quicker fancy, the truer *sprezzatura*. More than this, he was a better poet than has been recognized, a personal friend of (and in some ways a poetic parallel of) "Natural, easy Suckling."[53] On the other hand, for all the differences between father and son—the volatile courtier and the contemplative countryman—it is in the elder North's writing that one finds the most and the most interesting parallels for the images and ideas in the younger North's verse. Aside from an oblique reference to Virgil, the elder North is the only poet mentioned in the verse of the younger. In fact, one particular poem by the elder North is the sole subject of a poem by the younger. All things considered, it probably was

49. No. 21, ll. 7–8 (*The Poems of Sir Philip Sidney*, ed. William A. Ringler, Jr. [Oxford, 1962], p. 175).

50. *Light*, p. 131.

51. *Faerie Queene*, Bk. II, canto ix, esp. stanza 31 (*Works*, II, ed. Edwin Greenlaw et al. [Baltimore, 1933], esp. p. 117).

52. *Light*, p. 129.

53. The phrase is from Congreve's Millamant (*The Way of the World*, ed. Brian Gibbons [1971], p. 75: IV.i.87). It is striking that the elder North had long before referred to his own "easie and naturall nakednesse" of style (*Forest 45*, p. 4).

more than court holy water that Sir Dudley sprinkled at his father's shrine.[54]

A sympathetic reader of Sir Dudley's verse soon realizes that he had a variety of styles suitable to a variety of genres and subjects, and yet, taken as a whole, his writing tends to be thoughtful, earnest, responsible, sedate, conservative, moral, and devout. It is sometimes ingenious, sometimes even witty, but never merry; North was not one of those gentlemen who invite a reader to tipple verse. Sometimes his poems sound a lyric note, but seldom and as if from some distant room. Much more insistent and important are passages of morality and devotion, as befits a liberal Anglican gentleman who took his Christian duties seriously. Of all North's themes, two stand out as most thoroughly diffused throughout his *oeuvre*: the claims of this world versus the claims of the next, and liberty versus enthrallment. And passing back and forth, in and out of both of these is the fluid subject of love, profane and sacred, human and divine. Such subjects led other men to record glimpses of terrible depths or dazzling heights, but North's verse virtually always embodies and conveys respect for measure, authority, decorum, order, tradition, reason, and moderation—all of which, according to John North's perception, appeared to put his sixty-five-year-old father pretty much in step with the neo-classical times. As suggested here previously, however, the fact probably is that North's time simply had come round again.[55]

In fairness to North perhaps one should conclude by recalling that his poems were not written to be published. There are all too many prefaces in which a writer tells blushingly of being forced by friends to submit to the press, but here is a handful of poems that show what some unpruned private verse of the day really was like. Perhaps it is true, as Ruttkowski has argued,[56] that no literary work is totally without signs of a potential reader. On the other hand, our recollection that ninety-six percent of North's surviving poems never saw print in the seventeenth century should heighten our awareness of the fundamental reserve in most of them.[57] The demands of decorum,

54. Doubtless Sir Dudley knew other men who wrote verse, such as those who joined in mourning Anne, Lady Rich, but there is no evidence that he was ever part of any versifying circle.

55. Paul J. Korshin has observed that "The concept which seems most central to the poets of the middle and later seventeenth century is that of concord. The quest for stability in political and social life actuated the nation throughout the period . . . and, in the arts, an analogous search for orderly methods of creativity and aesthetic procedure was constantly under way" (*From Concord to Dissent: Major Themes in English Poetic Theory 1640–1700* [Menston, Yorkshire, 1973], p. 3). The point is too complex to be demonstrated here, but it is an interesting phenomenon that the regularity and avoidance of excess that in some sense constituted Dryden's goals at the end of the seventeenth century were similar to the goals of Ben Jonson at the century's beginning and also to the goals of certain Tudor writers.

56. Wolfgang Victor Ruttkowski, cited in discussion by Paul Hernadi, *Beyond Genre: New Directions in Literary Classification* (Ithaca, N.Y., 1972), p. 36.

57. Unpublished in North's own lifetime, ninety-eight percent (only No. 27, the elegy on Queen Anne, appeared before 1677); left unpublished after Hazlitt's 1870 volume, ninety-four percent.

position, and reserve were never far from North's mind, even when he mused in the privacy of his closet.

Bringing North's poems into the open, an act which North himself eschewed, ought not be construed as an effort to make him appear a better writer than he was. Despite the interest now attached to various kinds of documents so old as these poems, North was and will remain a minor writer, a man whose natural element was prose and whose poems seldom ascend above competence. Some years ago, when Ruth Wallerstein wished to share some things she had discovered about Martin Lluelyn (whose works, like North's, pose no threat to the reputations of Shakespeare or Milton), she explained her belief that such labors were worthwhile

> because, as may often be the case with a minor poet, in his spirit and his forms he defines the general poetic temper and poetic "school" of his day in a fashion impossible to the strong individual genius of a greater poet. With all the variety of the poetry of the seventeenth century, we are apt to forget how strong was the seventeenth-century *ars poetica*, the tradition, the definition of modes achieved by them, until such a poet as Lluelyn, so slight yet so little fumbling, and so varied, comes to make clear our scattered impressions.[58]

Something similar may be said for North. His poetic achievement, like Lluelyn's, is slight, but we surely will learn more by regarding it as in some sense a microcosm of seventeenth-century verse than as something unworthy of consideration because we have read better.

We may learn something also by regarding North's verse in the light of his life. Convention made it possible for North—indeed, for any seventeenth-century writer—to sidestep the stored details of his own experience, to protect himself by turning to a public pool of images and themes, and to give his verse a representative character by drawing on all sorts of accepted literary, social, and religious sources. From a base somewhere behind the lines of his complex cultural heritage, he could speak safely as a representative of a class, a sex, a faith, a place, a time. Yet room was still left for individual expression. Just as North's subject matter deals overtly with the tension between conventional authority and individual autonomy, so his writing in general embodies that dualism in more subtle and elusive ways. Of course he managed to subdue himself and affirm the necessity of authority, but no man ever wrote without revealing something of himself. Even in the selection of genre, subjective expression was possible. Furthermore, at the same time that genres required a writer to manipulate counters, they also opened up possibilities for something else. The funeral elegy and the meditative poem were capable of conveying a certain amount of real experience, and even that most frozen of

58. "Martin Lluelyn, Cavalier and 'Metaphysical,'" *Journal of English and Germanic Philology*, XXXV (1936), 94.

forms, the love sonnet, could be put to private uses. In fact, there is little doubt that the conventional surface of many an English poem of the sixteenth and seventeenth centuries shelters personal elements that once were apparent and important to writers and readers alike. It is in the nature of the problem that we can discern but few of these elements now, but we should be ready to recognize legitimate clues whenever we come upon them. In the case at hand, we may be rewarded by a growing awareness of how well Sir Dudley North's life and verse help to explain each other, and how often they are in accord.

THE TEXT OF THE VERSE

[Dedication]

Since freely of your selfe you have taken a resolution, to coppy out these imperfect essayes of myne in the way of poetry, and soe to give them a fayrer character, then otherwise they can deserve, it now becomes fitt that I should give you some accompt of theyr condition, least those few besydes your selfe (for they were never designed to bee made publike) whoe shall come to have a view of them should to the reading bring an exspectation too much to theyr disadvantage.[1] I may truly say, that some of them were borne, when theyr Muse was in her nonage, and soe cannot but merite the correction, of a more iudicious, and lesse partiall penn then myne, if not to bee quite obliterated.[2] Of others fresher in date and more serious, the greater part is of too rough and harsh a nature to admitt a curious dresse, and therefore can not yeild much delight in the reading, and well it is that they carry some kynd of remidy with them in theyr brevity.[3] The truth is, that the cheife vse of them was at theyr birth, for being grounded, eyther vpon some sadd occasion, or else vpon a burden of perplexed thoughts, the very being delivered (a terme well knowen to you Ladyes) could not but bring with it, much ease and satisfaction to mee the Parent.[4] Indeed many of the pieces are light and slight enough for recreation, yett can not but want much of the due lyfe and spiritt, since in theyr creation they were levelled at obiects of Love, not reall, but imaginary; in which case it is noe lesse hard, to give an exact colouring and touch, then for a paynter vndertaking to represent a true materiall fyre.[5] But some of them are not without a reall obiect, nor were it iniurious to any, if you should assume it to your selfe, to bee the person intended. The truth is that a rapsody, or masse of things, soe different in nature, and composed at tymes of lyfe, and coniunctures soe abhorrent one from the other, can very hardly appeare good, and the rather because theyr Author, as hee was noe wayes by nature designed to Appollo his lawrell, soe hee never affected the honor to attayne it; and where there is noe ambition, there can hardly arise perfection.[6] But for the collection it selfe, such as it is, you may take it to you as your own, if you please, and peradventure with lesse censure (at least from some) then hath fallen vpon those Ladyes, whoe out of an abundant affection, have called home theyr husbands spurious chyldren; for though this may bee taxed for levity in some parts, yett I hope, it will not bee found guilty of impurity, eyther in the conception, or exspression, and the chyld is as motherles, as Minerva her selfe.[7] You may safely therefore, doe it the honor to own it, and not vnfittly as I thinke, for in a true sence all may bee termed yours, that properly belongs to him, whoe is and delights to bee

Entirely and constantly yours

I

The Favorite of Loue and Honour

On High Olympus where the Gods reside,
And by the Rules of Fate our actions guyde,
There lately fell an vnexspected Jarr
Twixt Beautyes Souv'raigne and the God of warr.
The subiect of it Loue and Honor were,   5
Whether in worthyes ampler sway did beare?
Venus affirm'd, such was Loues influence,
As did in noblest brests benumm the sense
Of Honor, vnto Loue conserving still
Th'entyre subiection of the captiv'd will.   10
Mars call'd th'assaults of Loue but blasts of wynd,
Him but the offall of an honour'd mynd,
Bad Venus check the fondling, wish't her trye
To crush this monster in its infancye,
Least this presumption should begett another,   15
And make the overweener skorn his mother.
God Vulcan, if this fyre not quenched were,
Well knew the blaze would make his shame appeere,
And therefore wisely Joves com̃and hee gatt,
That Pallas she the cause should arbitrate.   20
Pallas concludes, that both must ioyne in one
To frame a true and full perfection,
And therefore will's them hold such amitye,
As eithers absence boths may signifye,
Bidds Loue bequeath to Lust as enimyes,   25
Those sensuallists whoe Honours worth despise,
Will's Honor those remitt to Vanitye
Whoe dare with spottlesse Loue haue enmitye,
And both as perfect freinds, to take some one
Choyse subiect, to conferr theyr guifts vpon.   30

The Doom's approov'd, and Verus tane to bee
Theyr bountye's marke, by all the Gods decree.
His person was that Center made by Loue,
Whither all eyes did naturally moove,
And pow'rfull Honor soe his mynd did wedd,   35
As all his actions admiration bredd.
Thus Verus did his meritts right obtayne
And Mars and Venus knitt theyr loves againe.

2

Musick and Poesy

Apollo	How comes it Nymphs, that you whose vertue drest My crown with lawrell, fill'd my court with praise, Whose vnion might fresh trophies hourely raise, Eclips your glory by this sharpe contest?
Poesy	Musick would my superior bee. 5
Musick	Else I were wrong'd by Poesy.
Poesy	Shall I whose powerfull words and Art Splendor to Gods and men impart, I who comand th'infernall race, To a poore empty sound give place? 10
Musick	My pretious sounds sublimb'd by Art Affect the Gods, dispose the heart Of man, and charme both earth and hell, If Poesy can truly tell
Poesy	Musicks defect my verse supplies. 15
Musick	But verses soule in Musick lies.
Both	Great Pythius wee appeale to Thee, Iudge who deserves Priority.
Apollo	Your equall worth for equall prayse doth call, Peeres to your selves peereles to others all. 20 I iudge that you, Deare Nymphs, your powers combine, And fix your Energie on things divine.
Chorus	The clouds retire, dispel'd by Phebus rayes, The Delphian God hath given vs Halcyon dayes. This pious harmony the earth will blesse, 25 And wee shall there a share of Heaven possesse

3

Sonnett

I doe not Love, it is most true,
Nor know I yett where Love is due.
For Love should not its growth prepare
But when perfections past compare
Attract and cherish like the Sunn,　　　　　5
And seeke t'enthrall all hearts to One.
Perfection such can hardly bee
In Man, whose spring is levity,
Whose summer is in faction spent,
Whose autumns fruit is discontent,　　　　　10
Old age is worse, yett women place
Theyr hearts on this vnhappy race.
　　　For mee I prize my freedome deare,
　　　And shall not till the glorious day
　　　When a new Phenix shall appeare,　　　　　15
　　　Or love or give my selfe away.

4

Sonnett

Alas you bid mee love and doe not tell
How in soe great a change I should doe well,
I'st well to banish selfe=contented rest
And feed on hope suckt from anothers brest?
T'afflict my soule anothers mynd to please　　　　　5
Forsaking health t'embrace a fond disease?
Is't well to forfeit precious liberty
And pay devotion wheres noe Deity?
To turne my calme into a restles passion
And make my greife anothers recreation?　　　　　10
　　　With pardon then till Love seeme fayre to mee
　　　Myne owne, not his, Idolater I'le bee.

5

Noe Noe, Selena, Now I playnly see,
Your coldnes springs from selfe=idolatry.
You thinke all tribute is from others due,
And iustly pay'd with rude neglect in you,
And soe my pursuit only would exspresse   5
Yo'ur Tropheyes raysd on my vnhappines.
I grant your tincture fayre, your sunshine bright,
Your features lovely obiects of delight,
Yett still those beautyes are possest with frost,
By which the hopefull'st blossoms may bee lost.   10
A more indulgent light in Her must raigne,
Whoe by my growth in love will honor gayne,
    I'le soon transplant, if you noe favor deigne,
    For Fyre alone will not it selfe mayntayne.

6

Vayne are thy doubts Selena, vayn thy feares,
Boast of thy flames for me noe trophy reares,
The Vestalls glory'd not in foolish fyres,
Nor Can I covett to delight those eares
That love reproach. T's vanity aspires   5
To glory from a womans fond desyres.

7

Thy Face, Selena, should not mee com̄and,
Were it the masterpiece of Natures hand,
Then thinke not borrow'd white or study'd grace,
The bastard offspring of thy hand and glasse,
Winning applause from those whoe of thy art   5
Are ignorant, can captivate my Hart.
Lett others choose vnstable habitation,
My Love must haue a true and sure foundation,
A Noble building, noe lesse firm then fayre,
Needing noe helpe for beautye but the Ayre,   10

Water'd with Vertu seen in many streames,
And arm'd with Constancye against extreams,
Not having snares in front to draw in guests,
Nor seeming like a court of Fond requests,
Yeelding to all, of goodnes fayre exspression,   15
But of it selfe to Mee the sole possession
Thus dwells my Loue, whylst others theyrs doe place
On thy Each=day=decayd=repayred Face

8

Sonnett

Wylye Cupid sett to proove,
Mynds averse must yeeld to Loue,
Straight on Mee his skill would trye
Lurking in Serena's eye.
Thence secure and free from sight   5
Comes an arrow hidd in light,
Strikes my heart, when Charmed I
Feareles was of enimye.

Cupid I thy power confesse,
Thou thy glory to encrease,   10
Lett Serena wounded bee
With the shaft that pierced mee,
Soe thy trophyes shalt thou see
Rear'd on her as well as mee,
Poorely else Thou winnst the feild,   15
If the Conqu'resse doe not yeeld.

9

Sonnett

I a wanton winning passion
Newly harbour in my brest,
By whose gentle vsurpation
All my freedom is supprest,
And in thralldom I delight   5
Fedd by fancy pleas'd by sight.

All my thoughts are now confyned
To the obiect of my love,
All designes are now declined
That on other grounds doe moove,   10
Venus charmes and Cupids darts
They possesse the noblest harts.

Yett when Reason musters forces,
And my freedome would regayne
Calling mee to actiue courses,   15
Then could I my selfe vnchayne,
But Serena with her eye
Gives mee fresh captivity.

10

Sonnett

Whence can that sweet force arize
Of those captivating Eyes
In the splendour of whose rayes
Liues the wonder of our dayes?
May bee Nature, to inferr   5
Age impayres not strength in her,
Would in little that comprize
Did a whole past age suffize.

Noe such sparkling brightnes (sure)
Springs from Elements impure,   10
But was form'd by powr's aboue,
To eclipse the Queen of Loue.
Lett not heav'nly semblance then
Bend its force to ruine men,
Shew in mee a power to blesse,   15
This full glory will expresse.

11

I'le not dispayre and dye, nor heav'ns accuse
That yett Serena doth my hart refuse,
Nor feare my want of merrit, and desist
Because my services theyr end have mist,
For since her mynd, and person soe transcend,   5
As noe perfection can with hers contend,
Desert must bee supply'd by love, and shee
In part designed for posteritye,
Will see the worlds defects, and choose for hers
As worthy'st, him whose love the best appeers,   10
Which yeelds the tryall, that must giue to mee
Eternall rest, or happy victorye,
For then my rivalls I in death must ioyne,
Or ells Serena, and all ioy is mine:
The first gives her in death my loves expression,   15
The last gives lyfe, and crown's it with possession.

12

Vpon a Poem of my Fathers

That this fayre Poeme doth much art exspresse,
In choyse of words, and order apt to clothe
The Verse intended, and its matter both,
The most austere of Criticks must confesse;
And all must grant, that perfect outsyde heere   5
Is animated by a soule of witt,
Fraught with conceipts vnto that subiect fitt
Which caus'd this matchles birth to vs appeere.
For had great Cupid neither shaft nor dart,
His Votaryes might heere compose fresh charmes   10
More pow'rfull then theyr patrons wonted armes,
To winn the most obdurate female hart.

This storehouse doth Celestiall fyre contayne,
Which gently breath'd into the stonye brest
Of such as Cupids pleasing law detest,   15
Conferr's new soule, but of a softer strayne.
In breife, This Garden of delight may clayme
All attributes peculiar to the Best,
And thus in little all may bee exsprest,
T'is worthy of the Noble Authors Name.   20

13

On Serena playing on the Lute

When by Serena's charming touch enclyn'd
Speech (fledd from vs) was to her strings confyn'd,
Seaz'd by a double admiration I
Felt discord springing from this harmony,
Two of my senses sweetly there opprest   5
By obiects in theyr kind the perfectest,
Strove for the choysest spirits, and thereby
To giue theyr organs capabilitye.
The Hearing, on such pleasing sounds intent,
As from Apollo's hand and harp were sent,   10
Affirm'd that those did more the Soule delight,
Then any obiect pertinent to sight.
The Sight, before the Soule this doubt to cleere
Presents Serena's lovely person there,
Whose winning shape th'astonisht soule to proove,   15
Consults th'Idea of the Queen of Love,
And finding that excell in ev'ery part,
Shee stay'd the figure, lodg'd it in my hart,
Where still it rests, and this adiudg'd the right
And gaue the choyse of spiritts to the Sight.   20

14

On Serena sleeping

Such a sweet stillnes doth the soule possesse,
When dead to sorrow, fill'd with blessednes,
From clogging earth emancipate, and free,
It only tends the great Divinitye.
Tymes vnrelenting messenger, to this   5
Fayre lovely semblance, ill compared is,
Were women sure, that death were thus attyr'd,
They'd sell theyr liues, and soules to bee admyr'd.
I Heav'n and lyfe in this fayre obiect see,
Not Earth, and death, theyr image rests on mee   10
Mee a poore plant bereft of verdure quite
By that too cleere a heav'ns abundant light:
Yett could those veyled Sunns theyr beams contract,
And on theyr mistris hart full warmth reflect,
Her frequent favors then, like tymely rayn,   15
Might make this plant to flourish once agayne.

15

Sonnett

When my heart was first enthrall'd
And Serena seaz'd on Mee,
Then noe freedom I recall'd
Blest in such captivitye,
Soe her eyes with love were fraught,   5
That in them all ioy I sought.

Now I feare my Hopes must dye
Starved at her thrifty hand,
Shee affords a pleased eye
Only where it winns comãnd,   10
And her smyles new conquests breed
Whilst on frownes her captives feed

Hopeles yett and helpeles I
Fetter'd must and will remayne,
Love of Her can never dye,   15
Though her love it never gayne,
If my suff'rings her doe please,
Her content shall bee my Ease.

16

Sonnett

Thinke not Disdayne can quench my Loue,
For my desire
Contaynes such fyre,
As Ages snow can not remoove,
Vayne then thy gentle frosts will proove.   5

My Fyre is of an essence pure,
And still would liue
Though Thou should'st giue
Thy sweets to worke my Rivalls cure,
And by a vow thy grant assure.   10

For though thy body Hymen bynd,
Yett Thou to Mee
Soe iust wilt bee,
As in thy nobler part thy mynd
A share shall bee to mee assign'd,   15

In which a plant of Love I'le sett,
And thereon feed
Till myne exceed
All blisse that haples Hee can gett
Whose Heart's on any other sett.   20

17

Lett not thy Husbands breach of Faith to Thee
Deprive thee, Laura, of thy Constancye,
Leaue not that glory to the faultye part,
To say in punishing Thou looser art,
For strokes, how ere deserv'd, are worse then lost,   5
When striking blemisheth the striker most.
Great faults should make Thee more thy Vertu prize,
Whose luster doubles when oppos'd to Vice,
And is like Gold, which till it passe the Touch
Though it bee perfect is not know'n for such.   10

I grant thy stock of beautye farr aboue
Her weaker store that triumphs in his love,
And all the world must straight conclude from this,
That punishment by him deserved is
Yett thy revolt would bee excus'd noe more,   15
Then Murder is where death's deserv'd before.
Lett then thy Soule her wonted purenes fynd,
For Beautyes highest throne is in the Mynd
And as thy outward features much are fam'd,
Soe lett thy Vertues euery where bee nam'd,   20
That by thy brightnes hee his fault may see,
And Thou mays't Queen of perfect Beauty bee.

18

You bynd, and say I may your bands vntye
By the fayre light that shynes in Laura's eye,
But how, Serena, can this bee, when I
Enthralld and charmed am by sympathy?
You are the North=starr that my lyfe doe sway,   5
I the true steele which points noe other way.

19

To Serena threatning to punish a supposed new
affection in her servant with a perpetuall
coldnesse in her selfe

Never, Serena, suffer soe to dye
The first born of thy soule, by thee once styl'd
Thyne only acceptable darling chyld,
Bee not deluded soe securely, by
A false misrepresenting iealousy,   5
Iudging that action worthy punishment
Whose ayme was to eternize thy content.

Most of the light in thy affections fyre
Was soe obscured by a Sunn in mee,
A Sunn of Zeale whose beames were fixt on Thee,   10
That fearing totall death of thy desyre,
For fyre, and light together doe exspyre,
I interpos'd a cloud, at whose retreat
I hop't to find in thee full light, and heat.

But Thou (Ixyon like) this cloud to bee   15
A Iuno thinking, rashly didst conclude
Thy love should cease, and never bee renew'd:
Lett Reason lyfe to love, and warmth to thee
Restore, and with it our loves harmonye,
Least Thou of Cupids wrath the obiect proove   20
Punisht with new, and vnrequitted Love.

20

An Ironicall perswasion to Serena seeming resolved to liue at Court

T'is true Serena thy perfections prize
Is admiration from Court=Deityes,
Thy christall Sunns should dim̃ all eyes but those
That guyde Joves birds, Soe fayre a springing rose
Should only rest, where its dilated sweete   5
High thrones may visite, and the Thunderer greet,
Such light in ayre (like meteors) should not bide,
But fixt aloft fayre Heav'ns first moover guyde.
Since purest bodyes earthlesse all ascend,
And Equalls blisse is noe perfections end,   10
Bee Nectar for the Gods, Lett Heav'n admyre,
And mighty Jove agayne feele Cupids fyre,
Rather then Equall's love should foyle thy story,
Like Bacchus mother, loose thy lyfe by Glory.

21

Come lett vs end our sorrowes with a Kisse,
And by a true loves knott confirme our blisse,
See Hymen crown's himselfe with choisest flow'rs,
T' exspresse by them our happy future how'rs,
Theyr beautye shewes the splendor of thy parts,   5
Theyr mixture testifyes Vnited Harts,
Theyr fullnes speakes the rypenes of our Loue,
And sweet, as they, shall our coniunction proove.
See how Hee stopps the mouth of those false freinds,
Whoe frustrate would our love for worthles ends,   10
See how hee banisheth thy fayned frownes,
And my distrusts in hop't fruition drown's,
See how hee turns with ease to sweet contents
My bitter playnts, and makes thy fayre intents
Securely in thy actions to appeare,   15
Arm'd with my Constant love against all feare.
Lett Hymen hasten then to ioyne our hands
Whose soules are linked in eternall bands,
Nought can dissolue the vnion of our mynd,
Why should our bodyes longer bee disioyn'd?   20
Since words may perfect all, and soe our ioyes
Rays'd with remembrance of our past annoyes,
May find theyr heigth and yeeld vs satisfaction
Farr aboue reach of Envye, or Detraction.

22

A Dialogue betweene Laura and Cloris

Laura   Come Cloris rest wee in this pleasing shade
            And count the croses which our loves have had

Cloris   My hopes are fledd

Laura   But are not dead

Cloris   Yes Laura plac't they are soe as I burne   5
            And yett the frigide soyle makes noe returne.

Laura   Thy fate is hard, but yett it were more crosse
       Should others rayse theyr trophyes on thy losse
         My fate is worse

Cloris   Theres noe such curse   10

Laura   Yes, for the persons love that should be mine
       Is prostituted at anothers shrine

Cloris   What may be done then to abate our greife

Laura   The Gods have only power to give releife

        Chorus
       Wee'l then Apollo pray   15
       Not for to take away
       Our love, but to refine
       And make it more divine
   To fixe on some eternall obiect pure
   That our content may bee both full and sure.   20

23

A Dialogue betwix Phillis and Daphne

Phillis   How comes it Daphne that Auroras hew
       hath left thy cheeks, and pensive looks take place
       Doth any foe thy pretious flock deface
       Or art thou struck by some Adonis new?

Daphne   My flock is safe, deare Phillis, nor am I   5
       Love struck though our old Prophett sayth t'is true
       That Cupids power must all at last subdue
       And that the Shepherds shall vnconstant bee

Phillis   I never will beleeve, my Thyrsis sighs
       Soe deepely fetcht, his earnest vowes soe free,   10
       Soe often iterated vnto mee,
       Can from a fond vnstable heart arise

Daphne   How ere, from doubtfull hearts Ile sever myne
       And nere depend on any fleeting swayne
       But though in perfect freedome I remayne   15
       With Phillis to avert this plague Ile ioyne

Chorus
To mighty Pan wee'l ioyntly sacrifice
Our whitest purest lambs of highest price
And put vp our request, that from the playnes
Hee'l banish false and double hearted Swaynes   20
Soe wee with confidence our flocks shall guard
And by our service meritt due reward

24

1627

Since fruitfull Nature thy imperfect mynd
For goodnes propagation nere design'd,
And more and more thy starrs malignant proove
Suff'ring Thee nought produce deserving Love,
Since other counsells Thou canst not impart,   5
Then such as wisedome and Exsperience th'wart,
All better thoughts, that Reason can suggest,
By a corrupt vnhallow'd will supprest,
Goe on, Great Lord and horrid mischeife make
Sole obiect of thy facultyes, Forsake   10
Small ills, lett thyne beare weight to yeeld a Name
May farr outlive Erostratus his Fame:
Perfect thy worke, and since thy fall's decreed
Make by thy pow'r the Christian world to bleed,
Of Europe one continew'd fyre create,   15
And soe thy Exequyes anticipate:
Thus Phebus sonns renown Thou shalt inherite,
And from the hand of Ioue like thunder meritt.

25

A Satyre. 1636

Since Sinn its cursed offspring still doth propagate
Hasting to pull from Heav'n this Kingdoms haples fate
(This Kingdome heeretofore soe much for vertu fam'd,
Soe blest, as by an author t'was Gods kingdome nam'd)
In this soe fruitfull age of Sinn, shall I help on   5
By guilty silence such our desolation?

Noe I'le dissect the wicked tymes, and strive to shew
The most destructive sinns even in theyr native hew,
And though I fayle in art, yett this will bee exsprest,
That I our cursed Achans and theyr deeds detest.   10
First I arraigne the court for its Idolatrye,
False Honor there and greatnes, perfect Idolls bee,
Idolls to which noe cõmon sacrifice is don
For they by prostituted soules are only won,
They whoe in adoration cheifest doe appeare   15
Tow'rds those bright starrs of magnitude (the Zenith neere)
Which haue most light and influence from the Royall Sunn,
They whoe those Lights, whose declination is begunn
And haplesly oppos'd to Sol ecclipsed stand,
With false and venimous aspersions seeke to brand,   20
They whoe can vary shapes with Proteus, and whose harts
Are furthest from intending what theyr toungue imparts,
Theyr Princes errors whoe applaud in Halcyon dayes,
And danger cõming, theyrs on his accompt doe place,
They only fitt the Curiall Empyrêan spheare,   25
And seldom leaue ascending till they governe there.
That part of vs, which is with sacred orders blest,
And of the name of Church would bee alone possest,
Whose words should only tend to Charity and Peace,
Whose lives, Humility should most encrease,   30
Whoe should confyne theyr labors to Gods Husbandry,
And thinke th'vnfolding of his truth Best policye,
Whoe Soules should only covett, and whose rock should bee
That never fayling treasure of Integritye,
These nourish strife at home for trifles, and vntye   35
The peace of Nations to mayntayne theyr Hyerarchye,
These ciuill Iudges are and Statesmen, and declare
That Lore for orthodoxe which with the tymes may square,
These in the brittle goods of Fortune place theyr Treasure,
And by theyr own advantage doe theyr Iustice measure;   40
Noe marvayle then if wee grow bold in Sinn, when they
(Our leaders) misinstruct, and goe themselves astray.
But now Mee thinks, I heare the people crye aloud,
That I too long haue spar'd the Esculapian brood,
Whose art th'affected party only should respect,   45
But now on th'Artists proffitt cheifly doth reflect,
These men for gayne the richer patients cure delay,
And these to trye theyr art (offt) cast the poore away;
In suñ, like cruell Iudges loftily they breathe,
And with the like indemnitye they putt to death.   50

The Lawes whose essence t'is to bee inanimate,
That Iustice noe ways forc't by Love or else by Hate,
T'incline th'impartiall ballance or to vse the Sword,
May distribute as each Case truly shall afford,
These by the pleader misrecited offt wee find,   55
Which stands for good if squaring with the Iudges mynd,
For toungue of mercenaryes silenc't is with ease
By feare of losse, The Advocate his Iudge must please
Or farewell Plutus, soe theyr oppositions fyre
Is quench't, for motion with i'ts cause must needs exspyre.   60
T'is strange that Statutes, which theyr makers sought t'expresse
In termes vnivocall, should by the wickednes
Of Glossers such a Spurious sence obtruded haue,
As of theyr very beeing seemes them to bereaue,
(Yett wonder not, that whoe to proffitt sold theyr youth   65
Should aged to Ambition sacrifize the truth.)
Our greater Nobles in theyr youth are bredd soe high,
They idolize theyr honors, feed on Vanitye,
Some to theyr country home themselves confyne, and spinn
Theyr bowells out in Table luxury, to winn   70
Applause from Clownes, who if the iealous court disgrace
Theyr cry'd=vp=Lord, scarse fayle to scorn him to his Face,
Some quarrell with theyr home, to Court and Citye flye
Of Plenty weary, sick of pretious libertye,
Thrifft's but vnnoble deemd, Most study vayn excesse,   75
And soe theyr fortunes waste, with sure vnhappines
To theyr posterity, whose birth makes them disdayne
By some fayre calling to exalt theyr house agayne:
Soe drownd in idlenes noe good by Them's effected,
A Burden to themselues they live and dye neglected.   80
Our Gentry they suck rudenes from theyr hyred Nurse,
Which in theyr youth's confirm'd by meane converse,
Theyr parents courses prompt them only to aspyre
To Hounds, Hauks, and the pleasures of a winter Fyre,
If any to our Athens doe themselves comend,   85
On Bacchus, not vpon Apollo, they attend,
By Court and Travell some are changed to the best,
But most in worthles Pryde and Affectation rest.
Of those whose Age them vnto Magistracy calls
Most seeke theyr private gayne, they factious grow and false,   90
Religion and the Publike are but empty names
Vs'd by the craffty to attayne theyr wicked Aymes.

Mars and his Votaryes with vs ecclipsed stand,
Whoe sometyme were the strenght and glory of our Land,
As well our Cheiffs as souldiers are Bisonians most,   95
And could a forraine Power attempt vs wee were lost,
Vnto our matchles selves wee equall matches are,
And want nor Art nor Courage for a civill warr.
But soft my wayward Satyre lett's not tyme mispend,
The tymes reforme wee cannot, therefore thus wee end.   100
This thrifftles People store of fitt materialls ha's
To nourish flames that may consume i'ts wicked Race,
And well wee may conceive, our stock of Sinn is even
With theyrs, whoe force down vengeance from the throne of Heav'n.
Lett vs then purge our wayes by timely Reformation,   105
Least A fifth Conquest snatch away our Name and Nation.

26

Made vpon the birth of my third Sonn on Sonday the 22th
of October 1637, to exspresse my desyre that
Hee may bee a Churchman.

Bee Thou, as is thy birthday in the seav'n,
Elect, and Holy to the Lord of Heav'n,
The houre of seaven first shew'd vs heere thy face,
And the same number ends thy yeare of grace,
Seav'n yeelds the Sabbath, Mayst Thou teach the way   5
To Happy rest, and fynd it in thy latter day:
The yeares tenth month thy race of lyfe begann
Ten giues the Church a share, Bee Thou Her man,
And as the rysing sunn did crown thy birth,
Soe lett thy guifts add light vnto the earth;   10
Winter, and stormes first wellcom'd Thee to lyfe,
The happyst man must troubles feele, and strife,
But steere Thou right, Afflictions must bee borne,
A crown of thorns was by our Savior worne.
By these prognosticks in thy Parents mynd,   15
Since Thou to sacred orders art design'd,
God moove thy heart that calling to desyre
With pious thoughts (not worldly) and inspyre
Thy Soule with graces, and thy person fitt
With helpes externall, to that service meete,   20

Thinke it beyond all earthly honor farr
To beare deservedly that Character;
Long not for prayse, To winn one soule from death
Is glory farr beyond applauders breath.
Thus may'st Thou, to abate the spreading night   25
Of Sinn, become a Burning=shyning Light.

27

ANna obit, æternâ in terris dignissima vitâ;
        Vitam si virtus, nobilitasue daret.
Hæc regis coniux, soror hæc, & filia regis:
        Hæc tua, quod magis est, Carole, mater erat.
Cur hunc? cur regem? cur tot, Regina, relinquis   5
        Regna? sapis; multò tu meliora petis.

28

To my deerest freind deceased.

Thy labours now are finish't, Thou possest
Of Joye's perfection in a blissefull rest,
That glorious prospect thou hast now attayn'd
Whereto all reall pleasure is restrayn'd,
Thy mansion is (like Pelions topp) above   5
All reach of tempest, and replete with Love
Love the fayre spring of Harmony, and peace,
The guyde that brought Thee to this happy place:
And couldst Thou in the sacred Trinitye
(As subtle Romanists affirme) espye   10
Our sublunary troubled sea, and there
What course each Pilot doth his vessell steere,
It would abate thy happines, to see
Natures best favors (which conferrd on Thee
And cultivated, gayn'd eternitye   15
In Ioyes) made weapons to supplant the Best
And instruments to fyre theyr proper nest.
Youth like to thyne, and strength thou shouldst behold
In comely persons allmost matchlesse, sold
Servants to vice, portending nought but shame,   20
And ruine vnto Body, soule, and name:

Nay lovely Vertue (glory of the mynd)
Soe liuely counterfeited heere wee fynd,
That Obiects of vnvsuall splendour Wee
May shunn, as Pearly Rocks in raging sea,   25
Whose luster is with hardnes soe combyn'd
As certayn wrack approching vessells fynd.
Temper was reconcil'd to youth in Thee,
Passion subscrib'd to Reasons Sov'raygntye,
Thy body from excesse, thy mynd was free   30
From storme, and this theyr fayre equalitye
A conversation form'd of pow'r to part
The foule Misanthropye from Timons heart.
A stone soe fayre as this, soe free from stayne,
Soe true, wee never heere shall see againe   35
Some conversations Diamond like doe shew
At first, but sifted at a stricter view
Proove full of spotts, or else at last confesse
Theyr falshood in a fragile brittlenes.
But whoe that peereles patience can exspresse   40
Which, seaz'd on by that multiforme disease
That spring of tortures, Thou, didst shew to proove
The fabrick of a mynd which nought can moove:
Surely the Deitye possest thy sense,
And inward Ioy conferr'd this indolence.   45
But now thy Soul's enlarg'd, and free from all
That fettred=wee doe most vnhappy call:
Thy blisses overflow, yett in thy gayne
The deerest of thy freinds great losse sustayne,
For that Perfection's fledd, wee still would haue,   50
And our cheife hopes lye bury'd in thy grave.

29

An Elegye composed vpon the buriall of
Ann Lady Rich

Could style and Fancy bee on Mee confer-r'd
To Character the Lady now enterr'd,
These should the smoothest richest lynes outgoe,
That can from any other subiect flow,
Her parts would to my verses luster giue,   5
And shee in them eternally might live.

Yett still my knowledge would my act accuse,
And shee her merrits prayses partly loose,
For how can numbers limited exspresse
The height of her perfections numberles, 10
Since verses then and lynes exspos'd to measure
Can nere describe this matchles=piece of treasure,
I'le pay my pressing debt in plaints and teares
The early'st truest fruit our sorrow beares,
Soe Natures mourners trewly shall lament 15
Natures great mayme in this our punishment.

30

An Elegy made vpon the Death of
Mary Lady Baesh

Can Shee whose fayre externalls, vertuous mynd,
Adorn'd her stem̃, gaue luster to her Kynd,
Whose prudence in the stations of her lyfe
A Patterne was to Virgin, widdow, wyfe,
In whom noe vice, or harshnes was t'offend, 5
But Piety encreasing even to th'end,
Could shee forsake this world without a herse
Strew'd with pathetique, and elegiaque verse?
Is Love exstinguisht? witt exhaust? or are
The tymes grown stupide vnto all but warr? 10
Awake my muse, shake off thy late restraynt,
Inspyr'd by sorrow, armed with complaynt
Exspostulate with Death, by whose dire frost
This pretious plant is soe vntimely lost,
I'st tyme when weeds abound, and corne growes thinn, 15
Then to destroy a well stor'd magazin?
When vessells wrack in Vices sea, and night,
Then to exstinguish Vertues fayrest light?
Surely thy dart had spar'd its deaths=wound now,
Had Iustice thee her ballance lent, to shew 20
How farr this new struck Ladyes worth outweigh's
The course of long liv'd matrones in our dayes
With them vaine levity in youth appeares,
Excesse and luxury in ryper yeares,
Her prime by modest carryage was protected, 25
Her ages strength a noble thrift affected.

Some dote on tytles, others on theyr ease,
And some with varyed shapes theyr lovers please.
Noe sloth, or pride with her, noe wanton glance,
In words and gesture noe extravagance,   30
Her presence gracefull, temper sweet and good,
Obliging all, but most those of her blood,
Yett to her marryage intrests soe confynd,
As there she fixed body, state, and mynd,
And doubtless shee, had shee not hence remoov'd,   35
Old ages vertues had to th'heigth improov'd.
But now her thredd is cut, and wee may mourne,
Yet this sure cordiall's left vs with her vrne.
Her lyfe excell'd, her end was most diuine,
The Sunn of Grace soe cleerely then did shyne,   40
As heer on earth shee seem'd of heaven possest,
And soe chang'd fraylty for eternall rest.

31

An Elegie vpon the Right Honble Dudley Lord North
by his Eldest Sonne Executor

What though thy thred be cut, and mine farr worn,
Thou liv'st in me as I of thee was born,
My heart thy Mansion is, Soe t'was before,
My pensive minde records the matchles store
Of thy abounding vertues, (happie t'were   5
If as imprest, soe they were rooted there)
My Eyes and feeble hands are thine by choyce
And could my prayers be thine I should reioyce
T'implore, But Orisons are vaine for thee
Surely possest of blest eternity,   10
Surely possest, for such a faith, such love
Such piety, nere faild reward above.
And were my fancy rich, and cleare as thine
Thy character should live in verse Divine
Apelles or Apollo were they here   15
Should neither paint nor penne thy fame soe cleare.
A heart inflam'd with love would raise my stile
Beyond what colder spiritts can compile
And for the later off=setts of thy stemme
Though equall Zeale, and fervour rest in them   20

Thy story yett like me they can't rehearse
More tyme I had, and more of thy converse.
But now, alas, I finde, my Muse she faintly sings
Aproach vnto thy luster melts her waxen wings.
I therefore dedicate to thee my latest verse,   25
And Sacrifice my penne, and lawrell at thy hearse.

32

A Body healthfull, strong, from blemish free
A Soule quicksighted full of pietye,
A Native promptnes, pow'rfull toungue and penn,
A Person favor'd both by God and men
A noble birth and competent Estate,   5
A Cheerefull spirit, and a timely fate,
 The Man thus born and blest appeares to mee
 The perfect modell of Felicitye

33

Youth is the cheerefull springtyme of our yeares,
In which our beautyes blossom soone appeares,
Love like the Sunn adds fervor to our mynd,
Hymen as gard'ner propagates our kynd,
Vertu our lasting winter fruit should bee,   5
Till Tyme at last devoure both fruit and tree,
And then young off=sets they supply our place
To wast theyr beeings in this fatall race,
Soe Lyfe preserves it selfe though wee exspyre,
And shall doe soe till allˢ destroyd by fyre.   10

34

Why should wee more for worldly losses care,
Then earlye pay of debts which wee may spare?
Great Blessings make vs on this world depend,
When crosses would prepare a happy End.

35
August .15. 1644

Could Wee live heere th'accepted life of Grace,
And Comfort only in our Savior place:
Could Wee externalls vse, but with distrust,
As those that wound vs may and leaue wee must,
Noe ebb of Fortune then, or wrack of State,   5
Could starve our ioy, or make vs desperate.
Stormes would but drive vs sooner to our Port,
And giue the Pilots care its due report.
Like Trees, our inward growth by winter's given,
And wanting roome to spread wee hast towards heaven.   10
Then court not Toyes, Lett's ayme at Crownes aboue
Steering our course by Fayth and holy Love.

36

As all by Natures fatall course must dye,
Soe all are shar'd in vast Eternity,
The wise as brightnes of the heaven shall shyne,
While others by theyr crimes obscur'd remayne.
    Lett Pious actings then adorn our story,   5
    Thus Death brings Fame and leads to endles Glory.

37
A Riddle. 1663

What beggars rarely want I must not gayne,
Though in my power and wish the thing remayne,
Past youth and strength yett vnder guardian still.
I have my own, but serve anothers will.
Worne out with tyme I tyme have allways wanted,   5
By a choise wast of tyme my tyme is scanted:
Others take wing, and sport them in the wynd,
Noe Eagle seen, noe remora in mynd
I fetters choose, and freely stand in aw,
Fatally bound by God, and Natures Law.   10

38

Deborah	Come Barack, as thy hands doe Trophyes rayse
	Soe lett thy toungue advance thy makers prayse.
Barack	Rather lett Deborah by grace inspyr'd
	Display his works, to bee by all admyr'd.
Chorus of	Lett both combine wee'l then accord and sing
Israelites	In sacred Hymns the mervayles of our King.
Deborah	By him Oppresion's fury was represt
	And pious innocence obteyned rest
Barack	Hee made the Prop'hetesse to battayle call
	And Sisera at Iaels feet to fall
Deborah	Stout Barack, armed by the God of might
	With ease destroyd th'insulting Cananite
Barack	Great Iabins steeled charyots needs must yeild
	When a devining Matrone tooke the feild.
Chorus	None can resist (noe not the gates of Hell)
	When God exalts his chosen Israell.
	Bow down yee nations then, for mercy crye
	Least in his burning wrath consum'd yee dye.

Line numbers: 5, 10, 15

39

Out of the 4ᵗʰ Chapter of Canticles

All fayre thou art my Love and blemish free,
Forsake the hills my Spouse and come with Mee.
My Heart is ravish't by thy peircing eye
And chayned by thy lovely locks I lye
How pure my sister is thy Love? how farr   5
Better then pretious wine? How alsoe are
Thy oyntments sweet for odour farr before
The choysest spices of the Indian store?
Thy lipps my spouse like hony combs distill,
Hony and milk thy mouth and tounge doe fill.   10
Of Lebanon thy comely garments smell
My Sister is a garden fenced well.
My spouse a fountayn shutt a sealed Spring
Thy plants yeild store of every pretious thing
Fruits fayre and pleasant proper for a feast   15
Of Gũms the sweetest and of spices best

Fountaine of gardens and a living well
With streames from Lebanon that most excell.
    Awake North wind and South awake
    Blow freshly on my gard'n and make   20
    I'ts fragrant spices flow, bring show'rs
    To deck our bridall bedd with flow'rs
    Lett my beloved come and find
    His wished store in every kind
    And give himselfe content entire   25
    By pleasing fruits at his desire
Soe shall our nuptialls bee complete and yeild
A pure and lasting seed vnto the feild

40

A Paraphrase vpon the Añuntiation

Haile Mary full of Grace by heav'n design'd
To be the height and Mirrour of thy kind,
Thou a pure Virgin shalt bring forth a Son
By Birth and choice entitled to a Throne,
With Pow'r not limited by time or place,   5
An everlasting King, who shall deface
Death and Hells Trophies at the last Assize,
And there the Penitent will Patronize,
As free from guilt, but Haughty sinners leave
The fruits of their rebellion to receive,   10
And happy Virgin know that this must bee,
For soone the Holy Ghost shall come on thee,
And so thou shalt conceive, and men thee style
Mother of God. Thy seed shall reconcile
Mankind to Heav'n, and breake the Serpents head,   15
That so his pow'r may be diminished.
    Blessed in thy selfe thou art
    By a pure and pious heart,
    Blessed in thy pretious Son,
    Blest by Angells every one,   20
    Blest by God, and Blest by all
    That wee on earth doe righteous call,
    But thou fully Blest must bee
    Planted in Eternity,
    When true Glory thou shalt gaine,   25
    And with Iesus ever raigne.

41

Who's this appears in crimson dye
Adorn'd with power and victory?
    It can bee none
    But hee alone
Whose death redeemed our liberty.   5

His bloud's an ever=springing well.
His merits all things else excell.
    That Fountayne lives,
    This Treasure gives
To clense from Sinn, To save from Hell.   10

Lord by thy suff'ring thou hast vanquisht all
O' lett thy servants never faynt or fall
    Halleluiah

42

A Paraphrase vpon the ascension

Disciples   What peereles exaltation's this wee see
That robbs vs of our cheife felicity
The presence of our Lord? whoe by his bloud
Having procur'd our everlasting good
Dissolv'd the frosty barrs and chayns of Death,   5
And powerfully inspir'd vs by his breath.

Angells   Why stand yee Galileans soe amaz'd
With eyes lift vp, to see your Saviour rays'd
From earth to Heaven? hee's gon to bee possest
Of Gloryes full extent, and there shall rest   10
Till iustice call, and thus hee'l come agayn
To Crown the iust, and iudge the wicked trayn.

Chorus   Glory to him whoe now ascends on high,
And voyd of sinn for sinners chose to dye.
Death is noe terror now, but made the way   15
To find an everlasting happy day.
Lett's strive to pay with love the love wee ow,
And seeke t'enlarge his kingdom here below.

43

Pentecost

This is the day that much repayres the losse
Of our deare Iesus slayne vpon the crosse,
For now the promis'd Comforter is here,
And now the fiery Cloven toungues appeare,
T'enflame our frozen hearts with fervent Zeale,   5
To cleanse our minds and hidden truth reveale,
Conferring strength, fell Tyrants to defye
And ev'n by Death our fayth to testifye.

Blest bee the Holy Father, and the Sonn,
Whoe guided by a free compassion,   10
To cure our weaknes, and our fall prevent,
Th'eternall comforter, and wittnes, sent,
Now since our Saviors mercy thus abounds,
Lett's Eccho out our ioyes in chearfull sounds.
And for the fuller prayses of our King,   15
Lett's new, and frequent Halleluiahs sing

Halleluiah.

44

Antiphona.

Votary.   Lord by thy pow'rfull hand distrest,
             Helples by nature, Spent in strife
             Of fragile elements, opprest
             Wth greife, to Thee I sue for lyfe.

Good Angell. Sweet soule, why crau'st thou lyfe of God?   5
             Life is a sea of Sinn and shame
             Where stormes of mynd haue theyr abode,
             And there the tempter playes his game.

Votary.   Fayre spiritt tis not lyfe I hold soe deere,
             But to advance our makers glory heere.   10

Angell   Then lett not carnalls that intent obscure,
                Least heav'n reiect thy prayer as impure.

Votary.   Soare then aloft my soule, and sing
                Casting away all frayle desyre
                Th' eternall prayses of our King   15
                Vnited with the heav'nly quire.

Angell   If thou Gods glory thus exalt,
                A treasure in his Sonn hee'l giue,
                By whose fayre light and grace thou shalt
                Eternally and purely live.   20

Votary   Then farewell outward obiects of delight,
                My soules accesses are by Faith not sight.

Angell   Yett when thy soule from drossy earth is free,
                Those ioyes thou shalt noe more beleeve but see.

Chorus   Thus they are blest   25
                    With happy rest
                  Whose hopes are fixt aboue
                  Rooted on pious love,
                On whom if pamperd worldlings frowne
                The crosse is answerd with a crowne.   30

                              45

                         Hymnus sacer

             Cantate Domino O vos dilecti eius,
             Cantate puro corde et voce canora,
             Eximias eius laudes iam promulgate,
             Nam restituta est in Christo vita nostra,
             Et stabilitur Ecclesia in cruore,   5
             Ex morte, Vitę surrexit arbor nova
             Quę Piis fructus vberiores reddit,
             Infirma fiunt per Fidem tela Averni,
             Nec sanctos lędit feri Draconis ira,
             Tam facilis et tuta est ad Cęlos via.   10

                Iô Triumphe.   Victoria Victoria.

46

A description of Man

Man is a structure fayre, compos'd of all
The choysest goods in Natures Arcenall,
A Citye fram'd for goverment, and state,
Enricht with Nobles to deliberate
For its direction, to whose watchfull care   5
Its weale, and flourishing entrusted are.
The Hart this Cityes center's placed in,
The source of spirits, and lyfes magazin,
This store abated, or corrupted, all
Mans other agents in theyr functions fall,   10
The counsell is without informers left,
And parts for action of theyr strenght bereft.
Of Microcosme the Head's the stately'st part.
I'ts frontispice beyond the hopes of art,
This glorious pyle for counsell is assign'd,   15
Iudgement the Soules Vicegerent heere you fynd,
Heere the fow'r noblest senses allwayes stand
As sentinells, account by Fancyes hand
To Iudgement's brought, hee circumstances sees
And consonant to Reasons law decree's,   20
His orders by the members are obey'd,
And in record by Memory are lay'd.
The Soule doth not heerein as Souv'raign raigne,
But Tenant at her makers will remayne.
Often when Shee her homage dares denye   25
Man is depriv'd of all fayre harmonye.
Nought's there but mutinye, all order dyes,
Th'affections they in fierce rebellion ryse,
Iudgement is first confyn'd, and Fancye plac't
As Governesse, then Reasons law defac't: 30
They last doe round the Soule, force her allow
Theyr Oligarchy, and her overthrow,
And ruin's certayne, if the Pow'r on high
Regayn'd by sorrow all not rectifye.
Thus man, in perfect, or deprav'd estate   35
His Makers Glorye still doth propagate.

47

Our Lyfe vnto a Garden I compare
A garden of the great Creator held,
The Tenant diverse services must yeeld,
His constant rent the Landlords prayses are:
This gardens entry bitter Aloes yeelds,   5
Afflictions bryars men in passage wound,
The wyly serpent everywhere is found,
But from his spreading poyson Herbgrace sheelds.
Labor's a prime effective agent heere,
Danger our only sure companyon is,   10
Our best designes doe often proove amisse,
Yett most of vs our troubles period feare.
Tyme doth by Nature in this garden grow,
Right vse of tyme must ever bee affected,
Tyme missapply'd may bee, or tyme neglected,   15
This works our hindrance that our overthrow.
When happy fruits this garden mother beares,
Theyr active Father is th'Eternall Sunn,
By show'rs of grace the midwyfes part is don,
And Industry, as nurse, the offspring reares   20
If Manhood water seeds by youth receiu'd,
And in our Autumn well wee fruits dispose,
Such cordialls Conscience then and Faith compose,
As make our ages winter scarse perceiv'd.
Oftner this ground is stor'd with hurtfull weeds,   25
These Nature as her own true births doth cherish,
Of which if Labor cause not many perish,
Theyr sure encrease our endles sorrow breeds.
If some of Natures brood possesse this land,
Theyr rootes with earth soe intermixed lye,   30
Noe art, or pow'r in man can make them dye
Without assistance from a higher hand:
That then these weedes may propagate noe more,
Nor frustrate labors vse and due intents,
By pray'rs, and teares and true obedience   35
Lett vs our gracious Patrons helpe implore,
His holy fyre will these intruders kill,

And make the clensed earth bring forth with ease
Those fruits whose fragrant odor may Him please,
The rule of choyse is his revealed will.   40
   Soe shall this lyfe abound with pretious flowers,
   And endlesse blisse shall crown our latest howers.

48

When after chyldhood Tyme had shew'd on mee
The Comick entrance of lyfes Tragedye,
And by discourse, and studye I had known
The rule of Microcosme to bee my own,
My Soule noe more in wardshipp claym'd her right   5
Of souvrayngtye, and fram'd her first delight
To visitt all her coasts, resolv'd to cleere
Each part from Vice, and settle Vertue there,
And least disorders should escape her sight
Shee governed her search by reasons light.   10
Much tender Vice discoverd is and kild,
And most of perfect growth is forc't to yeeld
Yett rooted out with payne, soe hard it prooves
To alter habitts, or dissolue old loves:
But after this successe the Soule doth fynd   15
Some helples naturall defects of mynd
Hind'rers of Outward Glory, for whose sake
The Soule enamourd, vertues part did take:
Then came she on the body to reflect,
Where much infirmity she doth detect,   20
Which charm'd her higher nobler thoughts, and drew
The Soule vnto a more externall view,
Then wants appear'd of Fortunes, Freedom, Freinds
All which might further fayre and noble ends,
Without whose helpe much vertue eyther dyes,   25
Or in the heart fruitlesse to others lyes;
With these discouragements the search exspires,
And much perplext the Soule her selfe retyres,
Devoyd of counsell, hopeles of releife
Shee agravates her ills, and feeds on greife   30
Till discontent had allmost form'd dispayre
Whose presence causeth ruine ev'ry where.

Then that Eternall God whose mercyes fill
All tyme, and place, whose pow'r but from his will
Can take noe bounds, whose will is ever bent   35
To acts of pittye, slow to punishment,
That wisedome infinite secur'd my Soule
From sharp dispayre, and purg'd my mynd from fowle
Terrene affections, taught new laws, new love,
Straight paths, desire of graces from above,   40
Contempt of things externall, wayes to gayne
And draw some proffitt ev'n from losse, and payne.
Nor came alone this pleasing change of mynd,
Some outward blessings with it were combyn'd,
Which make none happy whoe were not before,   45
But finding happines they make it more.
Thus to my selfe restor'd by pow'r divine
I am noe more my own but must confine
Mee to my Saviors gratious Laws, that Hee
May crown my hopes with blest Eternitye.   50

49

Noe Noe, I ever did and must denye
Him to bee happy that wants Libertye,
Discourse may make our ills afflict vs lesse,
But such defects admitt not happines;
Whoe is not master of his how'rs, but still   5
Must frame his actions to anothers will,
Hee may enioy a forc't content of mynd,
But force is nere with happines combyn'd.
Lyfe is scarse lyfe, if not with freedom blest,
Whoe craves not that with dullnes is possest,   10
If some imprison'd birds desyre it not,
T'is or vnknown to them, or quite forgott,
It is the cheife perfection of the Soule
That noe externall force can it controule,
And till t'is from the bodyes prison free,   15
It nere shall have a true felicitye.
But now I fynd my selfe deserve much blame
In thus discoursing on an empty Name,
For happy freedom evrywhere doth sound,
But (Eccho lyke) is noe where to bee found,   20

The greatest Prince some servitude must beare,
The happyst lyfe hath diverse crosses heere,
Lawes, Rules, Observances the bridles are
Which curbe our inclynations evry where,
By these the better natures are inclyn'd.   25
Theyre own perverse affections others bynd,
Hee whoe to his affections giues full sway
In taking freedome, freedome casts away,
And none lesse truly happy is then hee
Whoe happy in this life exspects to bee.   30
Since then the nature of our earthly ioye
Requyres a bitter mixture of annoye,
Lett vs not fondly anchor cast in these
These soe exsposed, soe tempestuous seas,
I the true Neptune dayly will implore,   35
To guyde mee till I find the blissefull shore,
To swell my sayles soe with his breath of grace
As I lifes western straights may safely passe,
And, ere my feeble tymber'd bark bee spent,
Find the Pacifick Sea of true Content,   40
Where wee, yett passengers, those ioyes may tast,
Which the blest hav'n shall fully yeeld at last.

50

An Essay in the way of Gratitude

What better can poore I to God returne
For many peereles mercyes, then to burn
In Zeale, and from that holy fyre to rayse
A lasting monument vnto his prayse
And could I silkworm = like my entrails wast   5
To yeild a webb, where letters rightly plac't
The perfect glory of my God might show
Yett must th'exspence fall short of what I owe
From Him at first my lyfe and being came
And to great length hee did extend the same   10
In dangers Hee secur'd mee, and by grant
Of signall bountyes sheilded mee from want
Some years in warr he gave me sure protection
And in sadd plagues he freed me from infection

Hee blest mee in relation coniugall   15
And in fayre inclinations filiall
Blest thus and more, yett could not I refrain
Of some thing still defective to complain
Well might I think my best of tyme was past
And that my Halcyon dayes would bee orecast   20
For discontent with other sins combind
Call'd for a rodd and of the smartest kind.
Then sicknes seiz'd on mee with tortures fell
Such as fall only short of those in Hell
A haples state, hopeles and helples too   25
Though for the cure each man pretends thereto
This made me cast away each touring thought
My heart became right humble and was taught
To leave externalls trusts and find content
In what so ère by Providence is sent   30
Yett still I knew all possible above
From whence all power doth naturally move
Powers fountayn it is there and that of Love
In power and Love my hopes I then did place
And cast me low before the throne of grace   35
Imploring ease from payne, yett leaving still
The issue to my Saviors holy will
God heard my prayer and comon meanes soe blest
As my nephritick tortures quickly ceast
And Natures strength enabled mee to voyd   40
Those ragged stones that mee so much annoyd
This was great mercy, yett it prov'd to mee
A Change but not an end of misery
A Stone in bladder grew so great as t'was
Impossible for it in bulk to passe   45
Which ston with vrine pressing, brought againe
A fearefull torment of the Hellish straine
This layd me once more prostrate full of greife
And sent me to my God to beg releife
When after new vnfain'd humilliation   50
By a most strange yett harsh evacuation
Of broken Stone I found a perfect ease
And seemingly am cur'd of my disease
This is Gods speciall hand for medicine none
Can in the bladder saffly breake a Stone   55
By this deliverance I am taught to place
Right confidence in each important case

Crye wee not vp our Earthly Monarchs then
Nor yett great artists of the sons of men
Tis true, they have a power to make vs dye   60
But life they cannot give vnto a flye
Seldome theyr own diseases they can know
And seldomer they cure them when they doe
Princes theyr subiects bodys may comand
But soules to rule they cannot vnderstand   65
Theyr outward power is but Vicegerency
Which can't be exercizd if God deny
Both life and greatnes seeme their own To day
But with the morrows light are blown away
But Gods existence all eternall is   70
Noe being ever can be soe but his
Nought can bee after it, or was before
When ere Hee speaks it, Time shall bee noe more
All things are present with him, nought forgott
Wee all obey him when wee know it nott   75
Nought from his goodnes can his being sever
His boundles mercy it endures for ever
His Spirit's allways present in the mind
That wee may bee to holines inclind
Yett still our will is in it's freedome left   80
Gods Iustice else were of its vse bereft
Glory to God whoe doth vs mortalls blesse
With Power t'attayne eternall happinesse

ANNOTATION OF THE VERSE

[Dedication]

North's introductory prose allows us a glimpse of his private attitudes when, an old man, he looked back over his collection of poems and, with quiet wit and affection, decided to dedicate them all to his wife. (In this section only, to minimize problems of lineation, notes are given sentence by sentence.)

1. *Since freely of your selfe*   For comments on the dimensions of Lady North's self-assigned task, see pp. 100–101. Roger North later observed that "she not only wrote over whatever her lord had for the entertainment of his solitude composed into books, but kept strict accounts of all the household affairs and dealings whatsoever," as well as carried on considerable correspondence (*Lives*, III, 285–286); *imperfect essayes* The adjective here may indicate that North uses the noun partly in its sense of "attempt." Whether or not one takes the phrase as an expression of genuine and justifiable modesty, one should recall that affected modesty was an ancient *topos* (see Ernst Robert Curtius, *European Literature and the Latin Middle Ages*, trans. Willard R. Trask [New York, 1953; orig. German ed., Bern, 1948], pp. 83–85); *character* a pun: style of handwriting and appearance betokening moral qualities; *accompt* account; *they were never designed to bee made publike* Some years before, in a letter that remained unpublished until after his death, North wrote: "*I never coveted the honour of the Press, much less should I do it in a time of so much prostitution*" (*Somes Notes*, p. 38).

2. *nonage* The mention of immaturity reinforces one's sense that some poems in the collection date from North's youth.

3. *the greater part is of too rough and harsh a nature* Variation in theme and treatment is related to decorum. When we come to a specific "rough and harsh" poem (notably No. 50), we might recall both this observation and Dryden's in "Religio Laici" (ll. 453–454): "this unpolish'd, rugged Verse, I chose; / As fittest for Discourse and nearest Prose. . ."; *a curious dresse* Apparently the phrase is an indirect comment on North's own early verse. "Curious" variously means ingenious, elaborate, exquisite, and carefully worked. Cf. North's statement about his "*rough and unpleasant Style*" in *Light*: "*But every man is not born to have a* Ciceronian *vein, and a fluency of Expression, neither is curiosity of Language necessary upon a Subject of this nature. . .*" (A4v). In *Observations* he says that books on economics give "*little occasion for pleasant conceits or curious terms*" (A6v). The word "dresse" conveys North's acceptance of the view (repeated in No. 12) that a poet clothes the matter of his poem.

4. *Ladyes)* The closing parenthesis was accidentally omitted from the Perkins manuscript.

5. *obiects of Love, not reall, but imaginary* See headnotes to Nos. 5 and 8.

6. *rapsody* A collection. More specifically, John Bullokar offers: "a ioyning of di-

uerse verses together" (*An English Expositor* [1616], M8r); *hee was noe wayes by nature designed to Appollo his lawrell*   An important and candid observation. Concerning Apollo, see No. 2 and note to No. 12 (l. 13); concerning North's "lawrell," cf. No. 31 (ll. 25–26).

7. *this may bee taxed*   I.e., this collection; *Minerva*   The Roman goddess (identified with Greek Athena) who sprang, motherless, from the head of Jove (Zeus).

1. The Favorite of Loue and Honour

First in the Perkins manuscript, this poem probably comes early in North's career. Not only does the traditional linkage of love and war relate naturally to North's youth, but the ideal it constitutes is embodied in a man named "Verus," and the one important "Verus" in North's life appears to have been Henry de Vere, eighteenth Earl of Oxford (1593–1625), North's commanding officer in the Low Countries. Beyond its general Roman connotations, appropriate to the classical cast of the poem, the pseudonym "Verus" ("truthful" or "true," "genuine") puns on "vir" ("man," "man of character or courage"); cf. Ben Jonson's "To Sir Horace Vere" (Epigram XCI) and George Chapman's "Pro Vere" (*Poems*, ed. Phyllis Brooke Bartlett [New York, 1941], pp. 340–342). It may also suggest Martial's valorous gladiator (Epigram XXIX, from *De Spectaculis Liber*). Besides being epideictic (a *laudatio*), North's poem combines elements of the debate poem with mythological and Petrarchan elements. Itself an original little "myth," it presents a dispute between Venus and Mars that is resolved so as to produce not only harmony among the gods but also a harmoniously elemented human being. The outcome is appropriate because one offspring of the two disputants (sometime lovers, as noted in l. 38) was said to be Harmonia.

l. 4 *Beautyes Souv'raigne and the God of warr*   North writes elsewhere that the ancients worshipped such deities "only as Representatives of the divine Attributes, . . . *Pallas* . . . representing the divine Wisedome [see l. 20], *Venus* the Beauty, . . . *Mars* the Power" (*Light*, p. 7). N.b., "pow'rfull Honor" (l. 35).

l. 6 *Whether*   Which one.

l. 7 *influence*   North plays with the concept of planetary or celestial influence in the sublunary world. Cf. ll. 29–30.

l. 11 *Loue*   Here, Venus's offspring, Cupid, nicely associated with verbiage ("wynd").

l. 13 *fondling*   A fond (i.e., foolish) person; also "one who is much fondled or caressed" (*OED*).

l. 15 *this*   The Rougham version gives "his."

l. 16 *overweener*   Presumptuous person.

l. 17 *fyre*   The "fyre" of the quarrel is contrasted implicitly with the amatory fire usually associated with Venus and Mars, and also with the fire of Vulcan, Venus's long-suffering mate.

l. 19 *Joves comand*   As the chief of gods, in charge of justice, Jove turns to his wise daughter, begotten of his brain, for judgment.

l. 20 *arbitrate*   In the manuscript an intrusive "r" produces "arbitrate," perhaps a sign of Lady North's difficulty in deciphering her husband's hand.

ll. 29–30 *one* / *Choyse subiect*   Cf. the son of "honor" who, "when he smiles / . . . shows a lover, when he frowns, a soldier" (Fletcher and Shakespeare [?], *Two Noble Kinsmen*, IV.ii.135–136); and North's father's "Reconcilement," a poem in which Beauty and Virtue agree to remain "in one mutuall mansion" (*Forest 45*, p. 30; title from *A Forest Promiscuous* [1659], p. 28).

l. 31 *Doom's*   Judgment (or sentence) is; *tane*   taken.

2. Musick and Poesy

Dependent for structure on dialogue rather than narrative, "Musick and Poesy" is another debate poem using divine adjudication to re-establish harmony. Music theorists in the late sixteenth and the seventeenth centuries believed in the independent powers of music and poetry, but had philosophical and historical authority (extending back to Plato) for holding that neither art alone could achieve as much as the two combined. Given a combination, it usually was assumed that music was the lesser partner, a point to recall in weighing the arguments North offers here. The thought of some theorists parallels North's suggestion that the combination of music and verse is finest of all when devoted to "things divine" (l. 22). Among North's poems in which music figures, see not only No. 13 but also, concerned with "things divine," Nos. 38, 39, 43, 44, and 45. Note that Apollo is assigned iambic pentameter and the "nymphs" iambic tetrameter—until their squabble is resolved, whereupon they, too, speak Apollo's more stately line.

l. 1 *Apollo*   The nature of Phoebus Apollo, god of the sun and master of the muses, is remarked in a note to No. 12, l. 13; *vertue*   power of a supernatural or divine being.

l. 2 *crown*   Apollo's "crown" as sun god is his golden hair.

l. 3 *vnion*   N.b. this anticipation of the solution to the wrangle.

l. 9 *I . . . comand th'infernall race*   Perhaps a recollection of Orpheus, who, to regain his wife, Eurydice, descended to the underworld and there, at the court of Pluto and Proserpine, sang so beautifully that the very shades wept. Orpheus usually was regarded as a poet, not a musician.

l. 13 *charme*   Not merely delight but also influence as by enchantment. Some of the appropriateness of Musick's argument is explained by Sidney's observation that "charm" comes from Latin "carmen"—i.e., song (*A Defence of Poetry*, in *Miscellaneous Prose of Sir Philip Sidney*, ed. Katherine Duncan-Jones and Jan van Dorsten [Oxford, 1973], p. 77). Cf. "comand" in l. 9.

l. 15 *supplies*   Compensates for.

l. 17 *Pythius*   Having been victorious over the serpent Python, Apollo was known as the Pythian god.

l. 22 *Energie*   Not merely activity but also force or vigor of expression; cf. Sidney, "that . . . forcibleness or *energia* (as the Greeks call it) of the writer" (*Defence*, p. 117); *on things divine*   The solution recommended by Apollo is paralleled in No. 22, ll. 15–20.

l. 24 *Delphian God*   Apollo's oracle was at Delphi on Mt. Parnassus; *Halcyon* peaceful, harmonious, after the mythical bird that could calm the winds and waves at sea.

3. Sonnett

Like other writers of his time, North uses the label "sonnet" for short lyrics composed in various forms and concerned with love, but the sort of fourteen-line poem regarded then and now as the most common form of sonnet appears nowhere in his work. It should be noted that the ordering of sonnets here (Nos. 3–21) adumbrates a sequence: the free young man, the young man involved with a less-than-satisfactory lady (Selena), and the young man experiencing ups and downs with an ideal lady (Serena), whom he finally contemplates marrying. The ordering is the editor's, however, not North's. In the Perkins manuscript the poems are tumbled together in such a way as to illustrate H. M. Richmond's comment on "the curiously contradictory impressions derived from reading the works of any one [Stuart] poet. . . . The writer seems to be running the whole gamut of attitudes in the course of a few love poems. . ." (*The School of Love: The Evolution of the Stuart Love Lyric* [Princeton, 1964], p. 222). Note that the present work, after twelve lines of couplets, achieves a sense of closure with a simple *abab* quatrain that is set off visually from the rest of the poem (see headnote to No. 31).

l. 5 *Attract and cherish like the Sunn*   Phototropism justifies the first verb; "cherish" = foster, give warmth to. Petrarchan comparisons of ladies to the sun are legion, of course, in Renaissance verse. A ready example occurs in "Aurora," by North's father: "And truth to say (faire Sun) I onely live / By that pure light and heat drawne from your eyes. . ." (*Forest 45*, pp. 16–17).

l. 6 *enthrall all hearts to One*   The two-sided theme of enslavement and liberty (see also l. 13), traditional in love poetry, is recurrent throughout North's work; cf., e.g., Nos. 37 and 49. Since the poem concerns perfection, capitalization here might be thought to carry Platonic-neoplatonic overtones.

ll. 8–11 A commonplace comparison of the seasons to the stages of man's life, here handled so casually that winter does not surface explicitly. Cf. Nos. 33 and 47.

l. 15 *Phenix*   The bird most common in sonnets of the period, the fabled phoenix was supposed to live for five hundred years or more.

4. Sonnett

The last poem on love in the Perkins manuscript, this "Sonnett" is in fact a rather neat if not altogether pleasant anti-love poem. Love as sickness (l. 6) is one of its several conventional motifs; others include the lover's servitude (l. 7) and inquietude (l. 9), the comparison of sacred and secular love (ll. 8, 11–12), and the lover as grieving plaything of the mistress (l. 10). The speaker is untouched by love, as is the speaker of No. 3, but someone has bidden him try it. Also as in No. 3, the close is emphasized visually by indentation.

l. 3 *I'st*   An option rather than an error, this form for "is it" appears in many Renaissance English texts; *selfe=contented*   When writers of the period wished to use a hyphen, they usually made it with two short, parallel, horizontal strokes such as Lady North uses here.

l. 6 *fond*   "Valued only by fools" (*OED*).

l. 11 *till Love seeme fayre*   A pun: until Cupid seem both even-handed and gracious in aspect. Cf. the "never" implied also at the close of No. 3.

l. 12 *Myne owne . . . Idolater*   Cf. No. 5, l. 2: "Your coldnes springs from selfe= idolatry."

5. [Noe Noe, Selena, Now I playnly see]

The speaker has become involved with a lady named Selena, whose name North may have derived from the moon goddess Selene (also Selena, Selina). The less attractive traits of a moon goddess are likely to include coolness (see the "coldnes" of l. 2 and the "frost" of l. 9) and inconstancy. On the other hand, Selene's most famous appearance in myth is as the aggressive female who threw Endymion into a sleep so that he would be unaware of her caresses. A lady named Selena in Drayton's verse was once his patroness but then transferred her favors elsewhere, thereby earning his indictment in the 1606 version of *Idea the Shepheards Garland* (1593); see Dick Taylor, Jr., "Drayton and the Countess of Bedford," *Studies in Philology*, XLIX (1952), 214–228. I know of no "Selena" figure in North's life, but one should recall the imaginary ladies referred to in his dedication, as well as Richmond's conclusion that the "fusion of actual and ingenious is the unique triumph of English poets of the seventeenth century" (*The School of Love* [Princeton, 1964], p. 184). One should also be aware that this poem (like Nos. 6 and 7) may be viewed against a striking old literary convention; as Richmond puts it, "The rather perverse denigration of a mistress . . . was a familiar motif in sixteenth-century satirical love poetry" (p. 6).

l. 2 *selfe=idolatry*   Concerning idolatry, cf. No. 4, l. 12.

l. 6 *Yo'ur*   Possibly an error, though the apostrophe in this instance appears to have been written carefully and general usage of the mark was loose (see No. 25, l. 60 and note). Elsewhere Lady North always writes "your."

l. 7 *sunshine bright*   A conventional reference to the lady's eyes, but somewhat surprising if Selena is a "moon" lady.

l. 12 *by my growth in love will honor gayne*   She whom I love will gain honor, conceivably with an allusion to North's family title.

l. 13 *I'le soon transplant*   North certainly was aware of Aristotle's three-part division of man's soul according to its vegetable, animal, and rational aspects, and also that, of the three, the vegetable is lowest ("Our first life is vegetable," writes his father in *Forest 45*, p. 166). Note that the speaker now has a relationship with Selena which he considers continuing.

l. 14 *Fyre*   The proverbial ring of this allusion to the speaker's passion makes the closing line, appropriately, the strongest in the poem (cf. F276, Morris Palmer Tilley, *A Dictionary of the Proverbs in England in the Sixteenth and Seventeenth Centuries* [Ann Arbor, Michigan, 1950], p. 215).

6. [Vayne are thy doubts Selena, vayn thy feares]

Related thematically to No. 5, this poem indicates that the speaker's "Fyre" (No. 5, l. 14) is answered now by Selena's "flames" (l. 2), and again trophies are involved.

l. 2 *Boast of thy flames*   One should recall the aggressiveness of Selena's probable prototype, the goddess Selene.

l. 3 *Vestalls*   In the temple of Vesta, goddess of the home, a fire tended by six virgin priestesses ("vestals") burned constantly. The speaker contrasts this sacred fire to the "foolish fyres" of a lesser woman.

ll. 4–5 *eares . . . / That love reproach*   I.e., the gossip-mongers.

7. [Thy Face, Selena, should not mee com̄and]

Beginning and closing with allusions to the superficial nature of her beauty, the speaker explains to Selena the kind of beauty required of the lady who is to "captivate" him. Although Selena herself lacks such beauty, the final couplet acknowledges that she is loved by some, and thus allows her to save face.

l. 3 *borrow'd white*   In the verse of Renaissance poets the ideal lady's colors, white and red, are not likely to be "borrow'd" from a pot. North's phrase is especially appropriate if, as seems likely, Selena is supposed to have moon-like qualities. Cf. Robert Greene, *Friar Bacon and Friar Bungay* (sc.i, ll. 54–55): "Her bashful white . . . / Luna doth boast upon her lovely cheeks" (Daniel Seltzer, ed. [Lincoln, Neb., 1963], p. 6).

l. 7 *vnstable habitation*   A reminder of Selena's (perhaps moon-like) inconstancy.

ll. 8–16 An extended metaphor comparing the speaker's ideal lady with a noble mansion. North writes at length of such a "habitation" in his *Observations*, where he has in mind the Norths' Cambridgeshire mansion, Kirtling.

l. 11 *seen in many streames*   Manifested in many ways. Late in life North wrote of the "well-spring of Charity, out of which continually there floweth water composing the river of Beneficence, or good works, which divideth it self into many streams, that it may the better water and refresh those dry and thirsty grounds which need it. . ." (*Light*, p. 51).

l. 13 *snares . . . to draw in*   Possibly like a drawbridge, which permits entry but may be raised to entrap "guests" who have been "drawn" in. Castiglione says that women should abstain from makeup because men are afraid of being tricked by such art (*Il Cortegiano*, Bk. I, chap. xl).

l. 14 *court of Fond requests*   The Court of Conscience or of Requests was a small debt court. The interpolated word "Fond" adds the idea of "foolish."

l. 15 *Yeelding to all, of goodnes fayre exsspression*   A puzzling line, but the first part seems to mean "pliant to all," with an implied contrast to the desirable "Constancye" of l. 12. The second part of the line would then resume the listing of positive attributes: the lady must be a fair means of manifesting goodness.

l. 17. *Thus dwells*   Probably "Thus *must* dwell."

l. 18 *Each=day=decayd=repayred*   An example of the fad for word compounding; an echo of "vnstable" (l. 7); and possibly an allusion to the fact that the moon goddess Selene's face, traveling across the sky, fades each day, then next night appears again, its beauty restored.

8. Sonnett

Although constructed entirely of conventional Petrarchan elements, this sonnet is of interest as one of the neatest of North's amatory poems. It also is one of his several attempts at trochaic tetrameter verse, and in form parallels No. 10. In the present ordering it serves to introduce the speaker's ideal lady, Serena (anticipated in Nos. 3, 5, and 7), whose name in Latin signifies "clear," "bright," "fair," "serene." Spenser had depicted a "faire *Serena*" in Bk. VI of *The Faerie Queene*; together with Timias, Prince Arthur's squire, she suffered from the poisonous wounds of the Blatant Beast. Raleigh addressed amatory verses to a lady named Serena (see *Poems*, ed. Agnes M. C. Latham [Cambridge, Mass., 1951], pp. 20, 118–119). And Drayton wrote not only of Selena but also of a woman named Sirena ("The Shepheards Sirena," *The Works of Michael Drayton*, ed. J. William Hebel, III [1932], 155–165)—which variant name points back to the classical sirens. Among classic poets Claudian wrote at length of a fair Spanish Serena ripe for marriage; she was niece and adoptive daughter of Theodosius, and eventually bride of the soldier Stilicho (see esp. "Laus Serenae," trans. Maurice Platnauer, in *Claudian*, II [1922], 238–257). It is impossible to say what North knew about other writers' use of the name, nor can one say to what extent North's Serena is a convenient organizing principle or a polite mask for a real woman. Very likely she is both, the proportion of components varying from poem to poem.

l. 4 *Serena's eye*   Love had entered through the eye at least since Plato's time (cf. below, headnote to No. 13).

l. 13 *trophyes*   Cf. Ben Jonson's observation on Cupid: "From the *center*, to the *skie*, / Are his *trophaes* rearèd hie" (*Haddington Masque*, ll. 111–112). Cf. also Nos. 5 and 6.

l. 16 *Conqu'resse*   Cf. the elder North's "My hearts faire Conqu'resse, author of my griefe" (*Forest 45*, p. 39).

9. Sonnett

Presenting the speaker as still but recently enthralled by Serena, this poem achieves its polished effect partly by means of an elegant handling of conventional themes in three six-line, trochaic tetrameter stanzas rhyming *ababcc*, a form used also in No. 15.

l. 6 *fancy*   Probably both amorous inclination, love (as in *Merchant of Venice*, III.ii.63: "Tell me where is fancy bred") and also imagination, mental image.

10. Sonnett

This "Sonnett" names no lady but is devoted almost entirely to a major theme of the Serena poems—"captivating Eyes" (l. 2). An air of trimness here (see also No. 8) derives in part from North's capable use of trochaic tetrameter.

l. 6 *Age impayres not strength in her*   I.e., Nature's powers, despite her longevity, are not declining. Belief in the world's decay, surviving from the *contemptus mundi* of medieval philosophy, gained strength in the late sixteenth and early seventeenth centuries.

l. 7 *in little that comprize*   A microcosm image: great splendor (sufficient for a "whole past age" [l. 8]) is compacted within the lady's eyes. Cf. North's No. 46 (esp. l. 13) and No. 48 (esp. l. 4).

l. 12 *eclipse the Queen of Loue*   The verb relates to Venus not only as Queen of Love but also as the most brilliant planet.

l. 14 *Bend*   Direct, aim (*OED*, v, 17).

11. [I'le not dispayre and dye, nor heav'ns accuse]

The "yett" of l. 2 indicates that Serena has refused the speaker for some while. As a conventional lover, he will be left to "dispayre and dye" if she does not choose him as "worthy'st" (l. 10). The eight-couplet form employed here occurs also in Nos. 14 and 29.

l. 3 *Nor feare my want of merrit*   An interesting glint of pride, given the conventional context.

l. 4 *services*   An allusion to the lover-as-servant tradition.

l. 7 *Desert must bee supply'd by love*   Love must be given to such transcendent worth.

l. 8 *In part designed for posteritye*   This parenthetical line is based on the fact that perfect things cannot decay, but it may include the idea that such a superb woman is "designed" for childbearing.

l. 11 *Which yeelds the tryall*   An ambiguous construction, possibly meaning "which one emerges [successfully] from the trial" or simply "whence arises my trial."

l. 13 *then*   I.e., in "Eternall rest"; *I*   A need to correct the manuscript "they" is shown by the statement on the lover's own projected death in l. 15. The error occurs also in the Rougham manuscript.

l. 16 *crown's it with possession*   The crown is one of North's recurring motifs (cf., for example, No. 35, l. 11). In the light of l. 8 on the woman "designed for posteritye," the juxtaposition here of "possession" with the opening words of the line ("The last gives lyfe") may not only refer to a new lease on life for the lover but also hint at impregnation.

12. Vpon a Poem of my Fathers

The title of this poem sends a reader searching in the elder North's *A Forest of Varieties* (1645). Given the younger North's hints (especially in l. 17), it is probable that the poem referred to is a rather long, untitled work addressed to a cruel mistress, Caelestia. The third, seventh, eighth, and eighteenth stanzas read as follows:

Thinke that you have a friend that doth possesse
A curious garden plentifully fraught
VVith all the pleasures nature can expresse,
And all delights that ever cunning wrought,
    And all these beauties singularly grac'd
    By a faire fountaine in the Center plac'd.

That cruell friend (faire love) are you to me,
And your perfections that faire garden are,
VVhither a welcome guest I seeme to bee;
My senses ravisht all with pleasures rare
Of beautie, enterchange of words and kisses,
VVhich yet all breed but thirst and further wishes.

And those as cheapely you may satisfie,
As you a water drop may easily give:
Why (cruell faire) is't then that you deny
That kindnesse, without which I cannot live?
    Deale plainly, may not this the true cause bee,
    You love my verses better farre then mee;

And if you like these off-springs of my brain
Whereto your self the *Heroine* mother are,
Suffer them not to die with drought, but daign
To water them from that your fountain faire,
    VVhich true *Parnassus* spring doth *Poets* breed,
    And tasted makes their Muse her self exceed.

(pp. 35, 36, 37)

Unfortunately the son's praise of the poem provides only the slightest glimpse of his own literary views: he considers word-choice and word-placement important, turns to the image of the poet as "clothing" his meter and matter, and praises wit and the fitness of "conceipts" (l. 7)—by which he probably means "thoughts." Though transcribed in both the Perkins and Rougham manuscripts as stichic verse, "Vpon a Poem" may have been designed as five four-line stanzas.

l. 6 *animated* With a pun on "anima," soul.

l. 10 *compose fresh charmes* At the same time "charmes" suggests "means to enchantment," the word "compose" reminds one that "charms" derives from Latin "carmen" (song, poem).

l. 13 *Celestiall fyre* This phrase puns on Caelestia's name and also alludes to divine inspiration. Sir William Temple observes in "Of Poetry" (1690) that Apollo was "esteemed among . . . [the ancients] the God of Learning in general, but more particularly of Musick and Poetry. The Mystery of this Fable means, I suppose, that a certain Noble and Vital Heat of Temper, but especially of the Brain, is the true Spring of these Two Arts or Sciences. This was that Coelestial Fire which gave such a pleasing Motion and Agitation to the minds of those Men. . ." (reprinted in J. E. Spingarn, ed., *Critical Essays of the Seventeenth Century*, III [Bloomington, Ind., 1968 printing], 80).

l. 14 *gently breath'd*   The phrase hints at divine afflatus.

l. 20 *T'is worthy of the Noble Authors Name*   Note the touch of North pride and the fact that writing love verse is here perceived as "worthy."

13. On Serena playing on the Lute

North's father wrote that "The first access of love is not ever [i.e., not always] by the eyes, it hath often a strong foundation and preoccupation begotten at the eare. . ." (*Forest Promiscuous* [1659], p. 8). Thus he raises a subject present in numerous poems here—the importance of the eye—while anticipating the problem of the specific poem at hand. The evaluative dilemma caused by a beautiful lady playing beautiful music was long a common theme in verse. This poem is generally characteristic of its time in drawing on neo-Platonism, and it is especially characteristic of North in that it is a form of verse debate leading to resolution through adjudication.

l. 1 *charming*   The magical connotations of the word are particularly clear here; *enclyn'd*   subjected.

l. 5 *opprest*   Pressed, forced, urged.

l. 7 *choysest spirits*   Perkins manuscript gives "choyest," one of Lady North's few errors, repeated in Rougham manuscript but elsewhere "choysest"; Robert Burton (*The Anatomy of Melancholy* [1651 ed.], p. 2) writes: "Spirit is a most subtile vapour, which is expressed from the *Bloud*, & the instrument of the soule, to perform all his actions; a common tye or *medium* betwixt the body and the soul, as some will have it; or as *Paracelsus*, a fourth soul of it self. . . . Of these spirits there be three kinds, according to the three principall parts, *Brain, Heart, Liver; Natural, Vital, Animal*." North himself explains that the choicest spirits come from the heart: "This is that part of the body which first liveth, and retaineth life the longest. Here the spirits are composed of the purest and most refined part of matter, and become the Mercury or chief Emissary of the Soul" (*Light*, p. 131).

l. 8 *giue theyr organs capabilitye*   Implying "greatest capability."

l. 13 *before the Soule*   As before a judge (cf. l. 19).

l. 16 *Consults*   Considers; *th'Idea of the Queen of Love*   the (Platonic) ideal form or pattern of Venus.

l. 18 *Shee stay'd the figure*   The speaker's soul "stayed" or "fixed" Serena's image as if making a permanent picture of it.

14. On Serena sleeping

North combines here the classical and Renaissance themes of the beloved asleep and the likeness of sleep to death, viewing both through the Petrarchan lens that he customarily chooses for his love poetry. The sixteen-line couplet form occurs also in Nos. 11 and 29.

ll. 1–4 The opening lines compare Serena's present stillness to that of religious ecstasy. Cf. Donne's "The Exstasie."

l. 4 *tends* Gives attention to; *the great Divinitye* The periphrasis somewhat softens and obscures the unusual presence of God (it *could* be Jove) in North's amorous verse.

l. 10 *theyr image* Image of heaven and life.

l. 13 *veyled Sunns* Reminiscent of one of the elder North's best passages, occurring in an untitled poem on a sleeping lady: "Shee seemed like an Evening cleare / VVhen absent is the Sunne. . ." (*Forest 45*, p. 31). *contract* concentrate.

15. Sonnett

This "Sonnett" is devoted to a relationship that occurs repeatedly in North's amatory verse: the lady's enthrallment of the speaker. The motif was used by ancient writers as diverse as Tibullus and Persius, popularized by Petrarch, and thence became so common in the seventeenth century that Francis Beaumont, in his famous farce of 1607, had his romantic hero Jasper assure his lady-love,

> You have caught me *Luce*, so fast, that whilst I live
> I shall become your faithfull prisoner,
> And weare these chaines for ever.
> (*Knight of the Burning Pestle*, III.i.15–17)

l. 13 *Hopeles . . . helpeles* Cf. Spenser's "haplesse, and eke hopelesse, all in vaine" (*Faerie Queene*, I, vii, 11); Shakespeare's "Hopeless and helpless doth Egeon wend" (*Comedy of Errors*, I.i.157); the elder North's "But Anchor hopelesse did, and helplesse prove. . ." ("Aurora," *Forest 45*, p. 14); and North's own "Essay," where he writes of "A haples state, hopeles and helples too" (No. 50, l. 25).

16. Sonnett

Selena's "frost" elicits a threat of departure from the speaker of No. 5 (l. 13), but here some "gentle frosts" (l. 5) of the unnamed lady (Serena?) do not keep the speaker from resolving to set "a plant of Love" (l. 16) in that part of her mind reserved for him. This poem shows the concern for form of which North is capable: four five-line stanzas rhyme *abbaa*, the *a*-lines in iambic tetrameter, the *b*-lines in iambic dimeter.

l. 4 *Ages snow*   Cf. Donne's "Ride . . . / Till age snow white haires on thee" ("Song," ll. 12–13).

l. 9 *Rivalls*   Rival's; instead of the plural rivals mentioned elsewhere (Nos. 11 and 15), a single lover here may be "cured" by a nuptial vow that grants him the lady's "sweets" (ll. 9–10).

l. 11 *Hymen*   The god of marriage appears in a context more cheering to the speaker in No. 21.

ll. 19–20 The poem closes with one of North's most graceful compliments: though the speaker lose the lady, his love will bring him greater joy than is known by any "Hee" who loves some other lady.

17. [Lett not thy Husbands breach of Faith to Thee]

The subject of the beautiful, virtuous woman appears here in an unusual guise: the paragon's husband is unfaithful. North assigns his lady the name "Laura," which for Petrarch had increasingly become a means of connoting moral ideas. What one most needs to recall, however, is that the laurel ("laurus," laurel>Laura) was generally symbolic of good fame and honor, and, more precisely, that it was a Christian symbol of chastity, heavenly bliss, and triumph. North uses the name in three poems (see also Nos. 18 and 22), treating it so as to suggest that it may allude to someone he knew.

ll. 1–2 *breach of Faith . . . / . . . Constancye*   Cf. North's comment that "our Levity and inconstancy is such, as the general unhappinesse would be much greater, if every man might be Divorced at pleasure" (*Observations*, p. 31).

l. 3 *faultye part*   Guilty party.

l. 7 *Great faults*   I.e., in your husband.

l. 8 *oppos'd to*   Contrasted to; with a suggestion of foil imagery.

ll. 9–10 *Gold . . . till it passe the Touch*   A reference to the touchstone as a means of testing the purity of gold.

ll. 11–14 *I grant thy stock of beautye. . .*   This passage utilizes the idea that physical beauty is proportional to moral beauty. Hence the husband's turning to a lesser woman carries its own "deserved" punishment.

l. 21 *thy brightnes*   Cf. ll. 7–9.

l. 22 *Queen of perfect Beauty*   "Perfect" because mind (l. 18), physical features (l. 19), and virtue (l. 20) all make their contribution; perhaps with a hint that Laura surpasses Venus, who is Queen of Beauty (as in No. 1, l. 4) but not noted for perfect virtue.

18. [You bynd, and say I may your bands vntye]

Though slight, this poem provides an interesting conjunction of a lady named Laura (perhaps the same as in Nos. 17 and 22) and the speaker's mistress, Serena. North deploys here a number of conventional motifs that he also uses elsewhere: enthrallment and enchantment by the mistress, the brightness of a lady's eyes, and astral influence. By means of the latter, the final couplet provides what appears to be a transparent paralleling of the speaker and North.

l. 4 *sympathy*   An affinity causing one thing to influence another.

ll. 5–6 *You are the North=starr . . . / I the true steele*   Since Serena is the speaker's North Star (i.e., North's star), and he "true steele," he must point towards her, not some other bright lady. North might claim the image as particularly appropriate to himself, but various forms of it may be found in emblem literature of the day (e.g., Otto van Veen, *Amorum Emblemata* [Antwerp, 1608], pp. 38–39), and in such poets as Petrarch (*Rime Sparse*, No. LXXIII), Spenser (Sonnet XXXIV), Carew ("To Her in Absence," *The Poems of Thomas Carew*, ed. Rhodes Dunlap [Oxford, 1949], p. 23), and Vaughan ("To Amoret," *The Complete Poetry of Henry Vaughan*, ed. French Fogle [New York, 1965], pp. 19–20). It is little surprise, therefore, to find John Jenkins using it in his elegy on North's father (Bodl. MS. Rawl. D.260, 34*v*). In fact, the elder North himself had used it ([In fruitlesse expectation], *Forest 45*, p. 36).

l. 6 *true*   The usefulness of the word here lies in its range of implications: constant, reliable, accurate, genuine, and (a scientific meaning) conformable to the accepted character of its kind.

19. To Serena threatning to punish a supposed new affection
in her servant with a perpetuall coldnesse in her selfe

Making use of both classical and Petrarchan traditions, the speaker here exonerates himself wittily from Serena's charge of infidelity. During the process one finds that previously she has allowed him to recognize her affection (l. 8). In fact, the headway achieved in their relationship—despite its present cooling—is made yet more clear when the speaker refers to "our loves [former] harmonye" (l. 19). Cf. Carew's "To His Jealous Mistris" (*The Poems of Thomas Carew*, ed. Rhodes Dunlap [Oxford, 1949], p. 110) and Habington's "To Castara, upon Disguising His Affection" (*The Poems of William Habington*, ed. Kenneth Allott [1948], p. 35).

title *servant*   Lover; cf. No. 11, l. 4.

l. 2 *first born of thy soule*   It is noteworthy that Serena's love for the speaker is said to be the "first born of . . . [her] soule," notwithstanding the various rivals who appear in other poems (cf. Nos. 11, 15, 16).

l. 4 *securely*   Carelessly, without misgiving. Cf. *Richard II*: "We see the wind sit sore upon our sails, / And yet we strike not, but securely perish" (II.i.265–266).

l. 9 *obscured*   Paradoxically, her flame was "enshadowed" to a dangerous degree (l. 11) by his greater one.

l. 13 *cloud*   The "supposed new affection" of the title, presumably a lady of lesser substance so far as the speaker is concerned (a good technique, according to Ovid, *Ars Amatoria*, II, 443–446).

l. 14 *full light, and heat*   Note how the speaker's words both convey and conceal a hope for physical ardor in his mistress.

ll. 15–16 *Ixyon like . . . / . . . Iuno*   The speaker assumes that Serena will recall how Ixion made love to a cloud that had the shape of Juno.

20. An Ironicall perswasion to Serena seeming resolved
to liue at Court

From time to time Renaissance writers compared court with country, generally to the advantage of the latter. Because the first two Stuart monarchs made repeated efforts to reduce the number of people at court, however, and because the Norths for various reasons found it advisable to retire to their Cambridgeshire seat, one may postulate a body of fact beneath the artifice of this poem (cf. the bitter passage on the court in No. 25, ll. 11–26). The major reason that "An Ironicall perswasion" ranks among North's better amatory writings, however, lies in the second word of the title. After ironically encouraging the lady to live at court among social superiors rather than elsewhere among equals, the poem ends with an emotion-charged warning about the consequences of such a decision. Note that this "sonnett" has fourteen lines as well as a full stop at the end of l. 8, inviting one to consider whether the poem consists of an octave and sestet; but the use of couplets forestalls any customary sonnet rhyme-scheme. The final two lines are lengthened (hypercatalectic), which serves to underscore their summarizing function.

l. 1 *perfections prize*   North's theme of perfection is nowhere more puzzling. A reader must decide to what extent Serena is set among ironies or encroached on by them.

l. 2 *Court=Deityes*   Apparently Serena already has won admiration in high places. Cf. Marston's "What a ravishing prospect doth the Olympus of favour yield!" (*The Malcontent*, I.v.32–33). In *Sejanus* Jonson writes of a ruler's favorite as a "court-god" (I.i.203), but later lines here suggest that the speaker has royalty itself in mind.

ll. 3–4 *christall Sunns . . . / . . . Joves birds*   The mistress's conventionally brilliant eyes (part of her "perfection") are put to good hypothetical use here as dazzling all eyes except those of Jove's eagles, who are monarchs among birds (eagles were said to test their young by making them gaze at the sun, driving from the nest all who flinched). In Rubens's famous painting on the ceiling of the Banqueting House at Whitehall, one of King James's feet rests on the imperial globe, the other on an eagle.

l. 4 *fayre . . . springing rose*   Cf. "Faire springing Rose, ill pluckt before thy time" (*Soliman and Perseda*, V.iv.81, cited in Thomas Kyd, *The Spanish Tragedy*, ed. Philip Edwards [Cambridge, Mass., 1959], p. 43). The context here suggests a variety of connotations: among Romans, the rose was symbolic of pride, victory, and love (George Ferguson, *Signs & Symbols in Christian Art* [New York, 1961], p. 37); and for Englishmen, according to John Gerard, it was esteemed not only for beauty and fragrance but also as "the honor and ornament of our English Scepter" (*The Herball or Generall Historie of Plantes* [1597], p. 1077). Cf. Campion's "Roses, the Gardens pride, / Are flowers for love and flowers for Kinges" (*The Lord Hay's Masque*, in *The Works of Thomas Campion*, ed. Walter R. Davis [Garden City, N.Y., 1969], p. 215).

l. 5 *dilated sweete*   The fragrance of the full-blown flower, probably with sexual overtones as in "hymeneal sweets" (Marston, *The Malcontent*, I.iii.121). Cf. l. 11.

l. 6 *High thrones . . . and the Thundrer*   A continuation of the royal-divine parallel; cf. Amintor's observation in Beaumont and Fletcher's *The Maid's Tragedy*: "Theres not the least limbe growing to a King / But carries thunder in't" (IV.ii.323–324). Like the eagle (l. 4), thunder is especially appropriate here because of its role in the story to which North alludes in ll. 12–14. See also No. 24, l. 18.

ll. 7–8 *in ayre . . . should not bide, / But fixt aloft* I.e., in mere air such as envelops the earth; such "Sunns" should be like the stars in the *Stellatum* (beyond Saturn), called "fixed" because their positions, relative to one another, are unchanging. Beyond the *Stellatum*, at the rim of the Ptolemaic universe, was the *Primum Mobile*. Rotation of the *Stellatum* was caused by rotation of the *Primum Mobile*, which in turn derived motion from the Prime Mover, God.

l. 9 *purest bodyes earthlesse all ascend* Of the four elements, the property of pure air and purer fire is to rise, and that of earth and water, to descend. The "divine" context of the present passage invites one to think also of angels, who, according to Richard Hooker, are "spirits immateriall and intellectuall, the glorious [cf. l. 14] inhabitants of . . . sacred palaces" (*Of the Laws of Ecclesiastical Polity*, ed. Georges Edelen, I [Cambridge, Mass., 1977], 69).

l. 11 *Nectar* The "sweete" of l. 5 recurs in this term, but reference to the gods' drink carries a troubling hint of consumption. In Occasional III, North compares sexual pleasures with honey and sweetmeats (*Light*, p. 75).

ll. 12–14 Since Serena is moving in high circles, let Jove himself be smitten rather than a mere equal. The myth North alludes to is that of Semele, who, granted a request by Jove, asked to see him in all his splendor. Jove came upon her in thunder and lightning, and, just before her body was consumed to ashes by his glory, their child Bacchus was snatched from Semele's womb.

21. [Come lett vs end our sorrowes with a Kisse]

In this love poem there is no enthrallment, freeze, or disease, but a linking of souls which is to issue in the "words" of a ceremony that "may perfect" all (l. 21). As J. W. Lever comments, "The main poetic tradition, from the Troubadour verse of Provence, through Dante and Petrarch to Sidney, treated romantic love as a state apart from, or even opposed to, that of betrothal and marriage. Only in the changed, post-Reformation climate of Elizabethan England could the two kinds of experience blend. The concept of a courtship leading through romance to marriage was a major element in Spenser's interpretation of life. . ." (*Sonnets of the English Renaissance* [1974], pp. 13–14). One may hope that Lady North had the satisfaction of knowing that this poem had been addressed, forty or so years earlier, to herself.

l. 1 *sorrowes* Note that the poem itself gives examples in ll. 9, 11, 12.

l. 2 *true loves knott* Literally a knot or bow, usually of ribbon, supposed to be a love token, but here perhaps an embrace to accompany the kiss. Such an embrace would be both a precursor and parallel of the marital "knot knit by God's majesty" (Thomas Dekker, *The Shoemaker's Holiday*, V.v.68; ed. J. B. Steane [Cambridge, 1965], p. 103).

l. 3 *Hymen crown's himselfe* Note how the crowning of the god of marriage serves to exalt the speaker and his mistress. Cf. No. 33, l. 4.

l. 22 *annoyes* Something troubling, stronger here than modern "annoyances"; cf. "our sorrowes" (l. 1) and No. 49, note to l. 32.

22. A Dialogue betweene Laura and Cloris

Like his sonnets and most pastoral verse, North's two pastoral dialogues, or eclogues (Nos. 22 and 23), concern love. Frequently pastoral elements in verse are garments for more than meets the eye (see, for example, Puttenham, p. 31; and Drayton's remark that *"the most High, and most Noble Matters of the World may bee shaddowed in them,"* *Pastorals* [1619], reptd. in *The Works of Michael Drayton*, ed. J. William Hebel, II [Oxford, 1932], 517); hence we should ask what each of these poems may be getting at. Judged by the chorus of the present poem, it is working in the direction of a palinode, commending a "more divine" love than may be found in mutable, mortal love. The name "Laura" appears to point further: in the two North sonnets concerning a "Laura" (Nos. 17 and 18) we learn that Laura's husband has taken up with another woman and that the speaker knows her well. We have no assurance that Laura in the present poem is the "same" Laura, but the possibility is arguable, for Laura here remarks that "the persons love that should be mine / Is prostituted at anothers shrine" (ll. 11–12). Perhaps the poem alludes to a real-life situation. The dialogue form had been traditional in pastoral verse since Theocritus; unusual, however, is the fact that the poem consists of couplets in a variety of meters.

title *Cloris*   Toward the close of the century Charles Sackville, Earl of Dorset, writes, "Methinks the poor Town has been troubled too long, / With *Phillis* and *Chloris* in every Song" ("A Song," ll. 1–2, in *Poems on Several Occasions, by the Earls of Roscommon and Dorset.* . . , II [1720], 56). Although the mythical strains associated with the name are confused, Chloris is "the chiefest Nymph of al" in Spenser's April eclogue (l. 122), and E. K. explains that her name "signifieth greenesse, of whome is sayd, that Zephyrus the Westerne wind being in loue with her, and coueting her to wyfe, gaue her for a dowrie, the chiefedome and soueraigntye of al flowres and greene herbes, growing on earth" ("The Shepheardes Calender," *The Minor Poems*, vol. I, ed. Charles Osgood and Henry Lotspeich, *The Works of Edmund Spenser*, ed. Edwin Greenlaw et al. [Baltimore, 1943], p. 44). Chloris corresponds to Roman Flora.

l. 2 *croses*   Frustrations or adversities, perhaps charged here with such overtones of Christian suffering as are useful for understanding the later lines of the poem. The idea that Christians need crosses was proverbial in North's England: "Crosses are ladders that do lead to heaven" (C840 in Morris Palmer Tilley, *A Dictionary of the Proverbs in England in the Sixteenth and Seventeenth Centuries* [Ann Arbor, Mich., 1950], p. 130).

ll. 5–6 *I burne / And yett the frigide soyle makes noe returne*   It is appropriate that frustration for Chloris, her name associated with flowers, should be expressed in terms of "frigide soyle." She burns with unrequited passion, of course, and she also refers to the country technique of burning the land in order to increase its yield. See note to No. 47, l. 37.

l. 8 *trophyes*   North utilizes the love-as-war theme in a variety of poems, including No. 17, where the speaker notes that Laura's rival for her husband now "triumphs in his love" (l. 12).

l. 15 *Wee'l then Apollo pray*   As frequently in North, a merging of discussants provides the resolution of the problem. In "Musick and Poesy" (No. 2), in fact, Apollo is the adjudicator, and his solution resembles that in the present chorus. Turning to Apollo here is appropriate in several ways: (1) the laurel (>Laura) is particularly beloved by Apollo; (2) Apollo was regarded as a patron of shepherds; (3) Apollo was thought to represent divine wisdom (*Light*, p. 7); and, (4) Apollo was sometimes associated with Christ. Virgil's famous fourth Eclogue thus announced the birth of a remarkable child, later taken to be Christ: "Thine own Apollo now is king!" (*Virgil*, vol. I, trans. H. Rushton Fairclough [Cambridge, 1953], pp. 28–29, l. 10).

23. A Dialogue betwix Phillis and Daphne

An eclogue like No. 22, this poem also treats inconstancy in love. Not only is the name "Phillis" ubiquitous among shepherdesses in literature (see note to title of No. 22); it sometimes suggests desertion in love because of the Thracian princess called Phyllis who died of grief over the supposed perfidy of her betrothed, Demophoon (son of Theseus). Equally striking is the name "Daphne," which calls to mind the nymph with whom Apollo became enamoured. Because it is the nature of Apollo (the sun) to move onward, he never would have been faithful to Daphne (the dawn), and in answer to her plea for aid, the gods changed her to a laurel tree. Because of the Daphne/laurel/Laura linkage, North's choice of name here may be partially explicable in terms of his poems that introduce the name "Laura" (Nos. 17, 18, and 22). It might be added that Marvell thought the Daphne-Apollo story useful ("The Garden," ll. 29–30) in bolstering an argument for what Warren L. Chernaik calls "asexual retirement and solitude" (*The Poetry of Limitation: A Study of Edmund Waller* [New Haven, 1968], p. 86). All we may be sure of, however, is that North's Phillis appears to enjoy a certain confidence in love, whereas his Daphne is conventionally melancholy about inconstancy. Virgil's Eclogue VII, which also involves a Phyllis and Thyrsis, is likewise built mainly with four-line stanzas.

l. 1 *Auroras hew*   The rosy color of dawn.

l. 3 *pretious flock*   If addressed to a married woman of the writer's acquaintance (cf. Laura in No. 17), this phrase might refer to children.

l. 4 *Or*   In both Perkins and Rougham manuscripts, "Or'," one of Lady North's few errors; *Adonis*   a type of the handsome youth. In myth, Adonis was reared by nymphs in pastoral surroundings.

l. 6 *our old Prophett*   Virgil (see John Webster Spargo, *Virgil the Necromancer: Studies in Virgilian Legends* [Cambridge, Mass., 1934]).

l. 7 *Cupids power must all at last subdue*   Virgil's famous "omnia vincit Amor" appears in his tenth eclogue (l. 69).

l. 8 *And that the Shepherds shall vnconstant bee*   I find no satisfactory source for this passage in Virgil's pastoral verse, but North may be thinking of *Aeneid* IV.373: "nusquam tuta fides" ("Nowhere is faith secure," trans. H. Rushton Fairclough, *Virgil*, I [Cambridge, Mass., 1953], 420–421). The words are those of the most famous jilted woman in classical literature—Dido.

l. 17 *mighty Pan*   Classical and Renaissance views of Arcady's god of shepherds derive in part from the supposed root of his name, the Greek word meaning "all."

T. Beverley observes that "Heathen Oracles [were] struck dumb by Christ, the Great *Pan*, or Shepherd, as *Plutarch* witnesseth" (*An Exposition of the Divinely Prophetick Song of Songs* [1687], B1*v*). Cf. E. K.'s gloss on "great *Pan*" from l. 54 of "Maye" in "The Shepheardes Calender": Pan "is Christ, the very God of all shepheards" (*The Minor Poems*, vol. I, ed. Charles Osgood and Henry Lotspeich, *The Works of Edmund Spenser*, ed. Edwin Greenlaw et al. [Baltimore, 1943], p. 55), and Milton's identical phrase, "mighty *Pan*" (ode "On the Morning of Christ's Nativity," l. 89); *ioyntly sacrifice*   Note that Phillis's part in the sacrifice is unnecessary except as insurance, since her last words expressed confidence in Thyrsis. Turning back to the seventh eclogue of Virgil, however, we find that *that* Thyrsis prefers Lycidas to Phyllis (ll. 67–68).

24. 1627

A "Great Lord" (l. 9) is at once the ostensible listener, chief subject, and target here of North's satiric outrage and contempt. Very likely this "Lord" was the King's favorite, George Villiers, Duke of Buckingham, whose large-scale corruption had nearly led to his impeachment in 1626. After years of malfeasance under James and, more recently, Charles, Buckingham in 1627 led a disastrous expedition to the Isle of Rhé to rescue the French Huguenots from French control at La Rochelle, the outcome being widely regarded as "the greatest dishonour that our nation ever underwent" (Christopher Hill, *The Century of Revolution 1603–1714* [Edinburgh, 1961], p. 59, citing a contemporary source). Although young North (he turned twenty-five in 1627) must have been impressed by the Isle of Rhé fiasco, he was apparently struck also by Buckingham's role in England's disastrous foreign policy elsewhere on the Continent. As Brian Morris writes, "The life and death of 'Steenie' Buckingham, the king's favourite and the people's scorn, aroused a hostility which found passionate expression in satire and invective quite unlike anything which had gone before" ("Satire from Donne to Marvell," in *Metaphysical Poetry*, ed. Malcolm Bradbury and David Palmer [Bloomington, Ind., 1971], p. 212; see also Frederick W. Fairholt, ed., *Poems and Songs Relating to George Villiers, Duke of Buckingham* [1850]). North makes use here of iambic pentameter couplets, which since the 1590s had been considered particularly suitable for satire.

l. 1 *Since*   This word, once repeated (l. 5), launches an eight-line introductory, subordinate construction which builds pressure and leads to the imperative of l. 9.

l. 2 *For goodnes propagation nere design'd*   Concerning evil's propagation, cf. No. 25, ll. 1, 5.

l. 12 *Erostratus his Fame*   In 356 B.C. Herostratus burned the Temple of Diana at Ephesus, one of the seven wonders of the ancient world, in order to make his name known forever. Hence Thomas Browne: "*Herostratus* lives that burnt the Temple of *Diana*" (*Hydriotaphia* [1658], pp. 75–76).

l. 13 *Perfect thy worke*   Cf. "thy imperfect mynd' (l. 1). The danger of the Great Lord, ironically, lies in his perverse ability to propagate (l. 2), "produce" (l. 4), "impart" (l. 5), and "make" (l. 14).

l. 15 *Of Europe one continew'd fyre create*   The Thirty Years War was then ravaging Europe. Fire, of course, is appropriate to a herostratic figure.

l. 16 *Exequyes anticipate* Presumably the Lord's funeral rites will involve fire. It is a curious and significant fact that many poems on Buckingham look forward to his death.

l. 17 *Phebus sonns renown* The fame of Phoebus Apollo's son Phaeton was also linked with fire. Granted a request to drive Apollo's chariot (the sun), Phaeton set the world ablaze, and Jove, calling on the gods to witness the need, hurled divine thunder to stop him.

25. A Satyre. 1636

North's longest poem, "A Satyre. 1636" has a convenient gloss in a Juvenalian passage composed in 1638 by North's father: "It is as familiar to carpe as hard to write of the times and not to become Satyricall. Errors in pretended Science, errors in wit, fashions, and manners, are so grosse, that they seldome faile to meet with as just an invective and derision, as refutation" (*Forest 45*, p. 81). "Invective" and "derision" are expressed in the poem by a dissection that concentrates on seven elements in society: the court, the church, medicine, law, the nobility, the gentry, and the military. Subject and stance alike are suitable to a conservative man who everywhere saw standards less high than his own and who perceived in 1636 that the English lacked neither "Art nor Courage for a civill warr" (l. 98). The poem is unusual for its period and for North in its use of iambic hexameter (alexandrine) couplets. Perhaps North is attempting to suggest the classical hexameters of Juvenal, Persius, and Horace.

l. 1 *Since Sinn* Cf. the "Since" and the ideas of propagation and fruitfulness in the opening lines of North's other satire, No. 24.

ll. 1–10 These lines constitute an introductory frame, balanced by ll. 99–106.

l. 4 *by an author t'was Gods kingdome nam'd* Cf. the elder North's observation of 7 December 1639: "*Polydor Virgill*, upon contemplation of the wonderfull extrications of *England* from divers ruine-threatning obsessions, attributes its subsistence to God alone, calling it *Regnum Dei*, and supported by his Grace in despight of all its own misgovernments and prevarications for private advantage against the publique good. . ." (*Forest 45*, p. 221). Both Norths allude to a passage that comes early in Bk. VIII of Vergil's *Anglicae Historiae* (p. 136 in the Basel ed. of 1546).

l. 7 *I'le dissect the wicked tymes* "Anatomical dissection . . . was an extremely popular topic; and the general interest in it is reflected in many titles of collections of satires and epigrams. . ." (Mary Claire Randolph, "The Medical Concept in English Renaissance Satiric Theory," *Studies in Philology*, XXXVIII [1941], 147).

l. 9 *though I fayle in art* This rare allusion of the speaker to his "art" is conventional, but may also point to North's belief in the primacy of his content.

l. 10 *our cursed Achans* Achan's sin was covetousness (Joshua 7.16–25).

l. 11 *First I arraigne the court* N.b. the wordplay. The sixteen-line passage beginning here may contain hints regarding the North family's retreat from court to country. Cf. No. 20 ("An Ironicall perswasion to Serena seeming resolved to liue at Court").

l. 15 *They* I.e., the prostituted souls; reiterated in ll. 18, 21, and 25.

ll. 16–17 *bright starrs of magnitude . . . / Which haue most light and influence from the Royall Sunn*   In referring to Charles, North designates a source for the starry "influence" of the chief persons at court.

l. 18 *declination*   Sinking or descent; suggestive of the astronomical term which refers to the angular distance of a heavenly body (north or south) from the celestial equator and also the angular distance from the ecliptic.

ll. 19–20 *oppos'd to Sol ecclipsed stand. . .*   Those opposed to the "Royall Sunn" (and therefore "ecclipsed") will be branded with "false and venimous aspersions" by the "prostituted soules" being satirized.

l. 21 *Proteus*   A sea-god famed for assuming different shapes; erroneously "Porteus" in both Perkins and Rougham manuscripts.

l. 23 *Theyr Princes errors whoe applaud in Halcyon dayes*   C. V. Wedgwood observes that during the 1630s "courtiers frequently congratulated the king and themselves on the era of peace and plenty he had inaugurated, and compared the tranquillity of England in the midst of European wars to the peace which the halcyon bird is supposed to create amid the raging of the sea" (*Poetry and Politics under the Stuarts* [Cambridge, 1960], pp. 35–36).

l. 24 *theyrs on his accompt doe place*   I.e., they blame their errors on him.

l. 25 *fitt*   Are suitable or proper for; *Curiall*   pertaining to a royal court; *Empyrêan spheare*   the sphere of fire or highest heaven. I.e., only the "prostituted soules" (introduced in l. 14) are suitable for the heaven of the court.

l. 28 *of the name of Church would bee alone possest*   North's dissatisfaction with Anglican clerics probably stemmed partly from their exclusive tendencies as indicated in this line, partly from his sense of various abuses (expressed later in the passage), and partly from his instinct for moderation. The fullest statement of his views is in *Light in the Way to Paradise* (1682); but see also, herein, pp. 63–64.

ll. 33–34 *whose rock should bee / That never fayling treasure of Integritye*   "Rock" not only suggests a firm foundation but also calls to mind such scriptural passages as Psalms 89.26 ("Thou art my father: my God, and the rocke of my saluation") and I Corinthians 10.4 (". . . they dranke of that spirituall Rocke . . . : and that Rocke was Christ"). Cf. the use of "Treasure" in l. 39.

l. 35 *nourish strife . . . for trifles*   North may have in mind current disputes such as those over vestments and altar rails.

l. 37 *ciuill Iudges . . . and Statesmen*   The prominence of England's three highest prelates (the Archbishops of Canterbury and York and the Bishop of London) in the Privy Council ran counter to tradition; and the courts of Star Chamber and High Commission were plainly being used to repress critics of the church. In particular, North probably alludes to William Laud, who became predominant in the Church of England after Charles's accession (1625) and, as Archbishop of Canterbury, exercised great influence in England's affairs before his impeachment (1640) and execution (1645). Closer to home was Matthew Wren, Bishop of Norwich (1635–1638), who came to be known as "the Laud of East Anglia." Shortly after he took office Wren startled his countrymen with the unbending rigor of his reforms (see, e.g., W. M. Palmer and H. W. Saunders, "The 1638 Visitation of Bishop Matthew Wren as It Concerned All Cambridgeshire Villages. . . ," *Documents Relating to Cambridgeshire Villages*, no. III, pt. 1 [1926], pp. 37–56).

l. 43 *I heare the people crye aloud*   A reminder that sometimes Roman satire was recited in public, this locution is also an indication that North is attempting to give his poem the sense of spontaneity a satire was supposed to have.

l. 44 *the Esculapian brood* Aesculapius was the Roman god of medicine, and the passage beginning here reflects the widespread distrust of physicians at the time (Thomas Browne writes of the "generall scandall of my profession," *Religio Medici* [1643], p. 1).

l. 45 *Whose art th'affected party only should respect* Whose professional skill should have only the patient in view. A man of "art" is a learned man, here a man of science.

l. 51 The sixteen-line section beginning here on abuses of the law has many antecedents and parallels; cf., for instance, Joseph Hall's *Virgidemiarum* (1597), Donne's *Satyres* (also from the 1590s); Jonson's *Volpone* (1605; 1st pub. 1607), and George Ruggle's *Ignoramus* (twice performed at Cambridge before King James, 1615).

l. 53 *th'impartiall ballance* Cf. No. 30, l. 20.

l. 55 *These* Appositive for "The Lawes" of l. 51; the intervening passage on justice (ll. 52–54) is parenthetic.

l. 59 *Plutus* God of wealth.

l. 60 *Is quench't, for motion with i'ts cause must needs exspyre* The line capitalizes on a pun between physics and law: "motion" is a legal term designating an application made to a court or judge. The form "i'ts" illustrates Samuel A. Tannenbaum's observation that "The position of the apostrophe seems to have depended to some extent on the writer's . . . caprice" (*The Handwriting of the Renaissance* [New York, 1930], p. 122).

l. 62 *vnivocall* Unmistakable, unambiguous.

l. 66 *Should aged to Ambition sacrifize the truth* Should, aged, sacrifice truth to ambition.

ll. 69–70 *spinn / Theyr bowells out in Table luxury* Connotations here may suffice, but a literal meaning is "extend their bowels with sumptuous food."

l. 71 *Clownes* Rustics, with implications of rudeness and ignorance.

l. 75 *Most study vayn excesse* One problem in assessing the facts about North's father is how culpable he was of such excess.

l. 78 *By some fayre calling* As we are reminded also in No. 26, North was intent on having all but the eldest of his sons learn to support themselves.

l. 85 *our Athens* For North, perhaps Cambridge. It is notable that he finds Bacchus (drinking) a problem and that he considers Apollo the proper tutelary god for "Athens." Joseph Hall believed that "our Land hath no blemish comparable to the mis-education of our Gentry" (Epistle VI, "The Sixt Decad" [t.p. "1643"] in *The Works of Joseph Hall* [1648], p. 357).

l. 89 *Magistracy calls* North writes in his *Observations* that a country gentleman "can hardly keep himself out of employment, under the Lievtenancy or Commission of the Peace. . ." (pp. 124–125); see above, pp. 70–71.

ll. 93–94 One should recall here that North was an aristocratic ex-soldier, descended from men who had soldiered. Cf. No. 1 and No. 50, l. 13; *strenght* Although this spelling occurs also in No. 46 (l. 12) and in the Rougham manuscript (74*v*), and although it has various precedents elsewhere (*OED* cites, e.g., "streinght"), the usual form in the Perkins manuscript is "strength."

l. 95 *Bisonians* "A recruit was called a *bezonian*, from the Spanish word *bisoño*, which means raw, undisciplined, and is used for a recruit inexpert in the use of arms"

(Clements R. Markham, *The Fighting Veres: Lives of Sir Francis Vere . . . and of Sir Horace Vere . . .* [1888], p. 62). The word was common among the English in the Low Countries.

l. 98 *civill warr*   In his *Narrative* North wrote later that no cause "can justifie an armed opposition by Subjects against their Sovereign" (p. 7).

l. 99 *my wayward Satyre*   Characteristically, North's satire is neatly structured, but this phrase indicates his awareness that satire was supposed to have a certain roughness.

l. 102 *flames*   Looking back later, North wrote of the "*fatal* [Long] *Parliament which set the whole Kingdom on fire*" (*Observations*, A4v). Cf. the fire imagery of "1627" (No. 24); *i'ts*   See note to l. 60.

l. 104 *theyrs, whoe force down vengeance from the throne of Heav'n*   The Lord says, "To me belongeth vengeance" (Deuteronomy 32.35) a few verses after references to Sodom and Gomorrah; but the "theyrs" here is general.

l. 106 *A fifth Conquest*   The Fifth Monarchy Men were a sect of fanatics who held that the four kingdoms described in Daniel 2 would be succeeded by a fifth, when Christ would reign a thousand years, and that their own task was to establish it by force. John Evelyn wrote of "the madness of the *Anabaptists, Quakers, fift Monarchymen* and a *Cento* of unheard of *Heresies* besides, which, at present, deform the once renowned *Church of England*. . ." (*A Character of England* [1659], pp. 25–26).

> 26. Made vpon the birth of my third Sonn on Sonday the 22ᵗʰ
> of October 1637, to exspresse my desyre that Hee may
> bee a Churchman.

A latter-day genethliacon ("with vs," writes Puttenham, "they may be called natall or birth songs" [p. 40]), this poem records North's hopes for the infant who was to become his most prominent son, Francis. "Frank," as he was known in the family, was born at Kirtling and baptized eleven days later (2 November). He was to become Lord Keeper of the Great Seal (1682) and Baron Guilford (1683) but die at the age of forty-seven (1685). During the course of his career he aided his family in many ways, and subsequently Roger, who benefited most, wrote a detailed and loving memoir in his *Lives*. It was not until the Norths' tenth child, John (b. 1645), that the family had a son who would become a "Churchman."

Immediately following this poem in both the Perkins and Rougham manuscripts are the proverbial words "Proponit Homo, Disponit Deus, / cuius fiat Voluntas in omnibus"—apparently a comment on the poem and probably deriving from Proverbs 16.9 ("A mans heart deuiseth his way: but the LORD directeth his steps").

l. 1 *seav'n*   Seven was symbolic of God's covenant of grace (Maurice H. Farbridge, *Studies in Biblical and Semitic Symbolism* [1923], p. 119). The *Catechisme* taught that "the number of seuen, forasmuch as in the Scripture it signifieth perfection, putteth vs in remēbraunce that we ought with all our force and endeuour continually to labour and trauayle toward perfection" (E1r).

l. 2 *Elect*   This reference to being chosen for salvation is a reminder that old-fashioned Calvinistic Anglicanism was more attractive to North than Laudian Arminianism. On the other hand, he wrote later of "the Presbyterian discipline being so strict, as made it unpleasing to most of the people; and especially to those of the Gentry, who found themselves likely to be over-powered by the Clergy, even in the places of their habitation" (*Narrative*, p. 51). When Francis was young, North sent him to an Isleworth schoolmaster who was, according to Roger, "a rigid presbyterian and his wife a furious independent" (*Lives*, I, 16); in fact, the boy "went from one of these fanatic schools to another for divers years, and afterwards being grown up was very averse to fanaticism." Roger adds, tellingly, "much may be attributed to the finishing of him . . . under . . . a cavalier master" (I, 16).

l. 5 *Seav'n yeelds the Sabbath* Leonard Barkan observes that "As early as Philo's *On the Creation*, there is an extremely lengthy treatment of the number seven, arising from the number of days of creation. . ." (*Nature's Work of Art: The Human Body as Image of the World* [New Haven, 1975], p. 39).

l. 8 *Ten giues the Church a share* A reference to the tithe, a tenth part of the annual increase in one's profits, paid to the church for religious or charitable use; *Bee Thou Her man* In his 1629 copy of Bacon's *Essayes* North could have read the following advice: "Let *Parents* choose betimes, the Vocations, and Courses, they meane their Children should take; For then they are most flexible. . ." (p. 34). In his own *Observations* (pp. 16, 17–18) North writes that parents of the chief gentry "are praiseworthy who cause all their Male Children to undertake some Profession of the more Noble way, whereof this Kingdom affordeth good plenty, as that of Divinity, of the Laws Common and Civil, of Soldiery, and of Physick."

l. 21 *beyond all earthly honor farr* Robert Burton writes of "our Divines" as "the most noble profession and worthy of double honor, but of all others the most distressed and miserable" (p. 135). Lawrence Stone observes that "Between 1560 and 1640 the Church was not the respected occupation it once had been and was to become again" and that "it was not until the early seventeenth century that a handful of well-born and well-connected younger sons began to trickle back into the Church" (p. 40).

27. [ANna obit, æternâ in terris dignissima vitâ]

Probably North's earliest surviving writing—certainly the earliest that is datable—this funeral elegy on the death of Queen Anne (d. 2 March 1619) was published in *Lacrymae Cantabrigienses: In Obitum Serenissimae Reginae Annae* (Cambridge, 1619), p. 26. Simonds D'Ewes reports that funeral observances for the Queen took place in Cambridge on 13 May ("D'Ewes's Diary," *The Eagle*, X [1878], 2). The brevity and succinctness of North's poem are reminders of the closeness of funeral elegy, epigram, and epitaph. Composed in elegiac couplets, the poem reminds us also that students of the day were expected to write Latin verse.

l. 1 *ANna obit, æternâ in terris dignissima vitâ* As Barbara Lewalski remarks of the epideictic verse occasioned by the deaths of Queen Elizabeth and Prince Henry, "By far the most common topic is the praise of the subject as an exemplar of virtues—often of the particular virtues appropriate to his station and role" (*Donne's Anniversaries and the Poetry of Praise: The Creation of a Symbolic Mode* [Princeton, 1973], p. 23).

l. 3 *Hæc regis coniux, soror hæc, & filia regis*   "Soror" is misprinted as "sorot" in the original text. Queen Anne (b. 1574), who had married James VI of Scotland (later James I of England) in 1589, was the daughter of Frederick II of Denmark and Norway and sister of his successor, Christian IV. Cf. the role-naming technique in No. 30, l. 4.

l. 4 *Carole*   Born to Anne and James in 1600, Charles became heir-apparent upon the death of Prince Henry in 1612. Three years before composing the present poem, at the time Charles became Prince of Wales, North was created Knight of the Bath. Cf. North's later verses on Charles's court (No. 25, ll. 11–26).

28. To my deerest freind deceased

Despite its conventional aspects, "To my deerest freind deceased" is a poem so private that the name of the deceased, which could be inferred by North's initial readers, is now lost. One difficulty is that the word "friend" was sometimes applied to a relative (John North addressed Francis North as "my Dearest Brother and cheifest Freind," Bodl. MS. North c.5, 71r). If not of a relative, conceivably North wrote of James Wriothesley, eldest son of the third Earl of Southampton, or of a young man whose surname was Stone (see l. 34). All that one may affirm safely is that the poem is relatively early if North was about the same age as his best friend, and that the poem illustrates anew the important Renaissance theme of friendship.

Immediately following the elegy are two lines of Latin which, like the lines following No. 26, appear to be North's own comment on his verse:

Si nulli gravis est percutus [for "percussus"] Achilles
Laudibus extincti nemo offendetur Achatis.

The first line is lifted from Juvenal's second satire (l. 163) and may be rendered, "it will hurt no one's feelings to hear how Achilles was slain" (*Juvenal and Persius*, trans. G. G. Ramsay [rev. ed., Cambridge, Mass., 1969], p. 17; North's "si" adds an "if"). The Juvenalian context suggests that the topic is safe because it makes no living men sweat with consciousness of their crimes. North's second line, which may be translated, "No one will be offended by praise of dead Achates," juxtaposes with Achilles a character who in ancient story is unrelated to him. The name "Achates" doubtless had alliterative attraction for North, but its greater usefulness is that the armor-bearer and companion of Aeneas, "fidus Achates" (Virgil, *Aeneid*, VI.158), was regarded as the type of the true friend.

l. 1 *Thy labours now are finish't*   Cf. "Blessed are the dead which die in the Lord, from hencefoorth, yea, saith the Spirit, that they may rest from their labours, and their workes doe follow them" (Revelation 14.13).

l. 4 *Whereto all reall pleasure is restrayn'd*   To which all true pleasure is limited.

l. 5 *mansion*   In his will (dated 1675) North would specify later that he had fixed his own hopes on "the eternall Mansion" prepared by his "pretious Saviour" (Bodl. MS. North c.32, no. 8). Cf. John 14.2: "In my Fathers house are many mansions." Of course there is an implicit comparison to earthly mansions of the day; Kirtling, for instance, had a fine "prospect." Cf. No. 7 (ll. 7–16) and No. 31 (l. 3).

l. 5 *Pelions topp* In an attempt to scale heaven and dethrone the gods, two young giants, devoted twin brothers, piled Mt. Pelion on Mt. Ossa.

l. 6 *replete with Love* "God is loue" (I John 4.8). Cf. No. 42, l. 17.

l. 10 *subtle Romanists* Presumably the dead would attain the Kingdom of God only at the end of the world, when Christ returned from heaven and the dead were raised. According to Roman Catholic doctrine, however, certain souls that died in a state of grace and were purged in purgatory could ascend to heaven and know perfect bliss before the general resurrection. In *Light* North writes of "the subtil *Roman* Doctors" (p. 80).

l. 11 *sublunary troubled sea* North combines the doctrine that all beneath the sphere of the moon is mutable with the ancient and ubiquitous image of human life as a voyage through what Hamlet called "a sea of troubles" (III.i.59). Cf. Wither's *Collection of Emblemes* (1635), pp. 13, 37, 221; Kathleen Williams, "Spenser: Some Uses of the Sea and the Storm-tossed Ship," *Research Opportunities in Renaissance Drama*, XIII–XIV (1970–71), 135–142; and below, No. 48, ll. 5ff.

l. 20 *Servants to vice, portending nought but shame* Although North is sparing in details, the passage is reminiscent of his revulsion from the life he knew as a youth in London.

l. 25 *Pearly Rocks* "Pearly" may describe rocks made to glisten by high-dashing waves, ice-covered rocks, or even rocks of ice (icebergs) such as seamen occasionally encountered. The irony of the passage is enhanced by the traditional association of pearls with virtue.

l. 28 *Temper* "Mental balance or composure. . . ; moderation in or command over the emotions" (*OED*).

ll. 31–32 *theyr fayre equalitye / A conversation form'd* The proper mix of characteristics produced a conduct or manner of living; see also l. 36. Cf. Psalms 50.23: "to him that ordereth his conuersation aright, will I shew the saluation of God."

l. 33 *Timons heart* Timon of Athens was renowned as a hater of men and gods alike.

l. 34 *A stone soe fayre* A contrast to the "Pearly Rocks" of l. 25 and a preparative for the diamond image of ll. 36ff.

l. 36 *Diamond like* In the iconology of the time, the diamond signified faithfulness, excellence. Diamonds appear in heraldic devices with such mottoes as "Bona fide" and "Sine fraude" (cited by Alastair Fowler, *Conceitful Thought* [Edinburgh, 1975], p. 5).

ll. 40–43 "But who can express the peerless patience which you exhibited (while seized by that multiform disease, that spring of tortures), demonstrating the makeup of a mind which nothing could move. . . ?"

l. 41 *multiforme disease* Since a number of diseases have multiple "forms," the friend's disease is not identifiable. Good possibilities include typhus, smallpox, and (often present together) bubonic and pneumonic plague.

l. 42 *spring of tortures* The phrase provides a striking contrast to "Love the fayre spring of Harmony, and peace" (l. 7). Note also the pun on "springe," meaning snare or trap.

l. 43 *fabrick* Considering the context, one might recall Latin "fabrica," the workshop or product of a "faber," that is, a worker in hard material such as stone; *nought can moove* A rock, especially in a turbulent sea, was a natural emblem of constancy.

Henry Peacham, *Minerva Britanna* (1612), p. 158, depicts "a mightie Rock" of *"MANLIE CONSTANCIE* of mind, / Not easly moou'd" (perhaps "nought can moove" it: North, l. 43). Nearby a "goodly ship" is about "to drowne" in "the *WORLD* the sea," "flaming in a pitteous fire" of *"HOT PASSIONS"* (cf. the passions that "subscrib'd to Reasons Sov'raygntye": North, l. 29), all that is opposite to the control and patience of the recently deceased friend. Cf. Wither, pp. 218, 236.

l. 45 *indolence* The friend's "inward Ioy" enabled him to manifest indifference to pain (from Latin "indolentia"); cf. "peereles patience" (l. 40).

29. An Elegye composed vpon the buriall of Ann Lady Rich

A sense of shock vibrates among the mortuary conventions in most of the poems occasioned by the death of Ann, Lady Rich, on her twenty-sixth birthday, 24 August 1638. The sole daughter of William Cavendish, second Earl of Devonshire, Ann in 1632, aged nineteen, had married Robert, Lord Rich, son of Robert Rich, second Earl of Warwick. (Perez Zagorin describes the Riches as "the principal landed family in Essex," the Earl being a man of vast wealth and "a great patron of the Puritans," *The Court and the Country* [New York, 1970], p. 93.) Said to have been ill with smallpox but four days, Lady Rich died at Kirtling. John Gauden, chaplain to Lord Rich, writes of the elder North as being "by this suddaine & most deplorable calamity, strucke with such a measure of Sorrow & astonishment, as if not capable of more. . ." (Bodl. MS. Eng. misc. e.262, 27r–v). Lady Rich, says Gauden, was the person whom Lord North "was chiefly ambitious to entertaine with many honorable guests at his house; esteeming her presence alone, able to make every meale a feast, & every house a pallace. . . ." It was a blow that "now she should turne his house, to an house of mourning; and by her unexpected death, imbitter all the mirth & contentment, of noble resort, & royall intertainment. . . ." North *père* wrote four poems on the death of his young friend (printed in *Forest 45*, pp. 77–80). North *fils*, who himself contracted the disease, was sufficiently debilitated to be still in a physician's hands in mid-November (*Forest 45*, pp. 58, 191, 194), but he rallied enough to write the present poem, a version of which Gauden included in his volume called "The Shadow of the (Sometimes) Right Faire, Vertuous, and Honourable Lady Anne Rich. . ." (34r). The eight-couplet form employed here by North occurs also in Nos. 11 and 14.

title *buriall* Lady Rich was buried at Felstead in Essex. Note that l. 2 reaffirms the occasion. One of the elder North's works is called "A Requiem at the Enterment" (*Forest 45*, p. 80).

l. 1 *Fancy* In a postscript to his *Observations* North explains that the "faculty of the intellect hath two others [besides will] attendant upon it, *viz.* the memory, and imagination or fancy. . . . The second is possest of a great perfection in ordering matters to the best advantage as to circumstances, and so becomes very usefull in most businesses that are to be transacted, affording also a promptness to apprehend or conceive that which shall be offered for consideration" (published in *Light*, p. 133). See also No. 9 (l. 6), No. 31 (l. 13), and No. 46 (l. 18).

l. 2 *Character* Characterize and perhaps make a character of (cf. the discussions of the deceased as symbol in Barbara Kiefer Lewalski, *Donne's "Anniversaries" and the Poetry of Praise: The Creation of a Symbolic Mode* [Princeton, 1973]).

l. 3 *richest* The elder North began one poem on Lady Rich, "In title *Rich*, in vertue all excelling" (*Forest 45*, p. 79). Long before, Sidney had punned on the name of Lord Rich's grandmother Penelope in *Astrophil and Stella*.

l. 7 *act* Performance.

l. 11 *exspos'd* Bodleian MS. Eng. misc. e.262, 34r gives the variant "confin'd."

l. 14 *sorrow* The Bodleian manuscript gives "natuer."

l. 15 *Natures mourners* The mourner's "natural" tears and laments.

l. 16 *punishment* The penalty for our sinful condition, contrasted to the perfection of Lady Rich; a common theme. *OED* regards "suffering" as a later, dialectal meaning.

30. An Elegy made vpon the Death of Mary Lady Baesh

Mary, youngest daughter of Sir Charles and Mary Montagu, was a sister of Sir Dudley North's wife, Anne. She married Sir Edward Baesh of Stansted Bury, Hertfordshire, one of the chamberlains of the Exchequer (Robert Clutterbuck includes a pedigree of the Baesh family in *The History and Antiquities of the County of Hertford*, III [1827], 243). After Sir Edward died on 12 May 1653, Mary took as second husband the surviving son of Sir Philip Cary, John (1612–1686; known as "of Stanwell" in Middlesex; see Fairfax Harrison, *The Devon Carys*, II [New York, 1920], 403–404). Mary died in 1657 and was buried the day before Christmas at Stanwell (John Gough Nichols, ed., "Cary, Viscounts Falkland," *The Herald and Genealogist*, III [1866], 33–54, 129–146). It is of interest that despite her second marriage, North refers to his sister-in-law as "Lady Baesh." Her death has led him to return to verse-writing after a period of unproductivity, he says, and in the process he calls our attention to the custom of pinning funeral poems to the "he[a]rse" (l. 7), the traditional, cloth-covered framework erected over a coffin. Note that the closing lines function as an epitaph which could be inscribed on an "vrne." Cf. the closing lines of Randolph's "An Elegie upon the Lady Venetia Digby" (*The Poems of Thomas Randolph*, ed. G. Thorn-Drury [1929], pp. 52–53) and Carew's "Elegy upon the Death of Doctor Donne." The technique is demonstrated with particular clarity in John Jenkins's elegy on the third Lord North (Bodl. MS. Rawl. D.260, 35r), where the final four lines are set off and labeled "*Epit.*"

l. 1 *fayre externalls, vertuous mynd* Cf. the elder North's "I will little esteeme the respect of man or woman who shall respect outward more than inward bravery, or rich apparell more then a rich mind. . ." (*Forest 45*, p. 93).

l. 2 *stem̃* *OED*: "In the 16th and 17th c. commonly associated with L. *stemma*, in pl. a genealogical tree, pedigree" (cf. "stemme" in No. 31, l. 19); *Kynd* class or group, perhaps meaning womankind here, as in No. 40, l. 2; the elder North writes of Lady Rich as the "glory of woman kinde" (*Forest 45*, p. 79).

l. 4 *Virgin, widdow, wyfe* The unusual order is justified by Lady Baesh's second marriage. Lewalski observes that Donne's "eulogy of Lady Danvers contains the conventional *topoi*: she is best wife, best mother, best neighbor, best friend, best example to the world" (*Donne's Anniversaries and the Poetry of Praise* [Princeton, 1973], p. 205).

l. 10 *warr*   Beyond the fighting of earlier years, the English had signed a new treaty with France in March 1657 whereby they agreed to furnish a fleet and six thousand soldiers, with Dunkirk and Mardyck (held by Spain) to fall into English hands. After the English arrived abroad in May, they spent a long while capturing places of benefit to France alone, but Mardyck (in Flanders) was captured in September and turned over to the English. The English then had to defend it from Don John of Austria— who was aided by England's own Duke of York.

ll. 13–14 *dire frost / . . . pretious plant*   Cf. No. 5, ll. 9–10.

l. 15 *I'st*   See note to No. 4, l. 3.

l. 16 *magazin*   Storehouse. In his *Observations* North writes of a householder's need to fill his "Magazines in due season," for "the very life of domestical frugality consisteth therein" (pp. 83–84). Cf. l. 26.

l. 17 *vessells wrack in Vices sea*   A variation on the life ≅ sea commonplace. Cf. Nos. 28 and 48.

l. 20 *ballance*   Cf. No. 25, l. 53.

l. 24 *luxury*   Perhaps in the sense of "lasciviousness" (cf. l. 29), but the context also allows "indulgence in costly things."

l. 26 *Her ages strength*   I conjecture that Lady Baesh lived to be no older than forty-three; *affected*   aimed at, sought.

l. 34 *state*   Many years later Montagu North wrote to his brother Francis about "Unckle Carys businesse" and recalled "our deceased aunt his wife, by whom he reaped so great a fortune. . ." (Bodl. MS. North c.5, 87r).

l. 37 *her thredd is cut*   With this conventional allusion to the Fates, cf. No. 31, l. 1.

31. An Elegie vpon the Right Honble Dudley Lord North
by his Eldest Sonne Executor

Dudley, third Lord North, died on 6 January 1667 at the age of eighty-four. It is noteworthy that this vivid, quick-tempered, pious old man is portrayed in Sir Dudley's funeral elegy quite conventionally, with few qualities save generalized virtue and piety. Whatever the nature of North's undoubtedly complex feelings at the time (he calls himself "feeble" in l. 7), he probably was distracted by the demands put upon him by death, and yet determined to honor his father in the old-fashioned way. His final line suggests that the poem was composed rapidly enough to be fastened to his father's hearse. It might be noted also that North reinforces his shift of thought in l. 23 ("But now. . .") with a shift from pentameter to hexameter. He and his father were aware that such a technique could be viewed as a blemish, and the elder North had long since penned a rationalization:

> my writings respect ease, duty, affection and profit [i.e., edification], not affectation, fame, perfection, or delight; I hate fetters and circumscriptions, more than Religion, government, and reason cast them upon mee. . . . Sometimes change of matter agrees to it; sometimes, as we have a Christian liberty, I will as well as my leaders make use of a Poeticall licence: VVhere is the law that restrains me?

VVhy not conclude with a longer proportion of lines, as well as to intermingle a
long and short? . . . I little respect old rules further than reason. Reason is the
rule of rules. . . .

(*Forest 45*, pp. 65–66)

title *Executor* If the word here jars modern sensibilities, it nonetheless preserves
an aspect of the moment that must have been prominent in North's own thinking. His
father left debts amounting to some £850, and the funeral charges and mourning came
to another £300 (Bodl. MS. North b.12, 355r).

l. 1 *thred be cut* Another such indirect allusion to the Fates occurs in No. 30, l. 37.

l. 4 *matchles store* Cf. "magazin" in the Baesh elegy (No. 30, l. 16).

l. 7 *My Eyes and feeble hands are thine by choyce* Cf. North's comments on such
choosing in No. 37.

l. 11 *such love* Despite its epideictic context, specification of this trait (which
could have been sidestepped) is a bit of counterbalance to some of the negative comments by Roger North.

l. 13 *were my fancy rich* North prided himself more on reason than fancy, but
sometimes praised both; cf. No. 9 (l. 6) and No. 29 (l. 1).

l. 14 *Thy character should live in verse Divine* Cf. North's praise of his father's verse
in No. 12. See also No. 29 (l. 6).

l. 15 *Apelles* The most celebrated painter of antiquity (fourth century B.C.);
Apollo See No. 12, note to l. 13.

l. 19 *off=setts* The term refers literally to the offshoots of a plant that is used for
propagation.

l. 22 *More tyme I had* Cf. No. 37, ll. 5–6.

l. 24 *melts her waxen wings* North's submerged allusion here to Icarus's flight may
be borrowed from praise which his father, in turn, had addressed to still better poets:
"*Bartas* and *Herbert* led, but flew so high, / Our flowry waxen wings dare not come
nigh. . ." (*Forest 45*, p. 160).

l. 26 *Sacrifice my penne, and lawrell at thy hearse* The decision to cease writing
when confronted with someone else's better verse is ancient in origin. In Virgil's
Eclogue VII Corydon asks the muses to let him sing as well as Codrus does or he will
hang up his flute. Ceasing to write as the result of a death also had various precedents.
Donne, for example, declared he would inter his muse in the grave of Lord Haring-
ton; and Henry King, writing on the loss of Lady Katherine Cholmondeley, flung
away his pen and resolved never to write again. Camden reported that when Spenser
died, various fellow poets threw into his grave the pens with which they had composed elegies for him (see R. W. Ketton-Cremer, "Lapidary Verse," *Proceedings of the
British Academy*, XLV [1960], 237–253).

32. [A Body healthfull, strong, from blemish free]

The five short moral and religious pieces that begin with this poem are best regarded
as epigrams. Richard Panowsky observes that this sort of poem had long since "proved
especially valuable in the schoolroom, where the student would exercise his Latin
style, rhetoric, and metrics and at the same time rehearse useful truths" ("A Descrip-

tive Study of English Mid-Tudor Short Poetry, 1557–1577," unpub. Ph.D. diss., University of California at Santa Barbara, 1975, p. 85). The "useful truths" in this first example relate to the classical *beatus vir* theme, which proved particularly attractive to seventeenth-century writers. Maren-Sofie Røstvig writes that "the figure of the classical *beatus vir*, re-interpreted in terms which suited the religious sensibility of the age, was definitely established during the Civil War as a Royalist counterpart to the Puritan pilgrim. In the years from Habington's *Castara* (1634–1640) to Cowley's essays (1668) no other poetic theme was more truly expressive of the spirit which prevailed in humanist circles in England" (*The Happy Man: Studies in the Metamorphoses of a Classical Ideal*, vol. I, 1600–1700 [1st pub. 1954; rev. ed., New York, 1962], p. 225). Neither pure Royalist nor Puritan, North was nonetheless very much a humanist. The closest parallel I know to the present poem is Martial's Epigram XLVII, Bk. X, which had long since caught Surrey's eye: "Marshall, the thinges for to attayne / The happy life be thes, I finde. . ." (*Henry Howard Earl of Surrey: Poems*, ed. Emrys Jones [Oxford, 1964], p. 34). Note the beginnings of the first six lines and the closing "thus" couplet, which is set off visually as well as conceptually.

l. 1 *A Body healthfull, strong*   Walter C. A. Ker's gloss on "vires ingenuae, salubre corpus" specifies that Martial referred to "the natural strength of a gentleman, not the coarse strength of a labourer" (No. XLVII, l. 6, in Bk. X, *Epigrams*, II [1930 printing of 1920 ed.], pp. 188–189).

l. 3 *Native promptnes*   Sir Dudley's father lamented the decline in his own early "alacrity of . . . spirits" (*Forest 45*, p. 125); *pow'rfull toungue and penn*   Note that the sole skill North mentions is verbal.

l. 5 *A noble birth and competent Estate*   The first desideratum is unusual, the second not; still, the two are compatible, as in Martial's "res non parta labore sed relicta" (Bk. X, No. XLVII, l. 3 [p. 188]).

33. [Youth is the cheerefull springtyme of our yeares]

Two of the more common tetrad symbols were the ages of man and the seasons of the year, which North links here in the service of the Renaissance theme of devouring time. He is so sure that a reader will recognize his pattern that, of the seasons, he mentions only spring and winter; of the ages of man, only youth. It is interesting that his scheme omits infancy but embraces—after youth (ll. 1–2)—maturity (ll. 3–4), age (l. 5), and death (l. 6).

l. 4 *Hymen as gard'ner*   The natural association of flowers and offshoots with the god of marriage leads North to make Hymen a gardener (cf. No. 21); *kynd*   i.e., mankind (cf. No. 30, l. 2).

l. 5 *lasting winter fruit*   The English had long known how to preserve fruit for winter—for example, apples, pears, cherries, and plums.

l. 7 *off=sets*   The family's scions; see note to No. 31, l. 19.

l. 8 *wast*   Exhaust or spend.

34. [Why should wee more for worldly losses care]

As North wrote in a prayer at the close of his *Observations*, "*We are fully bent, O Lord, to delight in our own wayes, and to be linked in Affection with the things of this World, which is enmity against thee*" (K6r). General and widespread as this topic is, the present quatrain nevertheless calls to mind the particular decline in fortune suffered by the seventeenth-century Norths.

l. 2 *debts* Cf. Seneca: "The properties that adorn life's stage have been lent, and must go back to their owners. . ." ("To Marcia on Consolation," *Moral Essays*, trans. John W. Basore, II [1932], 28–29; and, e.g., II Corinthians 4.18).

l. 3 *Great Blessings* I.e., great worldly blessings.

l. 4 *crosses would prepare a happy End* "Crosses" here are afflictions such as the "worldly losses" of l. 1, which paradoxically toughen one's virtues (cf. No. 22, note to l. 2). In his *Light* (p. 32) North explains the necessity of casting out covetous desires (though not one's riches) and making "God's glory the chief end of all our actions, and a full submission to him in all things, preferring his will before our own, for these will sweeten unto us all outward crosses that can befall us, while we are in this pilgrimage. . . ."

35. August .15. 1644

A pious poem (indeed, another editor might choose to group it with North's devotional verse), this epigram gains in interest when viewed in the light of its matter-of-fact title. In August 1644 Sir Dudley was a troubled member of the Commons. In February that year Edward Montagu, second Earl of Manchester, had begun implementing Parliament's policies for reforming religion in the Eastern Counties and regulating Cambridge University. Commander of the troops of the Eastern Association, the largest and most effective army of its time, Manchester was a cousin of North's wife, and back in 1619 had been a Cantabrigian lamenting the death of Queen Anne along with Sir Dudley (see headnote to No. 27). In June 1644 York was besieged by rebel armies under Manchester, Cromwell, and the Fairfaxes. Then on 2 July (six weeks before Sir Dudley's poem) Manchester led his men to victory over Prince Rupert at Marston Moor. That same month York surrendered. On 10 August (five days before North wrote his poem) the ordinance for naming a Committee for the Associated Counties was passed, citing "the great danger to the Protestant Religion" and noting "that the Earl of Newcastle with his whole army . . . is marching towards and ready to fall upon the Associated Counties" (Frederick John Varley, *Cambridge During the Civil War* [Cambridge, 1935], p. 90). Little wonder that Sir Dudley here contemplates the "wrack of State" (l. 5). Note that he builds his poem with a logical *if-then-therefore* structure.

l. 1 *life of Grace* What North means by this phrase is explored in his *Light in the Way to Paradise*. Basically he was a Church of England man who held "that the Fundamentals of Religion are neither many, nor abstruse" (p. 6). In fact, "my charity will not permit me to conclude under Eternal damnation those Heathen Philosophers and others, who in their reason having found out that there is a God, have applied themselves to doe Justice, love Mercy, and walk humbly with the Deity" (p. 7).

l. 2 *Comfort only in our Savior place*   Cf. North's *Light*: "*Christ* is the only Fundamental, proved I Cor. 3.11. *For other foundation can no man lay, than that is laid, which is Jesus Christ.* . ." (p. 6).

l. 3 *externalls*   One of North's frequent allusions to the perishability or inadequacy of outer, non-essential things. A major subject in the writing of his time, it receives his most thorough treatment in *Light* (p. 74):

> For my part, I think there cannot be an assertion more destructive to Vertue and Goodness, than that which shall deliver the delight by outward things, to exceed the satisfaction which is formed within. That by externals doth for the most part carry with it a whip, which punisheth either with satiety, or with a sudden change (for so it must be) in the want of the thing which was overmuch delighted in. This other, even when there is some bodily pain inflicted for Goodness-sake, yet carrieth with it a mixture of inward satisfaction or pleasure for the present, and finds another in the vacuity of pain when it is ended, and is always accompanied with the expectation of a reward to come.

BCP cites Romans 8.12 (I2r) and Galatians 5.16 (I6r).

l. 5 *wrack*   Wreck, ruin. Since the word had nautical overtones (cf. No. 28, l. 27), "ship of state" may be a submerged metaphor here (see ll. 7–8).

l. 7 *Stormes*   See note to No. 28, l. 11; *Port*   Cf. No. 49, l. 42.

l. 8 *due report*   Proper recognition.

l. 9 *Like Trees, our inward growth by winter's given*   I.e., inner development (in contrast to the "externalls" of l. 3) comes as a result of adversity (which functions like the "crosses" in such other North poems as Nos. 22 and 34). Cf. North *père*'s "Though Summer heighth and flourishing impart, / Winter gives strength and Timber to the Grove" ([Though friends be absent], *Forest 45*, p. 175).

l. 10 *And wanting roome to spread wee hast towards heaven*   Rather than developing the figure of a tree's winter growth, this line offers a different kind of arboreal adversity resulting in good. Note that lack of "roome to spread" carries on the "externalls" theme.

l. 11 *Toyes*   Cf., for example, "*Toyes of toyes, and vanities of vanities did withhold mee*" (John Hall, *Emblems with Elegant Figures* [1658], p. 5); *Crownes*   North's use of crowns has many precedents and parallels, e.g., I Corinthians 9.25, II Timothy 2.5 and 4.8, James 1.12.

36. [As all by Natures fatall course must dye]

This epigram is noteworthy among North's poems for reaching print in the seventeenth century. Because it appears in *Some Notes Concerning the Life of Edward Lord North, Baron of Kirtling, 1658* (p. 36), we have not only an approximate date for the poem but also a familial frame of reference. Charles North (twenty-three in 1658) is urged by his father, Sir Dudley, to "*Doe . . . as this Progenitor of yours did. . .*" (A2v). Here as elsewhere, North uses visual form (indentation) to reflect a shift in thought and enhance the sense of an ending.

l. 3 *The wise as brightnes of the heaven shall shyne*   Marginal notations in both manuscript and printed versions refer to Daniel 12, where the third verse reads: "And they that be wise shall shine as the brightnesse of the firmament, and they that turne many to righteousnesse, as the starres for euer and euer."

l. 5 *actings*   In the introductory address to his son, North speaks of the biography as "*an Historical Narration of the Life and Actings of the Raiser of your Family*" (A2r); *adorn our story*   The context suggests that, beyond generalized admonition, "our story" refers to that which will be told someday of the Norths.

l. 6 *Glory*   Besides the bliss of heaven, an effulgence of heavenly light (as in l. 3). Cf. No. 42, ll. 9–10. Note that the poem's final turn has man achieving secular goals of "fame" and "glory," but in a new key.

37. A Riddle. 1663

For North the riddle form provided a means of circling in words about a subject that was difficult to treat directly: at sixty-one, he was still subject to his father's will. Sir Dudley touched repeatedly on liberty in both verse and prose, his most extended verse treatment occurring in No. 49 ("Noe Noe, I ever did and must denye / Him to bee happy that wants Libertye. . ."). In *Light* (p. 82) he approached even the paternal aspect of the subject: "But how far the Paternal power extendeth it self beyond the government of Children in minority, it is very hard to define, especially among Christians. Yet that power whatsoever it is, and the filial reverence and observance due to Parents, is as well perpetual as natural, and cannot be extinguished justly by decree of any Magistrate whatsoever, if the Parent be *Compos mentis*." In the present riddle, which closes with the resolution that North apparently found in life, one senses what his stance cost in personal terms. On the other side of the ledger we have from the elder North such observations as the following: "I have dedicated my self (next to God) wholly to my Son, and have many years endevoured his good beyond my own. I have now made my self his Pensioner, and I wish no worldly happinesse more then his prosperity. . ." (*Forest 45*, p. 132).

l. 1 *want*   Lack; also l. 5.

l. 4 *but serve anothers will*   Cf. Sir Henry Wotton's "How happy is he born and taught / That serveth not another's will" ("The Character of a Happy Life," ll. 1–2, in *Poems by Sir Henry Wotton*, ed. Alexander Dyce [1843], p. 5).

l. 5 *I tyme have allways wanted*   Ironically, the idea that North's time has not been his own is prefigured in various passages in his father's writings.

ll. 7–8 *Others take wing, . . . / Noe Eagle seen*   It is safer for other birds to fly when no eagle is about. Perhaps also there is an allusion to the concept of caged versus uncaged (North uses such a comparison to discuss freedom in No. 49, ll. 11–12). The wind itself is a symbol of liberty; cf. Shakespeare's Jaques, "I must have liberty / Withal, as large a charter as the wind. . ." (*As You Like It*, II.vii.47–48).

l. 8 *remora*   A sucking fish of the family *Echeneididae*, anciently believed to have the power of staying a ship; it attaches itself to objects by means of a sucking disk on the top of its head. In his life of Edward North, Sir Dudley wrote: "he was not hasty in parting with his liberty, for he well knew the want of that to be one of the chief *remoras* to young men. . ." (*Some Notes*, p. 7). See Carroll Camden, "Spenser's 'Little Fish That Men Call *Remora*,'" *Rice Institute Pamphlet*, XLIV (1957), 1–16.

l. 9 *I fetters choose, and freely stand in aw*   That one may achieve freedom by choosing enthrallment is a time-honored paradox and frequently expressed in religious terms. Cf., for example, Seneca's "to obey God is freedom" ("On the Happy Life," *Moral Essays*, trans. John W. Basore, II [1932], 140–141); Donne's "Except you'enthrall mee, [I] never shall be free" (Sonnet XIV, l. 13); and—presumably said daily at morning prayer—God's "seruice is perfect freedome" (*BCP*, A6r).

l. 10 *Fatally bound by God, and Natures Law*   Bound for life by God (cf. Exodus 20.12) and by what North elsewhere calls the *Jus naturale*, supposed "to have been impressed by God in the heart of man at the first" (*Light*, pp. 4–5), i.e., before Christ. Cf. *Catechisme*, 19v; also, in the present headnote, the phrase "as well perpetual as natural."

38. [Come Barack, as thy hands doe Trophyes rayse]

North turns here to the common practice of paraphrasing a passage from scripture. He bases his poem on Judges 4 and 5, especially the latter, which conveys the so-called "Song of Deborah and Barak," probably the oldest extant example of Hebrew verse (J. Blenkinsopp, "Ballad Style and Psalm Style in the Song of Deborah: A Discussion," *Biblica*, XLII [1961], 69). Together the two chapters in Judges tell how Israel for its sins fell into the hands of Jabin, Canaanite king of Hazor, and how Deborah, the prophetess and judge, bade Barak raise an army against Sisera, the Canaanite captain. When Sisera's forces were destroyed, he fled for refuge to the tent of Jael, who, while he slept, drove a tent peg through his temples. There is reason to think that North composed his paraphrase in the earlier 1620s with his mind partly on current English military involvement in the Low Countries. One of the books that he owned attempted to rouse the English thus: "*Israell had a Deborah, who (though a wooman) had courage enough to daunt a whole Armye of Infidels; O then what a shame is it, that the King . . . [amongst] all this multitude, should finde never a man to stand, betweene him and reproach?*" (Thomas Scott, *Vox Dei* [1623], p. 12); North's copy is now in the Folger Shakespeare Library.

l. 5 *accord*   Not merely agree but also "To compose, sing, or play . . . in harmony; to attune" (*OED*).

l. 9 *Prop'hetesse*   Deborah prophesied the outcome of the battle. Cf. "devining" (l. 14).

l. 13 *Iabins steeled charyots*   Actually Jabin was dead at the time of the battle, but Sisera is said to have had nine hundred iron chariots which were mired because of a heaven-sent downpour.

l. 16 *chosen Israell*   It is worth pondering that the association of Israel with England was commonplace. For instance, the author of *Sions Charity Towards Her Foes in Misery* (1641) writes of "the troublers of this our Israel" (p. 2).

l. 18 *in his burning wrath* The association of deity with fire takes various forms in North; cf. Nos. 24, 33, 43, and 47.

39. Out of the 4ᵗʰ Chapter of Canticles

North's paraphrase of Solomon's Song 4.7–16 may be viewed in light of his observation elsewhere that the whole Song is made *"Poetical"* by its metaphoric quality, and that *"he who desires to win upon the opinion of others in writing, must endeavour to add some* [such] *delight to his more serious matter"* (*Light*, A3v–A4r). The meanings of the Song's metaphors, however, are *"unstable as Water,"* ready to "receive shape from every Vessel the Interpreter brings to it" (T. Beverley, *An Exposition of the Divinely Prophetick Song of Songs* [1687], A2v). Widely held to have been an epithalamion sung at the wedding of Solomon and Pharaoh's daughter, the Song was early viewed by the Jews as a celebration of Jehovah's love for Israel, and later by the Christians as a celebration of Christ's love for the Church and the soul. In the 1611 Authorized Version the fourth chapter is headed thus: "1 Christ setteth forth the graces of the Church. 8 He sheweth his loue to her. 16 The Church prayeth to be made fit for his presence." On the other hand, "Protestant tracts and sermons on marriage, such as Croft's *The Lover* (1638), not infrequently cite the allegorized Song as a presentation of the divine archetype which human marriage should imitate" (George L. Scheper, "Reformation Attitudes Toward Allegory and the Song of Songs," *Publications of the Modern Language Association*, LXXXIX [1974], 556; Scheper demonstrates the great popularity of the Song through the seventeenth century). Since North departs from his source to add the explicit idea of "our nuptialls" (l. 27), it may be correct to relate the poem to his marriage to Anne Montagu in April 1632 (cf. his other marriage poem, No. 21). As for form, Milton observes that "the Scripture . . . affords us a divine pastoral Drama in the Song of *Salomon* consisting of two persons and a double *Chorus*, as *Origen* rightly judges" (*The Reason of Church-government* [1642], *Complete Prose Works of John Milton*, Vol. I, ed. Don M. Wolfe [New Haven, 1953], p. 815). North's ll. 1–18 (in iambic pentameter) are spoken by the man, ll. 19–26 (iambic tetrameter) by the woman, and the closing couplet either by the man or (if North is following his usual practice) by a chorus of both.

l. 1 *blemish free* The biblical "there is no spot in thee" (Song 4.7) thus contributes to North's recurring perfection motif.

l. 4 *chayned by thy lovely locks* North goes out of his way to introduce the idea of chaining, which adds a pun and echoes the "enthrallment" motif of his amatory verse.

ll. 5–8 The punctuation of this passage illustrates that the modern differentiation between question marks and exclamation marks was not yet clearly established.

ll. 19–26 *Awake North wind. . .* These words of the woman, directly from Song 4.16, may remind one of the paraphraser's identity. Previously in the poem he has compressed his source, but here he expands, adding showers, bridal bed, and flowers.

l. 21 *I'ts* The intrusive apostrophe, which occurs in the same position in the

Rougham manuscript (86*v*), is repeated in No. 46, l. 14, and is probably just an indication of contemporary fluidity of punctuation; the Perkins manuscript also has "it's" and "its" as genitives; *fragrant*   Corrected here from Lady North's "fragant."

l. 28 *seed*   North's use of this word has simultaneous figurative and literal meanings, since one definition of "seed" was "semen." Elsewhere North notes that "the Body (if not the Soul *extraduce*) of Parents hath a partial continuance by the Seed, though not perpetuity" (*Observations*, pp. 14–15). Cf. Psalms 102.28: "The children of thy seruants shal continue: and their seed shall be established before thee."

40. A Paraphrase vpon the Añuntiation

Louis Martz comments on "the reluctance of conservative Anglicans" to relinquish devotion to the Virgin Mary (*The Poetry of Meditation* [New Haven, rev. ed., 1962], p. 96). During Charles's reign there was even an Anglican attempt to encourage such devotion (witness Anthony Stafford's *The Femall* [*sic*] *Glory: or, The Life, and Death of Our Blessed Lady* [1635]). Englishmen in general, on the other hand, were accustomed to a matter-of-fact naming of "the Feast of the Annunciation of the Blessed Virgin" in their business documents (e.g., Bodl. MS. North c.20, 63*r*), and even for the most irreligious, Lady Day (25 March) was important as the day from which England (until 1752) dated the calendar year. For religiously minded men like North it was significant as a festival relating to Christ. In the Book of Common Prayer the gospel reading for the day was Luke 1.26–38, telling how "the Angell Gabriel was sent from God, vnto a Citie of Galilee named Nazareth" (L1*v*). In the present poem the first and longer part (ll. 1–16), consisting of Gabriel's words, derives from Luke 1.28–35, and the second part (ll. 17–26) derives from the words of Elizabeth to Mary in Luke 1.42–45. In short, the poem is an antiphonal dialogue juxtaposing two speakers on the subject of Christ's Incarnation. North indicates the difference in speakers by assigning iambic pentameter to Gabriel, trochaic tetrameter to Elizabeth. Although the linkage here of the Fall with the Annunciation is not scriptural, it had long been traditional.

l. 1 *Haile Mary full of Grace*   This address, which appears in the gradual of the Roman mass on feast days to the Virgin, was best known among Catholics as part of the rosary prayer. The salutation is rendered in the King James bible as "Haile thou that art highly fauoured" (Luke 1.28), but the 1604 prayer book yields a closer "Haile full of grace" (*BCP*, L1*v*).

l. 2 *To be the height and Mirrour of thy kind*   Based on "Blessed art thou among women" (Luke 1.28), but cast in terms of the conventional old *speculum* figure.

l. 3 *bring forth a Son*   Luke 1.31. In the King James version, "bring forth a sonne"; in the Rheims bible and *BCP* (L1*v*), "beare a sonne."

l. 8 *Patronize*   Defend, support, stand by.

l. 10 *rebellion*   By definition, all sinners are rebels against God, but one might suspect that North's word choice relates also to the civil strife of his day. "*Rebellion is as the Sin of Witchcraft*" (I Samuel 15.23) is printed as an epigraph on the title page of his *Narrative*.

l. 14 *Mother of God* Cf. the King James bible: "that holy thing which shall bee borne of thee, shall bee called the sonne of God" (Luke 1.35); *seed* According to Nowell's *Catechisme* (28*v*), the "seede is (as saint Paul playnly teacheth vs) Jesus Christ the sonne of God very God, and the sonne of the virgin very man. . . ." In his *Light* North enumerates the basic beliefs of the Jews, beginning with their "expectation of the promised Seed or *Messias*" (p. 4).

l. 15 *breake the Serpents head* The *Catechisme* (28*v*–29*r*) relates that "In the head of the Serpent his poyson is conteyned, and the substaunce of hys lyfe and strength consisteth. Therefore the Serpentes head signifieth the whole strength, power, and kyngdome, or rather the tyranny of the deuill the old serpent: all whiche, Jesus Christ, that same seede of the woman, in whom God hath performed the full sūme of his promise, hath subdued by the vertue of his death. And so in breakyng the serpentes head, he hath rescued & made free from tyranny, all them that trust in hym." Cf. Genesis 3.15 and, herein, No. 45, l. 9, and No. 47, ll. 7–8.

ll. 23–24 *fully Blest* I.e., the fullness of Mary's blessedness will come about only when she is transplanted to heaven.

41. [Who's this appears in crimson dye]

The opening line of this poem is one of North's most arresting, and, in conjuring the presence of Christ at the time of the Passion, suggests momentarily the "composition of place" which plays such an important role in the meditative tradition (see Louis Martz, *The Poetry of Meditation* [New Haven, rev. ed., 1962]). The "crimson dye" of the line prepares for subsequent references to blood in ll. 6–10, which in turn derive from various scriptural passages, perhaps most importantly Matthew 26.28: "For this is my blood of the new Testament, which is shed for many for the remission of sinnes"—a passage spoken by the priest at every celebration of holy Communion (*BCP*, N3*r*). Blood and dye alike, combined with the idea of power (l. 2), are linked with a red garment that Christ is said to have worn: "Then the souldiers of the Gouernour tooke Jesus into the common hall. . . . And they stripped him, and put on him a scarlet robe. And when they had platted a crowne of thornes, they put it vpon his head, and a reed in his right hand: and they bowed the knee before him, and mocked him, saying, Haile king of the Jewes" (Matthew 27.27–29). North's opening question, furthermore, has typological implications (see *BCP*, E5*r*). The form of the poem (which was perhaps meant for music) is unusual in North: two five-line stanzas of iambic tetrameter (ll. 1, 2, 5) and iambic dimeter (ll. 3, 4), and a closing couplet of iambic pentameter (itself followed by a "Halleluiah" which might be yet another dimeter line; but cf. No. 43, l. 17, where the same word is clearly extra-metrical). Note that the shift in form after l. 10 marks a shift in focus: the final lines are addressed to Christ (see also headnote to No. 31).

l. 2 *power and victory* Ironically but appropriately, crimson was valued among the Romans for the robes of generals, princes, and especially emperors (John M'Clintock and James Strong, *Cyclopaedia of Biblical, Theological, and Ecclesiastical Literature*, I [New York, 1871, fac. ed., 1969], 566). Cf. the "vanquisht" of l. 11.

ll. 6–10 This stanza shows North attempting correlative verse: ll. 6 and 8 and the first half of l. 10 concern Christ's blood as fountain; ll. 7 and 9 and the second half of l. 10, as treasure.

42. A Paraphrase vpon the ascension

North's treatment of Christ's Ascension illustrates some of the breadth of seventeenth-century usage of the term "paraphrase." Related loosely to the brief accounts in Mark 16.19 and Luke 24.51, the poem owes most (particularly its second stanza) to the following passage in Acts 1.9–11:

> And when hee had spoken these things, while they beheld, hee was taken vp, and a cloud receiued him out of their sight. And while they looked stedfastly toward heauen, as he went vp, behold, two men stood by them in white apparell, Which also said, Yee men of Galililee [sic], why stand yee gazing vp into heauen: This same Jesus, which is taken vp from you into heauen, shall so come, in like maner as yee haue seene him goe into heauen.

After two stanzas beginning with questions—one for the disciples and one for the angels—the poem resolves itself in a stanza of praise by a chorus. Although the words of the latter are more appropriate for the disciples, North may have intended them to represent the harmonious merging of human and angelic voices.

l. 1 *exaltation*   The action of lifting or raising on high.

l. 2 *our cheife felicity*   Cf. No. 35, l. 2, and its annotation.

l. 6 *inspir'd vs by his breath*   The word "breath" is a reminder that "inspire" literally means to breathe or blow upon or into. For "inspire," *OED* gives: "Said of God or the Holy Spirit. . . : To influence or actuate by special divine or supernatural agency. . . ." Doubtless also there is an allusion to Christ's teaching.

l. 10 *Gloryes full extent*   Jesus said, "Father, the houre is come, glorifie thy Sonne, that thy Sonne also may glorifie thee" (John 17.1).

l. 12 *Crown*   Cf. No. 35 (l. 11) and No. 44 (l. 30); *trayn*   a set or class of persons.

l. 17 *pay with love the love wee ow*   Jesus said, "For God so loued the World, that he gaue his only begotten Sonne: that whosoeuer beleeueth in him, should not perish, but haue euerlasting life" (John 3.16); and "This is my Commaundement, that ye loue one another, as I haue loued you" (John 15.12). Cf. No. 28 (ll. 6–7).

43. Pentecost

The origin of the feast of Pentecost on the seventh Sunday after Easter is described in Acts 2.1–4:

> And when the day of Pentecost [i.e., the Jewish Shabuoth] was fully come, they [Christ's followers] were all with one accord in one place. And suddenly there

came a sound from heauen as of a rushing mighty wind, and it filled all the house where they were sitting. And there appeared vnto them clouen tongues, like as of fire, and it sate vpon each of them. And they were all filled with the holy Ghost, and began to speake with other tongues, as the spirit gaue them vtterance.

The manifestation of "the light of thy holy Spirit" (*BCP*, H1*r*) at Pentecost marked the commencement of the Christian church and hence was a time of particular joy. North's poem suggests both the restorative comfort of the day and also its appropriateness to song. If l. 16 is taken literally, the poem is not only epideictic but an invitation to epideictic singing or even an introduction to it, a possibility enhanced by the Norths' deep involvement in producing music. (Cf. No. 2, ll. 19–22, and No. 45, headnote. Several of Joseph Beaumont's poems for Whitsunday were composed for a bass and two trebles: *The Minor Poems of Joseph Beaumont, D.D. 1616–1699*, ed. Eloise Robinson [1914], pp. 194, 195, 196, 197.) Such force as North's poem has derives partially from its scriptural imagery and its sense of immediacy; beginning "This is the day," it insists that the holy time is "now." Cf. Milton's "This is the Month, and this the happy morn" ("On the Morning of Christ's Nativity," l. 1). The eight couplets that comprise the poem (cf. Nos. 11, 14, and 29) are divided into two stanzas, the first defining the nature of Pentecost, the second expressing a proper response to it.

l. 3 *the promis'd Comforter* According to the *Catechisme*, "In the manifold & diuers discomodities molestations & miseries of this life, the holy ghost with his secret cōsolatiō, & with good hope doth asswage, ease, & cōfort the griefes and mourning of the godly, which commonly are in this world, most afflicted, and whose sorrowes do passe all humane consolation: whereof he hath the true and proper name of Paraclete or the comforter" (43*r*&*v*). See also *BCP*, L1*v*–2*v* and Z1*r*.

l. 4 *fiery Cloven toungues* The fire, from Acts 2.3, provides physical evidence of the presence of the Holy Ghost.

l. 7 *fell* Ruthless, dreadful; *Tyrants to defye* Singling out this detail has the air of contemporary allusion.

ll. 9–12 Jesus said, "But when the Comforter is come, whom I wil send vnto you from the Father, euen the Spirit of trueth, which proceedeth from the Father, hee shall testifie of me" (John 15.26).

l. 15 *our King* An interesting tension is established between Jesus and the "fell Tyrants" of l. 7.

l. 16 *Lett's . . . Halleluiahs sing* The line may be a request to sing repeatedly the exclamation "Halleluiah" or to sing praise to God in songs known as "halleluiahs." According to St. Ambrose, "we receive the grace of the Holy Spirit who comes to us on the day of Pentecost. Fasting ceases, God is praised, and 'Alleluia' is sung" (John Gunstone, *The Feast of Pentecost* [1967], p. 35); and George Wither complains that "so innumerable are the foolish and prophane *Songs* now delighted in . . . that HALELVIAHS . . . are almost out of use and fashion. . ." (*Haleluiah or, Britans Second Remembrancer* [1641], Spenser Society, No. 26, pt. I [Manchester, 1879], pp. 11–12).

44. Antiphona

The title "Antiphona" invites comparison of this work with other verse or prose that is responsively sung in worship. Whether or not the connection with music is metaphorical, the poem illustrates North's penchant for dialogue. It illustrates also several of his recurring themes: life's "crosses," life as sea, the distraction of "carnalls," the desire for liberty, and the importance of love. The rhyme scheme varies systematically, and, in the chorus, the meter swells from two to three to four feet.

l. 1 *Lord by thy pow'rfull hand distrest*   Cf. note to No. 50, l. 22.

ll. 2–3 *Spent in strife / Of fragile elements*   Perhaps "wearied by strife amongst those frail things that constitute me."

l. 5 *Good Angell*   "God doth to our saluation vse the seruice of Angels, that wayte vpon vs, and therefore doe heare vs" (*Catechisme*, 54r). The adjective is a reminder that there are also bad (i.e., fallen) angels.

l. 11 *carnalls*   An unusual substantive, probably derived from the adjective "carnal" in its archaic sense of "Not spiritual, in a negative sense; material, secular" (*OED*). Cf. Romans 8.6: "For to be carnally minded, is death: but to be spiritually minded, is life and peace." See also "outward obiects of delight" (l. 21).

l. 18 *A treasure in his Sonn*   Cf. No. 41, l. 9.

l. 19 *By whose fayre light*   North elsewhere writes: "*If light external and light internal be of such excellence, what shall we say of light eternal flowing from the Sun of righteness, which lighteth every man that cometh into the world? This is the life of our Souls, which raiseth us up from the unclean sepulchre of Sin. . .*" (*Light*, A2r).

45. Hymnus sacer

The Book of Common Prayer highlights this scriptural advice: "be ye filled with the Spirit, speaking vnto yourselues in Psalmes, and Hymnes, and spirituall songs, singing and making melodie to the Lord in your hearts. . ." (Kiir; also D1v; cf. Psalms 33.3). North associates music and praise not only in this poem but also in Nos. 38, 39, 43, and 44. The mosaic of motifs in the "Hymnus sacer" may relate particularly to Easter. At morning prayer on Easter day, when certain "Anthemes shall be sung or sayd" (*BCP*, Giir), the first such anthem admonishes, "count your selues dead vnto sinne, but liuing vnto God in Christ," and the second speaks of Christ as "risen againe, the first fruites of them that sleepe." As in the present poem, furthermore, the second Easter anthem juxtaposes the story of Adam with that of Christ. Nevertheless, "Hymnus sacer" is a joyous hymn of general Christian relevance. It is comprised of rhythmical verses, generally of twelve or thirteen syllables, and since it does not occur in the Rougham manuscript, it may be one of North's later compositions.

l. 1 *Cantate Domino*   That the Psalms are described in the Vulgate as hymns may help to explain why "Hymnus sacer" begins with a line echoing the beginnings of Psalms 95, 96, 98, and 149. Psalm 95 ("O Come, let vs sing vnto the Lord" [*BCP*, Aiiv]) was to be said or sung daily at morning prayer, and Psalm 98 ("O Sing vnto the

Lord" [*BCP*, Aviir]) was assigned for evening prayer. Note the public, communal quality established by these opening words. A circumflex appears in the manuscript on the final "e" of "Cantate" both here and in l. 2, and also in "promulgate" in l. 3. Although circumflexes often were used as a means of accentuating seventeenth-century Latin verse, the nature of their occurrence in this poem is problematic—probably an error. Cf. the "cantate" of *Geor: Buchanani Scoti, Poemata* (Leyden, 1628), pp. 124, 126.

l. 6 *Vitę* The caudate "e" here is an old means of writing "æ"; *arbor nova* Through His death and resurrection, Christ made the cross a means to life, a "Tree of Life." The word "nova" invites comparison with the first Tree of Life, notably in Genesis 3.22. The point is that both trees symbolize the gift of immortality, the first long lost, and the second still available. North elsewhere writes: "The sweetness of . . . divine Providence appeared manifestly at first in our Paradise terrestrial, where the tree of Life (which Typically represented life Eternal) was no more under interdict, than any other fruit in the Garden" (*Light*, p. 3).

l. 9 *Nec sanctos lędit feri Draconis ira* See, for example, Revelation 12.9: "And the great dragon was cast out, that old serpent, called the deuill and Satan, which deceiueth the whole world. . . ." Cf. No. 40, ll. 14–15, and No. 47, ll. 7–8.

46. A description of Man

The final five poems beginning here have an affinity with North's devotional verse in that each concerns man's proper relationship with God. For various reasons, nonetheless, it seems best to regard them as meditative verse. This first poem, for instance, has many parallels with a particular prose meditation by Joseph Hall (*Meditations and Vowes Divine and Morall* [1605], Bk. I, no. LXXXIII, reptd. in *The Seventeenth-Century Resolve*, ed. John L. Lievsay [Lexington, Kentucky, 1980], p. 15; see also Louis Martz, *The Poetry of Meditation* [New Haven, Conn., rev. ed., 1962]; Barbara Kiefer Lewalski, *Protestant Poetics and the Seventeenth-Century Religious Lyric* [Princeton, 1979]; and my "Mode and Voice in 17th-Century Meditative Verse: A Discussion of Five Newly Discovered Poems by Dudley North," *Medieval and Renaissance Studies*, No. 9, Proceedings of the Southeastern Institute of Medieval and Renaissance Studies, ed. Frank Tirro [Durham, N.C., 1982], pp. 55–86). From the storehouse of traditional topics North draws forth for this poem the idea of man as a microcosm (see Leonard Barkan, *Nature's Work of Art: The Human Body as Image of the World* [New Haven, 1975], p. 28; David George Hale, *The Body Politic: A Political Metaphor in Renaissance English Literature* [The Hague, 1971]; and North's own No. 48, l. 4). He chooses a form of the commonplace that enables him to give it an emblematic cast, comparing man and city, as in Proverbs 25.28 and Donne's Sonnet XIV ("I, like an usurpt towne, to'another due," l. 5).

l. 2 *Arcenall* Cf. Pliny: "all Men with one consent, call him . . . *The little World*. For his Body is, as it were, a Magazine or Storehouse of all the vertues and efficacies of all Bodyes. . ." (cited by Helkiah Crooke, Μικροκοσμογραφία [2nd ed., 1631], p. 3).

l. 3 *goverment*   This form occurs also in the Rougham manuscript.

l. 4 *Enricht with Nobles to deliberate*   Note the assumption here and in the following lines that the welfare of the state is in the hands of the nobility.

ll. 7–8 *The Hart . . . / The source of spirits*   The heart was not the sole source of spirits but the best. See note to No. 13, l. 7.

l. 11 *counsell*   Presumably the "Nobles" that constitute the mind of this body; *informers*   There is a pun here on, (1) informants, and, (2) "One who or that which informs with life . . . ; an inspirer, animator, vitalizer" (*OED*).

l. 12 *strenght*   See note to No. 25, l. 94.

l. 13 *the Heads the stately'st part*   In a "Discourse" added to his *Observations*, North writes of "the most exalted part of Microcosm, which is the Head" (printed in *Light*, p. 132). More specifically, the head traditionally suggests superiority in government.

l. 14 *I'ts*   See note to No. 39, l. 21; *frontispice*   the face or front of a building.

l. 15 *pyle*   A large building or edifice.

l. 16   *Vicegerent*   A person appointed to act in the place of a king or other ruler (Donne follows the same tradition when he makes Reason man's viceroy in Holy Sonnet XIV). It is important that North seems to have regarded reason as his own strongest asset. In *Light* he says, "*I write not so much to the Learned, as to the rational part of men, and I confess that the use of Reason is my best weapon. . .*" (A3*v*).

l. 17 *the fow'r noblest senses*   Sight and hearing (see No. 13), smell, and taste are all situated in the noblest part of man's body. In the textbook on physics by Joannes Magirus (d. 1596), studied at St. John's by North's acquaintance D'Ewes, the senses are listed in the following order: sight, hearing, smell, taste, and touch (Harris Francis Fletcher, *The Intellectual Development of John Milton*, vol. II, *The Cambridge University Period 1625–32* [Urbana, 1961], p. 176).

ll. 18–19 *account by Fancyes hand / To Iudgement's brought*   I.e., any report brought by Fancy is subjected to evaluation by Judgment. North's apparently inconsistent attitudes towards fancy in various poems are resolved when one recalls that, although it is valuable, fancy is subordinate to reason. See note to No. 29, l. 1.

l. 21 *members*   Another pun: (1) parts of the body, (2) parts of an edifice, and, (3) individuals belonging to a society or assembly.

l. 22 *record*   Evidence of the proceedings or verdict of a court of justice. The stress on the second syllable is found in verse as late as the nineteenth century (*OED*).

l. 24 *Tenant*   God as landlord appears also in No. 47, ll. 2–3.

ll. 25–27 *when Shee her homage dares denye*   Probably North never relinquished this view, though he took sides against the King at mid-century. Cf. Shakespeare's famous "Take but degree away, untune that string, / And hark what discord follows" (*Troilus and Cressida*, I.iii.109–110).

l. 31 *They last doe round the Soule*   "Th'affections" (l. 28) finally surround the defecting Soul.

l. 34 *Regayn'd by sorrow*   I.e., through repentance.

47. [Our Lyfe vnto a Garden I compare]

As Louis Martz observes, the garden is "one of the great central symbols in the Christian literature of meditation and contemplation" (*The Paradise Within* [New Haven,

1964], p. 9). Commonly regarded as a place where "euerie *Species*" was "a character for Man, to read his Maker" (Henry King, *Two Sermons Preached at White-hall in Lent, March 3. 1625. And Februarie 20. 1626* [1627], p. 14), a garden was also a place where man could read about nature and himself. Though North elsewhere uses elements from nature and the pastoral (cf. esp. Nos. 22, 23, and 39), this garden piece is his closest approach to emblematic verse. Cf., for example, Henry Peacham, *Minerva Britanna* (1612), p. 183; and George Wither, *A Collection of Emblemes* (1635), pp. 70, 140, 144, 209.

l. 2 *A garden of the great Creator held*   Cf. No. 46, l. 24, and George Herbert's "Redemption," which begins, "Having been tenant long to a rich Lord. . ." (*The Works of George Herbert*, ed. F. E. Hutchinson [Oxford, 1964; 1st pub. 1941], p. 40). Rosemond Tuve points out Henry King's observation that "we have not *freeholds* but *farms*, are not *inheritors* but *tenants*, whereas the great landlord of Nature has everlasting titles. . ." (*Elizabethan and Metaphysical Imagery* [Chicago, 1961; 1st ed., 1947], p. 365).

l. 5 *bitter Aloes*   A genus of succulent plants with "a greuous sauour and a wonderfull bytter taste" (Turner, *A New Herball* [1551], Bvir). From the aloe was made "A drug of nauseous odour, bitter taste, and purgative qualities" (*OED*). Hence the aloe came to be associated with bitter experience.

l. 7 *wyly serpent*   Cf. the "wilye Serpent the deuill" (*Catechisme*, 66v); also No. 40, l. 15, and No. 45, l. 9.

l. 8 *Herbgrace*   Since the time of Aristotle, herbgrace or rue had been deemed effective against poisons (see, e.g., *Regimen Sanitatis Salerni* [1634], p. 49). North associates the plant with repentance in his *Light*. Citing I Peter 5.5 and James 4.6 (p. 50), he argues thus:

> Some there are (the *Antinomians* by name) who declare Repentance to be altogether unnecessary, *for Faith* (say they) *purifieth sufficiently, and God seeth no sin in the faithfull*; but certainly there are not so many Texts of Scripture, requiring Repentance in vain, so as it must be necessary in the way of Salvation. . . . From these waters [of affliction] by an ascent, become somewhat difficult, by reason of our fainting Spirits, we come to the garden of Spiritual consolation, a place not only pleasing, but usefull, for there we may discern at a considerable distance, the rock of Faith, and the temple of Holiness. . . . And in that Garden may be gathered herb of Grace usefull for Nutrition and Sustentation, and *Salvia* (or the hope of Salvation) as an incentive to Perseverance, from both which we may receive fresh vigour, enabling us to undergo the residue of our journey.
>
> (pp. 48–49)

Both repentance and grace are necessary if a soul is to be protected from the poison of sin.

ll. 13–16 *Tyme doth by Nature . . . grow*   Both time and wild thyme. Bacon, observing that "GOD *Almighty* first Planted a *Garden*," recommended planting "whole Allies" of "Wild-Time" for its fragrance ("Of Gardens," *Essayes* [1629], pp. 266, 270). Stewart discusses the close linkage of the ideas of time and the garden (*The Enclosed Garden: The Tradition and the Image in Seventeenth-Century Poetry* [Madison, Wis., 1966]).

ll. 17–18 *happy fruits*   Jesus said, "He that abideth in me, and I in him, the same

bringeth forth much fruit" (John 15.5); and the *Catechisme* teaches: "It is God alone
that geueth fruitefulnes to the grounde, that maketh the land plentifull, and to beare
fruite aboundantly, and therefore it is certaine that in vayne shall we wast and spend
out all the course of our lyfe in toyle of body and trauayle of minde vnlesse it please
God to prosper our endeuours" (64r). Sometimes "fruits" referred specifically to the
fruits of the spirit enumerated in Galatians 5.22–23.

l. 18 *th'Eternall Sun* Cf. Psalms 84.11: "For the LORD God is a sunne. . . ."
Maren-Sofie Røstvig observes that "The physical sun was usually viewed as the
shadow of God, and Marvell refers to it in this manner in 'The Garden', when he
characterises our great luminary as that 'milder sun'" (*The Happy Man: Studies in the
Metamorphoses of a Classical Ideal*, I [rev. ed., New York, 1962], 188). Cf. North's
own *Light*, A2r–v.

l. 19 *show'rs of grace* The *Catechisme* teaches that God "will with the diuine dew of
his grace so water & make fruitefull the drinesse and barrennesse of my harte, that I
may bring forth plentifull fruits of godlynes. . ." (79r).

ll. 21–24 *If Manhood water* Cf. Isaiah 58.11: "and thou shalt be like a watered
garden, and like a spring of water, whose waters faile not." Concerning "Manhood,"
it should be noted that the comparison between the seasons and the stages of man's
life is so much a habit of Renaissance mind that North feels moved to mention no
seasons but autumn and winter. Cf. No. 3, ll. 8–12, and No. 33.

l. 23 *cordialls* Fruits were a common ingredient in cordials. It is pertinent here
that "cordial" (from Latin "cor," "cordis") is defined as "that which comforteth the
heart" (John Bullokar, *An English Expositor* [1616], E3r).

ll. 30–32 *Theyr rootes with earth so intermixed lye* Twitch, known also as couch-
grass or dog's grass, is the sort of plant North has in mind. Gerard explains that "it
creepeth in the ground hither and thither with long white rootes, iointed at certaine
distances, . . . platted or wrapped one within another very intricately, in so much . . .
great labour must be taken before it can be destroied" (*The Herball or Generall Historie
of Plantes* [1597], p. 22). The point is worth mentioning because Sir Dudley's father
complains of it as "an evill Herb" that has overrun some of the Norths' land, and
"having once possessed a ground, the soyle must be wholly altered and over-come, or
no good thing will thrive committed unto it" (*Forest 45*, p. 162).

l. 37 *His holy fyre* The fire associated with divinity is of special use at this point
because burning was a means of controlling weeds and improving soil (Gerard, p. 22;
and Walter Blith, *The English Improver Improved or The Survey of Husbandry Surveyed*
[1653], pp. 61–62). A "twitch-fire" was "a fire for burning twitch or other weeds"
(*OED*).

l. 40 *The rule of choyse* It is God's will that men have free choice to sin or not
to sin.

48. [When after chyldhood Tyme had shew'd on mee]

The speaker of this poem reflects on his soul's past, and, coincidentally or not, the
movement of his thought parallels that which is commonly recommended for meditation: from memory through understanding to an arousal of the affected will. Probably
the autobiographical element is considerable.

ll. 1–10 North appears to describe a similar turnabout in his life in the introduction to *Observations* (A3v–A4r).

l. 2 *The Comick entrance of lyfes Tragedye* Cf. Plato's "the whole tragi-comedy of life" (J. C. B. Gosling, trans., *Plato: Philebus*, 50b [Oxford, 1975], p. 50). Among the most common of Renaissance commonplaces, the comparison of life to a stage play assumed many forms. Cf. these lines from Francis Quarles's *Divine Fancies* (1632):

> Our Life's a *Tragedy*: Those secret *Roomes*
> Wherein we tyre us, are our Mothers *Wombes*;
> The *Musicke* ush'ring in the *Play*, is Mirth
> To see a *Manchild* brought upon the Earth. . . .
>
> (Bk. I, No. 6, p. 4)

l. 4 *The rule of Microcosme* See headnote to No. 46. The sentiment is similar to that of Thomas Browne: "to call our selves a Microcosme, or little world, I thought it onely a pleasant trope of Rhetorick, till my neare judgement and second thoughts told me there was a reall truth therein" (*Religio Medici* [1643], p. 77).

ll. 5–6 *My Soule noe more in wardshipp claym'd her right / Of souvrayngtye* "Wardship," the guardianship of a minor, involves custody of his person and lands; the fact that the soul is about to take a sea-voyage may justify seeing a pun in the word. Regarding the soul and her sovereignty, cf. No. 46, ll. 23–24.

l. 6 *fram'd* Made (it).

l. 7 *To visitt all her coasts* Here begins North's most unusual treatment of the soul-as-ship-pilot *topos* (see No. 28, note to l. 11; also No. 49, ll. 33–42). Depiction of the rational soul as pilot of the bodily vessel was a common classical image (see Kathleen M. Grange, "The Ship Symbol as a Key to Former Theories of the Emotions," *Bulletin of the History of Medicine*, XXXVI [1962], 512–523). Most such souls, however, are troubled by the rough seas of vicissitude or sin (see, for example, No. 44, l. 6), whereas this youthful one starts out with "delight" (l. 6) on a cleanup-and-colonizing mission. Nevertheless, the journey partakes of the darkness of the profane; from the outset the cleanup is necessary, and eventually the soul is deflected by worldly things.

l. 10 *by reasons light* Man's rational soul *is* governed by reason. If it really is in good working order, says Donne, "the reasonable soul of man, when it enters, becomes all the soul of man, and he hath no longer a vegetative and a sensitive soul, but all is that one reasonable soul; so, sayes S. *Aug*[ustine]. . ." (Sermon XXIII, 1628, *LXXX Sermons* [1640], p. 225). See No. 46, ll. 16–21.

l. 12 *of perfect growth* An ironic pun which includes the meaning "fully developed." The adjective describes "old" vice (l. 14), largely controllable but more difficult to eradicate than "tender Vice" (l. 11).

l. 13 *rooted out with payne* Note that the soul's mission is presented in terms reminiscent of the vice/weed imagery of No. 47 (esp. ll. 25–39).

l. 16 *helples* Not merely incapable of self-help, but beyond help.

ll. 17–18 *Hind'rers of Outward Glory, for whose sake / The Soule enamourd, vertues part did take* An obscure passage, but explicable as a step in the soul's decreasing ability to cope. At first she had no trouble killing "tender Vice." Next, although she had problems rooting out more mature vice, she managed to conquer "most" (l. 12). "But after this successe" (l. 15) she was faced with a harder problem. It is all right for the soul to champion virtue against the mind's "defects" (l. 16) and to continue to "settle Vertue" (l. 8) where she can, but her motivation is sullied now because the mind's defects are "Hind'rers of Outward Glory," and she has become "enamourd" of this tawdry kind of "Glory." That is, she is now guilty of doing the right thing at least partly for the wrong reason. In the succeeding passage, she descends from "defects of mynd" which impede "Outward Glory" (i.e., from a relationship between internal and external elements) to "infirmity" of body (l. 20). In other words she descends to a still "more externall view" (l. 22), and thence to dangerous straits. North's continuing concern with the danger of "externalls" is noteworthy; see, for example, No. 35, note to l. 3; No. 44; and No. 50, l. 29.

l. 21 *charm'd*   Enchanted, with connotations of controlling, subduing.

l. 23 *Fortunes*   The matter is relative. The fortunes of the Norths were sadly shrunken, but young Simonds D'Ewes felt acutely that he was less well furnished at the University than Sir Dudley was (*The Autobiography and Correspondence of Sir Simonds D'Ewes*, ed. James Orchard Halliwell, II [1845], 147).

ll. 25–26 *vertue . . . / . . . fruitlesse*   Cf. No. 47, esp. note to ll. 17–18.

ll. 27–32 The causes and nature of the soul's descent are reminiscent of much writing on melancholy, most notably in Burton's *Anatomy of Melancholy* and the works of North's own father. Despair such as that approached by the speaker, says Burton, is "*opposite to hope, and a most pernicious sin*," "the Murderer of the soul, as *Austin* [St. Augustine] terms it"; "The part affected is the whole soul . . . ; there is a privation of joy, hope, trust, confidence, of present and future good, and in their place succeed fear, sorrow, &c." (1651 ed., pp. 694–695).

l. 37 *That wisedom infinite*   Appositive to "Eternall God" (l. 33). Note how both are amplified by the three intervening clauses beginning "whose."

ll. 37–38 *secur'd my Soule / From sharp dispayre*   Rendered it safe from attack by despair.

l. 39 *Terrene affections*   Desires for temporal, earthly things (the "things externall" of l. 41).

l. 42 *profitt ev'n from losse*   Relatable to North's theme of worldly "crosses."

l. 44 *Some outward blessings with it were combyn'd*   The presence of this thought is more easily justified if one views the poem as shadowing events in the writer's life.

49. [Noe Noe, I ever did and must denye]

This poem explores the nature of happiness and serves as a reminder that liberty exists in the eye of the beholder. It may be viewed to advantage in a frame provided by Lawrence Stone (p. 21):

> As the universe was ordered in a great chain of being, so the nation was regulated by obedience to a hierarchy of superiors leading up to the King, so society was composed of various estates of men all settled and contented in their degree, and so the family was ordered by obedience of wife and children to the *pater familias*. Whether in heaven or hell, in the universe or on earth, in the state or in the family, it was a self-evident truth that peace and order could only be preserved by the maintenance of grades and distinctions and by relentless emphasis on the overriding need for subjection of the individual will to that of superior authority.

An outstanding exemplar of filial duty, Sir Dudley reveals here that his self-containment was not achieved easily. This poem and "A Riddle" (No. 37) are his most forceful treatments of a theme that crops up repeatedly in his verse and prose.

l. 2 *happy*   Cf. the "perfect modell of Felicitye" which North devised in No. 32— in earlier days, one may suppose.

l. 11 *If some imprison'd birds desyre it not*   North also associates freedom and the flight of birds in No. 37. Cf., for example, the emblem of Nicholas Reusner, which depicts one bird flying, another in a cage, and gives as motto "Aurea libertas" (*Aureolorum Emblematum Liber Singularis* [Strassburg, 1587], D5*v*).

l. 15 *And till t'is from the bodyes prison free*   The image of the body as a prison may be traced to Plato (*Phaedo*, 62b, 67d, 82e–83a). In view of the "imprison'd birds" of l. 11, one should recall also, e.g., John Webster's *Duchess of Malfi* (IV.ii.128–130): "Didst thou ever see a lark in a cage? such is the soul in the body. . ."; and Quarles's *Emblemes* (1635), p. 281: "My Soule is like a Bird; my Flesh, the Cage."

l. 21 *The greatest Prince some servitude must beare*   Cf. North's Occasional VII:

It hath afforded me sometimes matter of no small admiration, to find in my self, and others, lovers of freedom, a desire . . . of being in a state of height and greatness. . . . I take this to be Vanity in the highest degree, and one of the scourges of the most High. The folly of it may appear in this, that our so much prized freedom would be utterly lost in such a way; outward freedom by a continual obtrusion of business, even at times most unseasonable to use in point of health and otherwise, and inward freedom by an inforcement of compliance in things no way to be approved of by a judicious and ingenuous spirit.

(*Light*, pp. 84–85)

l. 22 *crosses*   Cf. Nos. 22 (ll. 2, 7) and 34 (l. 4).

l. 23 *Lawes, Rules, Observances the bridles are*   The term "observances" encompasses customs and rituals as well as (with respect to another person) dutiful service. North says elsewhere that "generally in the new Testament the word Liberty standeth opposed to *Jewish* Ceremonies. . ." (*Light*, p. 37).

l. 26 *affections*   Note that North gives only the two major opposites in this passage (ll. 23–28), those bound by law and those bound by desire or feeling. Either he simplifies his views here or his position was more complex, less conservative, when, late in life, he wrote in *Light* "That no person is bound to doe any thing that is contrary to his Conscience, *for whatsoever is not of faith is sin*; but every man oweth that right to himself, to be informed carefully and fully in all things required by the Magistrate, and in case he cannot be satisfied, that Obedience in that particular is lawfull, then to submit himself to punishment" (p. 38).

l. 28 *In taking freedome, freedome casts away*   The statement that God's "seruice is perfect freedome" was supposed to be recited every day in the year (*BCP*, A6r).

l. 32 *annoye*   *OED*: "A mental state akin to pain arising from . . . subjection to circumstances, which one dislikes." The strength of the term is suggested by the contrasts in Thomas Kyd's line, "pleasure follows pain, and bliss annoy" (*Spanish Tragedy*, II.ii.11).

l. 34 *tempestuous seas*   Probably the best of North's life-as-sea passages (cf. Nos. 28 and 48).

l. 35 *the true Neptune*   Cf. Sir Dudley's father: "Thou, Oh God, art the Starre, the Loadstone, the *Neptune* of our voyage in this world, be thou my current, my guide. . ." (*Forest 45*, p. 144).

l. 38 *lifes western straights*   This passage blends traditions relating the West to the setting sun, death, and various "blest" lands (cf. ll. 36, 42) reachable by water, and it adds the dimension of a pun on "strait" (a narrow waterway or a time of sore need). Cf. Donne's "I joy, that in these straits, I see my West" ("Hymn to God, My God, in My Sickness," l. 11).

l. 40 *Find the Pacifick Sea of true Content*   The pun on "pacific" here has various parallels, its most effective perhaps in l. 16 of Donne's "Hymn" (cited above), but its most handy for North perhaps in the writing of his father (*Forest 45*, p. 163); the elder North's reference is dated 29 January 1637/8).

50. An Essay in the way of Gratitude

Although this final poem in the Perkins manuscript may be approached via the meditative mode, it fits neatly into no genre. In fact, North's decision to call it "An Essay" could indicate his awareness that he was creating a mixed form. Concerned with the age-old relationship between sickness and salvation, the poem gives every indication of being one of North's latest, most personal utterances. Along with other autobiographical matters, it relates the speaker's gratitude to God for allowing him to survive a recent attack of the stone. The second-longest of North's poems, it is constructed of plain, rough-hewn couplets, with a triplet at ll. 31–33.

l. 1 *What better can poore I to God returne*   From its opening, the poem expresses gratitude not *to* God, but for or about Him. Previously the speaker has forgotten the need to "returne" something to God; but see No. 42 (l. 17) and No. 47 (l. 4).

ll. 2–3 *burn / In Zeale*   In Isaiah 6.6–7 a six-winged seraph takes a live coal from the altar and puts it to Isaiah's lips to purify him and his speech. North utilizes the traditional association of fire and religious zeal also in Nos. 43 and 47; cf. No. 12, l. 13.

l. 4 *A lasting monument*   It is striking that this particular work should be the sole piece in which North speaks of his verse in terms of "lasting."

l. 5 *wast*   Expend. Far from the uselessness normally associated with "waste," the word here suggests the degree of the writer's commitment.

l. 6 *webb*   A pun referring both to a silkworm's thread and to a woven fabric. The latter, like a poem, might have "letters rightly plac't."

l. 10 *And to great length hee did extend the same*   An indication of the lateness of the poem.

l. 12 *signall bountyes sheilded mee from want*   An interesting line to juxtapose with No. 32 (l. 5) and No. 48 (l. 23), as well as with data on the North family's declining fortunes.

l. 13 *Some years in warr*   See pp. 34–36. Ll. 13–14 are written vertically in the margin of the manuscript with the notation that they should be inserted "between ye 12 & [former] 13 ver" (157r).

l. 14 *sadd plagues* North lived through a number of major outbreaks of plague (e.g., those of 1603, 1625, and 1665). The fact is, however, that between 1600 and 1670 Cambridgeshire suffered from outbreaks "at least every five years" (Ethel M. Hampson, in *The Victoria History of the County of Cambridge*, ed. L. F. Salzman, II [1948], 101). In August 1624, at a time when hundreds were dying of a spotted fever similar to the plague, his youngest sister, Elizabeth, fell ill. Taken to the Tunbridge Wells that had been discovered by their father, she died before having a chance to taste the water (Mary Anne Everett Green, ed., *CSP*, Domestic, 1623–1625 [1859], p. 329). It appears that the only specifically recorded illness of Sir Dudley connected with an epidemic was in 1638 (see p. 60 and the headnote to No. 29), but his son Roger later described the impact made on him by an outbreak of bubonic plague when the family was living in King Street, Westminster. Two of the children, Mary and Dudley (the latter born in 1641), were stricken, and Sir Dudley "removed because of his promiscuous converse," whereas his wife "stayed, and with her own hands nursed her two tender children" (*Lives*, II, 2).

l. 15 *blest mee in relation coniugall* The most unequivocal allusion to Anne in North's verse.

l. 22 *Call'd for a rodd* A minister coming to the home of a sick person was supposed to remind him that "whatsoeuer your sickenesse is, know you certainly that it is Gods visitation" (*BCP*, Aa2r). Cf. Milton's "That Golden Scepter which thou didst reject / Is now an Iron Rod to bruise and break / Thy disobedience" (*Paradise Lost*, V.886–888).

l. 23 *sicknes seiz'd on mee with tortures fell* North here introduces his affliction with the stone ("fell" = fierce, terrible). The earliest reference I know to a "fitt of the Stone" that North suffered occurs in a letter from a brother in October 1654, when North was approaching fifty-two (Bodl. North MS. c.4, no. 101). Bearing l. 10 in mind, the reader may decide whether this is early for the seizure North describes here. Lawrence Stone writes that "one in twelve of the English aristocracy of the time are known to have been sufferers from the stone, which suggests a true figure of one in six, or perhaps even higher still" (p. 562).

l. 25 *haples . . . hopeles . . . helples* Cf. No. 15, l. 13, and its note.

l. 29 *externalls* Possessive form here; a major North theme (see, for example, No. 35 and note to l. 3).

l. 30 *ēre* The circumflex sometimes was used to indicate contraction.

l. 33 *Powers fountayn* Cf., "the fountain of all power, which is of God himself" (Occasional VI, *Light*, p. 83).

l. 38 *comon meanes* North's wife was skilled at caring for the sick, in fact regarded within the family as "more than a match for a college of physicians" (*Lives*, II, 333). In his *Observations* North writes: "Much good ariseth to poor people by the application of . . . ordinary remedies, and it is of more certain benefit, then the dealing about Cures of extraordinary consideration, whereof observing the uncertain (and sometimes dangerous) event, some have taken occasion to doubt, whether there come more good, or harm, by those Arts in such difficult Cures" (pp. 60–61). His amplifying comment within the poem (at l. 40) confirms that he was spared the surgeon's knife on this occasion.

l. 39 *my nephritick tortures* An unusually specific touch in North's verse. Helkiah

Crooke defines "*Nephriticall* patients" as those "troubled about their Kidneyes, especially with the ston[e]. . . ." He explains that "the paine of the Stone is dull whilst it resteth in the Kidney, and acute when it mooueth into or toward the Vreter" (Μικρο-κοσμογραφία [2nd ed., 1631], pp. 189–190).

l. 41 *annoyd*   Injured, hurt. Cf. No. 49, l. 32 and note.

l. 52 *broken Stone*   A somewhat bizarre parallel of God's customary breaking of the stony human heart (l. 28) in order to prepare it for repentance; cf. Ezekiel 11.19.

ll. 59–63 *great artists*   A similar passage on medical men occurs in No. 25, ll. 44–50. As Sir Dudley's father had long since observed, a physician is "a Professor of a most conjecturall Art" (*Forest 45*, p. 98).

l. 66 *Theyr outward power is but Vicegerency*   North's ideas here on regal versus divine power are similar to those expressed at the close of Donne's "Satire III" (ll. 89–110). See also North's own Occasional X (*Light*, pp. 90–93).

l. 75 *Wee all obey him when wee know it nott*   North's approach here to foreordination is modified in the closing lines of the poem, especially l. 80, which asserts man's free will. Cf. No. 47, l. 40: "The rule of choyse is his [God's] revealed will."

l. 80 *it's*   A natural variant; elsewhere in the manuscript, "its."

V

TEXTUAL NOTES

These notes record substantive variants from the text of the poems as they appear in the (unnumbered) Perkins Library North manuscript. (A different copy text has been used for only one poem: No. 27 comes from *Lacrymae Cantabrigienses* [1619].) Variants derive from the Rougham Hall manuscript unless accompanied by the abbreviation *Bodl.* (Bodleian Library MS. Eng. misc. e.262, fol. 34*r*).

There are many additional but inconsequential differences in detail between the Perkins and Rougham versions, apparently reflective not only of Lady North's generally unfussy concept of faithful transcription but also of her greater concern for careful punctuation in the Perkins manuscript. Omitted here, these variations are recorded in the original typescript of the present volume, now on deposit in Perkins Library.

 1. The Favorite of Loue and Honour: 15 this] his
 14. On Serena sleeping: 7 women] woman
 20. An Ironicall perswasion to Serena seeming resolved to liue at Court: 6 Thundrer] Thunder
 25. A Satyre. 1636: 33 should only] should
 29. An Elegye composed vpon the buriall of Ann Lady Rich: *title* An elegy upon yᵉ buryall of yᵉ incomparable Lady An: Rich *Bodl.* 5 to my verses luster giue,] lustre to my Verses give *Bodl.* 7 my] mine *Bodl.* 11 exspos'd] confin'd *Bodl.* 14 sorrow] natuer *Bodl.*
 31. An Elegie vpon the Right Honᵇˡᵉ Dudley Lord North by his Eldest Sonne Executor: *title* vpon the Right Honᵇˡᵉ Dudley] vpon the death of Dudley Eldest Sonne] son
 36. [As all by Natures fatall course must dye]: 3 heaven] heavens
 44. Antiphona: 12 prayer] prayers
 47. [Our Lyfe vnto a Garden I compare]: 24 make] makes

A GENEALOGICAL CHART OF
THE NORTH FAMILY

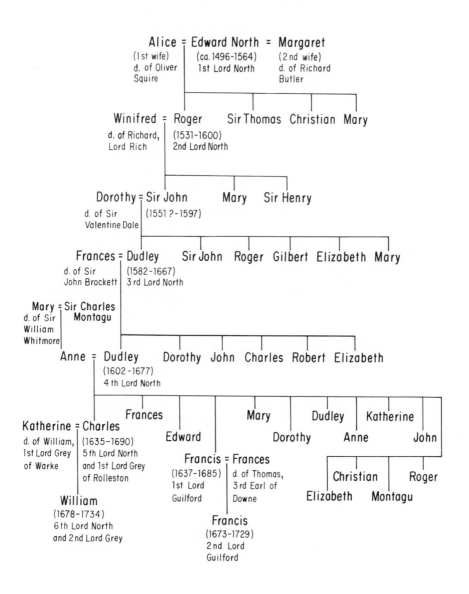

MISCELLANEOUS TRANSLATED FRAGMENTS

The following passages of verse occur in the discourse of North's *Observations and Advices Oeconomical* and his *Light in the Way to Paradise*.

1

Ask you why Wealth in Marriage I not crave?
'Tis that my Wife the Breeches should not have.
The Wife brings less in Birth, and Wealth then he,
Or else the Man shall not her equal be.

> *Observations*, p. 7; from
> Martial, *Epigrams*, VIII.xii.1–4.

2

Abroad good Wife, and there new dwelling find,
Or act at home, as I declare my mind.

> *Observations*, p. 14; from
> Martial, *Epigrams*, XI.civ.1.

3

A serious work to all of *Roman* name,
Useful to life, and limbs, and of good fame.

> *Observations*, p. 118; from
> Horace, *Epistles*, I.xviii.49–50;
> on hunting.

4

Let Verses gently charm the mind,
And as they will th'affections wind.

> *Observations*, p. 120; from
> Horace, *Ars Poetica*, l. 100.

5

Excess in Body makes the Soul decline,
And choaks with earth a share of breath divine.

> *Light*, p. 11; from Horace,
> *Satires*, II.ii.77–79.

6

That cause which conquers, Heav'n approves,
But Cato *he the conquer'd loves.*

> *Light*, p. 72; from Lucan,
> *Belli Civilis*, I.128.

APPENDIX C

THE ORDER OF ELEMENTS IN
THE PERKINS MANUSCRIPT

Entries in brackets are North's opening words of untitled writings, and entries in double brackets are labels added by the present editor. Entries that do not appear also in the "Index of Titles and First Lines" may be assumed to be in prose.

[[Dedication of poems]]
The Favorite of Loue and Honour
An Ironicall perswasion to Serena seeming resolved to liue at Court
On Serena sleeping
Sonnett [Whence can that sweet force arize]
[I'le not dispayre and dye, nor heav'ns accuse]
Sonnett [When my heart was first enthrall'd]
To Serena threatning to punish a supposed new affection in her servant with a perpetuall coldnesse in her selfe
On Serena playing on the Lute
Upon a Poem of my Fathers
Sonnett [Wylye Cupid sett to proove]
[Thy Face, Selena, should not mee comand]
[Lett not thy Husbands breach of Faith to Thee]
[Come lett vs end our sorrowes with a Kisse]
Sonnett [Thinke not Disdayne can quench my Loue]
An Elegye composed vpon the buriall of Ann Lady Rich
[Noe Noe, Selena, Now I playnly see]
Sonnett [I a wanton winning passion]
[Vayne are thy doubts Selena, vayn thy feares]
[You bynd, and say I may your bands vntye]
Sonnett [I doe not Love, it is most true]
Sonnett [Alas you bid mee love and doe not tell]
[Who's this appears in crimson dye]
[Come Barack, as thy hands doe Trophyes rayse]
A Paraphrase vpon the ascension
A Satyre. 1636
A description of Man
1627
To my deerest freind deceased
[Si nulli gravis est percustus (for "percussus") Achilles]
[Why should wee more for worldly losses care]
[When after chyldhood Tyme had shew'd on mee]

[A Body healthfull, strong, from blemish free]
[Our Lyfe vnto a Garden I compare]
[Noe Noe, I ever did and must denye]
Made vpon the birth of my third Sonn on Sonday the 22th of October 1637, to ex-
   spresse my desyre that Hee may bee a Churchman
[Proponit Homo, Disponit Deus]
August .15. 1644
An Elegy made vpon the Death of Mary Lady Baesh
[Youth is the cheerefull springtyme of our yeares]
Antiphona
Musick and Poesy
To the Reader [[introduction to "Occasionalls"]]
      1. [Truth is the best and most satisfactory reward]
      2. [When Aurelian had borne down all those]
      3. [I haue much wondred why the Philosopher Epicurus]
      4. [It is noe wonder, if those whoe haue eyther erroneous or wicked principles]
      5. [As the Essence of things resydeth in theyr substance]
      6. [That which wee call right or property]
      7. [It hath afforded mee sometymes matter of noe small admiration]
      8. [Religion is the serving of some Deitye]
      9. [I haue found by exsperience this to bee infallibly true]
     10. [I haue read in an Italian writer]
     11. [Ever since our first Father Adam sought to palliate his first transgression]
     12. [Of all my inward conflicts]
Doxologye. January the 8th 1655
An Appendix to the Occasionalls
Of Truth
Of Goodnes
Some Notes concerning the Lyfe of Edward Lord North Baron of Kirtling 1658
      To my eldest sonn
      [[The "Lyfe"]]
      [As all by Natures fatall course must dye]
      To the Reverend the Master of St Peters Colledge in Cambridge and to the Fel-
         lows and Schollers of the same
A Sundays meditation vpon Eternity June 17. 1666
An Elegie vpon the Right Honble Dudley Lord North by his Eldest Sonne Executor
Hymnus sacer
To the Reverend the Vice Chancellor and other the Heads and Governors of the
   Vniversity of Cambridge
[Being very much perplexed in my own thoughts]
A Riddle. 1663
A Dialogue betwix Phillis and Daphne
A Dialogue betweene Laura and Cloris
Pentecost
A Paraphrase vpon the Anuntiation
Out of the 4th Chapter of Canticles
An Essay in the way of Gratitude

Appendix D

THE ORDER OF ELEMENTS IN THE
ROUGHAM HALL MANUSCRIPT

Entries in brackets are North's opening words of untitled writings, and entries in double brackets are labels added by the present editor. Entries that do not appear also in the "Index of Titles and First Lines" may be assumed to be in prose.

Some Notes concerning the Lyfe of Edward Lord North Baron of Kirtling 1658
    To my eldest sonn
    [[The "Lyfe"]]
    [As all by Natures fatall course must dye]
To the Reader [[introduction to "Occasionalls"]]
    1. [Truth is the best and most satisfactory reward]
    2. [When Aurelianus had born down all those]
    3. [I have much wondred, why the Philosopher Epicurus]
    4. [It is noe wonder, if those whoe have eyther erronious or wicked principles]
    5. [As the Essence of things resydeth in theyr substance]
    6. [That which wee call right or property]
    7. [It hath afforded mee sometymes matter of noe small admiration]
    8. [Religion is the serving of some Deitye]
    9. [I have found by exsperience this to bee infallibly true]
    10. [I have read in an Italian writer]
    11. [Ever since our first Father Adam sought to palliate his first transgression]
    12. [Of all my inward conflicts]
Doxologye. January the 8th 1655
An Appendix to the Occasionalls
Of Truth
Of Goodnes
A Sundays meditation vpon Eternity June 17th 1666
To the Reverend the Vice Chancellor and other the heads and Governors of the Vniversity of Cambridge
To the Reverend the Master of St Peters Colledge in Cambridge and to the Fellows and Schollers of the same
[[Dedication of poems]]
The Favorite of Love and Honour
[A Body healthfull, strong, from blemish free]
An Ironicall perswasion to Serena seeming resolved to live at Court
On Serena sleeping

[I'le not dispayre and dye, nor heav'ns accuse]
On Serena playing on the Lute
Sonnett [Whence can that sweet force arize]
Sonnett [When my heart was first enthrall'd]
[You bind, and say I may your bands vntye]
To Serena threatning to punish a supposed new affection in her servant with a per-
    petuall coldnesse in her selfe
Sonnett [Wylye Cupid sett to proove]
Sonnett [Thinke not, Disdayne can quench my Love]
Sonnett [I a wanton winning passion]
Vpon a Poem of my Fathers
[Thy Face, Selena, should not mee comand]
[Vaine are thy doubts Selena, vayn thy feares]
[Lett not thy Husbands breach of Faith to Thee]
[Come lett vs end our sorrowes with a Kisse]
An Elegye composed vpon the buriall of Ann Lady Rich
[Why should wee more for worldly losses care]
[Noe Noe, Selena, Now I playnly see]
[Youth is the cheere full springtyme of our yeares]
Sonnett [I doe not loue, it is most true]
Sonnett [Alas you bid mee love, and doe not tell]
[Who's this appeares in crimson dye]
[Come Barack, as thy hands doe Trophyes rayse]
A Paraphrase vpon the ascension
A Satyre. 1636
A description of Man
1627
To my deerest freind deceased
[When after chyldhood Tyme had shew'd on mee]
[Our Lyfe vnto a Garden I compare]
[Noe Noe, I ever did and must denye]
Made vpon the birth of my third Sonn on Sonday the 22th of October 1637 to exspresse
    my desyre that Hee may bee a Churchman
[Proponit Homo, Disponit Deus]
August .15. 1644
An Elegy made vpon the Death of Mary Lady Baesh
Antiphona
Musick and Poesy
A Riddle 1663
A Dialogue betwix Phillis and Daphne
A Dialogue betweene Laura and Cloris
Pentecost
A Paraphrase vpon the Anuntiation
Out of the 4th Chapter of Canticles
An Elogy vpon the death of Dudley Lord North by his son Executor
[[Calendar of family dates in Roger North's hand]]

BIBLIOGRAPHY

The following bibliography is restricted to publications and manuscripts mentioned within this volume.

PRINTED SOURCES

(Unless otherwise specified, London is the place of publication.)

Acts of the Privy Council of England, ed. J. R. Dasent, E. G. Atkinson, J. V. Lyle, R. F. Monger, and P. A. Penfold: *1615–1616*, XXXIV (1st pub. 1925); *1619–1621*, XXXVII (1st pub. 1930); *1621–1623*, XXXVIII (1st pub. 1932); and *1623–1625*, XXXIX (1st pub. 1933; all vols. reptd. Nendeln, Liechtenstein, 1974).

Adolphus, John, *The British Cabinet; Containing Portraits of Illustrious Personages*, I (1799).

Arber, Edward, ed., *The Term Catalogues, 1668–1709 A.D.*, I (1903).

Ashley, Maurice, *The Stuarts in Love, with Some Reflections on Love and Marriage in the Sixteenth and Seventeenth Centuries* (1963).

Ashbee, Andrew, "John Jenkins," *The New Grove Dictionary of Music and Musicians*, ed. Stanley Sadie, IX (1980), 596–598.

———, "John Jenkins, 1592–1678," *The Consort*, XXXIV (1978), 265–273.

Ault, Norman, ed., *Seventeenth Century Lyrics* (New York, 1950, 2nd ed.).

Bacon, Francis, *The Essayes or Counsels, Civill and Morall . . . Newly Enlarged* (1629).

———, *The Twoo Bookes of Francis Bacon. Of the Proficience and Advancement of Learning, Divine and Humane* (1605).

Baker, C. H. Collins, *Lely and the Stuart Portrait Painters*, 3 vols. (1912).

Baker, George, *The History and Antiquities of the County of Northampton*, pt. II (1826).

Baker, Thomas, *History of the College of St. John the Evangelist, Cambridge*, ed. John E. B. Mayor, 2 vols. (Cambridge, 1869).

Barkan, Leonard, *Nature's Work of Art: The Human Body as Image of the World* (New Haven, 1975).

Barton, Margaret, *Tunbridge Wells* (1937).

[Barwick, John?], *Querela Cantabrigiensis: Or a Remonstrance . . . for the Banished Members of the Late Flourishing University of Cambridge* (Oxford, 1646).

Bearcroft, Philip, *An Historical Account of Thomas Sutton Esq. and of His Foundation in Charter-House* (1737).

Beaumont, Joseph, *The Minor Poems of Joseph Beaumont, D.D. 1616–1699*, ed. Eloise Robinson (1914).

Beaurline, L. A., "Dudley North's Criticism of Metaphysical Poetry," *Huntington Library Quarterly*, XXV (1962), 299–313.

——, "'Why So Pale and Wan': An Essay in Critical Method," *Texas Studies in Literature and Language*, IV (1963), 553–563.

Berry, William, *County Genealogies, Pedigrees of Hertfordshire Families* (n.d.).

Beverley, T., *An Exposition of the Divinely Prophetick Song of Songs* (1687).

Bible

> *The Holy Bible, Conteyning the Old Testament, and the New* (1611).
>
> *The New Testament of Jesus Christ, Translated Faithfully into English* (Rheims, 1582).

Billingsley, Martin, *The Pens Excellencie* (1618).

Birrell, T. A., "Roger North and Political Morality in the Later Stuart Period," *Scrutiny*, XVII (1950–51), 282–298.

Blenkinsopp, J., "Ballad Style and Psalm Style in the Song of Deborah: A Discussion," *Biblica*, XLII (1961), 61–76.

Blith, Walter, *The English Improver Improved or The Survey of Husbandry Surveyed* (1653).

Blunden, Edmund, and Bernard Mellor, ed., *Wayside Poems of the Seventeenth Century* (Hong Kong, 1963).

Blunt, Wilfrid, *Sweet Roman Hand: Five Hundred Years of Italic Cursive Script* (1952).

Bolton, Diane K., "Harrow," *A History of the County of Middlesex*, Vol. IV, ed. J. S. Cockburn and T. F. T. Baker, in *The Victoria History of the Counties of England*, ed. R. B. Pugh (1971), pp. 203–204.

The Booke of Common Prayer, and Administration of the Sacraments, and Other Rites and Ceremonies of the Church of England (1603; i.e., 1604).

Bradner, Leicester, *Musae Anglicanae: A History of Anglo-Latin Poetry 1500–1925* (New York, 1940).

Brayley, E. W., and John Britton, *A Topographical and Historical Description of the County of Cambridge* (n.d.).

British Museum General Catalogue of Printed Books (1963; photolithographic edition to 1955).

Brockett, Edward J., comp., asstd. by John B. Koetteritz and Francis E. Brockett, *The Descendants of John Brockett* (East Orange, N.J., 1905).

Browne, Thomas, *Hydriotaphia* (1658).

——, *Religio Medici* (1643).

Brunton, D., and D. H. Pennington, *Members of the Long Parliament*, introd. R. H. Tawney (1954).

Buchanan, George, *Geor: Buchanani Scoti, Poemata* (Leyden, 1628).

Bullokar, John, *An English Expositor* (1616).

Burke, Bernard, *The General Armory of England, Scotland, Ireland and Wales* (1884).

Burr, Thomas Benge, *The History of Tunbridge-Wells* (1746).

Burton, Robert, *The Anatomy of Melancholy* (1651; 1st ed., 1621).

Bush, Douglas, *English Literature in the Earlier Seventeenth Century: 1600–1660* (2nd ed., Oxford, 1962).

Bushby, Frances, "North, Dudley, Third Baron North," *Dictionary of National Biography*, ed. Leslie Stephen and Sidney Lee, XIV (Oxford 1959–1960 rept.), 594–596.

——, *Three Men of the Tudor Time* (1911).

Calendar of State Papers
> Green, Mary Anne Everett, ed., *Calendar of State Papers, Domestic . . . 1623–1625* (1859).
> Bruce, John, ed., *Calendar of State Papers, Domestic . . . 1627–1628* (1858).
> ———, *Calendar of State Papers, Domestic . . . 1633–1634* (1863).
> ———, *Calendar of State Papers, Domestic . . . 1637* (1868).
> ———, *Calendar of State Papers, Domestic . . . 1637–1638* (1869).
> ———, and William Douglas Hamilton, ed., *Calendar of State Papers, Domestic . . . 1638–1639* (1871).
> Hamilton, William Douglas, ed., *Calendar of State Papers, Domestic . . . 1640* (1880).
> ———, *Calendar of State Papers, Domestic . . . 1641–43* (1887).
> ———, and Sophia Crawford Lomas, ed. *Calendar of State Papers, Domestic . . . Addenda. March 1625 to January 1649* (1897).
> Daniell, F. H. Blackburne, ed., *Calendar of State Papers, Domestic . . . , September 1st, 1680, to December 31st, 1681* (1921).
> ———, *Calendar of State Papers, Domestic . . . January 1 to June 30, 1683* (1933).
> Hinds, Allen B., ed., *Calendar of State Papers . . . Venice, . . . 1619–1621, XVI* (1910).
> ———, *Calendar of State Papers . . . Venice . . . 1629–1632, XXII* (1919).
> Mahaffy, Robert Pentland, ed. *Calendar of the State Papers . . . Ireland . . . 1647–1660* (1903).
Calendar of the Proceedings of the Committee for Compounding, &c., 1643–1660, pt. IV (1892).
Camden, Carroll, "Spenser's 'Little Fish That Men Call *Remora*,'" *Rice Institute Pamphlet*, XLIV (1957), 1–16.
Camden, William, *Annales Rerum Anglicarum, et Hibernicarum* (1615).
———, *Remaines, Concerning Britaine* (1614; 1st pub. 1605).
Campion, Thomas, *The Works of Thomas Campion*, ed. Walter R. Davis (Garden City, N.Y., 1969).
Carew, Thomas, *The Poems of Thomas Carew*, ed. Rhodes Dunlap (Oxford, 1949).
Carter, Edmund, *The History of the County of Cambridgeshire* (1819).
"By a Carthusian," *Historical Account of Charter-house; Compiled from the Works of Hearne and Bearcroft, Harleian, Cottonian, and Private MSS.* (1808).
The Carthusian, A Miscellany in Prose and Verse (1839).
Cary, Henry, *Memorials of the Great Civil War in England*, 2 vols. (1842).
Chamberlain, John, *The Letters of John Chamberlain*, ed. Norman Egbert McClure, 2 vols. (Philadelphia, 1939).
Chapman, George, *The Memorable Maske of the Two Honourable Houses or Inns of Court; the Middle Temple, and Lyncolns Inne* (1614?).
———, *The Poems of George Chapman*, ed. Phyllis Brooke Bartlett (New York, 1941).
Chaucer, Geoffrey, *The Ellesmere Chaucer Reproduced in Facsimile*, pref. Alix Egerton, I (Manchester, 1911).
Chernaik, Warren L., *The Poetry of Limitation: A Study of Edmund Waller* (New Haven, 1968).
Claudian (Claudius Claudianus), *Claudian*, tr. Maurice Platnauer, II (1922).

Cleland, James, Ἡρωπαιδεία, or The Institution of a Young Noble Man (1607).

Clutterbuck, Robert, The History and Antiquities of the County of Hertford, III (1827).

Cokayne, George Edward, The Complete Peerage of England Scotland Ireland, ed. Vicary Gibbs, asstd. by H. Arthur Doubleday, IV (1916); IX, rev. and enl., H. A. Doubleday and Lord Howard de Walden (1936).

Colie, Rosalie L., The Resources of Kind: Genre-Theory in the Renaissance, ed. Barbara K. Lewalski (Berkeley, Calif., 1973).

Collins, Arthur, Collins's Peerage of England, aug. Sir Egerton Brydges, IV (1812).

———, Letters and Memorials of State, 2 vols. (1746).

Congreve, William, The Way of the World, ed. Brian Gibbons (1971).

Cooper, J. P., "Patterns of Inheritance and Settlement by Great Landowners from the Fifteenth to the Eighteenth Centuries," in Family and Inheritance, ed. Jack Goody, Joan Thirsk, and E. P. Thompson (Cambridge, 1976), pp. 192–327.

Cope, Esther S., The Life of a Public Man: Edward, First Baron Montagu of Boughton, 1562–1644 (Philadelphia, 1981).

Copinger, Walter Arthur, The Manors of Suffolk, VI (Manchester, 1910).

Costello, William T., The Scholastic Curriculum at Early Seventeenth-Century Cambridge (Cambridge, Mass., 1958).

Cotgrave, Randle, A Dictionarie of the French and English Tongues (1611).

Coxon, Carolyn, "A Handlist of the Sources of John Jenkins' Vocal and Instrumental Music," Royal Musical Association Research Chronicle, IX (1971), 73–89.

Cromwell, Oliver, The Writings and Speeches of Oliver Cromwell, ed. W. C. Abbott, asstd. by Catherine D. Crane, I (Cambridge, Mass., 1937).

Crooke, Helkiah, Μικροκοσμογραφία: A Description of the Body of Man (2nd ed., 1631).

Crum, Margaret, "The Consort Music from Kirtling, Bought for the Oxford Music School from Anthony Wood, 1667," Chelys, IV (1972), 3–10.

———, "Poetical Manuscripts of Dudley, Third Baron North," Bodleian Library Record, X (1979), 98–108.

Curtius, Ernst Robert, European Literature and the Latin Middle Ages, tr. Willard R. Trask (New York, 1953; orig. German ed., Bern, 1948).

Daniel, Samuel, Defence of Ryme, ed. G. B. Harrison (1925).

Darby, H. C., The Draining of the Fens (Cambridge, 1940).

———, and E. Miller, "Political History," in The Victoria History of the County of Cambridge and the Isle of Ely, ed. L. F. Salzman, II (1948), 377–419.

Darcie, Abraham, The Originall of Idolatries: Or, The Birth of Heresies (1624).

Davenant, William, The First Days Entertainment at Rutland-House (1657; produced 1656).

———, The Siege of Rhodes Made a Representation by the Art of Prospective in Scenes . . . at the Back Part of Rutland-House (1656).

Davies, Gerald S., Charterhouse in London: Monastery, Mansion, Hospital, School (1921).

Davies, Godfrey, The Early Stuarts: 1603–1660 (Oxford, 2nd ed., 1959; 1st pub. 1937).

———, ed. (1st ed.) and Mary Frear Keeler, ed. (2nd ed.), Bibliography of British History: Stuart Period, 1603–1714 (Oxford, 1970).

Davies of Hereford, John, *The Scourge of Folly* (1611).

Dawson, Giles E., and Laetitia Kennedy-Skipton, *Elizabethan Handwriting 1500–1650: A Guide to the Reading of Documents and Manuscripts* (1966).

Dawsons of Pall Mall, *Manuscripts and Autograph Letters from the 12th to the 20th Century*, Catalogue No. 200 (1969).

Dekker, Thomas, *The Shoemaker's Holiday*, ed. J. B. Steane (Cambridge, 1965).

D'Ewes, Simonds, *The Autobiography and Correspondence of Sir Simonds D'Ewes, Bart.*, ed. James Orchard Halliwell, 2 vols. (1845).

——, "D'Ewes Diary," *The Eagle*, IX (1875), 369–381; X (1878), 1–22.

——, *The Diary of Sir Simonds D'Ewes (1622–1624)*, ed. Elisabeth Bourcier (Paris, 1974).

——, *The Journal of Sir Simonds D'Ewes*, ed. Wallace Notestein, I (New Haven, 1923).

Donne, John, *The Complete Poetry of John Donne*, ed. John T. Shawcross (New York, 1968).

——, *LXXX Sermons* (1640).

——, *Poems* (1633).

Drayton, Michael, *Poly-Olbion* (1612).

——, *The Works of Michael Drayton*, ed. J. William Hebel, II and III (Oxford, 1932).

Druett, Walter W., *Harrow Through the Ages* (Uxbridge, 1956; 1st ed., 1935).

Edwards, Ralph, "Oil Miniatures by Cornelius Johnson," *The Burlington Magazine*, LXI (1932), 131–132.

Elliot, Adam, *A Modest Vindication of Titus Oates the Salamanca-Doctor from Perjury* (1682).

Elsing, Henry, *Notes of the Debates in the House of Lords . . . 1624 and 1626*, ed. Samuel Rawson Gardiner (Westminster, 1879).

Ephemeris Parliamentaria; or A Faithfull Register of the Transactions in Parliament, in the Third and Fourth Years of the Reign of Our Late Sovereign Lord King Charles (1654).

Evelyn, John, *A Character of England* (1659).

——, *The Diary of John Evelyn*, ed. E. S. deBeer, IV (Oxford, 1955).

Fairholt, Frederick W., ed., *Poems and Songs Relating to George Villiers, Duke of Buckingham* (1850).

Falk, Bernard, *The Way of the Montagues: A Gallery of Family Portraits* (n.d.).

Farbridge, Maurice H., *Studies in Biblical and Semitic Symbolism* (1923).

Ferguson, George, *Signs & Symbols in Christian Art* (New York, 1961).

Firth, Charles Harding, *The House of Lords During the Civil War* (1910).

——, and R. S. Rait, ed., *Acts and Ordinances of the Interregnum, 1642–1660*, 3 vols. (1911).

Fletcher, Harris Francis, *The Intellectual Development of John Milton*, II, *The Cambridge University Period 1625–32* (Urbana, 1961).

Foss, Michael, *The Age of Patronage: The Arts in England 1600–1750* (Ithaca, N.Y., 1972).

Foster, Joseph, *Alumni Oxonienses*, III (1891).

——, *The Register of Admissions to Gray's Inn, 1521–1889* (1889).

Fowler, Alastair, *Conceitful Thought: The Interpretation of English Renaissance Poems* (Edinburgh, 1975).

Gascoigne, George, *The Posies of George Gascoigne Esquire* (1575).

Gauden, John, *Funerals Made Cordials* (1658).

Gerard, John, *The Herball or Generall Historie of Plantes* (1597).

Girouard, Mark, *Life in the English Country House: A Social and Architectural History* (Harmondsworth, 1980; 1st pub. New Haven, 1978).

Grange, Kathleen M., "The Ship Symbol as a Key to Former Theories of the Emotions," *Bulletin of the History of Medicine*, XXXVI (1962), 512–523.

Greene, Robert, *Friar Bacon and Friar Bungay*, ed. Daniel Seltzer (Lincoln, Neb., 1963).

Guarini, Giovanni Battista, *Il Pastor Fido* (Venice, 1605).

Guicciardini, Francesco: Giovanni Francesco Lottini; and Francesco Sansovino, *Propositioni, overo Considerationi in Materia di Cose di Stato, sotto Titolo di Avertimenti, Avedimenti Civili, & Concetti Politici* (Venice, 1583).

Gunstone, John, *The Feast of Pentecost* (1967).

Hale, David George, *The Body Politic: A Political Metaphor in Renaissance English Literature* (The Hague, 1971).

Hall, John, *Emblems with Elegant Figures* (1658).

Hall, Joseph, *The Arte of Divine Meditation* (1606).

——, *Meditations and Vowes Divine and Morall* (1605).

——, *Quo Vadis? A Just Censure of Travell* (1617).

——, *The Works of Joseph Hall* (1648).

Hampson, Ethel M., "Social History, 1500–1900," in *The Victoria History of the County of Cambridge*, ed. L. F. Salzman, II (1948), 90–111.

Harrison, Fairfax, *The Devon Carys*, II (New York, 1920).

Hasted, Edward, *The History and Topographical Survey of the County of Kent*, I (Canterbury, 1778).

Hazlitt, W. C., ed., *The Complete Poems of George Gascoigne*, I (1869).

——, *Contributions Towards a Dictionary of English Book-Collectors* (1898).

——, ed., *Inedited Poetical Miscellanies 1584–1700* (priv. circ., 50 copies, 1870).

Heawood, Edward, "Further Notes on Paper Used in England after 1600," *The Library*, 5th ser., II (1948), 119–149.

——, "Papers Used in England after 1600," *The Library*, 4th ser., XI (1931), 263–299.

——, *Watermarks Mainly of the 17th and 18th Centuries*, vol. I of *Monumenta Chartae Papyraceae* (Hilversum, 1950).

Hendriks, Lawrence, *The London Charterhouse: Its Monks and Its Martyrs* (1889).

Herbert, George, *The Works of George Herbert*, ed., F. E. Hutchinson (Oxford, 1964; 1st pub. 1941).

Herbert of Cherbury, Edward, Lord, *The Poems English and Latin of Edward, Lord Herbert of Cherbury*, ed. G. C. Moore Smith (Oxford, 1923; rept. 1968).

Hernadi, Paul, *Beyond Genre: New Directions in Literary Classification* (Ithaca, N.Y., 1972).

Herne, Samuel, *Domus Carthusiana: or An Account of the Most Noble Foundation of the Charter-House Near Smithfield in London* (1677).

Hervey, S. H. A., *Biographical List of Boys Educated at King Edward VI. Free Grammar School, Bury St. Edmunds. From 1550 to 1900* (Bury-St.-Edmunds, 1908).

Heywood, Thomas, *Pleasant Dialogues and Dramma's* (1637).

Hill, Christopher, *The Century of Revolution 1603–1714* (Edinburgh, 1961).
His Majesties Message Concerning Licences Granted to Persons Going into Ireland (1641; i.e., 1642).
Historical Manuscripts Commission
 Fifth Report of the Royal Commission on Historical Manuscripts, pt. I, *Report and Appendix* (1876).
 Sixth Report of the Royal Commission on Historical Manuscripts, pt. I, *Report and Appendix* (1877).
 Seventh Report of the Royal Commission on Historical Manuscripts, pt. I, *Report and Appendix* (1879).
 Report on Manuscripts in Various Collections, vol. III (1904).
 Report on the Manuscripts of the . . . Marquess of Bath, vol. IV, ed. Marjorie Blatcher (1968).
 Report on the Manuscripts of the Duke of Buccleuch, vol. I (1899).
 Report on the Manuscripts of the Late Reginald Rawdon Hastings, vol. IV, ed. Francis Bickley (1947).
 Report on the Manuscripts of Lord Montagu of Beaulieu (1900).
 Calendar of the Manuscripts of the . . . Marquis of Salisbury, pt. X (1904).
 Calendar of the Manuscripts of the . . . Marquis of Salisbury, pt. XII (Hereford, 1910).
 Calendar of the Manuscripts of the . . . Marquis of Salisbury, pt. XIV, *Addenda* (1923).
 Calendar of the Manuscripts of the . . . Marquess of Salisbury, pt. XVI, ed. M. S. Giuseppi (1933).
 Calendar of the Manuscripts of the . . . Marquess of Salisbury, pt. XVII, ed. M. S. Giuseppi (1938).
Holmes, Clive, *The Eastern Association in the English Civil War* (Cambridge, 1974).
Hooker, Richard, *Of the Laws of Ecclesiastical Polity*, ed. Georges Edelen, I (Cambridge, Mass., 1977).
Horace (Quintus Horatius Flaccus), *Satires, Epistles and Ars Poetica*, tr. H. Rushton Fairclough (Cambridge, Mass., 1961 printing of 1929 ed.).
Hotson, Leslie, *The Commonwealth and Restoration Stage* (Cambridge, Mass., 1928).
Howard, Henry, Earl of Surrey, *Henry Howard Earl of Surrey: Poems*, ed. Emrys Jones (Oxford, 1964).
Howell, James, *Epistolae Ho-elianae*, ed. Joseph Jacobs (1890).
——, *Londinopolis* (1657).
Inderwick, F. A., ed., *A Calendar of the Inner Temple Records*, I (1896) and II (1898).
James I and VI, *A Proclamation Declaring His Majesties Pleasure Concerning Captaine Roger North, and Those Who Are Gone Foorth as Adventurers with Him* (1620).
Jeaffreson, John Cordy, ed., *Middlesex County Records*, II (1887?).
Jessopp, Augustus, "North, Dudley, Fourth Baron North," *Dictionary of National Biography*, ed. Leslie Stephen and Sidney Lee, XIV (Oxford, 1959–1960 rept.), 596–597.
Journals of the House of Commons, II (n.d.) and V (1803).
Journals of the House of Lords, V and XII (n.p., n.d.).
Juvenal (Decimus Junius Juvenalis), *Juvenal and Persius*, tr. G. G. Ramsay (rev. ed., Cambridge, Mass., 1969).

Keeler, Mary Frear, *The Long Parliament, 1640–1641: A Biographical Study of Its Members* (Philadelphia, 1954).

Ketton-Cremer, R. W., "Lapidary Verse," *Proceedings of the British Academy*, XLV (1960), 237–253.

———, "Roger North," *Essays and Studies*, ed. Dorothy Margaret Stuart, n.s. XII (1959), 73–86.

King, Henry, *Two Sermons Preached at White-hall in Lent, March 3. 1625. and Februarie 20. 1626* (1627).

Kingston, Alfred, *East Anglia and the Great Civil War* (1902 ed.).

Knowles, David, and W. F. Grimes, *Charterhouse: The Medieval Foundation in the Light of Recent Discoveries* (1954).

Korshin, Paul J., *From Concord to Dissent: Major Themes in English Poetic Theory 1640–1700* (Menston, Yorkshire, 1973).

Korsten, F. J. M., *Roger North (1651–1734): Virtuoso and Essayist* (Amsterdam, 1981).

Kyd, Thomas, *The Spanish Tragedy*, ed. Philip Edwards (Cambridge, Mass., 1959).

Lacrymae Cantabrigienses: In Obitum Serenissimae Reginae Annae (Cambridge, 1619).

LeNeve, John, *Monumenta Anglicana: . . . 1700 to the end of . . . 1715* (1717).

———, *Monumenta Anglicana: . . . 1650, to the end of . . . 1679* (1718).

Lenthall, F. Kyffin, "List of the Names of the Members of the House of Commons That Advanced Horse, Money, and Plate . . . ," *Notes and Queries*, XII (1855), 337–338, 358–360.

Letwin, William, "The Authorship of Sir Dudley North's *Discourses on Trade*," *Economica*, XVIII (1951), 35–56.

Lever, J. W., ed., *Sonnets of the English Renaissance* (1974).

Lewalski, Barbara Kiefer, *Donne's "Anniversaries" and the Poetry of Praise: The Creation of a Symbolic Mode* (Princeton, 1973).

———, *Protestant Poetics and the Seventeenth-Century Religious Lyric* (Princeton, 1979).

Lievsay, John L., ed., *The Seventeenth-Century Resolve: A Historical Anthology of a Literary Form* (Lexington, Kentucky, 1980).

Lyle, J. V., ed., *Acts of the Privy Council of England: 1621–1623* (1932).

Lysons, Daniel, *The Environs of London*, II (1795).

Macaulay, Thomas Babington, *The History of England from the Accession of James the Second*, I (1858).

MacCormack, John R., *Revolutionary Politics in the Long Parliament* (Cambridge, Mass., 1973).

M'Clintock, John, and James Strong, *Cyclopaedia of Biblical, Theological, and Ecclesiastical Literature*, I (New York, 1871; fac. ed., 1969).

Malcolm, James Peller, *Londinium Redivivum*, 4 vols. (1802–07).

The Manner of Creating the Knights of the Antient and Honourable Order of the Bath (1661).

Manningham, John, *Diary of John Manningham, of the Middle Temple, . . . 1602–1603*, ed. John Bruce (Westminster, 1868).

Markham, Clements R., *The Fighting Veres: Lives of Sir Francis Vere . . . and of Sir Horace Vere* (1888).

Markham, Francis, *Five Decades of Epistles of Warre* (1622).

Markham, Gervase, *Honour in His Perfection* (1624).

Martial (Marcus Valerius Martialis), *Epigrams*, tr. Walter C. A. Ker, II (1930 printing of 1920 ed.)

Martini, Fritz, "Personal Style and Period Style: Perspectives on a Theme of Literary Research," tr. Leila Vennewitz, in *Patterns of Literary Style*, Yearbook of Comparative Criticism, III, ed. Joseph Strelka (University Park, Pennsylvania, 1971), 90–115.

Martz, Louis L., *The Paradise Within: Studies in Vaughan, Traherne, and Milton* (New Haven, 1964).

———, *The Poetry of Meditation* (New Haven, rev. ed., 1962).

Members of Parliament: . . . the Names of Every Member Returned to Serve in Each Parliament, I (1878).

Metcalfe, Walter C., ed., *The Visitations of Hertfordshire*, Publications of the Harleian Society, XXII (1886).

———, *The Visitations of Northamptonshire Made in 1564 and 1618–19* (1887).

Miles, Josephine, *The Primary Language of Poetry in the 1640's* (Berkeley, Calif., 1948).

———, and Hanan C. Selvin, "A Factor Analysis of the Vocabulary of Poetry in the Seventeenth Century," in Jacob Leed, ed., *The Computer & Literary Style* (Kent, Ohio, 1966).

Millard, Peter T., "The Chronology of Roger North's Main Works," *Review of English Studies*, n.s. XXIV (1973), 283–294.

Miller, Edward, *Portrait of a College: A History of the College of Saint John the Evangelist Cambridge* (Cambridge, 1961).

Milton, John, *The Reason of Church-government*, in *Complete Prose Works of John Milton*, I, ed. Don M. Wolfe (New Haven, 1953).

Miner, Earl, *The Cavalier Mode from Jonson to Cotton* (Princeton, 1971).

Morison, Stanley, introd., Ambrose Heal, *The English Writing-Masters and Their Copy-Books 1570–1800* (Hildesheim, 1962).

Morris, Brian, "Satire from Donne to Marvell," in *Metaphysical Poetry*, ed. Malcolm Bradbury and David Palmer (Bloomington, Ind., 1971), pp. 210–235.

Mullinger, James Bass, *The University of Cambridge from the Royal Injunctions of 1535 to the Accession of Charles the First* (Cambridge, 1884).

Murray, James A. H., Henry Bradley, W. A. Craigie, C. T. Onions, ed. *The Oxford English Dictionary* (Oxford, 1933).

The Names of the Justices of Peace, in England and Wales . . . 1650 (1650).

Neville, Henry, *Newes from the New-Exchange, or The Commonwealth of Ladies* (1650).

Nichols, John Gough, ed., "Cary: Viscounts Falkland," *The Herald and Genealogist*, III (1866), 33–54, 129–146.

———, *The Progresses, Processions, and Magnificent Festivities of King James the First*, 4 vols. (1828).

North, Charles Augustus, untitled seven-page pamphlet on the fourth Lord North's *Some Notes Concerning the Life of Edward Lord North* (1889).

North, Dudley, third Lord North, *A Forest of Varieties* (1645).

———, *A Forest Promiscuous of Various Seasons Productions* (1659).

North, Dudley, fourth Lord North, *Light in the Way to Paradise: With Other Occasionals* (1682).

————, *A Narrative of Some Passages in or Relating to the Long Parliament* (1670); reptd. in *A Collection of Scarce and Valuable Tracts on the Most Interesting and Entertaining Subjects*, I (1748), 1–32; and by Sir Walter Scott in 2nd ed., *Collection*, VI (1811), 565–590.

————, *Observations and Advices Oeconomical* (1669).

————, *Some Notes Concerning the Life of Edward Lord North, Baron of Kirtling, 1658*, pub. with separate pagination but often bound with *Light in the Way to Paradise*.

North, Dudley (son of preceding), *Discourses upon Trade; Principally Directed to the Cases of the Interest, Coynage, Clipping, Increase of Money* (1691).

North, Francis, *A Philosophical Essay of Musick Directed to a Friend* (1677).

North, John, *Platonis de Rebus Divinis Dialogi Selecti Graece & Latine* (Cambridge, 1671).

————, *A Sermon Preached before the King at Newmarket October 8. 1671* (Cambridge, 1671).

North, Roger, *A Discourse of Fish and Fish-Ponds* (1713).

————, *Examen: Or, an Enquiry into the Credit and Veracity of a Pretended Complete History* (1740).

————, *The Lives of the Right Hon. Francis North, Baron Guilford; the Hon. Sir Dudley North; and the Hon. and Rev. Dr. John North*, ed. Augustus Jessopp, 3 vols. (1890); reissued with a new introduction by E. Mackerness (1972).

————, *Roger North on Music*, ed. John Wilson (1959).

North, Thomas, *The Lives of the Noble Grecians and Romanes, Compared Together by That Grave Learned Philosopher and Historiographer, Plutarke of Chaeronea* (1579).

Notestein, Wallace, and Frances Helen Relf, ed., *Commons Debates for 1629* (Minneapolis, 1921).

Nowell, Alexander, *A Catechisme, or First Instruction and Learnyng of Christian Religion*, tr. T. Norton (1577).

Ogg, David, *England in the Reigns of James II and William III* (Oxford, 1955).

Ong, Walter J., "The Writer's Audience Is Always a Fiction," *Publications of the Modern Language Association*, XC (1975), 9–21.

Palmer, William Mortlock, "The Fen Office Documents," *Proceedings of the Cambridge Antiquarian Society*, XXXVIII (1939), 64–157.

————, ed., *Monumental Inscriptions and Coats of Arms from Cambridgeshire Chiefly as Recorded by John Layer about 1632 and William Cole between 1742 and 1782* (Cambridge, 1932).

————, and H. W. Saunders, "The 1638 Visitation of Bishop Matthew Wren as It Concerned All Cambridgeshire Villages. . . ," *Documents Relating to Cambridgeshire Villages*, no. III, pt. 1 (1926), pp. 37–56.

Parks, George B., "Travel as Education," in *The Seventeenth Century: Studies in the History of English Thought and Literature from Bacon to Pope by Richard Foster Jones and Others* (Stanford, Calif., 1951), pp. 264–290.

Peacham, Henry, *The Compleat Gentleman* ("Inlarged" ed., 1634).

————, *Minerva Britanna* (1612).

Pepys, Samuel, *The Diary of Samuel Pepys*, ed. Robert Latham and William Matthews, I (1970), VIII (1974).

Peterson, Douglas L., *The English Lyric from Wyatt to Donne: A History of the Plain and Eloquent Styles* (Princeton, 1967).

Pevsner, Nikolaus, *Cambridgeshire*, vol. X of *Buildings of England* (1954).

Pitcher, John, *Samuel Daniel: The Brotherton Manuscript*, Leeds Texts and Monographs, n.s. 7 (Leeds, 1981).

Plato, *Plato: Philebus*, tr. J. C. B. Gosling (Oxford, 1975).

Porritt, Edward, asstd. by Annie G. Porritt, *The Unreformed House of Commons*, I (Cambridge, 1909).

Puttenham, George, *The Arte of English Poesie* (1589).

Quarles, Francis, *Divine Fancies: Digested into Epigrammes, Meditations, and Observations* (1632).

——, *Emblemes* (1635).

Raleigh, Walter, *The Poems of Sir Walter Raleigh*, ed. Agnes M. C. Latham (Cambridge, Mass., 1951).

Randall, Dale B. J., "Country Delights for the Gentry: A View from 1669," *South Atlantic Quarterly*, LXXX (1981), 222–232.

——, "Mode and Voice in 17th-Century Meditative Verse: A Discussion of Five Newly Discovered Poems by Dudley North," *Medieval and Renaissance Studies*, No. 9, Proceedings of the Southeastern Institute of Medieval and Renaissance Studies, ed. Frank Tirro (Durham, N.C., 1982), pp. 55–86.

——, and Robert J. Parsons, "A Concordance to the Poetry of Dudley North, Third Baron North, and Dudley North, Fourth Baron North," computer print-out (Cambridge, 1979).

Randolph, Mary Claire, "The Medical Concept in English Renaissance Satiric Theory: Its Possible Relationships and Implications," *Studies in Philology*, XXXVIII (1941), 125–157.

Randolph, Thomas, *The Poems of Thomas Randolph*, ed. G. Thorn-Drury (1929).

Redlich, Hans Ferdinand, "John Jenkins," *Die Musik in Geschichte und Gegenwart*, VI (Kassel, 1957), cols. 1876–80.

Regimen Sanitatis Salerni: Or, The Schoole of Salernes Regiment of Health (1634).

Reusner, Nicholas, *Aureolorum Emblematum Liber Singularis* (Strassburg, 1587).

Richardson, Walter C., *History of the Court of Augmentations 1536–1554* (Baton Rouge, La., 1961).

Richmond, H. M., *The School of Love: The Evolution of the Stuart Love Lyric* (Princeton, 1964).

Robinson, William, *The History and Antiquities of the Parish of Hackney in the County of Middlesex*, I (1842).

Røstvig, Maren-Sofie, *The Happy Man: Studies in the Metamorphoses of a Classical Ideal* (New York, 1958–62).

Rowzee, Lodwick, *The Queenes Welles: That Is, A Treatise of the Nature and Vertues of Tunbridge Water* (1632).

Sackville, Charles, *Poems on Several Occasions, by the Earls of Roscommon and Dorset. . .* , II (1720).

Sasek, Lawrence A., *The Literary Temper of the English Puritans* (Baton Rouge, La., 1961).

Scaliger, Julius Caesar, *Poetices Libri Septem* (Geneva, 1561).

Scheper, George L., "Reformation Attitudes Toward Allegory and the Song of Songs," *Publications of the Modern Language Association*, LXXXIX (1974), 551–562.

Schwoerer, Lois Green, "Roger North and His Notes on Legal Education," *Huntington Library Quarterly*, XXII (1958–1959), 323–343.

Scott, Thomas, *Vox Dei* (1623).

Selden, John, *The Table-Talk of John Selden*, ed. S. W. Singer, rev. W. S. W. Anson (n.d.).

Seneca (Lucius Annaeus Seneca), *Moral Essays*, tr. John W. Basore, II (1932).

Sheppard, Edgar, *Memorials of St. James's Palace*, II (1894).

Shipman, Thomas, *Carolina: Or, Loyal Poems* (1683).

Sidney, Philip, *Miscellaneous Prose of Sir Philip Sidney*, ed. Katherine Duncan-Jones and Jan van Dorsten (Oxford, 1973).

——, *The Poems of Sir Philip Sidney*, ed. William A. Ringler, Jr. (Oxford, 1962).

Simpson, Christopher, *The Division-Violist* (1659).

Sions Charity Towards Her Foes in Misery (1641).

Sleeper, Helen Joy, ed., *John Jenkins (1592–1678): Fancies and Ayres*, Wellesley Edition, no. 1 (Wellesley, Mass., 1950).

Sotheby & Co., *Catalogue of Valuable Printed Books Autograph Letters and Historical Documents* (day of sale: 14 March 1967).

Spargo, John Webster, *Virgil the Necromancer: Studies in Virgilian Legends* (Cambridge, Mass., 1934).

Spenser, Edmund, *The Works of Edmund Spenser*, ed. Edwin Greenlaw et al., 9 vols. in 10 (Baltimore, 1932–49).

Stafford, Anthony, *The Femall [sic] Glory: or, The Life, and Death of Our Blessed Lady* (1635).

The Statutes of the Realm, III (1817; rept. 1963).

Stevenson, Allan, ed., *Les Filigranes*, vol. I of Jubilee Edition of C. M. Briquet, gen. ed. J. S. G. Simmons (Amsterdam, 1968).

Stevenson, William, "Extracts from 'The Booke of Howshold Charges and Other Paiments Laid out by the L. North. . . ,'" *Archaeologia*, XIX (1821), 283–301.

Stewart, Stanley, *The Enclosed Garden: The Tradition and the Image in Seventeenth-Century Poetry* (Madison, Wis., 1966).

Stone, Lawrence, *The Crisis of the Aristocracy: 1558–1641* (Oxford, 1965).

——, *Family and Fortune: Studies in Aristocratic Finance in the Sixteenth and Seventeenth Centuries* (Oxford, 1973).

——, *The Family, Sex and Marriage in England 1500–1800* (New York, 1977).

Stoye, John Walter, *English Travellers Abroad 1604–1667: Their Influence in English Society and Politics* (1952).

Suckling, Alfred, *The History and Antiquities of the County of Suffolk*, 3 vols. (1846; 1848; and Ipswich, 1952).

Suckling, John, *The Works of Sir John Suckling: The Non-Dramatic Works*, ed. Thomas Clayton (Oxford, 1971).

Suffolk in 1674, Being the Tax Hearth Returns, Suffolk Green Books, no. XI, vol. XIII (Woodbridge, 1905).

Sutherland, James, *English Literature of the Late Seventeenth Century* (Oxford, 1969).

Tannenbaum, Samuel A., *The Handwriting of the Renaissance* (New York, 1930).

Tayler, Edward W., ed., *Literary Criticism of Seventeenth-Century England* (New York, 1967).

Taylor, Dick, Jr., "Drayton and the Countess of Bedford," *Studies in Philology*, XLIX (1952), 214–228.

Taylor, William F., *The Charterhouse of London* (1912).

Tebbutt, Louis, "The Lord Lieutenants of Cambridgeshire," *Proceedings of the Cambridge Antiquarian Society*, XLI (1948), 51–55.

Temple, William, "Of Poetry," in J. E. Spingarn, ed., *Critical Essays of the Seventeenth Century*, III (Bloomington, Ind., 1968 printing).

Thompson, Edward Maunde, ed., *Correspondence of the Family of Hatton*, Camden Society, ser. 2, vols. XXII, XXIII (Westminster, 1878).

Tilley, Morris Palmer, *A Dictionary of the Proverbs in England in the Sixteenth and Seventeenth Centuries* (Ann Arbor, Michigan, 1950).

Tipping, H. A., "Kirtling Tower, Cambridgeshire. A Seat of Lord North," *Country Life*, LXIX (24 January 1931), 102–108.

Todd, Henry John, *Memoirs of the Life and Writings of the Right Rev. Brian Walton*, 2 vols. (1821).

Topographical Miscellanies, Containing Ancient Histories, and Modern Descriptions, of Mansions, Churches, Monuments, and Families (1792).

A True Relation of Some Passages Which Passed at Madrid in the Year 1623 (1655).

Turner, William, *A New Herball* (1551).

Tuve, Rosemond, *Elizabethan and Metaphysical Imagery: Renaissance Poetic and Twentieth-century Critics* (Chicago, 1965; 1st ed., 1947).

Underdown, David, *Pride's Purge: Politics in the Puritan Revolution* (Oxford, 1971).

Varley, Frederick John, *Cambridge During the Civil War 1642–1646* (Cambridge, 1935).

Vaughan, Henry, *The Complete Poetry of Henry Vaughan*, ed. French Fogle (New York, 1965).

Veen, Otto van, *Amorum Emblemata* (Antwerp, 1608).

Venn, John, and J. A. Venn, comp., *Alumni Cantabrigienses*, pt. I, vol. I (Cambridge, 1922) and vol. III (Cambridge, 1924).

Vergil, Polydore, *Anglicae Historiae* (Basel, ed. of 1546).

Vermuiden, Cornelius, *A Discourse Touching the Drayning of the Great Fennes* (1642).

Virgil (Publius Vergilius Maro), *Virgil*, tr. H. Rushton Fairclough, I, *Eclogues, Georgics, Aeneid I–VI* (Cambridge, 1953).

Wallerstein, Ruth, "Martin Lluelyn, Cavalier and 'Metaphysical,'" *Journal of English and Germanic Philology*, XXXV (1936), 94–111.

Walpole, Horace, *A Catalogue of the Royal and Noble Authors of England: with Lists of Their Works*, II (Strawberry Hill, 1758); later enl. and con. by Thomas Park (1806).

Warwick, Philip, *Memoires of the Reigne of King Charles I. with a Continuation to the Happy Restauration of King Charles II* (1701).

Watson, Andrew G., *The Library of Sir Simonds D'Ewes* (1966).

Watson, Foster, *The Beginnings of the Teaching of Modern Subjects in England* (1909).

Watson, George, ed., *The New Cambridge Bibliography of English Literature*, vol. I, 600–1660 (Cambridge, 1974); vol. II, 1660–1800 (Cambridge, 1971).

Watt, Robert, *Bibliotheca Britannica*, II (Edinburgh, 1824).

Wedgwood, C. V., *Poetry and Politics under the Stuarts* (Cambridge, 1960).

Westrup, J. A., "Domestic Music under the Stuarts," *Proceedings of the Musical Association . . . , 1941–1942* (Leeds, 1942), pp. 19–53.

Whitmore, William H., *Whitmore Tracts* (Boston, 1875).

Willetts, Pamela J., "Autograph Music by John Jenkins," *Music & Letters*, XLVIII (1967), 124–126.

Williams, Kathleen, "Spenser: Some Uses of the Sea and the Storm-tossed Ship," *Research Opportunities in Renaissance Drama*, XIII–XIV (1970–71), 135–142.

Willis, Browne, *Notitia Parliamentaria* (1750).

Wilson, Arthur, *The History of Great Britain* (1653).

Wither, George, *A Collection of Emblemes* (1635).

———, *Haleluiah or, Britans Second Remembrancer* (1641), Spencer Society, nos. 26 and 27 (Manchester, 1879).

Wood, Anthony, *The Life and Times of Anthony Wood, Antiquary, . . . Described by Himself*, ed. Andrew Clark, I (Oxford, 1891).

Wotton, Henry, *Poems by Sir Henry Wotton*, ed. Alexander Dyce (1843).

Wynne, Richard, "An Account of the Journey of the Prince's Servants into Spain, A. D. 1623," in vol. II of *The Autobiography and Correspondence of Sir Simonds D'Ewes, Bart.*, ed. James Orchard Halliwell (1845), pp. 413–458.

Young, Percy M., *A History of British Music* (1967).

Zagorin, Perez, *The Court and the Country: The Beginning of the English Revolution* (New York, 1970).

UNPRINTED SOURCES

(In this section references to Dudley, third Lord North, and Dudley, fourth Lord North, are designated "DN1" and "DN2," respectively. The information in parentheses regarding subject matter is, of course, not complete.)

Bodleian Library

MS. Eng. hist. c.408 (Lady Frances Bushby, "Memoirs of Some of the North Family During the Tudor and Stuart Dynasties," 1893).

MS. Eng. misc. e.262 ("The Shadow of the [Sometimes] Right Faire, Vertuous, and Honourable Lady Anne Rich Now an Happy, Glorious, and Perfected Saint in Heaven").

MS. Eng. th.d.55 (65r–69v: DN2, "A Discourse Sometime Intended as an Addition to My Observations & Advises Oeconomicall afterwards Printed").

MS. North a.2 (243r–v: DN1 and Venice; 272r: warrant from Earl of Oxford to DN2 to raise company of soldiers).

MS. North a.16(R) (Brockett family).

MS. North b.12 (85r–90v, 113r–121r: DN1 abroad; 347v: DN2 daughters' portions; 355r: DN1, debts and funeral charges).

MS. North b.20 (308r: Kirtling).

MS. Eng. b.26 (145r: Kirtling).

MS. North c.4 (North family correspondence).

MS. North c.5 (North family correspondence).

MS. North c.10 (North family correspondence).

MS. North c.20 (North business documents).

MS. North c.25 (children of DN2).

MS. North c.29 (50–51: will of Sir John North, uncle to DN2).

MS. North c.32 (8: will of DN2).

MS. North c.44 (1: petition re Kirtling; 25.1 and 25.2, Lieutenancy of Cambridgeshire; 27, DN1's application to Charles II for pardon).

MS. North c.49 (book of accounts).

MS. North c.84 (Kirtling).

MS. North c.85 (no. 15: DN2's pardon).

MS. North d.49 (book of accounts).

MS. North e.37 (musical compositions by Jenkins).

MS. North g.1 (under "Printed Sources" above, see "Guarini").

MS. Rawl. B.314 (20*v*–21*r*: North pedigree).

MS. Rawl. D.260 (34*v*–35*r*: Jenkins elegy on DN1).

MS. Tanner 57.2 (395*r*: letter from DN2).

MS. Tanner 180 (75*r*: North pedigree).

MS. Tanner 226 (187*r*: DN2, J.P.).

R.6.104 (Mary Clapinson, "Index to the Calendar of North Family Papers in the Bodleian Library," 1972).

R.13.111 (C. M. Borough, "Calendar of the Papers of the North Family," 1960).

British Library

Add. MS. 5,819 (78*r*–80*r*, 114*v*–120*r*: North pedigree and inscriptions).

Add. MS. 18,220 (37*r*–*v*: Jenkins elegy on DN1).

Add. MS. 19,143 (175*v*–176*r*: North pedigree).

Add. MS. 29,571 (68*r*, 156*r*: Lady North's sister, Lady Hatton).

Add. MS. 29,580 (various family seals).

Add. MS. 32,500 (North family correspondence).

Add. MS. 32,510 (16*r*–19*r*: Roger North, "Advertisement," biographical writing on DN1).

Add. MS. 32,523 (Roger North, biographical writing).

Add. MS. 39,177 (113*r*: Montagu pedigree).

Harl. 806 (79*r*–80*v*: "Barones North de Cartelage," in "Baronagium Angliae," 1587).

Harl. 807 (104*r*: Montagu family).

Harl. 1,529 (99*r*: North pedigree).

Harl. 4,204 (233*r*: Montagu family).

Harl. 7,029 (269*r*: Sir John North, grandfather of DN2).

Cambridge, County Record Office, Shire Hall

MSS. G. N. Maynard, vol. IX (pp. 18–21: Kirtling).

L95/12 (North household accounts).

P101/1/1 (Kirtling Parish Registers, 1585–1649, 1654–1706).

Cambridge University

Cambridge University Library

MS. Ee.5.3 (DN2, "Some Notes Concerning the Life of Edward Lord North. . .").

Emmanuel College

MS. 48 (Richard Holdsworth, "Directions to Students").

St. John's College

MS. Bb, James 613 (Roger North, "Life of Lord Guilford").

Trinity College

MS. o.11a.3[35] (John North to DN2).

MS. o.11a.3[37] (John North to Lady North).

MS. o.11a.3[38] (John North to DN2).

MS. o.11a.3[46] (Francis North to DN2).

Charterhouse

Charterhouse MS., "The Inventorie of Charterhowse July . . . 1608" (transcribed by Francis Bickley).

Folger Shakespeare Library

MS. V.a.258 (DN2's coat of arms).

MS. W.b.96 (40r: Dr. John North).

Greater London Record Office, County Hall

P 79/JN1/21 (marriage of DN2 and Anne Montagu).

Guildhall Library

MS. 10,231 (baptismal record of DN1).

Houghton Library (Harvard University)

MS. Lat. 329 ("Alphonsus").

Huntington Library

MS. North 1 (Anne, Lady North, to Francis North).

MS. North 2 (Anne, Lady North, to Francis North).

MS. North 3 (Anne, Lady North, to Francis North).

MS. North 14 (Dame Anne North to DN2).

MS. North 15 (Francis North to DN2).

MS. North 45 (John Hallam to DN2).

Inner Temple

R. Lloyd, ed., "Admissions to the Inner Temple," 3 vols. (1950–1960).

Perkins Library (Duke University)

Dudley North, fourth Baron North, papers (prose and poetry; the copy text used herein).

Public Record Office

C 193/13 (5: DN2, J.P.).

C 193/13 (6: DN2, J.P.).

C 231/7 (p. 181: Crown Office Docquet Book; DN2, J.P.).

PROB 11/354.65 (174v–175v: will of Frances, Lady North).

PROB 11/354.69 (205v–206v: will of DN2).

PROB 11/366.61 (106r–v: will of Anne, Lady North).

SP 16/171 (no. 3: DN2 on London committee).

SP 16/531 (nos. 96 and 97: petitions to King Charles from DN1 and DN2).

SP 63/267 (20r–v, 24v, 25r: DN2, military service).

SP 81/27 (32r: fall of Heidelberg).

SP 84/118 (98r–v, 172r; troops in United Provinces).

SP 84/119 (179r: DN2, military service).

SP 84/121, pt. 2 (274r, 278r: DN2, military service).

SP 94/27, pt. 1 (22r: letter of King James).

Rougham Hall
>   Anne, Lady North, notebook.
>   DN2, manuscript volume of prose and poetry.
>   DN2, book of accounts (1632–1677).

Spencer Research Library (University of Kansas)
>   MS. E205, item 61 ("A True Relaĉon of euerie Daies proceedings in parlia-
>   ment since the begininge thereof this present Session 1628," i.e., Jan.–
>   March 1629).
>   MS. uncat. North 1J:47, packet 7:4 (Thomas Percivall to Francis North,
>   1679).
>   MS. uncat. North 1J:47:43 (marriage settlement of DN2 and Anne Montagu,
>   1632).
>   MS. uncat. North 1J:48:145 (Wyseman, letters patent, 1674).
>   MS. uncat. North 1J:48:184 (will of Dame Mary Montagu, 1649).
>   MS. uncat. North 1J:48:190 (indenture between DN2 and wife, and Dame
>   Mary Montagu, 1632).
>   MS. uncat. North 2A:32:38 (DN2, indenture, 1675).
>   MS. uncat. North 7:1 (sale of North properties, 1630).
>   MS. uncat. North 17:4 (DN2, Lady Dacre, and Katherine Lennard, 1638).
>   MS. uncat. North 17:5 (sale of Charterhouse, 1631).
>   MS. uncat. North 17:6 (supportive document regarding sale of Charterhouse,
>   1631).
>   MS. uncat. North 17:7 (North family properties, 1622).
>   MS. uncat. North 17:14 (John North's certificate of ordination, 1670).

Vatican Library
>   Biblioteca Chigiana, Q.IV.8.86 (song translated by DN2).

DISSERTATIONS

Lawniczak, Donald A., "George Herbert and His Classmates at Cambridge: 1609–
    1628," unpub. Ph.D. diss., Kent State University (1967).

Millard, Peter T., "An Edition of Roger North's *Life of Dr. John North* with a Critical
    Introduction," D.Phil. thesis, Linacre College, Oxford (1969).

Panofsky, Richard Jacob, "A Descriptive Study of English Mid-Tudor Short Poetry,
    1557–1577," unpub. Ph.D. diss., University of California at Santa Barbara (1975).

Parsons, Robert J., "Autobiographical and Archetypal Elements in the Verse of the
    Third Lord North," unpub. Ph.D. diss., Duke University (1980).

INDEX OF TITLES AND
FIRST LINES

Three types of entry are included: (1) titles as they appear in the Perkins manuscript, here set in italics; (2) first lines of titled poems, presented without distinguishing punctuation; and (3) first lines of untitled poems, indicated by brackets.

INDEX

Dale B. J. Randall is Professor of English, Duke University.